European Communication Research and Education Association (ECREA)

This series consists of books arising from the intellectual work of ECREA members. Books address themes relevant to the ECREA's interests; make a major contribution to the theory, research, practice and/or policy literature; are European in scope; and represent a diversity of perspectives. Book proposals are refereed.

Series Editors
Nico Carpentier
François Heinderyckx

Series Advisory Board
Denis McQuail
Robert Picard
Jan Servaes

The aims of the ECREA are

a) To provide a forum where researchers and others involved in communication and information research can meet and exchange information and documentation about their work. Its disciplinary focus will include media, (tele)communications and informatics research, including relevant approaches of human and social sciences;
b) To encourage the development of research and systematic study, especially on subjects and areas where such work is not well developed;
c) To stimulate academic and intellectual interest in media and communication research, and to promote communication and cooperation between members of the Association;
d) To co-ordinate the circulation of information on communications research in Europe, with a view to establishing a database of ongoing research;
e) To encourage, support and, where possible, publish the work of young researchers in Europe;
f) To take into account the desirability of different languages and cultures in Europe;
g) To develop links with relevant national and international communication organizations and with professional communication researchers working for commercial organizations regulatory institutions, both public and private;
h) To promote the interests of communication research within and among the of the Council of Europe and the European Union;
i) To collect and disseminate information concerning the professional position of researchers in the European region; and
j) To develop, improve and promote communication and media education.

The Independence of the Media and its Regulatory Agencies

The Independence of the Media and its Regulatory Agencies

Shedding New Light on Formal and Actual Independence Against the National Context

Edited by
Wolfgang Schulz, Peggy Valcke and Kristina Irion

intellect Bristol, UK / Chicago, USA

First published in the UK in 2013 by
Intellect, The Mill, Parnall Road, Fishponds, Bristol, BS16 3JG, UK

First published in the USA in 2013 by
Intellect, The University of Chicago Press, 1427 E. 60th Street,
Chicago, IL 60637, USA

A catalogue record for this book is available from the
British Library.

Series: ECREA
Series ISSN: 1742-9420 (Print), 2043-7846 (Online)
Cover image: Charlotte Moorman playing Nam June Paik's TV Cello in 1971.
    © Takahito iimuri.
Cover designer: Ellen Thomas
Copy-editing: Prufrock
Production manager: Bethan Ball
Typesetting: Contentra Technologies

Print ISBN: 978-1-84150-733-0
ePDF ISBN: 978-1-78320-320-8
ePUB ISBN: 978-1-78320-321-5

Printed and bound by Hobbs, UK

Contents

Editors' foreword

The independence of the media and its regulatory agencies is vital for democracies. This volume ventures to explore the complex relationship between media governance and independence of regulatory authorities within media systems in the European context, as this is part of the wider framework in which media independence may flourish or fade.

This book builds on two major European research networks, which both investigated media independence from an interdisciplinary and comparative perspective. A study on 'Indicators for independence and efficient functioning of audiovisual media services regulatory bodies for the purpose of enforcing the rules in the AVMS Directive', better known as INDIREG, was conducted on behalf of the European Commission by a European consortium led by the Hans Bredow Institute for Media Research. The study team mapped, compared and analysed the situation of independent media regulatory bodies in all European and four non-European countries, contributing to the theoretical understanding of media governance and the development of methodologies for assessing various dimensions of independence. The MEDIADEM project – called, in full, 'European media policies revisited: Valuing and reclaiming free and independent media in contemporary democratic systems' – is a collaborative European research project on media policy-making processes in EU member states and candidate countries. Its purpose is to identify which policy processes, tools and instruments can best support the development of free and independent media. The project was funded by the European Commission's Seventh Framework Programme, and it was concluded in 2013 after three years of productive research.

The various contributions to this book shed new light on formal and actual regulatory independence in the media sector in the national context. The special focus on media governance recognizes the connection between media freedoms and regulation, which determines important contextual factors that might influence independence externally. The contributing authors offer theoretical perspectives that combine law and public policy; review research methods; and offer a set of case studies that explore how the national socio-political context influences local institutions. As a whole, the book offers an accessible and relevant account of research into regulatory independence as applied to the audiovisual media sector in Europe.

As editors, we would like to thank, first of all, the contributors who have made this such a varied but coherent publication. Our thanks are extended to the ECREA book series editors Nico Carpentier and François Heinderyckx, as well as Manuel Puppis, the chair of ECREA's 'Communication Law & Policy' section. Additional thanks go to Bethan Ball at Intellect, our publisher, and our copy-editor Joost van Beek. The cover shows Charlotte Moorman playing Nam June Paik's TV Cello with TV glasses in 1971 and we are grateful to Takahiko iimura for his permission to use the image.

Most sadly, our distinguished colleague Karol Jakubowicz, who contributed the Preface to this book, passed away. We would like to dedicate this book to him, knowing that his thought-provoking scholarship will continue to inspire us.

Wolfgang Schulz
Peggy Valcke
Kristina Irion

Preface

Broadcasting regulatory authorities: Work in progress

Karol Jakubowicz

The concept and institution of an independent regulatory authority is today seen as the default choice for regulatory governance. That much we know. Beyond that, however, little is certain, as the term covers a multitude of sins (committed by or, more often, against these authorities) and problematic issues. To complement the information and findings presented in this book, we will seek in this preface to highlight some of these issues and to provide, however briefly, an interpretative and conceptual framework within which to consider the subject matter.

First, this preface will deal with the question of where broadcasting regulatory authorities come from and how their emergence and operation should be interpreted. The latter is a complex issue and there is no single answer, given that these public institutions, like most, are (as this book clearly shows) a product of what may be called 'systemic parallelism'.

Then we will take a look at a number of key issues, starting with the independence of these authorities and their position in the democratic system of separation of powers. In this context, we will also look at the process of 'ontogenesis' that these bodies undergo in young democracies. We will conclude this part with some comments on a further aspect of institutional evolution. Policy-makers and legislators in different countries are coming to different conclusions regarding the question of whether the authorities should remain 'sector-specific', concentrating exclusively or mainly on broadcasting, or be turned into 'integrated' regulatory bodies (dealing with both broadcasting and telecommunications). In the latter case, the question then emerges whether they should become truly 'convergent' or remain merely 'integrated'.

To conclude this preface, we will need to consider whether or not these regulatory bodies actually have a future. Given the tensions inherent to their existence and operation and the process of rapid change (technological and otherwise), we cannot discount the possibility that policy-makers will be taking a new, hard look at the rationale for their existence.

The views of some of the authors cited in this preface are at variance with the assumptions underlying some contributions to this volume. However, this is not to challenge those assumptions, but to provide a different perspective, as well as food for thought. The independence of regulatory authorities, for example, is not universally perceived as an unambiguously good thing. In fact, some authors believe that there may be not only malignant, but also benign and much-needed forms of politicization.

Knowledge of these alternative approaches should aid the reader in considering the ideas expressed in the body of this book and coming to his/her own conclusions.

The origin of broadcasting regulatory agencies

In Europe, regulatory agencies, for the broadcasting sector and in general, can be described as a product of ideology. More precisely, they are the result of an ideological shift from social-democratic systems in Western Europe, and from communist regimes in Central and Eastern Europe, to free-market, neoliberal social arrangements which involved the deregulation of many areas of the economy, and society in general. There are many useful theories explaining why this form of regulatory regime was chosen, but the root cause for the emergence of such authorities, as aptly explained by Jacobzone (2005: 33), was 'building a regulatory state where the regulatory function is clearly distinct from the ownership and policy-making function'. Independent regulators, Jacobzone wrote,

> have been established when setting up new market-oriented regulatory arrangements for utility sectors with network characteristics, for telecommunications, financial services, or for the social and environmental arena [...] This is part of the transition from the 'Owner State' to the 'Regulatory State'.

Schmitter and Trechsler (2004) define regulatory institutions as 'guardian institutions' (intended to be made up of experts) which serve the implementation of public policies. Their establishment, say the authors, reflects the demands faced by public decision making in developed societies, shifting the balance of political legitimacy from one based on democratic participation, access and accountability to one based on the superior performance of functions and satisfaction with improved output.

These observations place us squarely in the middle of the debate about whether the rise of regulatory authorities and the role they play should be interpreted as evidence of the strengthening, or – conversely – weakening of democracy. In other words, this debate questions whether regulatory authorities really should, or perhaps should not, be depoliticized.

Many authors place regulatory authorities within a process of democratization and democratic consolidation, with their establishment and operation providing evidence that such a process is indeed unfolding. One perspective could be that of 'democratic governance'. Hamelink and Nordenstreng (2007) note that Denis McQuail has described governance as 'government without politics', involving a more complex, differentiated and diffuse system of decision- and policy-making, and control, than is the case with the institutions and functions associated with 'traditional government'. As a result, any policy and the regulatory frameworks created in this process result from an interplay of divergent forces, seeking to achieve a workable compromise between their different interests and goals.

From the same democratic consolidation perspective, introduction of broadcasting regulatory authorities may also be seen as designed to reduce the discretionary rule of political society and protect media freedom (Grzymała-Busse 2004).

On the other hand, regulatory authorities are sometimes seen as reflecting a crisis of democracy. Christians, et al. (2009) identify several models of democracy, one of which they call 'administrative [or elite] democracy', which emphasizes the need for institutions of professional administration and other expert bodies to look after the people's welfare. This is based on the assumption that neither politicians nor ordinary citizens have the knowledge to govern a highly complex modern society. The trend has been away from direct public control and toward private ownership, subject to review by regulatory bodies.

Another possible interpretation along these lines can be derived from Colin Crouch's concept of an 'inevitable entropy of democracy', leading to a 'post-democratic revolution' (cited after Blühdorn 2006: 71). Political and public policy issues are relocated from the arenas of democratic contestation and decision into arenas which are governed by – at least supposedly – unambiguous and non-negotiable codes rather than contestable social values. Economic markets, scientific laboratories, regulatory bodies, courts of justice or international regimes are prominent examples of such supposedly apolitical arenas, and interest rates, educational standards, health provision and environmental quality are just a few examples of issues which have been transferred to them. However, deideologization, professionalization, pragmatism, managerial best practice and the pursuit of efficiency gains may also simply veil the essentially political character of political decisions and deprive democratic electorates of their right to deliberate and decide upon the affected issues.

We will return to these quandaries below, as we consider the particular issues under consideration here.

Independence

In Chapter 1 in this book, Wolfgang Schulz comes to the realistic conclusion that the independence of regulatory authorities depends on a culture of independence. Its existence (or otherwise) is, we believe, a manifestation of 'systemic parallelism'. Hallin and Mancini (2004) have introduced the concept of 'political parallelism' in media systems, but – as this book shows – we can also speak more broadly of 'systemic parallelism', whereby media systems are shaped by the socio-political and cultural features of the countries in which they operate. This notably includes the level of actual or potential societal conflict and the degree of democratic consolidation. Ample evidence of this is provided by an analysis of paradigm shifts in media regulation in Europe, conducted in Chapter 2 in this book by Kristina Irion and Roxana Radu. Indeed, a comparison of the situation in various groups of countries (e.g. those covered in Chapters 7–11) shows how different determinants (historical, cultural, political etc.) influence the prospects for regulatory authority independence. It is therefore of the utmost importance to take such determinants into account when devising indicators to measure the independence and efficiency of media regulatory bodies, as demonstrated in Chapter 6 in this book by Kristina Irion and Michele Ledger.

This 'systemic parallelism' also might help to explain the observation, which the Committee of Ministers of the Council of Europe underlined in its Declaration of 26 March 2008, that there is no clear link between the amount of detail in a country's legislation on broadcasting regulation and the regulatory authority's independence. In some cases, regulatory authorities governed by a very limited set of rules were nevertheless found to operate relatively independently, whereas in other cases, an extensive legal framework was promulgated without any effective impact in terms of the independent functioning of broadcasting regulators and their relation to public authorities or politics. Whether the legal safeguards – extensive or not – are effective depends, according to the Declaration, on the existence of a culture of independence in which lawmakers, government and other players, under the scrutiny of society at large, respect the regulatory authorities' independence without being explicitly required to do so by law.

Despite this observation, the Committee of Ministers considers an appropriate legal framework an essential condition for the establishment and proper functioning of a broadcasting regulator. Its Recommendation (2000)23 sets out guidelines regarding the organization, functioning, role and action of broadcasting authorities, and condemns any arbitrary controls or constraints on participation in the information process, on media content or on the transmission and dissemination of information. These guidelines, as well as the standards derived by the European Court of Human Rights from Arts 6, 10, 13 and 14 of the European Convention on Human Rights, are analysed in Chapter 3 in this book by Peggy Valcke, Dirk Voorhoof and Eva Lievens. Whereas the legal requirements for the independence of broadcasting regulators at the European Union level (specifically in the Audiovisual Media Services Directive) seem rather weak and difficult to enforce at first sight, the analysis carried out by David Stevens in Chapter 4 shows that this conclusion deserves to be nuanced in the light of the requirements they set out for a number of closely related sectors, including electronic communications, data protection and public service broadcasting.

In the end, however, the role of a regulatory authority is to enforce the law and implement public policy – both of which are formulated and adopted elsewhere. It seems fairly obvious, therefore, that by 'independence' we can at best mean functional or operational independence in what should be the impartial application of the law, without fear or favour.

In contrast to the above-mentioned regulations from the EU and recommendations from the Council of Europe on regulatory independence, there are also those authors who claim that democracy is not well served by a regulatory body's independence. For example, Schmitter and Trechsel (2004) believe that 'guardian' institutions, such as regulatory authorities, are non-democratic or non-majoritarian, existing outside of effective democratic control, disconnected from the circuits of democratic accountability and unaccountable to citizens for their decisions. The solution could, in their view, be to 'watch the guardians'; to assign to any 'guardian institution' another 'guardian' of its own, chosen by the parliamentary committee most relevant to its field of activity. This person would be a member of the permanent staff, paid by and responsible only to the parliament, serving as a sort of permanent whistleblower with privileged access to internal documents and discussions. This should serve to strengthen the general role of parliament within the usual system of inter-agency checks and balances. Schmitter and Trechsel (2004) call for 'special guardians' for 'media guardians': not only should members of media regulatory authorities be appointed for long terms with the approval of a parliamentary supermajority, but their subsequent renewal of contract or removal from office should be the exclusive responsibility of an especially convoked independent commission, perhaps comprising a random selection of members of the professional associations involved in the different media. We will return to this below.

IRAs and the separation of powers

The issue of the separation of powers can, as illustrated by the contributions to this volume, be examined from at least four interrelated points of view.

At the lowest level, it concerns the relative powers and positions of regulatory authorities with overlapping areas of competence, in this case primarily broadcasting, telecommunications and competition authorities. 'Turf wars' between such bodies are a fact of life in many countries, showing how difficult it is to clearly demarcate areas of competence and power. As discussed in Chapter 9 in this book by Pierre-François Docquir, Sebastian Müller and Christoph Gusy, this problem may be exacerbated in federal states like Germany and Belgium, where not only regulators, but legislators too are often competing rather than coordinating. In countries where the socio-cultural approach to broadcasting regulation remains strong, the broadcasting regulator will have a correspondingly strong position. Where the deregulatory, free-market, economic growth-oriented approach is dominant, meanwhile, telecom and competition regulators may have the upper hand.

At another level, IRAs pose a question mark in terms of constitutional arrangements, i.e. of fitting regulatory authorities into the classical and time-honoured concept of the division of powers. Stephan Dreyer notes in Chapter 5 that in the United States, regulatory authorities have been understood as 'governments in miniature', which combine legislative (e.g. rule-making), judicial (e.g. adjudication and dispute-settlement) and executive (e.g. enforcement) functions. This is not usually the case in Europe. Especially rule- and policy-making functions are mostly reserved for parliament and government: some authorities are given the competence to issue secondary, delegated regulations, but most are not, and even if it is granted, it is of limited character. For example, the Italian authority,

AGCOM, enjoys autonomous rule-making power in only three specific areas, and one of them is its internal organization. The UK Ofcom (2012: 15), which is particularly active and forceful in coming up with policy-oriented proposals, still describes its role as 'contribut[ing] to and implement[ing] public policy defined by Parliament [...] at the request of Parliament or government,' and expects that this will continue 'where Parliament identifies a clearly-defined role for Ofcom'.

To take a step further, we need to look at the relations between regulatory authorities and power centres in the establishment. In Greece, for example, as Evangelia Psychogiopoulou, Federica Casarosa and Anna Kandyla describe in Chapter 8, domestic audiovisual policy has been marked by strong politicization and the interweaving of interests between the political elites and powerful media moguls. As a result, the dominant political forces in the country have proven unwilling to release the broadcasting sector from their control and are consequently not given to strengthening the position of the Greek and Italian broadcasting regulatory bodies in the regulatory system.

As for the fourth and broadest framework for considering the issue of the separation of powers, Stephan Dreyer seeks in Chapter 5 to locate regulators in a governance structure composed of the government, parliament, industry and the public. Dreyer quotes with approval the view of Lamanauskas (2006) that the regulator is strongest and most independent if it can be located in an area where it keeps an equal distance from all possible interests. However, he recognizes that in addition to 'autonomizers,' i.e. factors strengthening the independence of the regulator, there are also 'dependencers' at play, factors that are detrimental to the regulator's autonomy.

Whatever equilibrium and balance are achieved at each of those four levels, they are highly unstable and subject to change as power relations change. To deal with at least one dimension of this, Schmitter and Trechsel (2004) propose, as already noted, to 'guard the guardians,' unambiguously locating regulatory authorities as directly subordinate in relation to government or parliament. Rather idealistically, however, they don't seem to foresee any possibility that the institutional solutions they propose would be abused. Their proposal for 'bringing democracy back' when it comes to regulatory authorities would in reality mean that less than fully democratic societies that subject regulatory authorities to formal and informal political control, and appoint politicians rather than experts as their members, are actually ahead of the game in terms of protecting democracy. This seems a very doubtful proposition.

'Ontogenesis' in young democracies

When societies reach a certain level of democratization, government ownership and control of the media begin to be seen as an embarrassment, out of keeping with present-day standards of democratic governance. That is often the point when state broadcasting is transformed into public service broadcasting, and when a broadcasting regulatory authority is established. In both cases, this is preceded by a search for 'models' to copy or adapt. And that is when a race for time begins.

Such a newly-established authority must quickly accumulate the requisite legal and technical expertise, enabling it to operate properly. Even more importantly, it must also fight to win and entrench its independence since, more likely than not, it will operate in a disabling, rather than an enabling environment. All this must happen in 'compressed time,' as Beata Klimkiewicz calls it in Chapter 7 in the context of Poland. Yet it has long been abundantly clear that legal and institutional solutions that are 'transplanted' to a country in a process of imitative (or mimetic) transformation rarely, if ever, perform as they do in the socio-political and cultural contexts within which they were originally designed. This is known as 'the transplant effect' which may take different forms in different socio-cultural circumstances (Berkowitz, Pistor and Richard 2000).

A process of democratic consolidation consists in large part of efforts to overcome the resistance of political forces that are seeking to preserve their discretionary power and draw material resources from the public domain of the state (Grzymała-Busse 2004; for an analysis and comparison of the situation in Southern Europe and Latin America see e.g. Hallin and Papathanassopoulos 2002; Prado 2008; 2009). The broadcasting regulatory authority is intended to serve as a constraint on the discretionary rule of political society, but it may be undermined and turned into its opposite – an extension of political society. This may be done in one of several ways:

- by constructing 'winner-take-all' or 'winner-take-most' institutions (e.g. by leaving the power of appointment to these institutions in the hands of the President or Prime Minister, or by introducing parity with the distribution of seats in parliament, filling the seats with political appointees and giving the ruling party or coalition an automatic majority in a collective body),
- by appointing academics, intellectuals and other worthy individuals to lead or oversee the institutions who do not have the power base in the political establishment needed to secure a sufficiently strong position for the authority in the political games in which it will unavoidably be involved or fall victim to,
- by creating 'Potemkin institutions,' lax or unenforced formal institutions, whose legal framework is often characterized by low regulatory standards, ambiguous language, and limited provisions for enforcement (or their informal abandonment). They exist on paper, often to satisfy the requirements of external actors (such as international donors or organizations), but they cannot fulfil their ostensible goals (cf. Grzymała-Busse 2004).

As a result, the transplanted institution of a regulatory authority may have to undergo all or most of the stages of evolution they originally went through in their countries of origin. This process is well described by Tarik Jusić in Chapter 11 in the context of Bosnia and Herzegovina. The authority needs to fight and win battles for what independence the law provides for, and for a position of autonomy and ability to act on the basis of the law and its expert knowledge.

Sector-specific, integrated or convergent?

Regulatory authorities cannot be described as anything like a 'finished product,' all the more so since the process of change is far from over. This is illustrated, for example, by how Ofcom, in 2011, was given the additional responsibility for the regulation of the United Kingdom's postal services. The emergence of issues regarding the Internet and the online environment is necessitating further change. Such issues include packet prioritization, online privacy, data protection and copyright. In the EU, there are new regulatory measures under the electronic communications regulatory framework to protect 'Internet freedom'; in the UK, Ofcom has been charged with new responsibilities to reduce online piracy. This suggests that legislation will continually need to evolve to keep abreast of technological change (ACMA 2011). Moreover, even when countries, like the UK, opted for so-called converged regulators, this has not prevented new co-regulators, such as the Authority for Television on Demand (ATVOD), from emerging and taking up specific duties. This has given rise to interesting discussions about the self- or co-regulatory nature of bodies operating in the media field (with the recent Leveson Inquiry and Report broadening the debate to also include bodies in charge of print media), and this issue is further elaborated upon by Rachael Craufurd Smith, Epp Lauk, Yolande Stolte and Heikki Kuutti in Chapter 10.

One of the major policy decisions which will determine the future of these authorities relates to whether they should remain sector-specific, and concentrate on broadcasting in its many manifestations, or whether there should be a process of integration with telecom regulators.

Such a process can theoretically happen in one of two ways: either the integrated regulator draws on separate pieces of legislation (as in the case of Canada, with its Canadian Federal Telecommunications Act and Broadcasting Act), or its establishment is preceded by 'legislative convergence,' on the principle that 'regulation should follow the logic of technological change and converge into one unified structure. This would represent the coming together of three historically different regulatory traditions – specific to communications, media and the internet – into one regulatory framework' (ACMA 2011: 1).

In addition to the United States and Canada, where this happened a long time ago, a number of other countries have integrated their media and telecom regulators. Yet an international overview has found that 'for most jurisdictions around the world, it is likely that separate media and communications laws remain the norm' (ACMA 2011: 1), implying the continued existence of separate, sector-specific regulators.

The term 'integrated regulator' is often treated as synonymous with 'convergent regulator'. Whether or not this is right merits close attention. First, it is sometimes pointed out that 'convergence' is incomplete as long as content regulation remains unchanged. Noam (2008) seems to take the same tack, noting that even when regulatory agencies are merged across media, this does not mean that regulations are harmonized. In the US as well as in Canada, the agencies operate under different laws or parts thereof. Different parts of the same agency may develop different approaches and philosophies towards different services, even if provided by the same company.

But is this necessarily bad? Regulation should be tailored to the nature of the service being regulated. This is why such 'harmonization' is deliberately avoided, with the express intention being, in the language of the EU Framework Directive, to 'separate the regulation of transmission from the regulation of content,' in order for the regulation of electronic communication networks to remain 'without prejudice to measures [...] to promote cultural and linguistic diversity [in broadcasting] and to ensure the defence of media pluralism'. Otherwise, traditional broadcasting regulation may be marginalized in convergent bodies because of the predominance of telecom issues over broadcasting ones (as the former ones are seen as more strategically important in terms of economy and growth; the industry players are more powerful and require a stronger regulatory partner; and the issues involved may be regarded as more important than in the case of broadcasting).

Regulatory convergence within an integrated agency may be aided, or hindered, by institutional or structural solutions. When AGCOM, the Italian authority, was originally created, it was based on the idea of 'processes' and 'knowledge' rather than on markets. Its staff was not structured into units and offices dedicated to each specific market (telecommunications, broadcasting, publishing), but into three departments, one in charge of regulation, one in charge of monitoring the operators' compliance with the regulation and one in charge of dispute resolution (Manacorda 2011). The intention was to create a fully convergent authority. Yet in 2006 a new organizational structure was introduced and the authority's services were reorganized into a number of directorates, dealing respectively with electronic communication networks and services; audiovisual contents and media (with the usual array of socio-cultural concerns); market analysis and competition; and consumer protection. Thus the authority's services became merely 'integrated': dealing with telecommunications and broadcasting separately and in much more focused ways, though still under one roof.

Another take on the issue is offered by Jeremy Hunt, UK Secretary of State for Culture, Media and Sports, who suggests that a 'convergent' regulatory authority should be taken to mean one that regulates, no doubt in a graduated way, *all* content services and all technology platforms. In Hunt's view, if British media organizations are to develop world-beating cross-platform offerings, with the newspaper industry moving to IPTV, sensible cross-platform regulation should be developed as well. 'It cannot be sensible to regulate newsprint through the PCC, on-demand websites through ATVOD and IPTV through Ofcom,' he said:

We have an opportunity to look to the future [and] establish a [...] *one-stop regulatory framework to be applied across all the technology platforms* [...] giving Britain the prize of being the first country in the world where a new generation of innovative, cross-platform media companies are able to grow on the back of the world's *first converged regulatory framework*.

(Hunt 2011; emphases added)

In any case, in this area (as in many others) nothing is fully certain and nothing is final about how particular regulatory authorities should be classified, in terms of their being sector-specific, integrated or convergent.

Any future for regulatory authorities?

As we stated at the outset, the concept and institution of an independent regulatory authority is today seen as the default choice for regulatory governance. The operative word here is 'today', as such authorities can by no means be certain that they have a future.

At least three possible reasons for this might develop:

1. changing technological, market and societal circumstances deprive the current model of broadcasting content regulation of the rationale for its continued existence,
2. neoliberal, free-market ideology leads to further deregulation of the broadcast media, and so of their regulatory regime,
3. history comes full circle and telecom and media regulation are returned to governments, as areas of strategic importance that must be politically controlled.

It could be argued that in the new media ecology, all the traditional rationales for broadcast media regulation – such as the special impact of broadcast media on the formation of opinion and their spread effect, suggestive power and immediacy (Grünwald 2003), or their pervasiveness, invasiveness, publicness and influence on mass communications (Verhulst 2002) – are much weakened. The same is true of 'spectrum scarcity'. Noam (2008) even argues there was never any real spectrum scarcity: 'Spectrum was scarce because governments chose to make it so, by allocating frequencies only grudgingly'.

The argument that there is not a major difference today between broadcast and print media in terms of their relative ease of entry into the market and providing content to the audience could be used to dismantle much of the traditional heavy-handed regulation of broadcast media.

However, Noam (2008) is right: the real reason for regulation is the public policy goals (as he puts it: 'The creation or distribution of "merit" programs, while preventing or reducing "non-merit" programs') that are pursued by means of broadcasting policy and regulation:

None of the societal objectives will vanish just because television signals travel over digital pipes rather than analog airwaves. It seems unlikely that societies will simply give up on their societal priorities [and] leave TV alone, whether analog, digital, or IP; whether over the air, over cable, or over IP networks, or whether there is a bottleneck or not. Instead, they will simply adjust the tools to the new environment.

In unchanged ideological and socio-cultural circumstances, the regulatory challenge for content regulation in a digital setting is thus to find appropriate legislative and other mechanisms based on a functional approach, i.e. one which does not depend solely on technology or forms of delivery, but proceeds from the nature of the content and the character of the audience receiving it.

Noam (2008) believes that television-specific regulation will largely disappear. This could (and according to some authors should) lead to the extension of the current non-interventionist regulatory regime (or absence thereof) for print media and the Internet (i.e. no regulation of content or conduit). However, Noam (2008) suggests that the model should actually be a combination of 'film + last mile common carrier' models. To create content serving some social and political objectives that is otherwise unavailable, the government must use positive mechanisms of creation, rather than negative ones of exclusion. To do so, the government should establish, as in the film industry, arrangements and institutions of funding, production and distribution for the favoured type of content. In search for a technologically-neutral approach, the Australian Government (2012) favours: 'a regulatory framework built around the scale and type of service provided by an enterprise rather than the platform of delivery'. Its Convergence Review developed the concept of a 'content service enterprise' to identify 'significant enterprises that have the most influence on Australians'.

However, and here we come to the second possible reason for the demise of broadcast regulatory authorities, a more pronounced neoliberal orientation that embraces further market liberalization in the name of economic growth and competitiveness may lead governments to renounce or significantly reduce public policy goals. Such an approach would favour eliminating sectoral regulators for telecommunications, broadcasting, etc. and leaving everything in the hands of competition regulators, possibly expanded to deal with essential technical issues.

These comments by Jaap Hoogenboezem (2002: 66) may be a portent of things to come:

> ITC companies should not fall under the regime of all sorts of specialist regulators, but should be treated as any other firm, and have to deal with a single regulatory office that judges their general adherence to competition principles.

The third possible reason why broadcasting regulatory authorities may not have a future would probably please supporters of bringing 'democracy back in' and putting an end to the 'harmful' depoliticization of the regulatory system in this field. As far back as in the early 1980s, John Howkins (1982) wrote that in the information society, information and communication policy would become a key platform for the pursuit of the national interest. Such a prospect would favour the reintegration of media and communications policy into the mainstream of government policy. After all, many of the key issues in this respect are already debated and decided upon at the international level, primarily in intergovernmental organizations, where they are the exclusive domain of government policy.

With convergence and the growing economic and strategic importance of information and communication technologies, there may be an even greater interlinking of communications policy and regulation and general government policy. Again, Jaap Hoogenboezem (2002: 66) describes 'the ideal system of regulation for the converged ICT-sectors' as follows:

> Technical matters are too important, because of their political and economic weight, to be outsourced to offices detached from the mainstream policy-making and politics. Technical matters should be considered, weighed, advised and decided by parliament and cabinets [...] This leaves no place for specialist independent regulators: technology is too important, as well as too politically sensitive, to be left to outsiders.

Conclusion

As is clear from the foregoing, the reasons for the establishment of broadcasting regulatory authorities, and the role they play, can be interpreted in a variety of ways. These authorities are perched precariously at the point of contact (or collision) of many power centres and societal forces. Whatever fate ultimately awaits them, no effort should be spared today and in the foreseeable future to turn them into, or reinforce them as, a force for democracy, capable of protecting the freedom and independence of the broadcast media, but also of applying and enforcing the law fairly and in a professional manner. Far from shrinking, their role in the new media ecology is now being expanded, as new segments of the media (e.g. non-linear audiovisual media services) are put under their supervision and as they are assigned new tasks in relation to new platforms and new content services.

Of course, on the principle of 'systemic parallelism', regulatory authorities can only be as free and as democratic as the societies around them. This must not, however, become an excuse for waiting passively for an enabling environment to emerge, where it is still lacking. This is what the concept of 'ontogenesis' relates to. Among its many duties, a regulatory authority has an obligation to strive for its own freedom and independence, and to create and cultivate a culture of independence for itself. By so doing, it will contribute to the general consolidation of democracy.

References

ACMA (2011), *Converged Legislative Frameworks – International Approaches*, Occasional paper, Melbourne: Australian Communications and Media Authority.

Australian Government (2012), *Convergence Review Final Report*, March, Canberra: Commonwealth of Australia.

Berkowitz, D., Pistor, K. and Richard, J.-F.(2000), 'Economic Development, Legality, and the Transplant Effect', *Working Paper 308*, Michigan: William Davidson Institute, University of Michigan, http://deepblue.lib.umich.edu/bitstream/2027.42/39692/3/wp308.pdf.

Blühdorn, I. (2006), 'The Third Transformation of Democracy: On the Efficient Management of Late-Modern Complexity', in I. Blühdorn, U. Jun (eds.) *Economic Efficiency – Democratic Empowerment. Contested Modernization in Britain and Germany*, Plymouth: Lexington Books, pp. 299–332.

Christians, C. G. et al. (2009), *Normative Theories of the Media. Journalism in Democratic Societies*, Champaign, IL: University of Illinois Press.

Grünwald, A. (2003), *Report on Possible Options for the Review of the European Convention on Transfrontier Television*, Doc. T-TT (2003)002, Strasbourg: Standing Committee on Transfrontier Television, Council of Europe.

Grzymała-Busse, A. (2004), 'Post-Communist Competition and State Development', *Working Paper Series #59*, Ann Arbor: Program on Central & Eastern Europe, Department of Political Science, University of Michigan.

Hallin, D. C. and Papathanassopoulos, S. (2002), 'Political clientelism and the media: Southern Europe and Latin America in comparative perspective', *Media, Culture and Society*, 24: 2, pp. 175–196.

Hallin D.C. and Mancini, P. (2004), *Comparing Media Systems: Three Models of Media and Politics*, Cambridge: Cambridge University Press.

Hamelink, C. J., and Nordenstreng, K. (2007), 'Towards Democratic Media Governance', in E. De Bens et al. (eds.), *Media Between Culture and Commerce*, Bristol: Intellect Books, pp. 225–240.

Hoogenboezem, J. (2002), 'Convergence and Regulation. Comments and Recommendations', in Jaap Hoogenboezem (ed.), *Convergence: A Special Issue of Trends in Communication*, 7, Amsterdam: Boom Publishers.

Howkins, J. (1982), *New Technologies, New Policies?*, London: BFI Publishing.

Hunt, J. (2011), *Boldness be my Friend*, Speech by Secretary of State to the Royal Television Society, London: Department for Culture, Media and Sport, http://www.culture.gov.uk/news/ministers_speeches/8428.aspx.

Jacobzone, S. (2005), 'Designing Independent and Accountable Regulatory Authorities: A Comparative Overview across OECD Countries', in *Designing Independent and Accountable Regulatory Authorities for High Quality Regulation. Proceedings of an Expert Meeting in London*, Paris: Working Party on Regulatory Management and Reform, Organisation for Economic Co-Operation and Development (OECD), pp. 33–36.

Lamanauskas, T. (2006), 'The Key Features of Independence of National Telecommunication Regulatory Authorities and Securing them in Law', *Law*, 61, pp. 73–80.

Manacorda, P. (2001), *The pros and the cons of convergent regulatory authorities*, Remarks delivered during the 14th meeting of the European Platform of Regulatory Authorities (EPRA), Malta.

Noam, E. M. (2008), *TV or Not TV: Three Screens, One Regulation?*, http://www.crtc.gc.ca/eng/media/noam2008.htm.

Ofcom (2012), *Annual Plan 2012/13*, London: Office of Communications.

Prado, M. M. (2008), 'The Challenges and Risks of Creating Independent Regulatory Agencies: A Cautionary Tale from Brazil', *Vanderbilt Journal of Transnational Law*, 41: 2, pp. 435–503.

Prado, M. M. (2009), 'Independent Regulatory Agencies, Patronage, and Clientelism: Lessons from Brazil', in I. Sandoval (ed.), *Corruption and Transparency: The Limits between State, Market and Society*, Mexico City: Siglo XXI and UNAM, pp. 299–322.

Schmitter, P. C. and Trechsel, A. H. (eds.) (2004), *The Future of Democracy in Europe: Trends, Analyses and Reforms, A Green Paper for the Council of Europe*, Strasbourg: Council of Europe Publishing.

Verhulst, S. (2002), 'About scarcities and intermediaries: the regulatory paradigm shift of digital content reviewed', in L. Lievrouw and S. Livingstone (eds.), *The Handbook of New Media*, London: Sage, pp. 432–447.

Introduction

Structural interconnection of free media and independent regulators

Chapter 1

Approaches to independence

Wolfgang Schulz
Hans Bredow Institute for Media Research

Abstract

This chapter presents different general concepts of independence, including philosophical ones, and their relationship with the concept of freedom of the media. It demonstrates how the concept of media freedom enshrines both the protection of independence of media organizations and, at the same time, the requirement to set a normative framework which reduces the independence of the media and their regulators.

Keywords: independence, legitimization of media systems, regulatory concepts, system theory

Introduction

At first sight the concept of independence appears to be appealing as well as simple. Media independence is obviously something that should be guaranteed in a free country and we can immediately cite examples of governments infringing the independence of the media we would eagerly condemn. As it is often the case, on closer examination the matter is more complex and we see that governments may hold media organizations accountable for good reasons.

Against this background the chapter explores the general concept of independence and its relationship with the concept of freedom of the media. It demonstrates that, and how, media freedom enshrines the protection of independence of media organizations but, at the same time, also the requirement to set a normative framework and, therefore, to reduce the independence of the media. Media regulators can, as demonstrated below, be a tool to control the media without hampering their independence in a disproportionate way – that is the case when they themselves enjoy some kind of independence.

The abstract concept of independence

It is interesting to observe that, at least in English and German, 'in-dependence' ('Un-Abhängigkeit') is construed in a negative way, as the absence of dependence. It is not easy to find a positive synonym: it may be 'autonomy', but this would already put a specific complexion on independence. While independence would also cover the logical relation to something else, autonomy refers rather to actions and rules.

Looking into the abstract concept of independence already shows that absolute independence is only seen in rather special cases. Spinoza sees what he called 'aseity' only in gods' existence because it is to be construed without any influence by others (Spinoza 2006). There is a certain similarity to the concept of the 'unmoved mover' described by Aristotle, which is itself not an effect of another cause (Aristotle 2008). However, the contemporaries of Aristotle already complained that the unmoved movers are powerless gods and therefore somehow unsatisfactory, because the concept puts them in another world, apart from the physical real universe.

Schopenhauer has most radically framed the in-dependence in the human existence (Schopenhauer 2010). He construes 'the will' as the starting point of action before all social or behavioural constraints. That the will does not depend on something external is crucial for his philosophical concept.

The above-mentioned examples – of course rather selective – show at least two things: first that we need a more down-to-earth concept for analysing media independence and, second, that some lines of thought in the history of ideas can be responsible for us framing independence as something inherently good.

Independence as the absence of, or the constraints to, control

The other side of the coin

We suggest acknowledging the negative semantic construction of in-dependence as a starting point, and frame independence from a perspective of dependence or, to be more concrete, of control. This pragmatic approach comes with a methodological advantage: if we look at independence from the viewpoint of someone who wants to control the object whose independence is in question, we can make use of regulatory theory to frame independence. On these grounds, the concept of independence appears as one side of a coin, the other side of which is regulatory theory.

In regulatory theory, there has generally been a shift from the regulation paradigm to the concept of governance (Keohane and Nye 2000: 18). It has become transparent that there is no rivalry between those concepts, but that within a governance framework one can ask what regulatory concepts a national state (or any other actor) does follow. This attempt can, at least by means of a snapshot, be seen as being linear as long as one keeps in mind that it is only a part of a complex procedure with feedbacks. Therefore a theoretical framing of independence should make use of a governance approach.

Governance is the most prominent approach in contemporary regulatory theory. Governance refers to a system of norms, rules, laws – and factual restrictions of similar effect – that guide and restrain the activities in society (based on Keohane and Nye 2000) and is not exclusively conducted by the government (for more details, see Chapter 5 in this book by Dreyer).

In line with regulatory theory we can look at regulatory resources like power, money and knowledge (Wilke 2001: 150; Hans Bredow Institute, et al. 2011: 47) and independence of an object can be construed by analysing 'dependencers' and 'autonomizers'. Dependencers are factors that enable another object to control the object of which the independence is in question and autonomizers refer to factors that make it more likely for that object to act according to its own rules rather than giving in to pressure from outside. Dependencers and autonomizers are further discussed in Chapter 5 in this book by Dreyer.

Media institutions or regulators can be seen as objects positioned within a parallelogram of power. This metaphor of a parallelogram of power already shows that we are not talking about organizations out of the economic or legal realities but about maintaining independence by systems of checks and balances. It allows for developing factors and finally indicators to really empirically measure the independence of organizations like publishers or regulators (cf. Chapter 6 in this book by Irion and Ledger).

Distinctions to be drawn

Before analysing the dependence or independence within the media sector another distinction has to be made, the distinction between different objects of control or subjects of independence. Within the context we are talking about in this book, the relevant thing is the production, in this case the production of media content. Theoretically, independence as regards production can mean production without any material from outside. This, however, seems to overstate the case. System theory teaches that even autonomous systems need material from outside for their production, be it cells in biology or social systems like the media (Kickert 1993: 271). What creates autonomy according to system theory is not the absence of elements from outside the system, but that the reproduction of the cell or the reproduction of communications within the social system is solely following the systems' own inherent logic. Differentiation of society has, to take an example, led to the creation of an autonomous media system that decides according to journalistic-editorial methods. In terms of systems theory this method can be described as being orientated to a specific *prime code* ('public/non-public' according to Marcinkowski 1993: 147). This autonomy of the media system is the basis for the media's societal function of enabling the self-observation of society.

As regards the level of production, again some distinctions can be drawn. One can analyse the single decision (to publish or not to publish an article, to take an example). Furthermore, one can focus on the decision-maker, the single person (here the journalist) or the organization (here the editorial department of a publishing company or a broadcaster). Organizational theory can help to analyse how organizations take decisions and what function organizations fulfil within the societal subsystems. Finally, the focus can be on the production within one of those societal systems (here 'the media'). Here again we see the link to the function of the respective specific subsystem of society – in this case the function of media as the self-observation of society.

Another general observation comes along with the understanding of independence as a specific positioning of an entity within the governance structure. How an organization is positioned in the structure and, therefore, what degrees of autonomy the organization can count on, is not solely determined by regulations laid down in formal law. There might be 'dependencers' as well as 'autonomizers' that are governed by social norms rather than formal legal regulation. The academic discourse around independence therefore focuses on the so-called 'real' or 'de facto' independence (Melody 1997: 197; Montoya and Trillas 2007: 183; Gilardi 2008: 4).

Social norms and even non-normative practices define the constraints a media organization or a regulator faces when making its own decisions. This is the theoretical reason why empirical studies are coming to the conclusion that the so-called culture of independence in a given society plays an eminent role when it comes to independence, especially of organizations. This culture of independence can be seen as the pattern of formal and informal norms and social practices as regards the type of object in question. This cultural independence might not be sector-specific, since the social norms might regard the behaviour of government bodies as a whole.

Independence and legitimization

Functions

The above-mentioned concept of independence already makes clear why independence is linked to functions. The autonomy of specific subsystems of society follows certain functions those subsystems fulfil for the society as a whole. Therefore, the whole concept of autonomy is seen as driven by the functional differentiation of society. In system theory the function of a subsystem can only be fulfilled if there is autonomy – that is the factual, not the normative pre-condition of the functional differentiation of societies (Luhmann 1997: 707). Only an autonomous media system can function as a kind of 'mirror' for all parts of society; a dependent media system would distort this mirror and would, eventually, lead to the collapse of the media system.

That does not, however, mean that the normative level is not relevant. Normative concepts can construe that it is reasonable to protect factual independence against interference and advocate for protecting the function of a specific entity for society.

The dreadfulness of absolute independence

As argued above in the section on the abstract concept of independence, absolute independence is reserved for gods or the framing of the free will of the subject. There are good reasons to have a critical view on the absolute independence of persons or organizations since the absence of control means arbitrariness.

Under normative theories an absolutely independent entity lacks democratic legitimacy and accountability (Hans Bredow Institute, et al. 2011: 24). If you are accountable to someone, this infringes on your autonomy and you are not absolutely independent any more. Thus a chain of legitimacy goes with a certain degree of dependence (Larsen, Pedersen, Sørensen and Olsen 2005: 6).

There is, furthermore, no theoretical or empirical evidence that absolutely independent entities are capable of fulfilling their functions better than others. Therefore, when someone calls for absolute independence, it is wiser to focus on his/her interest rather than on the suggested concept of absolute independence. On an EU-level there might be a simple reason for the call for independence of regulators or even absolute independence, to take an example. Independence makes it easier for the European Commission to create a network of regulators not linked with the national states' institutions and in doing so creating a European regulatory group. This might or might not be favourable for the efficiency and effectiveness of regulation.

Relativity of independence

When approaching independence from a normative perspective, the reason for granting or protecting independence has to be elaborated.

There are two different lines of approach here; one is that the normative framework sets constraints as regards interference with the action of the respective entity, most prominently when there are fundamental rights in play. The result is a greater degree of autonomy for that entity. Another track of thought is that the independence of the entity is connected with a higher degree of effectiveness or efficiency as regards the functioning of this entity. In that case the whole concept of independence has to be framed accordingly; that is to say that 'dependencers' and 'autonomizers' have to be framed in view of their effect on the functioning of the entity. In this book we will unfold the concept of independence of media regulators according to this approach (see Chapter 5 in this book by Dreyer).

Media independence in brief

Concepts and paradoxes

Independence is not the same concept as freedom, but there are, nevertheless, specific links between the two.

The construction of the freedom of the media under Art. 5 (1) 2 in the German Constitution (Grundgesetz, GG) by the Federal Constitutional Court in Germany (Bundesverfassungsgericht, BVerfG) is instructive in this respect. According to this Court there is a subjective element of media freedom and consequently the state has to refrain from interference with media production. In fact, a kind of graduated approach is applied, with the most restrictive test being applied when it comes to direct intervention in the content, whereas the interference with the organization can be justified more easily, and the least restrictive test concerns legal influence on procedures. However, the burden is high since the Federal Constitutional Court regards the freedom of speech and the freedom of the media as one of the most important freedoms within the system of basic freedoms in the German Constitution. The media, therefore, have a specific degree of independence protected by the constitution (for an overview see Hoffmann-Riem 1996: 119).

The specific protection of the media under Art. 5 (1), 2nd sentence of the German Constitution, in contrast to the general protection of freedom of expression under Art. 5 (1), 1st sentence GG, is – according to the Federal Constitutional Court's concept – already linked with a specific function of the media. Therefore one has to decide, according to the autonomous media system-based journalistic-editorial criteria, whether a published piece of content is protected under the constitution within the scope of media freedom or not. In another perspective, it is not the arbitrary decision of a publisher but the adherence to specific journalistic-editorial standards which is especially protected by the constitution. This provokes rather interesting constitutional debates right now, since on the Internet it is not easy to decide whether a service is journalistic-editorial or not (Rumyantsev 2008: 33; Held 2008: 990). However, autonomy in this context does not mean arbitrary decision making, but following one's own rules.

It is still under debate, yet accepted by the majority of legal scholars in Germany, that apart from guaranteeing subjective rights, Art. 5 (1), 2nd sentence GG does contain objective guarantees to protect the function of the media system as such as well (Hoffmann-Riem 2009: 211). According to the Federal Constitutional Court these even enshrine a constitutional mandate to protect the freedom of the media system and to create a legal framework in which a free and open process of public and private opinion-making is possible (BVerfGE 57, 295, 320; 73, 118, 159). That implies – for example – that the lawmaker has to set up an effective system to combat media concentration and curb any predominant influence of one person or a company on public opinion-making. This enhances the independence of the media system as a whole; at the same time, it reduces the leeway for media organizations, for example as regards mergers and acquisitions. It is a slightly paradoxical situation that the state has to reduce independence on one level to create a higher degree of independence on another.

We have chosen the German example because here the paradox is especially evident. However, on the level of Art. 10 of the European Convention on Human Rights (ECHR) one can see a similar structure. It is well established that the freedoms under Art. 10 ECHR contain both duties of abstention and duties of care (see for more details Chapter 3 in this book by Valcke, Voorhoof and Lievens). In media governance there is a tension between those duties when the state establishes legal rules to organize the media sector.

The European Court of Human Rights has held that the freedom of the media against state intervention has to be protected (see, for instance, ECHR, C-260/89 ERT, ECR I-2925).

However, protecting media pluralism is not only seen as a justification for limitations of freedom of the media under Art. 10 (2) ECHR; it has also been construed as part of the scope of protection under Art. 10 (1) to be actively protected by the Convention states. Under Art. 11 (2) of the Charter of Fundamental Rights of the European Union, this component is even more explicit.

Regulation and independent regulators

Under the above-mentioned concept of independence, media regulation is to some extent essential. It has, however, to be implemented while minimizing the infringement on the independence of the media organizations. This is the normative reason why most member states chose to have independent regulators in the media sector.

Apart from that, one reason for independence is the – assumed – effectiveness and efficiency of the regulator. Whether independence – and which kind of independence – supports the efficiency or effectiveness of a regulator in the media sector is not self-evident, but has to be construed according to the above-mentioned concept (this is done in Chapter 3 in this book by Valcke, Voorhoof and Lievens).

Conclusion

Current developments have drawn new attention to the independence of media systems and media regulators. Hungary and the changes in media legislation enacted by the Orbán government can be mentioned as an example without any definite conclusion as regards the development at this stage. While it is tempting to jump to conclusions, the analysis above has shown that a complex apparatus has to be put in place to frame independence. Hungary is not included in the case studies in Part 2 of the book, but one can consult the study *Hungarian Media Laws in Europe: An Assessment of the Consistency of Hungary's Media Laws with European Practices and Norms*, published by Central European University (Center for Media and Communication Studies 2012), or, if a more neutral reference is preferred, the entry written on 'Media Law in Hungary' in the International Encyclopaedia of Media Law (Bayer, Urban and Polyák 2012).

This chapter has argued that independence has to be seen as relative independence and that it relates to the functions that we have in mind when pondering about independence. Therefore, many chapters in this book will analyse the functions of the media and media regulation and explore links to the concept of independence.

Finally, the analysis has shown that independence cannot be adequately framed solely formally; de facto independence has to be taken into account as well. Therefore the patterns of formal and informal rules and practices are highly relevant, and will be systematically discussed in the case studies in Part 2 of this book.

References

Aristotle (2008), *Metaphysics*, New York: Cosimo.

Bayer, J., Urban, A., and Polyák, G. (2012), 'Media Law in Hungary', in P. Valcke and E. Lievens (eds.), *International Encyclopaedia of Media Law*, Alphen aan den Rijn: Kluwer Law International.

Center for Media and Communication Studies (2012), *Hungarian Media Laws in Europe: An Assessment of the Consistency of Hungary's Media Laws with European Practices and Norms*, Budapest: Central European University, https://cmcs.ceu.hu/news/2012-01-05/new-study-hungarian-media-laws-in-europe-an-assessment-of-the-consistency-of-hungary.

Gilardi, F. (2008), *Delegation in the Regulatory State: Independent Regulatory Agencies in Western Europe*, Massachusetts: Fabrizio Gilardi.

Hans Bredow Institute for Media Research, Interdisciplinary Centre for Law & ICT (ICRI), Katholieke Universiteit Leuven; Center for Media and Communication Studies (CMCS), Central European University; Cullen International; Perspective Associates (eds., 2011), *INDIREG. Indicators for independence and efficient functioning of audio-visual media services regulatory bodies for the purpose of enforcing the rules in the AVMS Directive*, Study conducted on behalf of the European Commission, Final Report. February 2011.

Held, T. (2008), *Beck'scher Kommentar zum Rundfunkrecht*, W. Hahn and T. Vesting, (eds.) § 54, Munich.

Hoffmann-Riem, W. (1996), *Regulating Media – The Licensing and Supervision of Broadcasting in Six Countries*, New York.

Hoffmann-Riem, W. (2009), *Wandel der Medienordnung-Reaktionen in Medienrecht, Medienpolitik und Medienwissenschaft*, Baden-Baden.

Keohane, R. and Nye, J. (2000), 'Introduction', in Joseph S. Nye, Jr. and John D. Donahue (eds.), *Governance in a Globalizing World*, Washington, D.C.: Brookings Institution Press, pp. 1–44.

Kickert, Walter J. M. (1993), 'Autopoiesis and the Science of (Public) Administration: Essence, Sense and Nonsense', *Organization Studies*, 14: 2, pp. 261–278.

Larsen, A., Pedersen, L. H., Sørensen, E. M. and Olsen, O. J. (2005), *Independent Regulatory Authorities in Europe*, Copenhagen: Institute of Local Government Studies.

Luhman, N. (1997), *Die Gesellschaft der Gesellschaft Band 2*, Berlin.

Marcinkowski, F. (1993), *Publizistik als autopoietisches System: Politik und Massenmedien. Einesystemtheoretische Analyse*, Opladen.

Melody, W. H. (1997a), 'On the Meaning and Importance of Independence in Telecoms Reform', *Telecommunications Policy*, 21: 3, pp. 195–199.

Montoya, M. Á. and Trillas, F. (2007), 'The Measurement of the Independence of Telecommunications Regulatory Agencies in Latin America and the Caribbean', *Utilities Policy*, 15: 3, pp. 182–190.

Rumyantsev, A. (2008), Journalistisch-redaktionelle Gestaltung: Eine verfassungswidrige Forderung? *Zeitschrift für Urheber- und Medienrecht*, 2008, pp. 33–40.

Schopenhauer, A. (2010), *The World as Will and Representation*, New York: Cambridge University Press.

Spinoza, B. (2006), *The Ethics*, Teddington: The Echo Library.

Wilke, H. (2001), *Systemtheorie III. Steuerungstheorie*, Stuttgart: Lucius & Lucius.

Part I

Assessing the independence of regulatory bodies
within the audiovisual media sector

Chapter 2

Delegation to independent regulatory authorities in the media sector:
A paradigm shift through the lens of regulatory theory

Kristina Irion
Central European University

Roxana Radu
Graduate Institute of International and Development Studies

Abstract

Today, it seems that independent regulatory authorities have almost become a natural institutional form for regulatory governance. This trend has economic and political roots, and numerous normative arguments for creating independent regulatory authorities have been put forward in the international economic, social science and legal literature, which this chapter will explore briefly. In the case of audiovisual media regulatory authorities the normative arguments for setting up independent regulators are more complex than just economic regulation. In the case of media there is a perceived need to prevent politicians and executive branches of government from exercising control over regulatory authorities because those would otherwise be highly susceptible to partisan interference. In this area, independence, as an institutional value of the regulator that should ensure the impartial and fair handling of its competences, has been a widely accepted media regulatory paradigm since the 1980s. This chapter will link regulatory theory and delegation to independent agencies with the inception of independent media regulatory authorities in Europe and introduce the various waves of development which have made this the leading institutional choice for audiovisual media governance.

Keywords: independent regulatory agencies, media, regulation, supervision, independence, delegation, liberalization, convergence, Europe

Introduction

From a European perspective, the existence of independent regulatory authorities (IRAs) in the television and now audiovisual media sector appears to be common sense. Salomon (2008: 17) asserts that it is accepted as best practice throughout the world to put an independent regulatory system in charge of licensing and overseeing the broadcasting sector. This general expectation can be found in a recent World Bank study by Buckley, Duerm, Mendel and Siocgru (2008: 160), who notice that '[t]he regulation of broadcasting should be the responsibility of an independent regulatory body established on a statutory basis with powers and duties set out explicitly in law'. The independence of audiovisual media regulators is enshrined in the relevant regional standards of the Council of Europe, which adopted a specific recommendation on this issue (Rec(2000)23) that was reinforced with a declaration (Council of Europe 2008a). At a programmatic level both documents, however non-binding, treat the matter of independence for media regulators as the only option to organize media supervision, for which there is no viable democratic alternative. They are discussed in more detail in Chapter 3 in this book by Valcke, Voorhoof and Lievens.

European Union (EU) law also carries statements on independent regulatory bodies overseeing the audiovisual media sector, which are further analysed in Chapter 4 in this book by Stevens.[1] The independence of functionally specialized independent media regulators is recognized as a value – either implicitly or explicitly – in an overwhelming majority of European countries (35 out of 39)[2] in which IRAs currently exist. In a few states, independence is explicitly recognized in a legal source higher than ordinary legislation, such as the constitution (Hans Bredow Institute, et al. 2011: 214).

This single conception of an independent media supervisor is best understood against the background of a democratic country's responsibility to observe and give full effect to the fundamental right to freedom of expression, from which media liberties are derived. Its dilemma is therefore: how to license broadcasting and introduce content regulation, but avoid the risk of stifling freedom of expression? How can countries ensure media pluralism and content diversity in a way that prevents political agendas from being imposed? Finally, how should countries enable public service television and new media without dominating it? IRAs offer an institutional solution to this dilemma because they move the regulatory function out of the purview of the administrative hierarchy in support of the presumption of non-interference by the state. In public service broadcast media, internal oversight represents another means of organizing independence from the state; some countries have opted for the latter in addition to their IRAs for the private sector (Hans Bredow Institute, et al. 2011, see also Chapter 9 in this book by Docquir, Gusy and Müller).

This chapter explores the delegation of responsibilities to IRAs in the media sector through the lens of regulatory theory and the wider phenomenon of IRAs as a mode of governance. This kind of delegation of functions originated in the financial sector, with the financial regulators and the national central banks being granted a greater degree of independence from central administration. The IRA model has become a feature of utility liberalization and peaked in the 1990s in the run up to the full liberalization of the telecommunications sector, which was imposed by EU legislation. For different rationales, IRAs have also become the first institutional choice for overseeing and enforcing the right to privacy and data protection regulation and, more recently, for expanding competences in the area of non-discrimination and equal opportunities in Europe.

In spite of the distinctiveness of the media sector, this comparative approach is grounded in recent advancements in the general theory on delegation to IRAs, which may offer a better understanding and propose new explanations for the overall phenomenon, and in particular for the proliferation of IRAs in the audiovisual media sector. We assume that such developments do not happen in isolation, but are to some degree influenced by the prevailing governance paradigm which emanates across sectoral boundaries and areas of public interest regulation. This interrogation is looking at the rationales and theories that offer an explanation for the proliferation of IRAs in Europe against the background of the literature on the regulatory state and prevalent modes of governance in the European context. It is important to note that IRAs are often introduced in a given context because of the advantage associated with this institutional form of governance, regardless of whether the local context and conditions facilitate the crucial independence needed to produce the desired regulatory outcomes.

Ultimately, this chapter relates its findings back to the various stages that can be observed in the evolution of IRAs in the broadcasting and audiovisual media sector, and answers questions regarding the viability and sustainability of a concept that is, from the very outset, a relative one (Machet 2007: 2). It also attempts to uncover trends that contribute to explaining the recent backlashes and strains on the IRA principles, which can be observed in a fair number of European countries. In today's radically altered technological, cultural and geopolitical world, the independence debate is as topical as ever, because the formal independence of institutions continues to be contested by politicians, governments and other powerful interests groups. This chapter draws to a substantial degree from the INDIREG study on *Indicators for independence and efficient functioning of audiovisual media services regulatory bodies for the purpose of enforcing the rules in the AVMS Directive* (Hans Bredow Institute, et al. 2011). However, the integration of regulatory theory and of the literature on delegation to IRAs in the audiovisual media field has been taken further in this chapter and enriched by additional analysis.

The chapter is structured as follows. The first part scrutinizes the rationales behind instituting independent sectoral regulators and the challenges emphasized by each of the theoretical approaches under investigation. The subsequent sections put into perspective broadcasting and audiovisual media regulation in Europe and the creation and functioning of IRAs, comparatively incorporating empirical evidence from their historical evolution. Accounting for the broader regulatory trends and the political conditions in which they emerged, we identify five main regulatory shifts that have occurred in the European context, from the 1950s to the present. These shifts have involved the paradigms of public service, competitive deregulation, media transition, convergence and marginalization, as well as several relevant phases within each of these. The final part of the chapter draws conclusions and points to potential future research directions.

Delegation to independent agencies in regulatory theory

Despite its relatively short history, the phenomenon of IRAs performing a wide range of different state functions has proliferated throughout Europe. This type of economic and social regulation by means of agencies operates outside the hierarchical control or oversight by the central administration (Majone 1994: 83). Thatcher (2002: 125) defines an IRA as 'a body with its own powers and responsibilities given under public law, which is organizationally separate from ministries and is neither directly elected nor managed by elected officials'.

IRAs play a crucial role not only in a number of utility or network-based sectors (e.g. rail, water, energy, electronic communications etc.), but also in other economic (e.g. competition, banking and financing) and non-economic areas (e.g. the protection of fundamental rights such as privacy, freedom of expression and non-discrimination) where independence from the state is a virtue and IRAs are put in place to further the public interest. By now, IRAs are considered an established alternative to centralized bureaucracy and in certain sectors they are almost 'the natural institutional choice for regulatory governance' (Hans Bredow Institute, et al. 2011: 12).

This particular institutional development is characteristic of the 'rise of the regulatory state in Europe' (Majone 1994: 76) which has attracted much scholarly attention. Majone's theory of the regulatory state is part of the wider paradigm shift from the positive and interventionist state to a new form of public management.[3] New public management refers to a range of state reforms aimed at modernizing the public sector towards a better management of public resources that emphasizes outcomes and efficiency (Hood 1991: 3). It entails the disaggregation of traditional bureaucratic organizations and the introduction of private sector styles of management, performance measurement and output controls. In many ways, the growth of indirect 'third party' government though IRAs is based on these principles inasmuch as it is a strategy that is leading the transition to the regulatory state (Gilardi 2008: 21). The literature discusses this phenomenon interchangeably in terms of as IRAs, non-majoritarian institutions (Thatcher and Stone Sweet 2002: 2), and – mainly in the UK context –'quangos', which stands for quasi-autonomous non-governmental organizations. It has regularly been argued that independent regulatory bodies which operate 'at arm's length from central government' (Majone 1997: 152) are a central feature of modern regulatory governance. According to this approach, the state can no longer credibly exercise all functions and tasks itself, but needs to delegate them to specialized agencies and control these agencies through regulation.

A significant amount of research has been dedicated to the rationales for setting-up IRAs and explaining their widespread diffusion in the European context. This trend has economic and political roots, and corresponds to the increasingly refined questions of conflicts of interest between the public and the private sector, as well as between different private interests. Nicolaïdes (2005) underlines two basic aspects with regard to governance: first, regulatory competences should be delegated to an independent body primarily for effectiveness considerations; and second, it is important for the regulatory authority to be independent due to a need for consistency. For Majone (1994: 84; 1997: 152), the main reasons are credible long-term commitment and expertise, resulting into better regulation (see also Gilardi 2008; Thatcher and Stone Sweet 2002).

At an abstract level, the literature proposes several different rationales for independent regulators in Europe. Besides the protection of fundamental rights, the most influential explanations fall under the principal-agent framework derived from rational choice theory. Much of the dynamic of 'agencification' in Europe, however, can be captured with the sociological institutionalists' theory on institutional isomorphism and Europeanization.

This literature is shortly revisited below as a first step before exploring its relevance to IRAs in the broadcasting and now audiovisual media sector.

Safeguarding fundamental rights

According to a normative argument that is invoked in the area of protecting fundamental rights and corresponding public interest regulation, an independent body functions as an institutional safeguard vis-à-vis the state in order to keep oversight and enforcement at arm's length from politicians (Council of Europe 2000 and 2008a; for France see Thatcher 2002: 133). Media, data protection and to a lesser extent non-discrimination and equal opportunities are areas susceptible to partisan interference from politicians and executive branches of government. In these areas, independence is an institutional value of the regulator that should ensure impartial and fair handling of its competences. The paradigmatic example is the media sector, where many countries put IRAs in charge of commercial broadcasting and maintain a system of independent oversight for public service broadcasting.

There are, however, effects which have certainly amplified the proliferation of IRAs in Europe which are discussed in the section on European integration and Europeanization below. It suffices to observe that relevant international standard-setting, institutional mimetism and Europeanization did play a role in reinforcing the creation of IRAs, which are modelled after regionally accepted best practices. The EU Data Protection Directive 95/46/EC and the Council of Europe's Recommendation (Rec(2000)23) on independent media authorities are supra-national benchmarks for IRAs in these respective areas, despite the fact that the latter is non-binding.

Principal-agent approach

The delegation of competences to agencies brings benefits, but also entails costs for the government. This dilemma is referred to as the principal-agent problem (Pollack 2002: 202; Majone and Stone Sweet 2002: 3f). Initially designed to explain the delegation of legislative authority within the US Congress committees, this schema has also been used to analyse the delegation of executive functions to federal agencies. It describes the framework where the principal confers on the agent the power to regulate a specific area, based on the assumption that any public authority is moved primarily by a cost-benefit calculation: an authority will therefore regulate a given field on its own as long as the benefits outweigh the costs (Magnette 2005: 5). Accordingly, the challenge is to find the particular governance structure that maximizes the net benefits to the principal(s), subject to various constraints.

From the point of view of self-interested politicians, different kinds of functional pressure can provide increased incentives to create IRAs and delegate decision-making competences to them. Among the reasons why an authority may believe that it has an interest in delegating one of its functions to an agent, four stand out as highly influential, and they are by no means mutually exclusive:

- Delegation can help to reduce the problem of credible commitment and political uncertainty.
- A non-governmental agent can also provide policy expertise needed by governments at low cost, and reduce their workload.
- The efficiency of decision making can be enhanced, particularly in fields characterized by a high level of technicality.
- It is also used for blame-shifting for unpopular decisions (Magnette 2005: 5; Pollack 1997; Thatcher and Stone Sweet 2002: 3f.).

Apart from the more obvious blame-shifting, these hypotheses are explained in more detail below.

Credible political commitment and overcoming political uncertainty

The main reason for granting independence to agencies may be their role in limiting 'government failure' by making a credible political commitment. Independent regulators were often introduced to replace public ownership together with sector-specific regulation. The bigger the country's investment in the respective industry sectors, the stronger the government's need is to separate regulatory agencies from its short-term political goals. An independent regulatory body can serve as a guarantor to companies that their investment in infrastructure (which involves substantial sunk costs) would be honoured in the future and that short-term political interest cannot interfere with their long-term operational interest. IRAs are a vehicle that can decrease the 'time inconsistency' problem, where policies change over time, and thus it can increase the long-term credibility and predictability of regulation (Gilardi 2008: 30f.). A working IRA model is able to limit political influence on business decisions, thereby making the risk of regulation more predictable. It has often been argued that such bodies have the benefit of not being necessarily tied to election cycles and can thus work on specific issues continuously, and ideally develop long-term solutions (Majone 1994: 84).

Political uncertainty is a normative argument which resonates somewhat with the earlier hypothesis on credible political commitment. In effect, delegation to IRAs can serve as a common solution to both. To Gilardi (2008: 49), the main difference is that political commitment is an act of self-binding (that can outlast a government), while political uncertainty is an attempt to bind subsequent governments. Gilardi argues that 'by insulating policy-making from politics, current [governments] lose some control when they are in office, but this will ensure that their choices will last longer' (2008: 48f.). Placing regulation into the hands of an independent regulatory body could allow regulations to outlive the current government's time in office and prevent future governments from revoking the policies of the current one. However, this theory is limited in that it does not adequately capture legislative reforms of subsequent governments with the aim of leaving their distinct footprint on the institutional design of a given authority.

Expertise and better regulation

This hypothesis emphasizes the quality and effectiveness of regulatory intervention where specialized IRAs are better placed to focus on regulation without being distracted or misled by political calculation. Regulation has become much more technical and complex, often in the presence of high levels of information asymmetries vis-à-vis the regulated entities, which require specialist knowledge and scientific expertise that can be better concentrated in an IRA (Thatcher 2002: 132). Flexibility, expertise and the 'continuity of concerns' in the IRA model set it apart from the traditional bureaucratic arrangement (Landis 1938/1996: 23). IRAs have – in many cases – the combined competences of rule-making and rule-application in a particular field, which distinguishes them from an executive branch of the government or the courts. Agencies can, furthermore, overcome information asymmetries in technical areas of governance and enhance the efficiency of rule-making. For Gilardi (2005a: 102) the flexible organizational structure of independent regulators – as opposed to central bureaucracy – can create attractive work conditions for experts.

In general, the broader the delegation is (i.e. the more independence given to the agency), the greater the reduction in decision-making costs and the increase in expertise and policy credibility. To be able to fulfil its regulatory tasks, the agent must be granted a certain amount of discretionary power, which might at the same time cause a divergence between the interests of the principal and the agent and affect the ability of regulators to act in their own interest (referred to as 'agency loss'). Such agency costs may be reduced by strict procedural requirements, transparency and public participation in agency decision making, and reliance on judicial review. The institutional design of an agency matters and principal-agent theory analyses how the governance structure and formal control mechanisms can constrain an agency's ability to pursue of its own preferences (Pollack 2002: 201). Ultimately, retaining and using formal controls by elected officials is bound to have an impact on the independence of agencies in various ways.

European integration and Europeanization

The theory of 'institutional isomorphism' suggests that if an apparently successful model of a regulator exists, it is likely to be copied (Thatcher 2002: 136). One of the drivers for institutional isomorphism or 'mimetism' (133) is the experience with an independent regulatory body in a specific domain, which can then be copied in other areas of regulation, or can become international policy learning. Europeanization can be perceived as a subset of institutional isomorphism or can be acknowledged as a self-standing normative explanation of the proliferation of independent regulatory agencies in this region. Gilardi (2005b: 89f.)

explains the diffusion of independent regulatory agencies across Europe as both a top-down process of Europeanization and a horizontal emulation between European countries.

The EU has significantly catalysed the inception of independent regulatory authorities in its member states and beyond. Though it may at first appear surprising that the delegation of competences to the EU is connected to an increase of regulation at national level, this is easily explained by the necessity of building new regulatory agencies and of adjusting existing authorities in order to implement the EU legislation. In practice, the creation and/or strengthening of IRAs was often imposed on member states by the EU regulatory framework for a specific sector, where liberalization and harmonization measures explicitly require the establishment of such bodies (Thatcher 2002: 133f.). This is the case for utilities sectors, such as electronic communications, energy, railways, post etc., but also, under EU harmonized regulation, regarding data protection and non-discrimination issues (see Chapter 4 in this book by Stevens for more details). Successive new member states and candidate countries have created IRAs in preparation for EU accession and the implementation of the *acquis communautaire*.

The changing role of independent regulatory agencies

In the early 2000s, the IRA model reached the peak of its popularity in Europe and there are now signs of a decline or hollowing-out. As regulatory practice evolves in response to globalization and the increasing complexity of public policy, new tensions around the IRA model surface in a growing scholarly debate about new approaches to governance in the twenty-first century – aptly labelled 'new modes of governance' (Héritier and Lehmkuhl 2011).[4] New governance entails a range of novel approaches to policy-making across all aspects of public policy, i.e. processes, institutions and instruments. It is characterized by an increasing reliance on soft means of regulation, such as self- and co-regulation, the exchange of good practices, industry standards and peer pressure. Another trend is the rise of networked governance, which involves the collaboration of a variety of policy stakeholders. According to Rhodes (2000: 61), the key features of governance networks include diplomacy, reciprocity and interdependence.

For this discussion two ongoing developments are pertinent: first, the changing role of government in prescribing governance mechanisms for achieving public goals, which has become less direct and provided more space for multi-stakeholder participation, involving NGOs, industry professionals and market actors in the process of regulatory development, enforcement and implementation. Second, the replacing of fixed and static regulatory commands with mandates that allow for evolution and dynamism in the face of technological and normative developments. In the light of these developments, IRAs face new demands with respect to their role in the governance system in which flexibility and expertise, networking and collaboration are emphasized over top-down intervention. In response to such pressures, IRAs are increasingly acting as brokers between the various interests, with the aim to pursue an amorphous public interest. To fulfil this role, they conduct research and collect evidence, which is infused into the public discourse among the stakeholders concerned by forging coalitions and steering networks towards finding appropriate solutions.

Emerging modes of governance reshape the IRA model fundamentally. On the one hand, they bring about a diversification of competences that include soft governance mechanisms, such as standard-setting and benchmarking for co- or self-regulation, alongside the more traditional responsibilities delegated to sectoral authorities. With the menu of regulatory tools greatly diversified, the assessment of the most effective instrument is no longer straightforward. Currently, IRAs need to engage in extensive research to acquire the highly specialized knowledge required. However, cooperative means are more and more frequently used, including consultation and deliberation processes with other relevant actors within a specific policy domain. In the case of environmental regulation, Jordan, Wurzel and Zito (2005: 492) note that, for new policy instruments, 'co-existence appears to be the most dominant, although there is some incipient *fusion* and *competition*' (original emphasis), thus allowing for the emergence of a multitude of hybrid types.

On the other hand, the delegation of powers no longer only takes place from the national government to the independent regulator, but also to the EU level, thus altering the practices of IRAs. In effect, we are facing the creation of multiple expert fora for exchanging specialized information and sharing best practices, as well as the fast institutionalization of regulatory networks at the European/EU level, set in place for fostering regulatory harmonization and uniformity of policy implementation across Europe. Such bodies, known as European regulatory networks (ERNs), provide expertise and reduce the cost of gathering information in a transnational environment, while promoting international regulatory learning. For example, in telecommunications, the European Regulators Group (ERG) was founded in 2002 under EC law and replaced in 2009 with the Body of European Regulators for Electronic Communications (BEREC), which has enhanced competences for harmonization and is composed of the heads of the national IRAs of member states (Regulation (EC) No 1211/2009). This represented the first instance of formal engagement by the European Commission with the implementation of EU directives at the national level (Coen and Thatcher 2008: 58). ERNs are now common for sectors such as banking, securities, data protection, electricity and gas, etc.

The supranational networks of regulators appear as 'functional and informal means of establishing best practice and procedures for sector regulation' (Coen and Thatcher 2006: 7), while epitomizing a double delegation of power and functions: from national governments to domestic IRAs and to the EU, at the supranational level. In line with the principal-agent theory, the IRAs thus become the common agent of both the national government and the European Commission, which might bring about agency loss concerns. Nevertheless, the delegators retain a degree of control over the ERNs not only in allocating resources, but also in designing the distribution of responsibilities, in particular by minimizing the rights of initiative.

Section conclusions

In this section, various hypotheses and normative arguments have been presented to explain the shift towards delegating powers to IRAs. Three important caveats must be made. First, delegation to IRAs is primarily discussed in relation to the privatization and re-regulation of utilities, which is of little relevance to other areas of regulation. Thatcher (2002: 133f.) observes that these pressures on elected officials to delegate authorities 'were particularly strong in the regulation of markets, especially after privatisation, liberalisation and EU legislation', but weaker in other fields where regulatory bodies were established. This has become evident at the level of formal independence and powers, where regulatory bodies in other fields tend to underperform compared to IRAs in network and utility markets. Second, these are alternating hypotheses for the emergence of the IRAs as a governance mode. Hence, the pressures to delegate to IRAs stemming from functional advantages (rational-choice mode), on the one hand, and from institutional mimetism and Europeanization, on the other hand, are not interrelated (Thatcher 2002). Nevertheless, policy diffusion has the potential to create a positive feedback loop. It was even suggested that IRAs have been created because this is the prevalent mode for institutional governance and because it is happening elsewhere.

Third, the reasons for creating independent regulatory authorities can differ depending on which country is the focus of research. Legal, economic, political and cultural factors also influence the shaping of regulators, resulting in varying institutional designs and even organizations, which, though similar at the formal level, can nevertheless vary widely at the level of implementation and efficient functioning. Some of the arguments presented in this section, such as the hypotheses on credible commitment and political uncertainty, have been developed against the background of countries that have been through an organic development in which independent regulators became the preferred mode of governance in certain areas in public policy. This may not adequately capture exogenous effects stemming, for example, from Europeanization, where countries implemented independent regulators in line with, and as a consequence of, EU legislation. Where exogenous factors have prompted the establishment of independent regulatory authorities, there is a risk that these bodies remain essentially anomalous and not embedded in the administration system, since administrative and procedural reforms do not automatically accompany the spread of the IRAs (Hans Bredow Institute, et al. 2011: 15).

Paradigm shifts and independent media regulatory authorities in Europe

National media systems take different forms in accordance not only with alternative underlying logics and technological developments, but also with political traditions and legacies binding the decision-makers and relevant stakeholders. After scrutinizing the normative considerations, we now turn to investigating the interactions between historical developments, political trends and the transformation of governance in media regulation in specific European contexts. Drawing on the theory of media policy paradigm shifts developed by Van Cuilenburg and McQuail (2003), we expand the scope of inquiry to reflect on the development phases of media-specialized IRAs and their subsequent impact on the audiovisual landscape in Europe. Analysing the conditions under which structural shifts occur, we emphasize the extent to which broadcasting and audiovisual media regulation is subject to general regulatory trends (public service, delegation to independent authorities, network governance), developments in the market (the advent of private broadcasters in the beginning of the 1980s and the current convergence of television broadcasting and other forms of audiovisual media services and means of transmission), as well as structural political transformations (the fall of communism, post-conflict reconstruction, re-politicization and neo-authoritarian tendencies).

Nowadays, any communications and media policy is aimed at 'securing the free and equal access' (Van Cuilenburg and McQuail 2003: 205) to broadcasting media markets and to the means of transmission, while protecting a range of content standards in order to serve the needs of society. Different forms of state intervention[5] – legitimized in the name of the public interest – have dominated the history of media systems. The establishment of supervisory authorities originally coincided with the acknowledgement that media structures should no longer act as the operational arm of politics. Additionally, once the spectrum scarcity justification for government regulation lost credibility with the emergence of satellite and cable distribution platforms in the 1980s, liberalization of market access and delegation of powers were seen as an alternate means to regulate the nascent commercial television landscape. At that time, independent regulators were established across Europe in order to oversee the numerous commercial broadcasters; however, in most of these cases, their competences would also extent to public service broadcasting.

The rationales for IRAs in the broadcasting sector are thus bifurcated: independent supervision was established in the public interest and in response to liberalization. These two paradigms constitute the building blocks for an array of new regulatory arrangements that would combine elements of both, and would also increase the variation in IRA practices across Europe throughout the 1990s and 2000s. According to our extrapolation of Van Cuilenburg and McQuail's theory, later creations of IRAs are more likely to have followed the trend under Europeanization and institutional isomorphism theories. The latest media regulatory shift which post-dates the theory of Van Cuilenburg and McQuail (2003) is the wider trend to governance and new modes of governance that has been characterized as a hollowing-out of traditional regulation and regulatory institutions. Thus, our reference to the marginalization paradigm must be read as a wider distribution of regulatory functions to stakeholders and governance networks at national and European levels.

Table 2.1 below summarizes our interpretation of the evolution of media regulation going back to the early days of radio and television. The five distinctive shifts we identify and their specific phases are analysed in the subsequent sections.

Table 2.1: Overview of paradigm shifts in broadcasting and audiovisual media regulation in Europe, their necessary conditions and their implications.

Paradigm shift (time period)	Necessary conditions and determinant factors	Implications for the regulator and its independence
Public service paradigm (1950s – late 1970s)	In Western Europe: – scarcity of spectrum (for radio and television) – social equity and equal access considerations (universal service) – nature of programming fostering national identity	State television, acting as the operational arm of the government, or exceptionally public service broadcasting organization under internal oversight
Competitive deregulation paradigm (1980s – mid 1990s)	In Western Europe: – market liberalization due to the expansion of cable and satellite television, resulting in a diversification of content (except where protectionism prevailed for longer) – internationalization of broadcast media markets (the advent of satellites) – minimal state ideology in commercial broadcasting (based primarily on economic rationales) – transformation of state television into independent public service broadcasters	Establishment of independent regulatory agencies to oversee the new and numerous commercial broadcasters and in many instances also the public service broadcaster
Media transition paradigm Post-communist media (1989 – mid 2000s)	In Central and Eastern Europe: – large-scale transition process towards a liberal democratic model (political, economic and social change) – legacy of communism in the approach to audiovisual media markets – pressure from the international community to reform the media – transformation of the state-controlled broadcaster into a public service broadcaster	Establishment of regulatory agencies which: – retained a high degree of political control, or – were shaped as independent bodies, after the available Western models
Post-conflict intervention (1995 – mid 2000s)	In countries of Ex-Yugoslavia: – sharp ethnic divisions – post-conflict general reconstruction – attempts by ethnic groups to take control over broadcasting for nationalist propaganda purposes – International intervention and institution building	Establishment of independent media regulatory authorities to provide safeguards against a monopoly of the media by partisan groups

Paradigm shift (time period)	Necessary conditions and determinant factors	Implications for the regulator and its independence
Re-politicization and neo-authoritarian tendencies (early 2000s – present)	In new EU member states: – politically-motivated reforms that affect the broadcasting sector – neo-authoritarian tendencies	Remodelling the IRAs' practices through highly politicized procedures, while maintaining the appearance of independence
Convergence paradigm (late 1990s – present)	In Europe: – fast-changing globalized environment – technological developments, converging trend of audiovisual platforms – horizontal regulation of all audiovisual media services (AVMS)	Establishment of some converged independent authorities for electronic media and communications. Different models of supervision introduced by on-demand audiovisual media services.
Marginalization paradigm (late 1990s – present)	In the EU: – co- and self-regulation gaining more ground – network governance and the use of soft governance tools – Internet regulation – globalization/internationalization	Expanding the responsibilities of existent IRAs to perform co-regulatory functions or establishing new IRAS for this purpose. IRAs to enhance deliberative capacity as public-facing institutions. The spread and institutionalization of regulatory networks at the EU level.

Source: Adapted from Hans Bredow Institute, et al. (2011: 87f).

Back in 2003, van Cuilenberg and McQuail observed that a new communications policy paradigm was taking shape, representing a third major shift since the first attempts at regulating communication systems. According to them, in the early phase of emerging communications industry policy, regulation had revolved around the promotion of national interest, the separation of regimes for different technologies and the strategic development of the communications industry. The three spheres which policy distinguished between were: print media, common carriers (telephony and telegraph) and broadcasting. Whereas the first sector remained minimally regulated for many decades, the other two came under the control of governments as soon as they appeared.

In Europe, radio became a mass medium in the 1920s, developing technologically from the postal, telephone and telegraph (PTT) services, which were owned by the state. Whereas in the United States the radio industry was from the start a private sector activity, soon after the expansion of airwaves across Europe, the governments took control over them by invoking the need to foster the public interest (Van Cuilenburg and McQuail 2003: 188). The crucial importance of radio during the First World War created both the incentive and the justification for imposing an exclusive state monopoly in countries such as Germany, Sweden and France. Switzerland followed a different model, by having small public corporations running the radio stations in large cities to serve different communities. In other countries, such as Belgium, Denmark and Norway, radio transmission began as a commercial enterprise but was later transformed into a state-operated enterprise.

In the period leading up to the Second World War, the German and British regulatory developments were the two models that largely influenced the history of European media thereafter. In Germany, broadcasting was perceived as a function of public administration, and an exclusive state monopoly over the radio was imposed from the start. During the Weimar Republic (1918–1933), all the transmission facilities belonged to the *Reichspost*, which became part of the centralized Imperial Broadcasting Company in 1925. In sharp contrast, in Britain the liberal state tradition initially allowed for a representation of private interests. The British Broadcasting Company Ltd. – established in 1922 by the British General Post Office as a commercial venture – had the primary task of allocating frequencies and distributing licenses and the resulting revenues. By 1927, the British Broadcasting Company turned into a non-commercial entity, the British Broadcasting Corporation (BBC). Later on, some of the features of the BBC model were replicated in the evolution of the German media system regulation (OSI 2005: 34), supporting the idea of transnational policy learning.

The need for expanding regulation to wireless and, subsequently, television, was subordinated to three different rationales: technical, economic and political (Humphreys 1996). Apart from the state intervening in allocating spectrum (Elstein 2005: 68–72), socio-political motivations prevailed in the interwar period (Van Cuilenburg and McQuail 2003: 191), at a time in which 'mass democracy', state reconstruction and nation-building took precedence. The use of broadcast media for political purposes reached a peak during World War II, when most European governments directly conducted their propaganda by taking control over the channels of communication.

The public service paradigm – internal oversight

After the Second World War, the importance of separating broadcast content from political interests was acknowledged as a safeguard against the instrumentalization of mass media, and this also implied that broadcasting organizations should be structurally independent from the state. At the same time, there was pressure to ensure the democratic accountability of broadcasters. Eventually, this led to the gradual establishment of public service broadcasters (PSBs); nonetheless, they inherited the state operation of radio and television. In contrast with the independence enjoyed by the printed press, television broadcasting received a different regulatory treatment, resulting in less freedom to decide on the content provided or to manage a diversity of standpoints. This was primarily justified by the idea that this new medium exerted opinion-forming powers over 'captive audiences', in the context of the limited choice of broadcasters that was available due to the prevailing spectrum scarcity, a consequence of the technical limitations of the time.

PSBs reproduced, to a large extent, the characteristics of both the political system and the particular historical context in which they emerged (Jakubowicz 2008). Autonomy was derived, in the beginning, from the PSB statute. The BBC, established through a Royal Charter and not by an act of parliament, from the outset had a considerable amount of independence from interference by political actors and protected this by a ten-year renewable statute. Starting in 1927, the BBC services were monitored by a Board of Governors, nominated by the government; today, this is the function of the BBC Trust.[6]

Diverging from the BBC model, the internal control of the German public service broadcasting system was ensured by granting appointment and dismissal rights to representatives of the plural interests in society, the so-called 'socially significant groups' or organized interests (such as political parties, federal, state and local government representatives, churches, trade unions and employers' associations, professional associations of journalists etc.). Germany was also among the pioneers of decentralized public broadcasting (Humphreys 1996: 132). In accordance with the federal construction of the country and with the 1949 Basic Law, the regulation of broadcasting services fell under the jurisdiction of the 16 constituent states (*Länder*). By 1956, nine regional public broadcasting corporations[7] had been established, governed by independent broadcasting councils (*Rundfunkräte*).

Decentralization of broadcasting took place at the end of the 1950s in many other European countries as well, following different underlying logics. In states such as Norway and Belgium this happened in order to cater for the linguistic and cultural needs of the countries' constituent groups. In these cases, the broadcasting system remained 'purely public' (Brants and Suine 1992: 104) until liberalization in the 1980s. In France, the governmental control of broadcasting continued even after the establishment of regulatory agencies (Coppens and Saeys 2006: 272). In most Western European countries the activities of commercial broadcasters remained, to a large extent, confined to the public service paradigm.

The competitive deregulation paradigm

Cable and satellite technologies became widespread in the 1980s and this eliminated the technical constraint of scarcity of frequencies, and allowed a gradually higher number of commercial broadcasters to operate. The reasons for which many Western European states reconsidered their degree of intervention in media markets at that time were primarily economic: minimal state ideology, inward investment and revenues from advertising (see Table 2.1). In the late 1970s, this paradigmatic change occurred primarily due to 'the ambitions of media corporations and governments alike to benefit from the economic opportunities offered by communication technologies' (Van Cuilenburg and McQuail 2003: 197). In the Cold War context, the implications of the move towards deregulation were twofold: on the one hand, it further reduced political control; and on the other hand, it imposed few or no public service obligations on private broadcasters (OSI 2005: 45), whose number increased continuously after liberalization.[8]

Yet, in order to maintain a strong role for the PSB, many Western European governments pursued a different strategy, one of public investment or protectionism (Van Cuilenburg and McQuail 2003: 195). This manifested itself in a late liberalization and was applied in Greece, Spain and France – where the practice was also known as *dirigisme* (Venturelli 1998: 189). In contrast, broadcasting in small countries such as Andorra and Monaco, which could be received in the larger neighbouring countries, remained purely commercial (Humphreys 1996: 125). Likewise, Luxembourg developed from the start a commercial broadcasting market, whose regulation was entrusted to a for-profit monopoly, the *Compagnie Luxembourgoise de Télédiffusion* (CLT), with a limited public service remit.

These different patterns of deregulation also affected the type of relations that existed between the PSBs and national governments in Europe (Dragomir 2008: 24–25). On the one hand, the proportionality model was employed in countries such as Germany, Austria and the Netherlands to retain the influence of political parties and civil society groups in the governance of the public broadcaster). On the other hand, the insulated PSB model – requiring the juxtaposition of intermediary non-political bodies – dominated in the Scandinavian countries, as well as in the UK and Ireland.

Establishing independent regulatory authorities for the broadcasting sector

The late 1980s witnessed the rise of the pan-European Eutelsat and Astra satellites, as well as the expansion of commercial satellite television platforms in Europe. As a reaction to these fundamental changes occurring in a short time span, and to the pressure from commercial entities, further deregulation was envisioned. At the same time, several safeguards were set in place to limit political interference in the work and functioning of public and commercial broadcasters through the establishment of national independent regulatory agencies. These safeguards included conferring the legal status of autonomous corporations to PSBs; regulation by special internal boards (e.g. the BBC Board of Governors and German broadcasting councils), special external bodies (e.g. the IBA in the UK) or a combination of internal and external supervision (as in Sweden); and a degree of financial autonomy of PSBs.[9] In the light of such developments in several of the larger European states, the introduction of independent regulators also took precedence in other parts of the continent, where governments were compelled to create new regulatory authorities to oversee the broadcasting sector and to move away from political control. The shift from interventionist to deregulatory policies, primarily influenced by the minimal state ideology and market liberalization, gave rise to a great variation in regulatory patterns across Europe.

In the UK, the 1954 Television Act introduced the Independent Television Authority (ITA), a public corporation with the mandate to create the first independent television broadcaster (Scannell 1990: 18). The Independent Broadcasting Authority (IBA), evolving from the ITA, was founded in 1972 to oversee the allocation of frequencies for fifteen regional independent television (ITV) companies[10] and a large number of independent local radio stations. In 1984, the United Kingdom established an independent regulatory agency for telecommunications, Oftel. The successor of the IBA and Oftel were two of the five bodies that merged into the Office of Communications (Ofcom) in 2003.

In Germany in the 1980s, commercial broadcasting was regulated by the individual states (*Länder*) within the parameters set by the German Constitutional Court. This resulted in a new layer of media authorities overseeing non-public service broadcasting. Inspired by the practice of PSB's internal oversight, membership in these bodies would be assigned according to the principle of interest diversity (ensuring all main parties would have a voice) and fair representation of 'socially significant groups'. For pieces of legislation that would require national frameworks, a system of inter-state treaties based on collective agreements was established. In 1990, following the re-unification with East Germany, the same rules were used as model for the audiovisual media system in the former communist part of the country.

In France, the state monopoly over broadcasting was only lifted in 1982, with the introduction of the Law on Audiovisual Communication (OSI 2005: 645). The same act established the first independent regulatory agency for broadcasting in the country, the High Authority for Audiovisual Communications (*Haute autorité de la communication audiovisuelle*), which started supervising the appointments for PSBs, licensing radio and television programmes and oversee certain aspects of programming. The privatization of the cable sector in France was implemented during the first period of 'cohabitation' under President Mitterand (1986–1988), and made the French media market 'one of the most marketised' (Humphreys 1996: 165) in Europe by the early 1990s. The 1988 Law on Freedom of Communication created the legal framework for the operation of a dual private-public system; at the same time, the Higher Audiovisual Council (*Conseil Supérieur de l'Audiovisuel*) was given extensive powers, including the power to suspend the transmission of broadcasters in case of non-compliance with the existent regulation.

In Italy, the first restructuring of the national broadcaster, RAI, occurred in 1975. The media market was characterized by strong regulation for public service broadcasters and 'wild de-regulation' (Humphreys 1996: 179) for commercial broadcasters, relying heavily on entertainment and advertising. The 1975 reform transferred the control of public television from the executive branch to the political parties represented in parliament. Consequently, the Italian public broadcasting system remained highly politicized; the largest political parties came to dominate different channels of RAI under a system known as *Lottizzazione*. This context resulted in a specific institutional arrangement: a parliamentary commission known as 'the Guarantor'. With the passage of the 1990 Broadcasting Act, the authority to decide on a wide range of issues (such as ownership structures or compliance with viewers' interests) was entrusted to a single individual, usually a magistrate.

Satellite broadcasting and the re-broadcasting via cable networks of satellite television programmes created new pressures on closed national media systems. Transborder television, as it was then called, intensified regulatory competition between countries in the European region. In 1989, the European Convention on Transfrontier Television (Council of Europe CETS No. 132), as well as the Television without Frontiers Directive, instituted the country of origin principle and minimum harmonization of television services in the sector. Thus, the transnational dynamics in the European television landscape could be interpreted as creating a sector-specific functional pressure to maintain and strengthen independent supervisory bodies at a national level as a strategy to attract the establishment of television companies. Some smaller countries in Western Europe, most notably Luxembourg and Andorra, succeeded as television companies' headquarters heavyweights (Humphreys 1996: 178). Progressing internationalization made standard-setting and regulation at the supra-national level recurrent features over the next two decades.

Media transition paradigm

At a time when media market internationalization and liberalization flourished in Western Europe, the Eastern part of the continent was marked by fundamentally different media systems, with a tightly-controlled state broadcaster in each country and limited or no access to a plurality of views. With the 1989 regime change, the countries of Central and Eastern Europe (CEE) embarked on a democratization process that was characterized by multiple simultaneous transitions that were still marked by the communist legacy. Consequently, the challenge of restructuring the media after 1989 revolved primarily around minimizing the interference of the state – but not per se of politics – in the functioning of the newly transformed PSB and of the IRAs in the broader context of democratic institution-building. Against the background of the former regime, there was a strong desire in many CEE countries to structure the audiovisual media and their supervision according to the highest European standards and best practices.

The involvement of foreign donors and the Europeanization process have been the main drivers in turning the independence of broadcast media regulation into a widely acknowledged value. The international community also shaped media reforms in the post-conflict environments in ex-Yugoslavia, where the creation and strengthening of IRAs was encouraged as a means of reducing partisan monopolies over the audiovisual media landscape. More recently, some of the new EU member states have witnessed a series of politically motivated reforms that challenge the independence of the media regulatory bodies, while preserving the appearance of democratic change implementation.

Post-communist media transition

In spite of a slight liberalization brought about by Gorbachev's *glasnost* reforms in the Soviet Union in the 1980s, the PSBs in CEE remained largely under a state monopoly. After the 1989 revolutions in the region, media freedom 'was not granted to the sector by governments via negotiations, but grew independently within most countries once it became clear that there were no longer any communist barriers to prevent free speech' (Mungiu-Pippidi 2003: 32). To a large extent, both liberalization and media plurality pressures came by virtue of acquiring membership to the Council of Europe and, later on, candidate status for EU membership (OSI 2005: 43). Although the EU lacks the competence to determine the structure of media supervision in the member states, which should effectively preclude EU harmonization and integration as an explanation, the EU has nevertheless promoted IRAs in the audiovisual media sector during the EU accession process.

In the early days after the regime change, when the public broadcaster was still controlled by the government, reluctance to liberalize the media market produced different patterns of developments in CEE countries. In addition to the Czech Republic and Slovakia, two Baltic countries were pioneers of the dual private-public system in the early 1990s: Lithuania and Estonia. The monopolistic position of the state ended in Albania and Bulgaria in the mid-1990s, in Latvia in 1996 and in Hungary in 1997 (OSI 2005: 35–36). In Poland and Romania, the licensing of commercial broadcasters took place between 1993 and 1997 (see also Chapter 7 in this book by Klimkiewicz in the context of Poland). In Lithuania, until 2000, no regulation applied to the commercial sector, whereas the public broadcasting sector was heavily regulated.

The new audiovisual landscape of the CEE countries was shaped by two contradictory objectives: retaining political control and following Western models (Petković 2004). The first objective was closely linked to the communist legacy. In Poland, for example, the National Broadcasting Council (*Krajowa Rada Radiofonii i Telewizji* – KRRiT) that was instituted by the 1992 Broadcasting Law, although considered to be the first democratic body of the country (OSI 2005: 1089), was defined by statute as a 'state institution'.[11] The allocation of broadcast licenses was not delegated to IRAs in countries such as Estonia, where it remained with the Ministry of Culture, or the Former Yugoslav Republic of Macedonia, where it was run until 2005 by the government in cooperation with the Broadcasting Council (Dragomir 2008: 7). Traditionally, the CEE media markets also relied on state financing for broadcasting regulatory bodies. While most of the broadcasting and public service media laws in the region were passed by 1994, the independence of regulatory agencies remained hampered by heavily politicized appointment procedures (Petković 2004), such as those governing the appointment of the members of the Radio and Television Broadcasting Council in the Czech Republic or those which required IRA members in Poland to have no political past (OSI 2005: 1092). In Romania, Lithuania, the Former Yugoslav Republic of Macedonia and Croatia, regulatory agencies were granted independent status from the beginning, yet political interference in the functioning of the body was not entirely absent.

The second objective reflected the influence of Western European models and practices (OSI 2005: 34–38) and entailed a degree of institutional mimetism and international policy learning. Post-communist countries tried to follow the European media standards by imitation or adaptation (Petković 2004: 10). For example, the 1993 Albanian press law was drafted after the law of one of the German states (*Länder*), but was considered too restrictive and was replaced in 1997. In the Lithuanian case, two separate regulators were established for public and commercial broadcasting[12] and, in line with the German model of involving 'socially significant groups', nine out of the thirteen members of the Radio and Television Commission of Lithuania – which regulated commercial broadcasters – were appointed by professional organizations (OSI 2005: 45). Following the French example, IRAs appoint the governing bodies of the public broadcasters in Bulgaria,[13] Estonia, Latvia and Poland.

For many years, the regulation of the audiovisual sector remained subordinated to the ideologies of the political elites driving the transformation. The shift came through the infusion of values promoted by the international organizations and the multitude of foreign donors operating in the region, which fuelled a strong respect for and adherence to the rule of law, considered to be the necessary condition for the 'emergence of a genuine legal culture of standards related to freedom of expression and freedom of the media' (Kaminski 2003: 64). Additionally, the international actors provided support for the establishment of professional organizations, trade unions and training organizations. The impact of Europeanization manifested itself in the attempts of the candidate countries to comply with accepted European standards and best practices and harmonize their national legislation accordingly, in particular with regard to the transformation of the public broadcaster from a state-controlled to a public service oriented entity (Jakubowicz and Sükösd 2008: 16).

By 2007, ten of the countries in the region had become full members of the EU. Similar to the prevailing governance approach after liberalization and re-regulation in the utilities sectors, independent regulation was introduced after the transformation from state broadcasting to public service broadcasting and the deregulation phase. Across all sectors, part of the dynamic that transformed regulatory governance, in particular in the countries of Central and Eastern Europe, is attributed to European integration and Europeanization. Nonetheless, the transformations in post-communist broadcast regulation occurred within a limited time frame and thus their systematization was more prone to political influence, especially in cases in which the democratic institutions supposed to counterbalance such politicization were themselves undergoing reform.

Media intervention in post-conflict states
The restructuring of broadcasting following the end of the wars in former Yugoslavia in 1995 (Bosnia and Herzegovina) and 1999 (Kosovo) represented a new instance of media intervention by the international community, with the aim of preventing national monopolies or ethnic domination. A historical precedent for this kind of intervention was set by the Allied Occupation Forces' efforts to influence the media system in Germany and Japan after the Second World War (Price and Thompson 2002: 4). In the Western Balkans, the

intervention was intended to limit the effects of politically-fuelled nationalist propaganda. As illustrated in Table 2.1, the need for establishing IRAs was subsumed to the broader objective of limiting partisan interference in a post-conflict environment. It was, in the words of Karlowicz (2003: 116), 'an entirely new experiment in the field of media'.

Once the Dayton Peace Accords put an end to the war in November 1995, the involvement of the Office of the High Representative (OHR), the Organization for Security and Co-operation in Europe (OSCE) and numerous NGOs represented a real test in reshaping and reforming the media space as part of the democratic institution-building process. Bosnia and Herzegovina represented a special case, as the media were divided along ethnic lines in three distinct spheres: Bosniak, Serb and Croat. Thus the process of disentangling the media from nationalist propaganda and the struggle to create an enabling environment were further complicated, as Chapter 11 in this book by Jusić explains in more detail. In Bosnia and Herzegovina, an Independent Media Commission (IMC), was introduced in 1998 as a temporary body for print media and broadcasting, as well as for establishing codes for the press and for the Internet, and was expected to transfer its authority to a local body as soon as possible.

The establishment of a country-wide public service broadcaster in Bosnia and Herzegovina, as well as a public broadcaster for the Federation entity, was decreed by the international community's High Representative in 1999 and again in 2000. Due to political resistance, however, it was not until 2002 that the old state broadcasting system was formally replaced by the Public Broadcasting Service of Bosnia and Herzegovina (PBSBiH), later renamed Radio and Television of Bosnia-Herzegovina (BHRT), as well as public broadcasters in both entities – the Radio-Television of the Federation of Bosnia & Herzegovina (RTFBiH) and the Radio-Television of Republika Srpska (RTRS), respectively (OSI 2005: 294–296). In 2001, the IMC and the telecommunications regulator were merged into a new converged regulatory body, the Communications Regulatory Agency (CRA) – the first of its kind in the region.

The case of Kosovo is not entirely different. During the Milosevic regime, the Albanian-speaking media were banned in Kosovo (Karlowicz 2003), while the media system was appropriated by the state, which controlled all information channels (Thompson and de Luce 2002). Just as the 1995 Dayton Peace Accords in the Bosnian case, the Rambouillet Accords ending the Kosovo conflict did not include any specifications for media reform, except for guaranteeing freedom of expression. As part of the UN Interim Mission in Kosovo (UNMIK), the OSCE was mandated to develop 'civil society, non-governmental organizations, political parties, and local media' (Mertus and Thompson 2002: 260). In spite of the peace proceedings, ethnic tensions continued to be fuelled by the partisan media in Kosovo. In response, the Temporary Media Commissioner (TMC) was created in June 2000 as a provisional entity mandated up to 2004. From the outset, the TMC was given extensive powers, ranging from establishing codes of ethics – which became prerequisites for granting broadcast licenses – to the imposition of substantial fines for promoting hate speech. To balance these powers, an independent three-judge Media Appeals Board was put in place. A public broadcaster, Radio-Television Kosovo (RTK), and two commercial televisions with a public service orientation (KTV and TV 21) were funded primarily by international donors. As of 2003, a public financing system based on licence fees has been established for RTK. The Bosnian model inspired the OSCE to establish an Independent Media Commission in Kosovo in 2005.

The paradigmatic change of introducing independent regulators in post-war environments at a time of general power transition poses both conceptual and practical concerns for media freedoms safeguarding approaches and delegation models. Bosnia and Herzegovina and Kosovo represent special cases in which influence was exerted by international donors on audiovisual policy at critical moments of post-conflict reconstruction. This was done at the expense of having local stakeholders significantly involved or getting real needs articulated in a bottom-up process (Price and Thompson 2002). Several pieces of regulation which constituted rather advanced achievements on paper in fact remained inefficient in practice and not adapted to local specificities. De facto, in both cases, media reform was delayed because the peace accords included almost no specific provisions on this subject,[14] thus considerably underestimating the role played by the media in the reconciliation process.

Re-politicization and neo-authoritarian tendencies

The politicization of media supervision has always been a challenge, given its potential to erode the IRA model from inside. The delicate relationship between politics and the media remains a constant source of temptation to exert influence on the IRA. In the Berlusconi era, the Italian media system achieved notoriety because of the dominance of the prime minister's company, RTI/Mediaset, in commercial broadcasting in combination with his influence over the Italian public service broadcaster RAI. In this context, moreover, the Italian regulator AGCOM was affected by appointments of its president and commissioners that were considered highly politicized. There are currently several countries, notably in the CEE region, where governments engage more or less bluntly in the reverse modelling of IRAs away from international best practice enshrined in the recommendation of the Council of Europe (Rec(2000)23). The early 2000s have marked a paradigm shift because re-politicization has gained ground. The resulting marginalization of IRAs is just the visible result of the mismatch between independent media supervision as an ideal and the regular operation of such bodies.

The politicians who have the primacy to define the formal institutional framework can at any time pass or amend laws to model their preferred version of an IRA (Hans Bredow Institute, et al. 2011: 34). Changes to the IRA's constituting laws are therefore a potent vehicle to re-align regulators with a country's political majorities at any given time. In order to avoid the appearance that these changes are exclusively politically motivated, a reform need is established, and this offers a ready narrative to pursue the IRA's reorganization. Quite often, the context for a reform of the media regulation is set by the EU itself with the passing of a Directive that requires transformation into national law, as was the case with the 2007 Audiovisual Media Services Directive (2007/65/EC) (in its consolidated version

Directive 2010/13/EU, European Parliament and the Council 2010). Examining the record of changes to the original statute can reveal whether these were related to changes in a country's political majorities and if the independence of the respective IRA has deteriorated as a consequence of it. There are many examples of the proximity between a change of government and a change in media supervision, for instance by effectively replacing the board members or the chairman of an IRA's highest decision-making organs. One such case occurred in Poland after the 2005 elections, as the restructuring of KRRiT can be linked to political motivations much more than to an objective reason.

What is remarkable in this regard is the new tendency of negative yet accepted practices in media regulation to diffuse in Europe. For instance in 2011, the Hungarian government made an effort to defend their highly controversial media reforms by referring to specific similar legislations in other European countries. If such negative policy learning had an empirical basis beyond Hungary, it would significantly alter our understanding of institutional isomorphism in Europe. This theory holds that countries copy apparently successful models of regulators elsewhere (Thatcher 2001: 3). If, however, in a political value system an IRA is considered successful if it complies with minimum requirements of formal independence, while allowing enough leverage for political influence, this model may have export value for governments attempting to regain influence over the media sector. Attempts to enshrine in EU legislation firm requirements for independence of regulatory bodies in the audiovisual media sector have so far been unsuccessful. The rules in the relevant instrument, the Audiovisual Media Services Directive (hereafter: AVMS Directive), are intentionally limited to internal market aspects of media services, leaving the responsibility for designing regulatory supervision in the audiovisual media sector to the member states. The effect of the reference in the AVMS Directive on independent supervisory bodies is limited (Hans Bredow Institute, et al. 2011: 316f.). The details of this complex legal arrangement are explained in Chapter 4 in this book by Stevens. Currently, EU member states retain a wide discretion as to how they want to model the institutional design of their IRAs, which leaves potential for engineering the dimension of independence by introducing weaker formal frameworks at the national level, especially in the absence of a strong system of checks and balances.

Politicization is taken to a higher level when a country displays the characteristics of a neo-authoritarian media system. This is the case once the freedom of the media is significantly jeopardized, yet still backed by the government's attempt to uphold the appearance of commitment to democratic values (Coyne and Leeson 2009: 129). Russia under Putin has been identified as the prototype of such a system, but other countries have also embarked on strategies which blur the line between free and controlled media by combining political influences through media ownership, regulation, supervision and litigation. The 2010 media law reforms in Hungary and the Former Yugoslav Republic of Macedonia are believed to be inspired by neo-authoritarian media politics, although both have already been corrected to some extent by subsequent developments.

Convergence paradigm

Technological convergence continues to blur boundaries between the formerly distinct information technology, media and telecommunications sectors, and this is largely attributable to digitalization. The broad conditions that have facilitated this shift since the late 1990s were: the introduction of mixed broadcasting systems in the post-communist countries; new technological advancements, including digital delivery infrastructures; and the advent of non-linear audiovisual services and hybrid services that are situated somewhere in between individual communications and electronic media (Buckley, Duerm, Mendel and Siocgru 2008: 36). Convergence manifests itself at the level of content (audiovisual media services), transmission (digitalization) and terminal equipment (devices). Its emergence coincided with the advent of the Internet and the challenges of regulation in the online space. In Europe, convergence has affected the organization of regulatory supervision in two distinct ways. On the one hand, the trend to create converged regulators has made some inroads in Europe, even if it is by no means the predominant model and the prevailing model remains one of IRAs specialized in television and radio regulation. On the other hand, regulatory competences in the field of television in Europe are quite routinely expanded to certain television-like formats distributed over the Internet.

Converged independent media regulatory authorities

The idea of a single regulator dates back long before the convergence phenomenon, to the creation of the Federal Communications Commission (FCC) in the United States in 1934. Yet the first two converged national regulatory bodies to appear in Western Europe have completely different histories: AGCOM, the Italian regulator, was created directly as a converged authority in 1997, whereas Ofcom in the United Kingdom was the result of merging five different regulators in 2003.[15] Technological convergence certainly spurred the emergence of converged regulators in Europe, as it offered a compelling argument for the need for regulatory reform, which politicians would readily invoke as a trigger for significantly improving effectiveness.

The main rationale of the converged regulatory model is avoiding the duplication of functions and costs of regulation. Because of the interdependency of content and distribution, converged regulators are a structural means to forestall the passing of inconsistent cross-sectoral decisions (Council of Europe 2008b: 10). Along with this, the reorganization of regulatory tasks and simplification of procedures can stand out as important advantages. The primary challenge to converged regulation on the other hand, is the adaptation from a sector-based perspective to a technologically neutral approach (McGougan 1999). Notably, the different sectors within the converged agency might have divergent agendas (Council of Europe 2008b: 10), which might delay the adoption of policies by making the negotiation process longer. The creation of a single point of contact for information is believed to facilitate communication with both the industry and the public. At the same time, it can raise concerns revolving around the loss of transparency and a decreased level of accessibility to the consumer (Lunt and Livingstone 2012: 3).

Converged regulators with competences for broadcasting or audiovisual media operate to date in seven European countries. In addition to Italy and the United Kingdom, there is the CRA in Bosnia and Herzegovina, the Federal Office of Communications in Switzerland, FICORA in Finland, APEK in Slovenia and, as the most recent addition, the National Media and Infocommunications Authority (NMHH) in Hungary (Hans Bredow Institute, et al. 2011: 211f.). What they have in common is that the different sectoral competences are combined under the roof of a formally independent regulatory authority. Beyond that, they are distinctly different regulators, which necessarily reflect the institutional history and administrative culture of their countries. The fact that national specificities tend to be replicated in both converged and non-converged models could be the main reason why there is no empirical evidence that would support the superiority of the converged regulator over the more traditional IRA specialized in television and radio regulation, in particular with regard to the issue of political interference (Manchet 2007: 7).

In specific contexts, the creation of a converged regulator has likely been used as a pretext for abolishing an unwanted one. Establishing a converged regulator necessarily involves a reorganization of existing regulatory structures, in the course of which members of the decision-making organs are ousted. The European Commission raised concerns over institutional independence in the case of the attempts to establish new converged regulatory structures in Slovakia in 2004, the Former Yugoslav Republic of Macedonia in 2007 and Romania in 2008.[16] In other CEE countries, such re-structuring efforts have succeeded or are under way, which could significantly alter the arm's-length relationship between governments and IRAs. In 2010, Hungary created the NMHH by merging the former regulators overseeing broadcast media and telecommunications. Its constituting law grants broad and unprecedented powers to the newly converged regulatory agency. The agency's independence is affirmed in its statute, but may not be reflected in practice. Specific provisions, such as the appointment procedures, terms in office and entrusted responsibilities of the NMHH's officials, have a strong impact on the independence of the converged regulator, especially in the light of the legacy of prior similar uses resulting in political favouritism (CMCS 2012, p. ix f.; Jakubowicz 2010; OSCE 2010).

The new notion of audiovisual media services

Convergence is behind the notion of audiovisual media services, i.e. a combination of *linear* television formats and new, *non-linear*, on-demand audiovisual services. It entered the stage of the EU's media policy with the 2007 AVMS Directive (2007/65/EC) which member states had to transpose into their laws by 2009 (European Parliament and the Council 2010). The Directive introduced three tiers of regulation of audiovisual media services and the basic tier includes new on-demand audiovisual services. Consequently, different models of supervision have appeared, with most EU member states opting to expand the competences of their existing regulators that oversee commercial broadcasting to non-linear services

(Hans Bredow Institute, et al. 2011: 211). In a large majority of European countries (31 out of 39 countries surveyed), the supervision of the implementation of AVMS rules is left to the IRA that already oversees commercial broadcasting, and in some countries also PSB (Hans Bredow Institute, et al. 2011: 501).

So far, the regulation of on-demand audiovisual media services has been delegated to an independent co-regulator only in the UK. The British Authority for Television On Demand (ATVOD) was entrusted with specialized functions and powers by Ofcom in 2010.[17] ATVOD works in partnership with the industry, with the aim of protecting the users' interests in accordance with the law. To that purpose, the ATVOD established a dialogue platform, called the ATVOD Industry Forum. In general, it appears that the new EU member states – but also the countries of Southern Europe – have little experience with co-regulation as an alternative to regulatory supervision, outside the area of traditional press, and tend to use it much less (see the country reports in SEENPM 2009).[18] When it comes to implementing EU regulation, these countries are also path-dependent insofar as competences for new regulation are vested in the existing IRAs.

The marginalization paradigm – new modes of governance

New modes of governance have non-discriminatingly entered the sphere of media supervision and any interrogation must take into account the larger transformation in governance and in the twenty-first-century media. IRA structures continue to evolve as a result of their new roles and functions, gradually increasing tensions around the concept of agency independence. In particular in the North-Western European countries, certain aspects of media regulation are now dealt with in a more discursive fashion and self- and co-regulatory schemes flourish in certain contexts.

Self- and co-regulation and onward delegation
In the UK, where this trend has advanced considerably, Lunt and Livingstone characterize agencies like Ofcom, the converged regulator with responsibilities for the media, as 'public-facing institutions in the public sphere' (2012: 4), intended to enable governance in the era of globalization. Ofcom's role extends beyond economic and media regulation to 'fostering partnerships and networks of connection among stakeholders' (Lunt and Livingstone 2012: 6). In addition to this new policy steering function, transnational media and communications demand coordination across borders and at all levels among a diverse range of stakeholders. In view of the new role of IRAs in the media sector, the traditional means of intervention decline in favour of a more orchestrated and concerted governance approach, which almost render IRAs a public interest broker.

The AVMS Directive (European Parliament and the Council 2010) encourages self- and co-regulation in line with the European inter-institutional commitment to 'better regulation' (European Parliament, the Council and the Commission 2003). It recognizes the role which effective self- and co-regulation can play in achieving the objectives of the regulation and encourages member states to use co-regulation and self-regulation where appropriate and on a voluntary basis (Audiovisual Media Directive, Recital 44 and Art. 4 par. 7). Such endeavours, which subscribe to the logic of new governance modes, are indicative of efforts to pre-empt legislation. Following this, the UK introduced an independent co-regulator, the ATVOD.

Austria's and Germany's governance approach in the field of media advances 'regulated self–regulation', understood as 'self-regulation that fits in with a legal framework or has a basis laid down in law' (Schulz and Held 2001: 3). In this way, the expertise of the industry actors is built into the new governance modes. Such a modus operandi rests on two fundamental principles: first, that there is a statutory framework in place allowing for the proper functioning of self-regulation; second, that the conduct of the regulating body influences the process of self-regulation through direct intervention in the process (introducing legal safeguards, creating a supervisory body etc.) or indirect control (definition of responsibilities, procedures and membership rules for the relevant bodies etc.). According to Héritier and Eckert (2008), industry self-regulation is more likely to appear when positive incentives are provided, or when the threat of legislation is present. Importantly, regulated self-regulation – as distinct from 'pure self-regulation' where there is no state involvement – can be complemented by other forms of regulation, such as the traditional 'command-and-control' intercession, industry codes or industry standards (Schulz and Held 2001, HBI/EMR 2006).

European regulatory networks in the media sector

Turning now to the role of ERNs in the media landscape, two entities with overlapping membership exist at European level. For broadcasting, the European Platform of Regulatory Authorities (EPRA) functions as a discussion forum for regulators in the broadcasting sector, while the independent regulators have established the Independent Regulators Group (IRG). However, in both cases the national level retains all regulatory competences, which is the reason to disregard the independence of both cooperation bodies. The INDIREG study (Hans Bredow Institute, et al. 2011: 60), however, stresses the positive effect of cooperation in European (or international) networks on the independence of national IRAs, due to best practice exchange, policy-learning and enhancement of the agency's overall self-promotional value.

The emerging paradigm of marginalization complements the changes stemming from the need to consider forms of media oversight beyond national borders, while including a wide array of stakeholders. Within this framework, co- and self-regulation operate alongside network governance arrangements, in which delegation procedures become strongly intertwined. To a large extent, these reflect alternative means of exerting governmental influence over the functioning of the media sector, in most cases by reducing the role played by the IRAs in new regulation domains, be it by creating the institutional design for encouraging voluntary regulation by the industry or by indirectly pressuring the suppliers to apply specific standards of content regulation (for example, on the Internet).

Adding to the complexity of contemporary media policy, regulatory shifts continue to follow a non-uniform path, with multiple paradigms co-existing and different ones prevailing at different moments in time, in an era of globalization and multi-layered interdependence. Double delegation instances accompany national struggles to maintain domestic competences for regulation. An exemplary case of this is the advent of ERNs, created by national governments, IRAs and the European Commission for the purpose of mitigating the effects of the uneven development of sectoral regulators in EU member states. Entrusting more powers to regulatory networks creates the conditions for the role of the national IRAs to be curtailed in what we identified as the marginalization paradigm.

Conclusion

This chapter scrutinized the normative considerations for, and the empirical development of, media specialized IRAs in the European context. Starting from the early days of radio and television, the direct control of the government over the channels of information was recognized as problematic. With the introduction of PSB, the need to separate broadcasters from the state and to ensure their accountability was addressed by instituting internal oversight as a mechanism to safeguard independence, yet the governing bodies often remained subordinate to political purposes. When the market continued to expand as the number of satellites increased, the need for regulating the new and numerous commercial broadcasters made it more urgent to establish IRAs, which, in turn, responded to the regulation efficiency agenda under the new public management ideology in Western Europe. Delegating decision-making competences to IRAs served, primarily, the purposes of institutionalizing credible political commitment beyond electoral terms and pooling expertise for better regulation. These developments also permeated media transition environments, from post-communist transformation to post-war reconstruction in the 1990s.

Arguably, it was primarily functional pressures, in particular in relation to commercial broadcasting, that motivated elected officials to establish the first IRAs in some Western European countries, but there may have also been a symbolic intention in the delegation of supervision over audiovisual media, as the guarantee of independence became more widely accepted. The change from direct interventionism to delegation, which occurred throughout the 1980s and 1990s in Western Europe, was replicated in CEE in a much shorter time span, which made the newly established IRAs much more vulnerable to political pressures. The lack of experience with the tradition of entrusting responsibilities to expert independent bodies pre-empts the choice of institutional governance and continues to be visible in the path-dependent way of vesting attributions for new regulation in the existing institutions, which can be better described as IRAs that were reverse engineered according to political preferences. In addition, national practices around the functioning of the IRAs differed considerably, sometimes allowing the establishment of regulatory bodies whose independence is questionable, in particular in contexts in which re-politicization has emerged as a strong tendency.

IRAs have further evolved or adapted in response to the convergence of audiovisual media services as well as the increasing reliance, starting in North-Western European countries, on new governance instruments. The impetus for regulatory reform in the member states is sometimes set by the necessity to transpose EU directives into domestic law. However, the relevant EU instrument for the broadcasting sector does not prescribe any organizational primate for IRAs, although it does contains a mentioning of the competent independent supervisory authorities. To date, IRAs have primarily expanded their responsibilities to include harmonized AVMS legislation, while in some cases member states have adopted the converged regulator's model. Where countries responded by establishing converged structures one should expect that the converged body combines some of the institutional characteristics of traditional IRAs, but what if convergence is used by politicians as a pretext to create legislative disruption for an existing IRA? How can one tell apart the necessity for organizational reform from political interference with an IRA in the field of media? Recently, the role of IRAs is challenged by new modes of governance that no longer require the implementation of the traditional top-down regulatory approach and instead place increased emphasis on self- and co-regulatory regimes, which affects IRAs role and conception as a regulator.

Our politico-historical investigation into the delegation to IRAs in the audiovisual media sector in Europe through the lens of regulatory theory allows us to identify a number of parallels. With some modifications that take into account the specific evolution of the media sector, the observed commonalities with the trajectories followed by IRAs in other sectors lead us to conclude that the general theories on regulation and delegation hold strong in the former broadcasting and now audiovisual media sector as well. The media sector's own dynamic development can explain some variations in the pattern of delegation which are necessarily specific to the supervision of audiovisual media. Posing a challenge to the notion of IRAs, however, is the frequent recurrence of political influence over national media regulators that renders the prevailing media governance model a symbolic rather than functionally driven delegation, with all the consequences this entails regarding the lack of political commitment.

In addition, in the European context, the operation of IRAs remains strongly influenced by national institutional developments that are marked by the legacy of the country's traditional government culture, which cannot be shrugged off in spite of all the modernizations in law and in the sector supervised. During the 1990s, liberalization and media transformation in the CEE region moved the European countries closer in terms of the functional solutions delegated to IRAs and best practices adhered to. More recent developments, however, point to new major differences: while IRAs in some Western European countries reinvent themselves with new modes of governance, other regions grapple with the very essence of independence.

Future research should investigate the possible need to accept that politicized appointments are a recurring feature in this area and is not limited to any specific region of Europe. The US theory on delegation handles such issues much more openly and does not assume it could be entirely avoided. With our contemporary understanding of media governance, we should consider whether to relinquish the attribute of 'independence' and instead re-focus on governance mechanisms which encourage adherence to transparency, deliberation, participation and accountability in the operations of any media supervisory body. Research in this direction would actually support the quest for EU-level safeguards against undue interference with IRAs in the audiovisual media sector, similar to those known in the area of national central banks and recently in electronic communications.[19] However, in the aftermath of the discussion around the adoption of the AVMS Directives, member states are likely not prepared to turn such safeguards into a credible commitment that would constrain the ability of national governments to temper with media supervision.

Acknowledgements

We would like to acknowledge the contribution of the entire INDIREG research team as listed in the acknowledgement section of Hans Bredow Institute, et al. (2011).

Notes

1   Article 30 of the Audiovisual Media Services Directive, which is the short name for Directive 2010/13/EU of the European Parliament and of the Council of 10 March 2010 on the coordination of certain provisions laid down by law, regulation or administrative action in Member States concerning the provision of audiovisual media services (Audiovisual Media Services Directive) (Official Journal L 95, 15/4 2010, p. 1). This Directive repealed Council Directive 89/552/EEC on the coordination of certain provisions laid down by law, regulation or administrative action in Member States concerning the pursuit of television broadcasting activities (Official Journal L 332, 18/12/2007, pp. 27–45), as amended by Directive 97/36/EC of 30 June 1997 and by Directive 2007/65/EC of 11 December 2007.
2   The following European countries were included in the INDIREG study by Hans Bredow Institute, et al. (2011): the 27 EU member states, candidate countries to the European Union (Croatia, Former Yugoslav Republic of Macedonia, Turkey), potential candidate countries to the European Union (Albania, Bosnia and Herzegovina, Montenegro, Serbia, Kosovo) and EFTA countries (Iceland, Liechtenstein, Norway, Switzerland).
3   Majone (1997: 140) identifies three sets of strategies leading from the positive to the regulatory state: privatization, Europeanization and the growth of indirect 'third party' government.
4   According to the wide definition of Héritier and Lehmkuhl (2011: 126) these are 'modes of public policy-making which include private actors and/or public policy-making by

public actors occurring outside legislative arenas, and which focus on delimited sectoral or functional areas'. The creation of IRAs is in itself considered a new mode of governance; however, here the focus is more on outsourcing policy-making and policing to self- and co-regulatory schemes.

5   Hallin and Mancini (2004) identify the following forms of state intervention: libel; privacy; defamation; right-of-reply laws; hate speech laws; professional secrecy laws for journalists; laws on access to information; laws regulating media concentration, ownership and competition; laws regulating political communication (especially during electoral periods); broadcast licensing laws; and laws regulating broadcast content. They conclude that 'the most important form of state intervention is surely public service broadcasting' (2004: 43).

6   According to section 7(1a) of the BBC Charter, the Governors should set and monitor a set of 'clear objectives and promises for the Corporation's services, programmes and other activities and monitor how far the Corporation has attained such objectives and met its pledges to its audiences'.

7   The nine regional broadcasting entities jointly act, to this day, in the Association of Public Broadcasting Corporations in Germany (*Arbeitsgemeinschaft der öffentlich-rechtlichen Rundfunkanstalten Deutschlands – ARD*).

8   Liberalization is understood here as a process through which exclusive rights to provide television broadcasting services have been lifted in order to allow market access by private and commercial television stations.

9   In most cases, however, this autonomous funding of PSBs was based on user licence fees that were still determined by the government.

10 The ITVs were established as regional monopolies and comprised 14 regions plus London, which had two companies. In London, one company would broadcast during weekdays and the other one during weekends.

11 The KRRiT remains accountable to the Chamber of Deputies (Sejm), Senate and Presidency, which are also the appointing institutions.

12 The Council of Lithuanian Radio and Television and the Radio and Television Commission of Lithuania.

13 In Bulgaria, the Communications Regulation Committee (CRC) operates alongside the Council for Electronic Media, but the appointment procedure for this body remains divided between the Parliament and the President of the Republic.

14 Except for Annexe 3, art. 1 and Annexe 7, art. 1.3b of the Dayton Peace Accords (full text available at http://www.nato.int/ifor/gfa/gfa-home.htm).

15 Namely, the five previous regulatory bodies were: The Radiocommunications Agency (RA), The Office of Telecommunications (Oftel), The Independent Television Commission (ITC), The Broadcasting Standards Commission and The Radio Authority (RA).

16 Per prime ministerial emergency ordinance the Romanian government has dissolved the National Regulatory Authority for Communications and Information Technology (ANRCTI), replacing it with the National Authority for Communications (ANC) (Global Insight 2008).

17 The designation act legally prescribes that 'ATVOD is sufficiently independent of providers of on-demand programme services' (Section 5, par. IV of the Designation pursuant to section 368B of the Communications Act 2003 of functions to the Association for Television

On-Demand in relation to the regulation of on-demand programme services, http://www. atvod.co.uk/uploads/files/designation1803101.pdf).

18   In the new sphere of Internet content, which is not part of the regulatory system applying to television and audiovisual media, many European countries are experimenting with self-regulation and industry standards.

19   Article 3 of the Framework Directive (2002/21/EC) amended by Regulation 544/2009 and Directive 2009/140/EC provides: 'Member states shall ensure that the head of a national regulatory agency (NRA), or where applicable, members of the collegiate body fulfilling that function within a NRA [...] may be dismissed only if they no longer fulfil the conditions required for the performance of their duties'.

References

Brants, K. and Siune, K. (1992), 'Public Broadcasting in a State of Flux', in K. Suine and W. Truetzschler (eds.), *Dynamics of Media Politics: Broadcast and Electronic Media in Western Europe*, London: Sage.

Buckley, S., Duerm, K., Mendel, T. and Siocgru, S. O. (2008), *Broadcasting, Voice and Accountability. A Public Interest Approach to Policy, Law, and Regulation*, Washington, D.C: The World Bank Group.

Center for Media and Communication Studies (CMCS) (2012), *Hungarian Media Laws in Europe: An Assessment of the Consistency of Hungary's Media Laws with European Practices and Norms*, Budapest: Central European University, https://cmcs.ceu.hu/sites/default/files/field_attachment/news/node-27293/Hungarian_Media_Laws_in_Europe_0.pdf. Accessed 20 February 2012.

Coen, D. and Thatcher, M. (2006), 'After Delegation: the Evolution of European Networks of Regulatory Agencies', in *The First Conference of the ECPR Standing Group on Regulatory Governance: Frontiers of Regulation. Assessing Scholarly Debates and Policy Challenges*, Bath, United Kingdom, 8–10 September, ECPR Standing Group on Regulatory Governance.

Coen, D. and Thatcher, M. (2008), 'Network Governance and Multi-level Delegation: European Networks of Regulatory Agencies', *Journal of Public Policy*, 28: 1, pp. 49–71.

Coppens, T. and Saeys, F. (2006), 'Enforcing Performance: New Approaches to Govern Public Service Broadcasting', *Media, Culture and Society*, 28: 2, pp. 261–284.

Council of Europe (2000), *Recommendation (Rec(2000)23) of the Committee of Ministers to the Member States on the independence and functions of regulatory authorities for the broadcasting sector*.

Council of Europe (2008a), *Declaration of the Committee of Ministers of 26 March 2008 on the independence and functions of regulatory authorities for the broadcasting sector*.

Council of Europe (2008b), *Converging Media – Convergent Regulators? The Future of Broadcasting Regulatory Authorities in South-Eastern Europe*, Strasbourg: Directorate General of Human Rights and Legal Affairs.

Coyne, C. J. and Leeson, P. T. (2009), *Media, Development and Institutional Change*, Northampton, MA: Edward Elgar Publishing.

Dragomir, M. (2008), 'The Structure and Functions of the Broadcasting Industry as a Public Forum', in The CommGAP Program, World Bank and the Joan Shorenstein Center on the Press, Politics and Public Policy, Harvard Kennedy School of Government, *Harvard-World Bank Workshop on The Role of News Media in the Governance Reform Agenda*, Cambridge, MA, United States, 29–31 May, http://www.hks.harvard.edu/fs/pnorris/Conference/Conference%20papers/Dragomir%20Broadcasting%20Industry.pdf. Accessed 23 October 2010.

Elstein, D. (2005), 'Public Service Broadcasting in the Digital Age', *Economic Affairs*, 25: 4, pp. 68–72.

European Parliament, the Council and the Commission of the European Union (2003), Inter-institutional Agreement on better law-making 2003/C 321/01of 16 December 2003, *Official Journal of the European Union* of 31.12.2003.

European Parliament and the Council of the European Union (2002), Directive 2002/21/EC of the European Parliament and of the Council of 7 March 2002 on a common regulatory framework for electronic communications networks and services (Framework Directive), *Official Journal of the European Union* of 24.04.2002 L 108/33.

European Parliament and the Council of the European Union (2007), Directive 2007/65/EC of the European Parliament and of the Council of 11 December 2007 amending Council Directive 89/552/EEC on the coordination of certain provisions laid down by law, regulation or administrative action in Member States concerning the pursuit of television broadcasting activities, *Official Journal of the European Union* of 18.12.2007 L 332/27.

European Parliament and the Council of the European Union (2009a), Regulation (EC) No 544/2009 of the European Parliament and of the Council of 18 June 2009 amending Regulation (EC) No 717/2007 on roaming on public mobile telephone networks within the Community and Directive 2002/21/EC on a common regulatory framework for electronic communications networks and services, *Official Journal of the European Union* of 29.06.2009 L 167/12.

European Parliament and the Council of the European Union (2009b), Directive 2009/140/EC of the European Parliament and of the Council of 25 November 2009 amending Directives 2002/21/EC on a common regulatory framework for electronic communications networks and services, 2002/19/EC on access to, and interconnection of, electronic communications networks and associated facilities, and 2002/20/EC on the authorization of electronic communications networks and services, *Official Journal of the European Union* of 18.12.2009 L 337/27.

European Parliament and the Council of the European Union (2010), Directive 2010/13/EU of the European Parliament and of the Council of 10 March 2010 on the coordination of certain provisions laid down by law, regulation or administrative action in Member States concerning the provision of audiovisual media services (Audiovisual Media Services Directive), *Official Journal of the European Union* of 15.4.2010 L 95/1.

Gilardi, F. (2005a), 'Evaluating Independent Regulators', in OECD Working Party on Regulatory Management and Reform, *OECD: Designing Independent and Accountable Regulatory Authorities for High Quality Regulation. Proceedings of an Expert Meeting in London, United Kingdom, 10–11 January 2005*, OECD, pp. 101–125.

Gilardi, F. (2005b), 'The Institutional Foundations of Regulatory Capitalism: The Diffusion of Independent Regulatory Agencies in Western Europe', *The ANNALS of the American Academy of Political and Social Science*, 598: 1, pp. 84–101.

Gilardi, F. (2008), *Delegation in the Regulatory State: Independent Regulatory Agencies in Western Europe*, Cheltenham, UK: Edward Elgar Publishing.

Global Insight (2008), 'Romania – Europe: Romania Dissolves Telecoms Regulator, Faces EU Inquiry', Newsletter of 24 September 2008 (on file with the authors).

Hallin, D. and Mancini, P. (2004), *Comparing Media Systems: Three Models of Media and Politics*, Cambridge: Cambridge University Press.

Hans Bredow Institute for Media Research and the Institute of European Media Law (EMR) (2006), *Final Report: Study on Co-regulatory Measures in the Media Sector*, study conducted on behalf of the European Commission, DG Information Society and Media, http://ec.europa. eu/avpolicy/docs/library/studies/coregul/final_rep_en.pdf.

Hans Bredow Institute for Media Research; Interdisciplinary Centre for Law & ICT (ICRI), Katholieke Universiteit Leuven; Center for Media and Communication Studies (CMCS), Central European University; Cullen International; Perspective Associates (eds., 2011),

INDIREG. Indicators for independence and efficient functioning of audio-visual media services regulatory bodies for the purpose of enforcing the rules in the AVMS Directive. Study conducted on behalf of the European Commission. Final Report. February 2011, http://ec.europa.eu/avpolicy/docs/library/studies/regulators/final_report.pdf.

Héritier, A. and Lehmkuhl, D. (2011), 'New Modes of Governance and Democratic Accountability', *Government and Opposition*, 46: 1, pp. 126–44.

Héritier, A. and Eckert, S. (2008), 'New Modes of Governance in the Shadow of Hierarchy: Self-regulation by Industry in Europe', *Journal of Public Policy*, 28: 1, pp. 113–138.

Hood, C. (1991), 'A Public Management for All Seasons?', *Public Administration*, 69: 1, pp. 3–19.

Humphreys, P. (1996), *Mass-media and Media Policy in Western Europe*, Manchester and New York: Manchester University Press.

Jakubowicz, K. (2008), 'Finding the Right Place on the Map: Prospects for Public Service Broadcasting in Post-communist Countries', in K. Jakubowicz and M. Sükösd, (eds.), *Finding the Right Place on the Map: Central and Eastern European Media Change in a Global Perspective*, Bristol: Intellect Books, pp. 101–124.

Jakubowicz, K. (2010), *Analysis and assessment of a package of Hungarian legislation and draft legislation on media and telecommunications*, prepared for the Office of the OSCE Representative on Freedom of the Media, http://www.osce.org/documents/rfm/2010/09/45942_en.pdf. Accessed 20 October 2010.

Jakubowicz, K. and Sükösd, M. (2008), 'Twelve concepts regarding media system evolution and democratization in post-communist societies', in K. Jakubowitz and M. Sükösd (eds.), *Finding the Right Place on the Map: Central and Eastern European Media Change in a Global Perspective*, Bristol: Intellect Books, pp. 9–41.

Jordan, A., Wurzel, R. K. W. and Zito, A. (2005), 'The Rise of "New" Policy Instruments in Comparative Perspective: Has Governance Eclipsed Government?', *Political Studies*, 53: 3, pp. 477–96.

Jusić T. and Dzihana, A. (2008), 'Bosnia and Herzegovina', in S. Basic-Hrvatin, M. Thompson and T. Jusić (eds.), *Divided They Fall: Public Service Broadcasting in Multiethnic States*, Sarajevo: Mediacentar, pp. 81–119.

Kaminski, I. (2003), 'Applying Western media law standards in East Central Europe', in M. Sükösd and P. Bajomi-Lázár (eds.), *Reinventing Media. Media Policy Reform in East-Central Europe*, Budapest: Central European University, pp. 63–84.

Karlowicz, I. (2003), 'The difficult birth of the fourth estate: media development and democracy assistance in the post-conflict Balkans', in M. Sükösd and P. Bajomi-Lázár (eds.), *Reinventing Media. Media Policy Reform in East-Central Europe*, Budapest: Central European University, pp. 115–135.

Landis, J. M. (1938/1966), *The Administrative Process*, New Haven, CT.: Yale University Press.

Lunt, P. and Livingstone, S. (2012), *Media Regulation: Governance and the Interest of Citizens and Consumers*, London: Sage.

Machet, E. (2007), 'The Independence of Regulatory Authorities', Background document EPRA/2007/02, in European Platform of Regulatory Authorities (EPRA), *25th EPRA Meeting*, Prague, Czech Republic, 16–19 May, http://epra3-production.s3.amazonaws.

com/attachments/files/1799/original/Prague_independence_final_public.pdf?1327491949. Accessed 22 February 2012.

Magnette, P. (2005), 'The Politics of Regulation in the European Union', in D. Geradin, R. Muñoz and N. Petit (eds.), *Regulation through Agencies in the EU – A New Paradigm of European Governance*, Cheltenham and Northampton, MA: Edward Elgar Publishing.

Majone, G. (1994), 'The Rise of the Regulatory State in Europe', *West European Politics*, 17: 3, pp. 77–101.

Majone, G. (1997), 'From the Positive to the Regulatory State: Causes and Consequences of Changes in the Mode of Governance', *Journal of Public Policy*, 17, pp. 139–167.

McGougan, J. (1999), 'The Challenge of Convergence to Audiovisual Regulation: is the Current Regulatory Framework Approaching its Sell-by Date?', in C. Marsden and S. Verhulst (eds.), *Convergence in European Digital TV Regulation*, London: Blackstone Press Limited, pp. 175–191.

Mertus, J. and Thompson, M.(2002), 'The Learning Curve: Media Development in Kosovo', in M. Price and M. Thompson (eds.), *Forging Peace. Intervention, Human Rights and the Management of Media Space*, Edinburgh: Edinburgh University Press, pp. 259–86.

Mungiu-Pippidi, A. (2003), 'From State to Public Service: the Failed Reform of State Television in Central Eastern Europe', in M. Sükösd and P. Bajomi-Lázár (eds.), *Reinventing Media. Media Policy Reform in East-Central Europe*, Budapest: Central European University, pp. 31–62.

Nicolaïdes, P. (2005), 'Regulation of Liberalised Markets: A New Role for the State?', in D. Geradin, R. Muñoz and N. Petit (eds.), *Regulation through Agencies in the EU – A New Paradigm of European Governance*, Cheltenham and Northampton, MA: Edward Elgar Publishing, pp. 23–42.

OSCE (Organization for Security and Co-operation in Europe) (2010), 'OSCE media freedom representative calls on the Hungarian Government to halt media legislation package, start public consultations', 24 June, http://www.osce.org/item/44817.html. Accessed 17 October 2010.

OSI (Open Society Institute) (2005), *Television across Europe: Regulation, Policy and Independence. Monitoring Reports*, Budapest: OSI.

Petković, B. (2004), *Media Ownership and Its Impact on Media Independence and Pluralism*, Ljubljana: Peace Institute.

Pollack, M. A. (1997), 'Delegation, Agency and Agenda Setting in the European Community', *International Organisation*, 51: 1, pp. 99–134.

Pollack, M. A. (2002), 'Learning from the Americanists (Again): Theory and Method in the Study of Delegation', *West European Politics*, 25: 1, pp. 200–219.

Price, M. and Thompson, M. (2002), *Forging Peace. Intervention, Human Rights and the Management of Media Space*, Edinburgh: Edinburgh University Press.

Rhodes, R. A. W. (2000), 'Governance and Public Administration', in J. Pierre (ed.), *Debating Governance: Authority, Steering, and Democracy*, Oxford: Oxford University Press, pp. 54–90.

Salomon, E. (2006), *Guidelines for Broadcasting Regulation*, 2nd ed., London: CBA.

Scannell, P. (1990), 'Public Service Broadcasting: the History of a Concept', in A. Goodwin and G. Whannel (eds.), *Understanding Television*, London: Routledge, pp. 11–29.

Schulz, W. and Held, T. (2001), *Regulated Self-Regulation as a Form of Modern Government*, Interim Report for a study commissioned by the German Federal Commissioner for Cultural and Media Affairs, Hans Bredow Institute for Media Research, http://www.humanrights.coe. int/media/documents/interim-report-self-regulation.pdf. Accessed 10 January 2012.

SEENPM (South-East European Network for the Professionalization of the Media) (2009), *The Impact of Regulating On-demand/Non-linear services by the EU Audiovisual Media Services (AVMS) Directive on Freedom of Speech in Post-Communist Democracies of Central and South Eastern Europe*, http://www.mminstitute.org/files/SEENPM_AVMS_report.pdf.

Thatcher, M. (2001), 'Delegation to Independent Regulatory Authorities in Western Europe', in European Consortium for Political Research (ECPR), *29th ECPR Joint Sessions of Workshops*, Grenoble, France, 6–11 April.

Thatcher, M. (2002), 'Delegation to Independent Regulatory Agencies: Pressures, Functions and Contextual Mediation', *West European Politics*, 25: 1, pp. 125–147.

Thatcher, M. and Stone Sweet, A. (2002), 'Theory and Practice of Delegation to Non-majoritarian Institutions', *West European Politics*, 25: 1, pp. 1–22.

Thompson, M. and De Luce, D. (2002), 'Escalating to Success? The Media Intervention in Bosnia and Herzegovina', in M. Price and M. Thompson (eds.), *Forging Peace. Intervention, Human Rights and the Management of Media Space*, Edinburgh: Edinburgh University Press, pp. 200–235.

Van Cuilenburg, J. and McQuail, D. (2003), 'Media Policy Paradigm Shifts. Towards a New Communications Policy Paradigm', *European Journal of Communication*, 18: 2, pp. 181–207.

Venturelli, S. (1998), *Liberalizing the European Media. Politics, Regulation, and the Public Sphere*, Oxford: Clarendon Press.

Chapter 3

Independent media regulators: Condition sine qua non for freedom of expression?

Peggy Valcke
KU Leuven ICRI-iMinds and HU Brussel

Dirk Voorhoof
University of Ghent and University of Copenhagen

Eva Lievens
KU Leuven ICRI-iMinds

Abstract

This chapter will explore the impact of the European Convention on Human Rights and Fundamental Freedoms (ECHR) on the characteristics and the functioning of independent regulatory bodies in the audiovisual media sector in Europe. Does states' duty of care under Art. 10 ECHR, which protects freedom of expression, entail an obligation to establish independent media regulators (IMRs)? Is independence of regulatory bodies a conditio sine qua non *for freedom of expression and for the media to fulfil their important role in democratic societies? What standards have been put forward with regard to institutional and procedural requirements in relation to regulatory oversight of the media sector? The chapter will first discuss the so-called 'soft law' instruments developed by the Council of Europe on the independence and functions of regulatory authorities for the broadcasting sector: the Recommendation Rec(2000)23 of 20 December 2000 (Council of Europe 2000) and the Declaration of 26 March 2008 (Council of Europe 2008). Although from a legal perspective both documents, adopted by the Committee of Ministers, are not binding on the member states, they do have moral authority and are politically persuasive. They express principles and guidelines for a common policy in the 47 member states of the Council of Europe which the Committee of Ministers has agreed on and is actively promoting. The importance of the Declarations, Recommendations and Resolutions of the Council of Europe is also reflected in the jurisprudence of the European Court of Human Rights (ECtHR) applying Art. 10 ECHR. The principles and guidelines on IMRs elaborated in Recommendation (2000)23 and Declaration 2008 are explicitly reflected in reports and opinions of the Commissioner for Human Rights of the Council of Europe, requesting or urging member states to review their legislation or transform their practices accordingly.[1] The second part of the chapter will clarify how the ECHR is applied in cases where IMR are involved in, or interfered with, the right to freedom of expression of audiovisual media. Therefore the relevant jurisprudence of the ECtHR will be analysed: on the one hand, Art. 10 ECHR guaranteeing the right to freedom of expression and information, and, on the other hand, Arts. 6 and 13 ECHR safeguarding two procedural fundamental rights, i.e. the right to a fair trial and the right to an effective remedy. The case law of the Strasbourg Court has clarified that the right to freedom of expression and information or the right to a fair trial can be violated if structural or procedural requirements are not sufficiently guaranteed or applied by judicial or administrative authorities when they make decisions that interfere with the rights of (audiovisual) media. A fourth article also deserves attention in this context, namely Art. 14*

ECHR which prescribes that the enjoyment of the Convention's rights shall be secured without discrimination on any ground.

Keywords: independent media regulators, Art. 10 ECHR, freedom of expression, Arts. 6, 13 and 14 ECHR, right to fair trial, right to effective remedy, non-discrimination, independence

Standard-setting by the Council of Europe's Committee of Ministers

The Council of Europe has adopted an array of international treaties and other normative standards containing central or incidental focuses on freedom of expression and the media, such as journalistic freedoms, access to information, public service media, media pluralism etc. (McGonagle 2011: 4). In relation to the independence and functions of regulatory authorities for the broadcasting sector, its Committee of Ministers has adopted two specific texts: the Recommendation (2000)23 of 20 December 2000 and the Declaration of 26 March 2008 (Council of Europe 2000; 2008). These texts emphasize the importance for a democratic society of the existence of a wide range of independent and autonomous media. They also underline the pivotal role that IMRs fulfil in creating a diverse and pluralistic media landscape and they offer a set of guidelines as to the organization, functioning, role and action of IMRs, condemning any arbitrary controls or constraints on participation in the information process, on media content or on the transmission and dissemination of information.[2] These guidelines will be discussed in the subsequent sections.

The establishment of IMRs and their basic characteristics

Recommendation (2000)23 clearly stipulates that member states should 'establish, if they have not already done so, independent regulatory authorities for the broadcasting sector'. As the ECHR member states are under positive obligations to safeguard media pluralism (see also *infra*), this implies the organization of an effective enforcement system of the regulatory framework guaranteeing the right of freedom of expression and media pluralism. Hence there is a need for well-functioning bodies in order to monitor the practices in the audiovisual media sector and eventually to compel the audiovisual media service providers to comply with law and regulation. Taking into regard the broad margin of appreciation in this area of positive obligations derived from Art. 10 ECHR, it is up to the member states to decide which bodies are competent or are to be established in order to organize and to monitor the functioning of audiovisual media or to interfere otherwise when legal provisions or other regulations are allegedly violated.

Recommendation (2000)23, developments in EU-law (for instance Art. 30 of the AVMS-Directive)[3] and in national law, and actual practices in (nearly) all member states of the Council of Europe all demonstrate that competences of regulation, allocation of frequencies, and monitoring and sanctioning in the sector of audiovisual media have gradually and systematically been transferred from legislative bodies, governmental institutions and judiciary authorities to IMRs. As the European Platform of Regulatory Authorities (EPRA) mentions: 'the most common organization form in Europe is that of the independent regulatory authority which is characterised by the fact that it is not part of the actual structure of governmental administration' (EPRA 2011). This does not exclude that, to a certain extent, some parts of broadcasting regulation may be exercised by governmental administrative authorities, while other issues may be dealt with by judicial authorities or courts, applying general legislation such as provisions of civil law, criminal law or commercial law. In some countries self- or co-regulatory bodies also oversee some aspects of the scope of media regulation, especially regarding journalistic ethics, commercial communications in the media or public service broadcasting. In any case, from the moment an IMR or other authority interferes with the rights of a broadcaster or audiovisual media service provider, that body must guarantee 'structural' or 'objective' impartiality to comply with the fair trial requirements of Art. 6 ECHR (cf. *infra*).

Recommendation (2000)23 underlines the importance of devising an appropriate legislative framework that sets out the organization of the broadcasting regulator. The rules and procedures governing or affecting the functioning of regulatory authorities should clearly affirm and protect their independence. The duties and powers of regulatory authorities for the broadcasting sector, as well as the ways of making them accountable, the procedures for appointment of their members and the means of their funding should be clearly defined in law (Council of Europe 2000: para. 2). Further details on what these rules should entail will be discussed in the respective sections below.

Whereas the Committee of Ministers considers an appropriate legal framework a necessary condition (it uses the term 'essential') for the setting up and proper functioning of a broadcasting regulator, it also acknowledges that it is not a sufficient condition. In its overview of the implementation of Recommendation (2000)23, attached to its Declaration of 2008, it underlines the absence of a clear link between the amount of detail in a country's legislation on broadcasting regulation and the regulatory authority's independence. In some cases, regulatory authorities governed by only a very limited set of rules were found to operate relatively independently, whereas in other cases an extensive legal framework was promulgated without any effective impact in terms of the independent functioning of IMRs and their relation to public authorities or politics. Whether the legal safeguards – extensive or not – are effective also depends, according to the Declaration, on the existence of a 'culture of independence' where lawmakers, government and other players, under the scrutiny of society at large, respect the regulatory authorities' independence without being explicitly required to do so by law.

Appointment, composition and functioning

To protect the members of the media regulator against interference from, in particular, political forces or economic interests, three categories of legal rules should be put in place according to Recommendation (2000)23. A first category concerns incompatibility rules, which should (a) preserve the regulator's members from being under the influence of political powers – for instance, by prohibiting them from holding political office – and (b) prohibit them from holding interests in enterprises or other organizations in the media or related sectors. Declaration 2008 notes that certain countries have extended the incompatibility rules beyond these guidelines; by excluding members of regulatory authorities from working in the media business or engaging in politics for several years after the expiry of their mandate, or by requiring that close relatives of members also give up commercial interests in the media, they intend to cover a broader range of potential conflicts of interest.[4] As part of a second category of regulations, intended to guarantee the integrity of the members, Recommendation (2000)23 also calls for rules to ensure that members of regulatory authorities are appointed in a democratic and transparent manner. In addition, this second category should also include rules preventing the nominating or appointing bodies from exerting pressure on the members after their appointment. Recommendation (2000)23, however, formulates the latter as rules that are to be respected by the members themselves: they may not receive any mandate or take any instructions from any person or body; and they should not make any statement or undertake any action which may prejudice the independence of their functions, nor take any advantage of them. In order to guarantee specific know-how, IMRs should include experts in the domain of audiovisual media or other areas which fall within their competences.

A third category of rules called for in Recommendation (2000)23 are rules regarding the conditions and procedures under which members can be dismissed. To prevent dismissal being used as a means of exerting political pressure, the grounds for dismissal should be limited to cases of non-respect of the incompatibility rules, duly noted incapacity to exercise a member's functions and conviction (by a court of law) for a serious criminal offence. A judicial review should be available for members of an IMR who have been dismissed.[5]

In short, this set of principles should not only guarantee the independence of IMRs from any interference by political forces or economic interests. They should also guarantee that the members of IMRs are appointed in a democratic and transparent manner, may not receive a mandate or instructions and cannot be dismissed as a means of exerting political pressure.

Financial independence

Financial independence is defined by Recommendation (2000)23 as another key element of the independence of audiovisual regulatory authorities. Funding arrangements should be specified in law in accordance with a clearly defined plan, and with reference to the estimated cost of the regulatory authority's activities. It is obvious that a regulator which is underfinanced will not be able to carry out its functions fully and independently. According to Declaration 2008 this is a problem in several countries where the regulator is not given the means (in particular human resources) to adequately perform its duties. In some cases, despite the existence of a legal obligation to provide for an independent funding plan, regulatory authorities reported feeling threatened or pressured by governments which go back on agreed funding plans and/or use funding decisions as leverage in political power struggles.

The Recommendation, however, explicitly states that public authorities should not use their financial decision-making power to interfere with the independence of regulatory authorities. This is especially relevant in countries where the regulatory authority is financed by the state budget.[6]

In addition, recourse to the services or expertise of the national administration or third parties should not affect the independence of the regulatory authority. Finally, it is proposed that funding arrangements should take advantage, where appropriate, of mechanisms which do not depend on ad hoc decision making of public or private bodies.

Powers and competence

Recommendation (2000)23 distinguishes between four different tasks of regulatory authorities, three of which it considers as indispensable. First, it underlines that the legislator should entrust the regulatory authority ('subject to clearly defined delegation') with the power to adopt regulations and guidelines concerning broadcasting activities, as well as internal rules ('within the framework of the law').

Second, it considers the granting and renewal of broadcasting licences as one of the essential tasks of regulatory authorities, stating that regulatory authorities should also be involved in the process of planning the range of national frequencies allocated to broadcasting services.[7] Since licensing activities can be considered one of the most intrusive interferences in a (candidate) broadcaster's freedom of expression – the refusal or non-renewal of a licence implying the impossibility to broadcast – a number of safeguards should be installed:

- The basic conditions and criteria governing the granting and renewal of broadcasting licences should be clearly defined in the law.
- The regulations governing the broadcasting licensing procedure should be clear and precise and should be applied in an open, transparent and impartial manner.
- Calls for tenders should be made public, should define a number of conditions to be met by the applicants (such as type of service, minimum duration of programmes, geographical coverage, type of funding, licensing fees or technical parameters) and should specify the content of the licence application and documents to be submitted (in particular, information about the company structure, owners and capital, content and duration of proposed programmes).[8]
- The decisions made by the regulatory authorities should be made public (see also 'Accountability' below).

Third, according to the Recommendation, the monitoring of broadcasters' compliance with the conditions laid down in law and in the licences is another essential function of regulatory authorities. The Recommendation stresses that monitoring should always take place *after* the broadcasting of programmes, and not *a priori*. In the context of monitoring compliance, regulatory authorities should have the following powers: to request and receive information from broadcasters; to consider complaints; and to impose sanctions in cases of violations. These sanctions have to be defined by law, starting with a warning, and have to be proportionate. The broadcaster in question should be given an opportunity to be heard before the decision is taken, and should also have the right to appeal the decision before the competent jurisdictions according to national law.

The fourth task identified in Recommendation (2000)23 relates to public service broadcasters (nowadays called 'public service media' in documents of the Council of Europe) and is formulated in an optional manner. Regulatory authorities *may* be given the mission to carry out tasks often incumbent on specific supervisory bodies of public service broadcasting organizations. At any time, however, they have to respect the public service broadcaster's editorial independence and institutional autonomy. It can be noted that the recent Declaration and Recommendation of 15 February 2012 on public service media governance does not oblige member states to entrust an independent media regulator with the task of supervising public service broadcasters (or media). The Declaration underlines the importance of ensuring that external oversight 'by government or independent regulators' does not undermine the public service media's independence, while the Recommendation (merely) prescribes that the legal framework should provide 'clarity about the responsibility of the regulator in relation to the public service media'. This regulator, so it continues, is required to operate openly and transparently in respect of regulatory action, and is itself guaranteed independence from the State in its decision-making powers.[9]

Not all Council of Europe member states have implemented the aforementioned guidelines relating to media regulators' tasks and powers. Although Declaration 2008 states that the majority of regulatory authorities seems to award licences in a manner consistent with the recommendation, it also notes that in a number of Council of Europe member states, the broadcasting licensing procedure allegedly lacks transparency, is arbitrary or politically biased. This can be due to a lack of, or unclear, regulations and licence selection criteria. According to the Declaration, the legislation of no fewer than nine member states fails to clearly define the basic conditions and criteria for the granting and renewal of broadcasting licences. In almost one in two member states, the legal framework is either silent or provides insufficient details on the content of licence applications. Moreover, frequent revisions of the law apparently add to the confusion. Regarding the monitoring activities of regulators, the practice is not always in compliance with the requirements in Recommendation (2000)23 either. The Declaration refers to cases where regulators have been accused of applying sanctions arbitrarily or inconsistently. It also mentions complaints about sanctions that were either too harsh or too lax, and sanctions motivated by archaic moral ideas or political reasons.

Accountability

According to Recommendation (2000)23, regulatory authorities should be accountable to the public for their activities, for example by means of publishing annual reports. The Recommendation also underlines that all decisions taken and regulations adopted by the regulatory authorities should be duly reasoned, open to review by the competent jurisdictions and made available to the public.

Regulatory authorities should only be supervised in respect of the lawfulness of their activities as well as the correctness and transparency of their financial activities – and with respect to the legality of their activities, this supervision should be exercised *a posteriori* only.

The majority of regulatory bodies in Council of Europe member states publish their decisions in annual reports. Declaration 2008 notes, however, that regulatory authorities are accountable by law to the public in only a few countries, and that there is often a lack of active transparency. Mostly, they are accountable to state bodies or authorities, such as the parliament, the head of state or auditing authorities. The Declaration mentions that it has been alleged that, in countries where regulatory bodies are accountable by law to parliament and/or the head of state, annual reports were rejected and regulatory authorities dissolved not on objective grounds but for political reasons.

The impact of the ECHR on the functioning of IMR: the case law of the European Court of Human Rights

The following section will explore the impact of Arts. 6, 10, 13 and 14 ECHR on the organization and functioning of IMRs by analysing the relevant case law of the ECtHR. First the main characteristics of these articles are briefly introduced. In the second part of this chapter the application of these articles is analysed and illustrated with reference to relevant cases and judgments in which (decisions of) IMRs were involved.

Relevant ECHR articles and general characteristics

Art. 10 ECHR[10]

Art. 10 ECHR guarantees the right to freedom of expression and information as a fundamental right in a democratic society. In its Grand Chamber judgments of 7 February 2012 and 4 April 2012, the ECtHR has reiterated that:

> freedom of expression [...] constitutes one of the essential foundations of a democratic society and one of the basic conditions for its progress and for each individual's self-fulfilment. Subject to paragraph 2 of Article 10, it is applicable not only to 'information' or

'ideas' that are favourably received or regarded as inoffensive or as a matter of indifference, but also to those that offend, shock or disturb. Such are the demands of pluralism, tolerance and broadmindedness without which there is no 'democratic society'. [...] As set forth in Article 10, this freedom is subject to exceptions, which must, however, be construed strictly, and the need for any restrictions must be established convincingly.[11]

States not only need to refrain from interfering with the freedom of expression of their citizens or media, they also have an active duty of care to ensure that the freedom of expression can be effectively exercised by their citizens and the media (Voorhoof 2004: 925).[12] In this respect, the ECtHR has stated that '[g]enuine, effective exercise of freedom of expression does not depend merely on the State's duty not to interfere, but may require it to take positive measures of protection, through its law or practice. Given the importance of what is at stake under Art. 10, the State must be the ultimate guarantor of pluralism'.[13]

Hence ensuring pluralism and diversity of media output is considered part of this active duty of care. Throughout its case law, the ECtHR has reaffirmed that media pluralism is essential for the functioning of a democratic society and is the corollary of the fundamental right to freedom of expression and information as guaranteed by Art. 10.[14] The ECtHR has emphasized that, in the field of broadcasting, the state has a duty to ensure, 'first, that the public has access through television and radio to impartial and accurate information and a range of opinion and comment, reflecting *inter alia* the diversity of political outlook within the country and, secondly, that journalists and other professionals working in the audiovisual media are not prevented from imparting this information and comment'.[15]

In some areas the ECtHR accepts a broad margin of appreciation by the member states, such as in cases where interferences are based on the protection of morals,[16] and regarding restrictions on commercial communication,[17] although in each of these areas the ECtHR has also found violations of Art. 10 (Voorhoof 2009).[18] In cases where the ECtHR refers to positive obligations by member states, domestic authorities also have a wide margin of appreciation at their disposal, reducing the supervisory control of the ECtHR substantially,[19] but as we shall see, not eliminating it.

Art. 6 ECHR

The impact of the ECHR on IMRs is not restricted to Art. 10 ECHR: as IMRs can interfere with the right to freedom of expression and sanction media over breach of provisions of law or other regulation, they affect the (fundamental) civil rights of the media. The media shall therefore have the right to a fair trial guaranteed in accordance with Art. 6 ECHR.

Art. 6 ECHR guarantees the right to a fair trial, which is essential in a democratic society. One of the requirements laid down in Art. 6 ECHR, and the most relevant to the subject of this chapter, is that cases need to be dealt with by 'an independent and impartial tribunal established by law'. The ECtHR has acknowledged that a tribunal does not need to be 'a court of law of the classic kind, integrated within the standard judicial machinery of the country'.[20] Tribunals must be capable to take legally binding decisions, and its members should usually be professional judges. The latter requirement, however, is not an absolute one (Harris, et al. 2009: 286). The requirements of independence and impartiality are usually considered jointly by the Court. First, the 'independence' requirement aims to guarantee that the tribunal and its members are 'independent of the executive and also of the parties'.[21] The ECtHR has clarified in *Campbell and Fell v the United Kingdom* how independence is assessed: 'In determining whether a body can be considered to be "independent" – notably of the executive and of the parties to the case [...] –, the Court has had regard to the manner of appointment of its members and the duration of their term of office [...], the existence of guarantees against outside pressures [...] and the question whether the body presents an appearance of independence [...]'.[22]

Second, impartiality requires that 'the court is not biased with regard to the decision to be taken, does not allow itself to be influenced by information from outside the court room, by popular feeling or by any pressures whatsoever, but bases its opinion on objective arguments on the ground of what has been put forward at the trial' (van Dijk, et al. 2006: 614). The requirement encompasses two aspects: impartiality needs to ensure not only that there has been no actual bias on the part of a judge (subjective or personal impartiality), but also that there is no legitimate doubt that there was any partiality (objective or structural partiality) (Harris, et al. 2009: 284). In the objective test it is to be determined whether, quite apart from the judge's conduct, there are ascertainable facts which may raise doubts as to his impartiality. In this respect even appearances may be of some importance. What is at stake is the confidence which the courts in a democratic society must inspire in the public. This implies that in deciding whether in a given case there is a legitimate reason to fear that a particular member of a judiciary body lacks impartiality, the standpoint of the applicant is important but not decisive. What is decisive is whether this fear can be held to be objectively justified. A lack of impartiality, for instance, can be derived from the fact that a judge has regular and close professional relations with one of the parties.[23]

If a dispute over a civil right occurs and the regulatory body in question does not meet the requirements of Art. 6 § 1 ECHR, the dispute must be 'subject to subsequent control by a judicial body that has full jurisdiction'.[24] This is required by the 'doctrine of full review' the ECtHR has developed specifically with respect to administrative and disciplinary authorities, which do not always comply with the requirements of Art. 6 ECHR (Kuijer 2004: 133).

Art. 13 ECHR
Another relevant fundamental right is the right to an effective remedy before a national authority, included in Art. 13 ECHR. This Article (along with Art. 5 paras 4–5 and Art. 6 para. 1) holds the obligation for Contracting States to secure for everyone within their jurisdiction the Convention rights and freedoms included in Art. 1. A claim under Art. 13 ECHR can occur, for example, when persons are complaining of an infringement of certain provisions of media regulation by audiovisual media service providers, to the extent that the applicants, as private persons or as commercial organizations, can also invoke an infringement of a Convention right (e.g. the right of privacy in its very broad application, property rights etc.).

With regard to the subject of this chapter, the question arises whether remedies provided by regulatory bodies can be qualified as 'remedies before a national authority'. The ECtHR has clarified that Art. 13 ECHR guarantees the availability at national level of a remedy to enforce the substance of the Convention rights and freedoms in whatever form they may happen to be secured in the domestic legal order. The effect of Art. 13 is thus to require the provision of a domestic remedy to deal with the substance of an 'arguable complaint' under the Convention and to grant appropriate relief. In this context, it has been noted that remedies must not necessarily be judicial; ombudsman procedures and other non-judicial remedies could also be considered adequate (Ovey and White 2006: 463). Neither does the ECtHR require the national authority to be a judicial authority in the strict sense.[25] However, in such a case, the Court will assess the 'powers and procedural guarantees an authority possesses' when it determines whether a remedy can be considered accessible, adequate and effective.[26] The Court will, for instance, check whether the 'national authority' is independent, impartial and provides certain minimal procedural guarantees. Such a national authority should be competent to receive a complaint, to investigate the merits of the complaint and to take binding decisions regarding the provision of redress.

Another aspect of Art. 13 ECHR requires that there must be effective remedies available against decisions, regulations or actions by IMRs that can be considered as interferences with the right to freedom of expression and information or other Convention rights of audiovisual media service providers.

Art. 14 ECHR

According to the Court's case law, discrimination, for the purposes of both Art. 14 of the Convention and Art. 1 of Protocol No. 12 to the Convention, means treating differently, without an objective and reasonable justification, persons in relevantly similar situations. This means that not every difference in treatment will amount to a violation of these provisions. It must be established that other persons in an analogous or relevantly similar situation enjoy preferential treatment and that this distinction is discriminatory. While it is true that the guarantee laid down in Art. 14 has no independent existence in the sense that under the terms of that Article it relates solely to 'rights and freedoms set forth in the Convention', a measure which in itself is in conformity with the requirements of the Art. 10 may however infringe this Article when read in conjunction with Art. 14 for the reason that it is of a discriminatory nature.

Case law of the European Court of Human Rights related to IMRs

Sigma RTV v Cyprus[27]

In this case, a broadcasting company, *Sigma RTV*, challenged a number of decisions of the Cyprus Radio and Television Authority (CRTA) in which it had been fined for several violations of the country's broadcasting legislation (e.g. in relation to children's advertising, rules on sponsoring and product placement, objectivity of news programmes, protection of minors, and hate speech). The company invoked Art. 10 ECHR, claiming that the provisions of the broadcasting rules in Cyprus had not been formulated with sufficient precision and clarity and hence that the interference by CRTA had not been 'prescribed by law' in the meaning of Art. 10. According to Sigma RTV these rules were drafted in too general terms, were excessively rigid and did not keep pace with changing circumstances and evolving societal attitudes. Sigma RTV argued that this vague and unclear regulation left too much space for interpretation to the CRTA applying these provisions, and did not sufficiently protect Sigma RTV against arbitrary application of the broadcasting legislation. Sigma RTV also maintained that the interference did not pursue a legitimate aim and that the interference was not necessary in a democratic society. Moreover, Sigma RTV complained about CRTA's alleged lack of 'structural impartiality', arguing it had been denied a fair hearing before an independent and impartial tribunal, invoking Art. 6 ECHR. It also invoked a breach of Art. 13 ECHR, claiming that its cases before the Supreme Court had not been adequately examined.[28] Finally, Sigma RTV complained about a violation of Art. 14 of the Convention, in conjunction with Art. 10 ECHR, as the CyBC, Cyprus' public service broadcaster, had not been subject to the same restrictions (CyBC was not monitored by CRTA, not subject to fines at that time, and did not have to obtain an annual licence). Sigma RTV argued that there was no reasonable and objective justification for the differential treatment in the exercise of the right to freedom of expression.

Regarding the claim that the provisions of the Broadcasting Law and regulations had not been formulated with sufficient precision and clarity and could lead to arbitrary application, the Court held that:

> whilst certainty in the law is highly desirable, it may bring in its train excessive rigidity and the law must be able to keep pace with changing circumstances. Accordingly, many laws are inevitably couched in terms which, to a greater or lesser extent, are vague and whose interpretation and application are questions of practice. The Court notes that Law 7(I)/1998 and the Regulations constitute a detailed legislative scheme aimed at regulating broadcasting. The violations found in respect of the various broadcasts in question were based on an array of different provisions of the Law and Regulations, some more specific than others. It cannot be said, however, that any of these provisions or Regulations were so vague and imprecise as to lack the required quality of law.

The ECtHR was satisfied that the interference with Sigma RTV's rights under Art. 10 § 1 was 'prescribed by law' within the meaning of Art. 10 § 2 (para. 195).

The ECtHR also found that all decisions and sanctions by the CRTA interfering with Sigma RTV's rights under Art. 10 were proportionate and pertinently justified on the basis of legitimate aims. The CRTA had imposed sanctions on Sigma RTV because of breach of a whole set of provisions in the Broadcasting Act and regulation in Cyprus, such as provisions regarding unethical advertising practices, the protection of minors, the protection of pluralism of information, the need for a fair and accurate presentation of facts and events and the protection of the reputation and privacy of persons involved in, or affected by, the broadcast. The ECtHR found that the interference with Sigma RTV's exercise of its right to freedom of expression could reasonably be regarded as having been necessary in a democratic society for the protection of the rights of others. The Court declared therefore inadmissible, as manifestly ill-founded, the complaints under Art. 10 in respect of the CRTA's decisions. One complaint, however, received a more thorough analysis on the merits: the complaint regarding the racist and discriminatory content of a fictional series. The Court emphasized that it was particularly conscious of the vital importance of combating racial and gender discrimination in all its forms and manifestations, and that the CRTA could not be said in the circumstances to have overstepped its margin of appreciation given the CRTA's profound analysis, even though the remarks had been made in the context of a fictional entertainment series. Lastly, as to the proportionality of the impugned measure, the ECtHR referred to the repeated violations by the applicant in other episodes of the same series, justifying that the fine imposed (approximately €3500) was proportionate to the aim pursued. Accordingly, there had been no violation of Art. 10 of the Convention.

The claim which Sigma RTV made relating to Art. 6 concerned the structural characteristics an IMR needs to comply with as an impartial and independent authority. Sigma RTV argued that the CRTA combined an unacceptable multiplicity of functions in prosecuting, investigating, trying and deciding cases and imposing sanctions. In addition, according to Sigma RTV, the members and staff of the CRTA had a direct and personal interest in imposing fines, since the amounts thus collected were deposited in the CRTA's Fund from which their salaries and/or remuneration were paid. Such characteristics of an IMR were considered by Sigma RTV as not complying with the required standards under Art. 6 ECHR in terms of 'structural' or 'objective' impartiality. The European Court, however, noted the presence of a number of procedural guarantees in the proceedings before the CRTA: the broadcaster is provided with details of the probable violation or the complaint made against it and is given the opportunity to make written and/or oral submissions during the hearing of the case. The CRTA is also required to give a reasoned decision. But these safeguards by themselves, even combined with the fact that no concrete irregularities had been reported in this case and that there was no evidence of members of the CRTA being personally biased, was not sufficient to consider the CRTA as meeting the threshold of the requirement of structural or objective impartiality. Indeed, the ECtHR emphasized that, in its view, despite the existence of a number of safeguards, the combination of different functions (investigating, prosecuting, judging and deciding cases) within the CRTA, and in particular the fact that all fines were deposited in its own fund for its own use, gave rise to legitimate concerns that the CRTA lacked the necessary structural impartiality to comply with the requirements of Art. 6. But this still does not necessarily create a problem from the scope of Art. 6 ECHR. The Court reiterated that even where an adjudicatory body which determines disputes over 'civil rights and obligations', including administrative ones such as the CRTA, does not comply with Art. 6 § 1 ECHR in some respect, no violation of the

Convention can be found if the proceedings before that body are 'subject to subsequent control by a judicial body that has "full" jurisdiction and does provide the guarantees of Art. 6 § 1' (paras 149–151). To that end the Court is satisfied where it is found that the judicial body in question has exercised 'sufficient jurisdiction' or provided 'sufficient review' in the proceedings before it. The consequence of this approach is that when an IMR lacking guarantees of structural impartiality has come to a decision and interfered with the rights of a broadcaster or media service provider, there is still no breach of Art. 6 § 1 as long as a judicial body has exercised sufficient jurisdiction or has provided sufficient review, in accordance with all 'fair trial' requirements of Art. 6 ECHR. In assessing the sufficiency of a judicial review in such circumstances the Court will have regard to the powers of the judicial body in question and to such factors as (a) the subject matter of the decision appealed against and, in particular, whether or not it concerned a specialized issue requiring professional knowledge or experience, and whether it involved the exercise of administrative discretion and if, so, to what extent; (b) the manner in which the decision was arrived at and, in particular, the procedural guarantees available in the proceedings before the adjudicatory body; and (c) the content of the dispute, including the desired and actual grounds of appeal (para. 154). Whether the review carried out is sufficient for the purposes of Art. 6 will very much depend on the circumstances of a given case: the European Court will confine itself as far as possible to examining the question raised in the case before it and to determining if, in that particular case, the scope of the review was adequate. The case of *Sigma RTV v Cyprus*, however, shows that the ECtHR does not require or apply strict standards in this regard. The ECtHR admitted that the Supreme Court which executed the judicial review in this case could not substitute its own decision for that of the CRTA and that its jurisdiction over the facts was limited. For the ECtHR, however, it was sufficient that the Supreme Court could have annulled the decisions of the CRTA on a number of grounds, including if the decision had been reached on the basis of a misconception of fact or law; if there had been no proper enquiry or a lack of due reasoning; or on procedural grounds (para. 159). The ECtHR also noticed that the Supreme Court, with an extensive reasoning, had examined all the issues raised by Sigma RTV, point by point, without refusing to deal with any of them. In conclusion, the ECtHR found that the scope of the review of the Supreme Court in the judicial review proceedings in the present case was sufficient to comply with Art. 6 ECHR.

All in all the judgment in the case of *Sigma RTV v Cyprus* is a clear example of how a decision by an IMR that does not meet the requirements of Art. 6 ECHR itself can be justified from the scope of Art. 6 ECHR if sufficient judicial review has taken place.

A third claim in this case was related to Art. 14 ECHR. The Court observed that the alleged discriminatory treatment by the CRTA which Sigma RTV claimed to have been a victim of laid in the distinction drawn between private stations like Sigma RTV and the CyBC, the public broadcaster of the Republic of Cyprus (para. 221). Sigma RTV had indeed complained that the CyBC did not have to pay a licence fee and that, at the material time, it was not monitored by the CRTA and subjected to fines. The ECtHR noted that Sigma RTV compared the situation of the stations it runs, which are private stations, with that of the public broadcaster. Given, however, the differences in the legal status and the applicable legal frameworks and the different objectives of private stations and the CyBC in the Cypriot broadcasting system, the Court considered that they were not in a comparable position for the purposes of Art. 14 of the Convention. The Court therefore found that the case in Sigma RTV did not disclose any appearance of discrimination contrary to Art. 14 ECHR (paras 222–225).

Impact on IMRs

The judgment in *Sigma RTV v Cyprus* clarifies that a combination of a multiplicity of functions of an IMR in prosecuting, investigating, trying and deciding cases and imposing sanctions does not in itself amount to a breach of the fair trial principle, as long as there are a number of procedural guarantees in the proceedings before the IMR itself, combined with a sufficient judicial review of the decision taken by the IMR afterwards, in conformity with Art. 6 ECHR. Moreover, an IMR, such as the CRTA, can apply the provisions of broadcasting law and regulations and can sanction a broadcasting company or provider of audiovisual media services even where the provisions and rules are couched in terms which, to a greater or lesser extent, are vague and whose interpretation and application are questions of practice. When there is a detailed legislative scheme aimed at regulating broadcasting, the ECtHR is willing to accept that the provisions or regulations at issue were not so vague and imprecise as to lack the required quality of law. The judgment also illustrates that domestic authorities, including IMRs, have a wide margin of appreciation in interpreting and applying the provisions of broadcasting law and regulations.

Manole and others v Moldova[29]

In the case of *Manole and others v Moldova*, the European Court formulated what it called the 'general principles regarding pluralism in audiovisual media'. The Court took as its starting point the fundamental truism that there can be no democracy without pluralism. One of the principal characteristics of democracy is the possibility it offers of resolving a country's problems through dialogue, without recourse to violence, even when they are irksome. Democracy thrives on freedom of expression. Freedom of the press and other news media affords the public one of the best means of discovering and forming an opinion of the ideas and attitudes of political leaders. On many occasions, the Court has stressed that it is incumbent on the press to impart information and ideas on political issues and on other subjects of public interest. Not only does the press have the task of imparting such information and ideas: the public also has a right to receive them. According to the Court, the audiovisual media, such as radio and television, have a particularly important role in this respect. Because of their power to convey messages through sound and images, the audiovisual media have a more immediate and powerful effect than print. It is therefore imperative to avoid situations whereby a powerful economic or political group in a society is permitted to obtain a position of dominance over the audiovisual media and thereby exercise pressure on broadcasters and eventually curtail their editorial freedom (paras 95–98).[30]

The ECtHR confirmed that the choice of the means by which to achieve media independence and pluralism may vary according to local conditions and, therefore, falls within the state's margin of appreciation (para. 100). However, in this case the ECtHR found a breach of Art. 10 of the Convention, because of the lack of guarantees for pluralism and independence of the public broadcaster. The Court stated (para. 101):

> Where a State does decide to create a public broadcasting system, it follows from the principles outlined above that domestic law and practice must guarantee that the system provides a pluralistic service. Particularly where private stations are still too weak to offer a genuine alternative and the public or State organization is therefore the sole or the dominant broadcaster within a country or region, it is indispensable for the proper functioning of democracy that it transmits impartial, independent and balanced news, information and comment and in addition provides a forum for public discussion in which as broad a spectrum as possible of views and opinions can be expressed.

In this judgment the Court also referred to the principle that 'the supervisory bodies of public service broadcasters should be defined in a way which avoids any risk of political or other interference' (para. 102).

The Court concluded that the Moldovan authorities violated the right to freedom of expression by not sufficiently guaranteeing the independence of Teleradio-Moldova (TRM), the public service broadcaster: 'The legislative framework throughout the period in question was flawed, in that it did not provide sufficient safeguards against the control of TRM's senior management, and thus its editorial policy, by the political organ of the Government' (paras 109–111).

Impact on IMRs

This judgment explains that even though it falls within a State's margin of appreciation to decide how to realize media pluralism, the State must ensure that the legislative framework contains sufficient guarantees to protect the independence of the public service broadcaster, so that it is able to broadcast impartial news and information to the public, without interference from the government.

Demuth v Switzerland[31]

In *Demuth v Switzerland* the Court considered that 'the authorities' margin of appreciation is essential in an area as fluctuating as that of commercial broadcasting' (para. 42). The Court referred to 'the particular political circumstances in Switzerland [...] (that) necessitate the application of sensitive political criteria such as cultural and linguistic pluralism, balance between lowland and mountain regions and a balanced federal policy'. Hence the Court saw no reason to doubt the validity of criteria and considerations which are of considerable importance for a federal state: 'Such factors, encouraging in particular pluralism in broadcasting, may legitimately be taken into account when authorising radio and television broadcasts or when refusing a licence to a certain broadcaster not sufficiently guaranteeing the goals of pluralism'. The ECtHR also emphasized that 'in view of their strong impact on the public, domestic authorities may aim at preventing a one-sided range of commercial television programmes on offer', legitimizing regulatory provisions established to secure pluralism in broadcasting. The fact that the criteria in the broadcasting regulation were both aimed at guaranteeing pluralism and validly applied justified the finding by the Court that there was no violation of Art. 10.

Impact on IMRs

This judgment demonstrates that it falls within the member state's margin of appreciation to impose specific licensing criteria that aim to guarantee pluralism based on national particularities, if those criteria are prescribed by law and applied accordingly. In deciding whether or not an applicant broadcasting company can be allocated a licence on the basis of criteria aiming to guarantee pluralism, an IMR will need to weigh, in particular, the legitimate need for ensuring the quality and balance of programmes in general, on the one hand, against the applicant's freedom of expression, namely his right to impart information and ideas, on the other.

Centro Europa 7 S.R.L. and Di Stefano v Italy[32]

In 2009 Centro Europa 7 complained in Strasbourg that, for a period of almost ten years already, the Italian Government had not allocated the company any frequencies for analogue terrestrial television broadcasting, notwithstanding the fact that it had already obtained a licence for TV broadcasting in 1999. In this regard Centro Europa 7 argued that the private broadcaster Mediaset – owned by the family of Prime Minister Silvio Berlusconi – was being treated preferentially, and that this was the reason for the long delay in making frequencies available for other broadcasting companies. The European Court affirmed that the Convention is intended to guarantee rights that are not theoretical or illusory, but rights that are practical and effective. *In casu* '[t]he failure to allocate frequencies to the applicant company deprived the licence of all practical purpose since the activity it authorised was de facto impossible to carry out for nearly ten years' (para. 138). According to the Court, this constituted an interference with Centro Europa 7's exercise of its right to impart information and ideas. In addition, the Court concluded that, given its vagueness and lack of clarity, the legislative framework in Italy at the time did not satisfy the foreseeability requirement under the Convention and deprived the company of the measure of protection against arbitrariness required by the rule of law in a democratic society (paras 152–154). This shortcoming resulted, among other things, in reduced competition in the audiovisual sector. It therefore amounted to a failure by the State to comply with its positive obligation to put in place an appropriate legislative and administrative framework to guarantee effective media pluralism. These findings were sufficient to conclude that there had been a violation of Centro Europa 7's rights to freedom to express and impart ideas and information under Art. 10 of the Convention (paras 156–157). The Court reached the same finding in relation to Art. 1 of Protocol No. 1 (right of property) being violated, as the interference with Centro Europa 7's property rights did not have a sufficiently foreseeable legal basis either, within the meaning of the Court's case-law.[33]

Impact on IMRs

In this judgment the Court explicitly confirmed that member states have a positive obligation to enact an appropriate, clear and precise legislative and administrative framework with regard to licensing and the attribution of frequencies, as a safeguard for achieving media pluralism. The case demonstrates that a media policy aimed at countering monopolization of the electronic media and possible abuse of power will be more efficient when decisions on the allocation of frequencies and their implementation are not made by, or dependent on, administrative bodies that act under influence of political parties or interests of some media groups. Media service providers must also have effective means at their disposal to compel the authorities or any administrative body to abide by the law and the judgments by domestic courts. If such means are lacking, there are no sufficient guarantees against arbitrary interferences in the freedom of expression of (certain) media.

Glas Nadezhda EOOD and Elenkov v Bulgaria[34]

In the case *Glas Nadezhda EOOD and Elenkov v Bulgaria*, the Court was of the opinion that the refusal by the Bulgarian authorities to grant a broadcasting licence to the applicants did not meet the requirements of lawfulness as prescribed by Art. 10 § 2 of the Convention. The refusal to grant the licence was based on a decision by the National Radio and Television Committee (NRTC). The NRTC, however, had not held any form of public hearing and its deliberations had been kept secret, despite a court order obliging it to provide the applicants with a copy of its minutes. Furthermore, in its decision, the NRTC had merely asserted that Glas Nadezhda EOOD had not, or only partially, met a number of its criteria, but no reasoning was given to explain how the NRTC had come to that conclusion. Neither had redress been given for that lack of reasoning in the ensuing judicial review proceedings, because it had been held that the NRTC's discretion was not reviewable. This, together with the NRTC's vagueness concerning certain criteria for programmes, had denied the applicants legal protection against arbitrary interference with their freedom of expression. The Court noted that the guidelines adopted by the Committee of Ministers of the Council of Europe in the broadcasting regulation domain call for open and transparent application of the regulations governing the licensing procedure and specifically recommend that '[a]ll decisions taken […] by the regulatory authorities [be] duly reasoned [and] open to review by the competent jurisdictions' (Recommendation 2000/23). Consequently, the Court concluded that the interference with the applicants' freedom of expression had not been lawful and held that there had been a violation of Art. 10. In such a situation it is not even required to determine whether the interference by the IMR pursued a legitimate aim and, if so, whether it was proportionate to the aim it sought to attain.

Apart from a violation of Art. 10, the European Court also found that the lack of effective remedies against the decision of the NRTC and the State Telecommunications Commission (STC) to not grant a broadcasting licence to the applicant violated Art. 13. The Court observed that the Supreme Administrative Court of Bulgaria had made it clear that it could not scrutinize the manner in which the NRTC had assessed the compliance of Glas Nadezhda EOOD's programme documents with the relevant criteria, that assessment being within the NRTC's discretionary powers. The Supreme Administrative Court had thus refused to interfere with the exercise of NRTC's discretion on substantive grounds, and had not examined the issues going to the merits of the applicants' Art. 10 grievance. Referring to its case law in some similar cases, the Court concluded that the approach taken by the Supreme Administrative Court – refusing to interfere with the exercise of the NRTC's discretion on substantive grounds – fell short of the requirements of Art. 13 of the Convention (paras 66–71).

Impact on IMRs
This judgment clarified that Art. 10 may be violated when basic procedural requirements for administrative bodies are not met. Not only the law or the broadcasting regulation itself must contain guarantees against the arbitrary refusal of broadcasting licences, the IMRs are also obliged in practice to motivate explicitly on what grounds or motives a refusal to allocate a frequency or licence is based. Any decision of an IMR with a restrictive impact on the right to freedom of expression and information must be motivated, transparent and open to a substantive review, according to the requirements of Art. 13 ECHR.

Meltex Ltd and Mesrop Movsesyan v Armenia[35]
In the case *Meltex Ltd and Mesrop Movsesyan v Armenia*, the applicant was refused a licence by the country's National Television and Radio Commission (NTRC), which was entrusted with regulating the licensing process and monitoring the activities of private television and radio companies in Armenia. The Court reiterated that states are permitted, under the third sentence of Art. 10 § 1, to regulate the way broadcasting is organized in their territories, particularly in its technical aspects, by means of a licensing system. The granting of a licence may also be made conditional on such matters as the nature and objectives of a proposed station, its potential audience at national, regional or local level, the rights and needs of a specific audience and the obligations deriving from international legal instruments. However, the compatibility of such interferences must be assessed in the light of the requirements of paragraph 2 of Art. 10 ECHR, including the condition 'prescribed by law'. In matters affecting fundamental rights it would be contrary to the rule of law, one of the basic principles of a democratic society enshrined in the Convention, for a legal discretion granted to the executive to be expressed in terms of an unfettered power. Consequently, the law must indicate the scope of any such discretion conferred on the competent authorities and the manner of its exercise with sufficient clarity, having regard to the legitimate aim of the measure in question, in order to give the individual adequate protection against

arbitrary interference. As regards licensing procedures in particular, the Court reiterated that the manner in which the licensing criteria are applied in the licensing process must provide sufficient guarantees against arbitrariness, including a proper reasoning by the licensing authority of its decisions denying a broadcasting licence. The ECtHR noted that the NTRC's decisions granting broadcasting licences were based on the criteria defined in the Broadcasting Act and other complementary legal acts. These included 'the predominance of programmes produced in-house', 'the predominance of programmes produced in Armenia', 'the technical and financial capacity of the applicant' and 'the professional level of the staff'. While these criteria in themselves appear to be sufficiently precise, the Broadcasting Act did not explicitly require at the material time that any reasons be given by the licensing authority in applying these criteria. Even though the NTRC held public hearings, no decisions containing reasons for the granting or denial of a licence were announced at such hearings. The competing companies simply presented their bids, after which a points-based vote was taken, without a reasoning being given as to why this or that company's bid met the requisite criteria more than those of the other applicant companies. The applicant company and the public were thus not informed about the basis on which the NTRC had exercised its discretion to deny broadcasting licences. The Court therefore concluded that the interferences with the applicant's freedom to impart information and ideas, namely the seven denials of a broadcasting licence, did not meet the Convention requirement of lawfulness. Accordingly a violation of Art. 10 of the Convention was found.

Impact on IMRs
This judgment demonstrates that a licensing procedure wherein the licensing authority gives no reasons for its decisions does not provide adequate protection against arbitrary interferences by a public authority with the fundamental right to freedom of expression.

Özgür Radyo, Nur Radyo Ve Televizyon Yayıncılığı A.Ş. and Özgür Radyo-Ses Radyo Televizyon Yayın Yapım Ve Tanıtım's v Turkey[36]

In 1998 and 1999 the Turkish radio station Özgür Radyo, based in Istanbul, was given three warnings and its licence was twice suspended by the Turkish broadcasting regulatory authority Radio and Television Supreme Council (Radyo Televizyon Üst Kurulu, RTÜK). The first suspension was for a period of 90 days, the second suspension period lasted 365 days. Some of the programmes of Özgür Radyo had touched on themes such as corruption, the methods used by the security forces to tackle terrorism and possible links between the state and the mafia. The radio station was sanctioned by RTÜK because one of its programmes was considered defamatory and other programmes had incited the people to engage in violence, terrorism or ethnic discrimination, stirred up hatred, or offended the independence, the national unity or the territorial integrity of the Turkish State. The radio station applied to the administrative courts for an order setting aside each of the penalties, but its applications were dismissed. The ECtHR observed that although certain particularly acerbic parts of the programmes had made them hostile in tone to some degree, they had not encouraged the use of violence, armed resistance or insurrection and did not constitute hate speech. The Court strongly underlined that this is an essential factor to be taken into consideration. The Court also referred to the severity of the penalties that had been imposed on the applicant company, especially in terms of the suspension of the licence, first for a period of 90 days and in a second decision for a period of one year, the latter being the maximum penalty prescribed in Art. 33 of the Turkish Broadcasting Act n° 3984. The ECtHR considered the penalties disproportionate to the aims pursued and, therefore, not 'necessary in a democratic society'. Consequently, the Court held unanimously that there had been a violation of Art. 10.

In the case of *Nur Radyo Ve Televizyon Yayıncılığı A.Ş.*, the applicant company complained about the temporary broadcasting ban which had been imposed on it by the RTÜK. In 1999, RTÜK censured *Nur Radyo* for broadcasting certain comments by a representative of the Mihr religious community, who had described an earthquake in August 1999 in which thousands of people had died in the Izmir region of Turkey as a 'warning from Allah' against the 'enemies of Allah', saying Allah had decided on their 'death'. Since the applicant company had already received a warning for breaching the same rule, the RTÜK decided to suspend its radio broadcasting licence for 180 days. In this case the ECtHR acknowledged that the comments might have been shocking and offensive, but observed that they did not in any way incite violence and were not liable to stir up hatred against people. The Court reiterated that the nature and severity of the penalty imposed were also factors to be taken into account when assessing the proportionality of interference. It therefore considered that the broadcasting ban imposed on the applicant company had been disproportionate to the aims pursued, which constitutes a violation of Art. 10 of the Convention.[37]

In another case, RTÜK had suspended *Özgür Radyo-Ses Radyo Televizyon Yayın Yapım Ve Tanıtım's* licence for 365 days on account of a song which it had broadcast. The RTÜK took the view that the words of the offending song infringed the principle set forth in s. 4(g) of Law no. 3984, prohibiting the broadcasting of material likely to incite the population to engage in violence, terrorism or ethnic discrimination, and of a nature to arouse feelings of hatred among them. In its judgment, the ECtHR considered that the song reflected a political content and criticized the military. The song, however, referred to events that took place more than 30 years previously. Moreover, the lyrics of the song were very well known in Turkey and the song had been distributed for many years, with the authorization of the Ministry of Culture. According to the Court the song did not hold a risk to incite hatred or hostility amongst the population. There was no pressing social need for the interference and the sanction suspending the broadcaster's licence for such a long period was not proportionate to the legitimate aim of the protection of public order. The ECtHR found a violation of Art. 10 of the Convention.[38]

Impact on IMRs
These judgments show that severe sanctions that are imposed by IMRs on audiovisual media service providers, such as lengthy suspensions of licences, may be considered

disproportionate to the legitimate aim pursued, leading to a violation of Art. 10. Offensive or defamatory statements related to issues of public interest that have some factual basis and do not incite violence, hostility or hatred are under a very high level of protection of Art. 10 ECHR, also when these statements are broadcast on radio or television. In applying the provisions of the domestic broadcasting legislation, often implementing the EU Broadcasting Directive 89/522 and more recently the Audiovisual Media Services Directive 2010/13, IMRs are under an obligation to integrate the binding character of Art. 10 ECHR in their decision making and any sanctioning of audiovisual media service providers under their jurisdiction.

Conclusion

The European Court of Human Rights has clarified how the ECHR imposes various obligations on the member states regarding the organization and functioning of the IMRs applying domestic provisions of broadcasting law and regulations. Although an obligation to create an IMR cannot be directly deducted from the relevant Articles of the ECHR and the Court's case law, a set of principles based on the ECHR can be identified. The principles put forward by the ECtHR in different cases that IMRs were involved in largely echo, clarify and enforce the guidelines adopted by the Committee of Ministers in their Recommendation (2000)23 and Declaration 2008. The ECtHR has attached particular importance to the positive obligations for member states to enact a legislative framework which contains sufficient and clear guarantees to achieve media pluralism. Such frameworks should be characterized by the foreseeability of the legal provisions applied by IMRs; the existence of effective and efficient procedural guarantees, including in particular the obligation for IMRs to motivate their decisions; guarantees to avoid arbitrariness; access to substantive judicial review of IMR decisions; and the proportionality of sanctions imposed by IMRs.

On the other hand, the ECtHR often leaves a wide, sometimes a very wide, margin of appreciation to the domestic authorities, including IMRs, in interpreting and applying domestic provisions of the broadcasting law and regulation. Whereas such an approach is acceptable and in line with the general jurisprudence of the Strasbourg Court regarding advertising and regulation of commercial communications, or regarding morals and religion or protection of minors, a (too) wide margin of appreciation becomes problematic when it comes to developing positive action and securing media pluralism, or restricting journalistic reporting or political speech. In the Sigma RTV case it has been noted that the ECtHR left a broad margin of appreciation to the national media regulator CRTA, by accepting that sanctioning a TV station for stereotyping women, inappropriate language, offensive remarks and (alleged) incitement to discrimination in a fictional TV series was a necessary interference with the broadcaster's right to freedom of expression. Compared to other case law of the ECtHR such an approach risks neglecting the importance and the characteristics of the protection of freedom of expression and information as guaranteed by Art. 10 ECHR.[39]

The need for IMRs will be felt in the future as well, with the advent of an era of new media and media-like mass-communication services. In a Resolution of 29 May 2009, 'Towards a new notion of media' (Council of Europe 2009), the Council of Europe Ministers responsible for Media and New Communication Services emphasized that all media and media-like service providers have to respect certain benchmarks and should be adequately informed of their responsibilities. It is mentioned in the Resolution that 'media or media-like regulatory or accountability mechanisms, whether self- or co-regulatory or, if necessary, state driven, must be effective, transparent, independent and accountable'. Steps need to be taken in order to improve the functioning of those mechanisms, in particular regarding 'the access to those mechanisms for persons or groups who consider that their rights have been breached by media or media-like service providers'. The 2009 Reykjavik Action Plan annexed to the Resolution urges to 'pursue reflection on possible means of ensuring the effective, transparent, independent and accountable operation and functioning of complaints bodies and procedures for media and media-like mass-communication services'.

Notes

1 See e.g. Council of Europe Commissioner for Human Rights, Opinion of the Commissioner for Human Rights on Hungary's Media Legislation in Light of Council of Europe Standards on Freedom of the Media, 25 February 2011, CommDH(2011)10. Notice that reports and opinions of the Commissioner for Human Rights in their turn are considered part of the relevant law and practice the ECtHR is referring to in its case law, as e.g. in ECtHR (Grand Chamber) 26 June 2012, No. 26828/06, *Kurić and Others v Slovenia*, para. 223.

2 For a critical analysis that applies the COE standards to a situation of lacking guarantees for an adequate level of independence of members of an IMR, see Council of Europe Secretariat General, *Expertise by Council of Europe Experts on Hungarian Media Legislation*, Directorate General Human Rights and Rule of Law, Strasbourg, 11 May 2012.

3 'Member States shall take appropriate measures to provide each other and the Commission with the information necessary for the application of this Directive, in particular Articles 2, 3 and 4, in particular through their competent independent regulatory bodies'.

4 The Declaration, however, also notes that in a number of member states, the framework that seeks to guarantee the independence of members of regulatory authorities is far less satisfactory.

5 Recommendation (2000)23 also stresses that, given the broadcasting sector's specific nature and the peculiarities of its mission, regulatory authorities should include experts in the areas which fall within their competence.

6 Many regulatory authorities in Council of Europe member states receive their funding directly through fees in order to be independent from the decision-making of public authorities. However, in a number of countries where the law foresees that the regulatory

authority should be financed independently, in practice it receives its revenue from the state because of a weak broadcasting market or because the licence fee collecting system is ineffective (Council of Europe 2008, paras 20, 22).

7   Recommendation CM/Rec(2011)7 of 21 September 2011 on a new notion of media confirms this, stressing, however, that licensing is nowadays only justified in exceptional cases, i.e. by the need to manage scarce resources (for example the electromagnetic wavelength spectrum). The Recommendation also stresses that licensing or authorization should pursue the public interest, namely to guarantee the existence of a wide range of independent and diverse media (paras 77–78). It can be noted that similar limitations, i.e. that individual licences can only be required in the case of scarce resources, in particular numbers and frequencies, have already been imposed since 2003 under EU Electronic Communications Directives.

8   Recommendation (2000) 23 notes that, given the general interest involved, member states may follow different procedures for allocating broadcasting frequencies to public service broadcasters (para. 16).

9   Recommendation of 15 February 2012 on public service media governance, Appendix, para. 25.

10 The following paragraphs are mainly based on Lievens (2010: 303–310) and Voorhoof (2009: 3–49).

11 ECtHR (Grand Chamber) 7 February 2012, No. 39954/08, *Axel Springer AG v Germany*, para. 78 and ECtHR (Grand Chamber), 4 April 2012, No. 41723/06, *Gillberg v Sweden*, para. 82.

12 See, for instance, ECtHR 16 March 2000, No. 23144/93, *Özgür Gündem v Turkey*, paras 42–43 and ECtHR 16 December 2008, No. 23883/06, *Khurshid Mustafa and Tarzibachi v Sweden*.

13 ECtHR 17 September 2009, No. 13936/02, *Manole and others v Moldova*, para. 99.

14 For an analysis of the broader concept of pluralism in the case law of the ECtHR, also outside the media sphere, see: Nieuwenhuis 2007.

15 ECtHR 17 September 2009, No. 13936/02, *Manole and others v Moldova*, para. 100.

16 See for instance: ECtHR 20 September 1994, No. 13470/87, *Otto-Preminger-Institut v Austria*, ECtHR 25 November 1996, No. 17419/90, *Wingrove v the United Kingdom* and ECtHR 13 September 2005, No. 42571/98, *I.A. v Turkey*. See also ECtHR 10 July 2003, No. 44179/98, *Murphy v Ireland*.

17 See for instance: ECtHR 20 November 1989, No. 10572/83, *Markt Intern Verlag GmbH and Klaus Beermann v Germany*; ECtHR 24 February 1994, No. 15450/89, *Casado Coca v Spain*; ECtHR 5 November 2002, No. 38743/97, *Demuth v Switzerland*; ECtHR 5 March 2009, No. 26935/05, *Société de Conception de Presse et d'Edition and Ponson v France* and ECtHR 5 March 2009, No. 13353/05, *Hachette Filipacchi Presse Automobile and Dupuy v France*. See also ECtHR 10 July 2003, No. 44179/98, *Murphy v Ireland*.

18 See for instance: ECtHR 4 December 2003, No. 35071/97, *Gündüz v Turkey*; ECtHR 31 January 2006, No. 64016/00, *Giniewski v France*; ECtHR 2 May 2006, No. 50692/99, *Aydin Tatlav v Turkey*; ECtHR 28 June 2001, No. 24699/94, *VGT Verein gegen Tierfabriken v Switzerland*; ECtHR 4 October 2007, No. 32772/02, *VGT Verein gegen Tierfabriken (n° 2) v Switzerland*.

19   ECtHR 6 May 2003, No. 44306/98, *Appleby and Others v U.K.*

20   ECtHR 28 June 1984, No. 7819/77, 7878/77, *Campbell and Fell v the United Kingdom*, para. 76.

21   ECtHR 23 June 1981, No. 6878/75, 7238/75, *Le Compte, Van Leuven and De Meyere v Belgium*, para. 55.

22   ECtHR 28 June 1984, No. 7819/77, 7878/77, *Campbell and Fell v the United Kingdom*, para. 78.

23   ECtHR 17 June 2003, No. 62435/00, *Pescador Valero v Spain*, paras 21–29.

24   ECtHR 23 October 1995, No. 16841/90, *Pfarrmeier v Austria*, para. 38.

25   ECtHR 6 September 1979, No. 5029/71, *Klass and others v Germany*, para. 67; ECtHR 26 October 2000, No. 30210/96, *Kudla v Poland*, para. 157.

26   ECtHR 26 October 2000, No. 30210/96, *Kudla v Poland*, para. 157 and ECtHR (Grand Chamber) 26 June 2012, No. 26828/06, *Kurić and Others v Slovenia*, paras 295–372. See also ECtHR 28 January 2003, No. 44647/98, *Peck v the United Kingdom*, in which the applicant had been able to assert and vindicate his claims before the Broadcasting Standards Commission (BSC), the Independent Television Commission (ITC) and the Press Complaints Commission (PCC), bodies which could be considered to be self- or co-regulatory bodies. According to the ECtHR, however, these bodies could not provide an effective remedy for the applicant to have his right of privacy protected, resulting in the finding of a violation of Article 13 in conjunction with Article 8.

27   ECtHR 21 July 2011, Nos. 32181/04 and 35122/05, *Sigma Radio Television Ltd v Cyprus*.

28   With regard to this claim, the Court stated that 'this complaint is the same in substance as that raised under Article 6 § 1 concerning the alleged insufficiency of the scope of jurisdiction of the domestic courts. The Court reiterates that the role of Article 6 § 1 in relation to Article 13 is that of a *lex specialis*, the requirements of Article 13 being absorbed by the more stringent requirements of Article 6 § 1 (see *Brualla Gómez de la Torre v Spain*, 19 December 1997, para. 41, *Reports of Judgments and Decisions* 1997-VIII). Consequently, it will consider this part of the application solely under Article 6 § 1 of the Convention'.

29   ECtHR 17 September 2009, No. 13936/02, *Manole and others v Moldova*.

30   In line with this judgment and referring to Article 10 ECHR, the Committee of Ministers in its Recommendation and Declaration of 15 February 2012 on Public Service Media Governance emphasizes that 'freedom of expression, and free and pluralist media, are indispensable to genuine democracy. Media are the most important tool for freedom of expression in the public sphere, enabling people to exercise the right to seek and receive information.' See https://wcd.coe.int/ViewDoc.jsp?id=1908241&Site=CM&BackColorInternet=C3C3C3&BackColorIntranet=EDB021&BackColorLogged=F5D383, accessed: 13 March 2012.

31   ECtHR 5 November 2002, No. 38743/97, *Demuth v Switzerland*.

32   ECtHR (Grand Chamber) 7 June 2012, No. 38433/09, *Centro Europa 7 S.R.L. and Di Stefano v Italy*.

33   Centro Europa 7 also claimed that Article 6 and Article 14 were violated. The Court, however, held that it was not necessary to examine separately Centro Europa's 7 complaint under Article 14, and found its other complaint, under Article 6 § 1, inadmissible.

34   ECtHR 11 October 2007, No. 14134/02, *Glas Nadezhda Eood & Elenkov v Bulgaria*.

35   ECtHR 17 June 2008, No. 32283/04, *Meltex Ltd. and Mesrop Movsesyan v Armenia*.

36 ECtHR 30 March 2006, Nos. 64178/00, 64179/00, 64181/00, 64183/00, 64184/00, *Özgür Radyo-Ses Radyo Televizyon Yayın Yapım Ve Tanıtım A.Ş. v Turkey*.

37 ECtHR 27 November 2007, No. 6587/03, *Nur Radyo Ve Televizyon Yayıncılığı A.Ş v Turkey*.

38 ECtHR 4 December 2007, No. 11369/03, *Özgür Radyo-Ses Radyo Televizyon Yayın Yapım Ve Tanıtım A.Ş. v Turkey*.

39 ECtHR (Grand Chamber) 15 March 2012, Nos. 4149/04 and 41029/04, *Aksu v Turkey*. See also ECtHR 11 December 2008, No. 21132/05, *TV Vest As & Rogaland Pensjonistparti v Norway*.

References

Council of Europe (2000), *Recommendation Rec(2000)23 of the Committee of Ministers to member states of 20 December 2000 on the independence and functions of regulatory authorities for the broadcasting sector.*

Council of Europe (2008), *Declaration of the Committee of Ministers of 26 March 2008 on the independence and functions of regulatory authorities for the broadcasting sector.*

Council of Europe (2009), *Resolution MCM(2009)011 of the 1st Council of Europe Conference of Ministers responsible for Media and New Communication Services of 29 May 2009, Towards a new notion of media.*

European Platform of Regulatory Authorities (EPRA) (2011), *About Regulatory Authorities*, 9 November 2011, http://www.epra.org/articles/about-regulatory-authorities. Accessed 19 June 2012.

Harris, D., O'Boyle, M., Warbrick, C., Bates, E. et al. (eds.) (2009), *Harris, O'Boyle and Warbrick Law of the European Convention on Human Rights*, Oxford: Oxford University Press.

Kuijer, M. (2004), *The Blindfold of Lady Justice: Judicial Independence and Impartiality in Light of the Requirements of Article 6 ECHR*, Leiden: E.M. Meijers Instituut.

Lievens, E. (2010), *Protecting Children in the Digital Era: the Use of Alternative Regulatory Instruments*, Leiden: Martinus Nijhoff Publishers.

McGonagle, T. (2011), 'Freedom of Expression and the Media: Standard-setting by the Council of Europe's Committee of Ministers', *IRIS Themes Series 2011 Volume 1*, http://www.obs.coe.int/oea_publ/legal/CM_intro.pdf. Accessed 19 June 2012.

Nieuwenhuis, A. (2007), 'The Concept of Pluralism in the Case-Law of the European Court of Human Rights', *European Constitutional Law Review*, 3, pp. 367–384.

Ovey, C. and White, R. (2006), *Jacobs and White: The European Convention on Human Rights*, 4th ed., Oxford: Oxford University Press.

Van Dijk, P., van Hoof, F., van Rijn, A. and Zwaak, L. (eds.) (2006), *Theory and Practice of the European Convention on Human Rights*, Antwerp: Intersentia.

Voorhoof, D. (2004), 'Vrijheid van meningsuiting', in J. Vande Lanotte and Y. Haeck (eds.), *Handboek EVRM*, Antwerp and Oxford: Intersentia, pp. 837–1061.

Voorhoof, D. (2009), 'Freedom of Expression under the European Human Rights System. From Sunday Times (n° 1) v U.K. (1979) to Hachette Filipacchi Associés ("Ici Paris") v France (2009)', *Inter-American and European Human Rights Journal/Revista Interamericana y Europa de Derechos Humanos*, 1/2, pp. 3–49.

Chapter 4

Media regulatory authorities in the EU context: Comparing sector-specific notions and requirements of independence

David Stevens
KU Leuven ICRI - iMinds

Abstract

This chapter compares the requirements imposed under EU law for independence of regulatory authorities in the information and communication technology sectors. It starts by examining the provisions that are most relevant for media regulators (which form the focus of this book), notably those in the Audiovisual Media Services Directive (European Parliament and the Council of the European Union 2010, hereafter: AVMS Directive). These provisions might seem rather weak at first sight, which is the result of a sensitive compromise struck between the European Commission, the European Parliament and the European Council.

The subsequent sections of this chapter will elaborate on the requirements – both regarding independence and powers – which apply to regulatory authorities in a number of closely related information and communication technology sectors, such as electronic communications, data protection and public service broadcasting. The relevance of this analysis goes further than merely providing a comparative overview. Considering the close relationship between the audiovisual sector and, for instance, the electronic communications sector, it is highly probable that rules imposed in these closely related sectors will influence the concept of regulatory bodies in the audiovisual media sector (either because these rules directly apply to them when they perform certain tasks in 'the other sector', or indirectly, by indicating a trend in Europe towards more empowered and more independent regulatory authorities, centred around the objective to guarantee the impartiality of their decisions).

Hence the conclusion that requirements for independence of audiovisual media regulatory authorities in the AVMS Directive might seem rather weak and difficult to enforce needs to be nuanced in the light of the requirements applicable in a number of closely related sectors.

Keywords: independent regulatory bodies, independent regulatory authorities, legal position and powers, impartiality of decisions, audiovisual media, electronic communications, data protection, public service broadcasting

Introduction

Everywhere around the globe, an increasing number of regulatory tasks, traditionally falling under the responsibility of parliaments or governments, are being transferred to independent regulatory authorities.[1] Regulation, powers of regulatory authorities and their autonomy are all increasing. Regulators not only play a crucial role in a number of utility or network-based sectors (e.g. rail, water, energy, electronic communications), but also in other areas of our daily lives, whether economic (e.g. banking and financing, audiovisual media) or non-economic (e.g. the protection of fundamental rights and independent privacy commissions). As in most European information and communication technology sectors, the objectives to guarantee fair competition on the market and to effectively protect fundamental rights are the main normative arguments for creating independent regulatory bodies in the audiovisual media sectors as well (Hans Bredow Institute, et al. 2011: 12–16).

This chapter analyses the concept of independent regulatory bodies in the audiovisual media sector in the context of European Union legislation. The first section analyses the requirements applicable to independent regulatory bodies under the Audiovisual Media Services Directive (European Parliament and the Council of the European Union 2010, hereafter: AVMS Directive). The subsequent sections will contrast these requirements with those imposed in a number of closely related sectors, such as electronic communications, data protection and public service broadcasting. Examining the institutional design of the regulatory bodies in those sectors is relevant, not only because the normative arguments are similar, but also because they might serve as *best practices* for the audiovisual media sector. Moreover, the audiovisual media regulatory bodies often perform tasks in these other sectors as well, and therefore also need to comply with these additional requirements.

The analysis is limited to requirements imposed under sector-specific rules, and does not explicitly take into account general principles of European Union law, such as the obligation for member states to implement directives (Art. 288 para. 3 TFEU). Nor does it discuss the impact of fundamental rights, such as freedom of expression, as enshrined in the European Convention on Human Rights and Fundamental Freedoms (ECHR), as this is the topic of Chapter 3 in this book by Valcke, Voorhoof and Lievens.

Audiovisual Media Services Directive

Objectives

The starting point in determining the requirements for independence and efficient functioning of regulatory bodies in the audiovisual media sector is the AVMS Directive.[2]

The general objectives of this directive are summarized in its recital 2, stating that audiovisual media services provided across frontiers by means of various technologies are one way of pursuing the objectives of the Union. Therefore certain measures are necessary to permit and ensure the transition from national markets to a common programme production and distribution market, and to guarantee conditions of fair competition without prejudice to the public interest role to be discharged by the audiovisual media services. Furthermore, other recitals also explicitly refer to the growing importance of the audiovisual media sector for societies, democracy (in particular by ensuring freedom of information, diversity of opinion and media pluralism), education and culture as a justification for the application of specific rules (AVMS Directive, recital 5), and to the fact that it is essential for member states to ensure the prevention of any acts that may prove detrimental to freedom of movement and trade in television programmes, or which may promote the creation of dominant positions which would lead to restrictions on pluralism and freedom of televised information and of the information sector as a whole (AVMS Directive, recital 8).

Relevant provisions on institutional design

The core Article on institutional design is Art. 30 AVMS Directive,[3] being part of Chapter XI ('Cooperation between regulatory bodies of the Member States'). It requires member states to:

> take appropriate measures to provide each other and the Commission with the information necessary for the application of this directive, in particular Arts. 2, 3 and 4, in particular through their competent independent regulatory bodies.

The scope and impact of this provision is further elaborated in two specific recitals of the directive:

> (94) In accordance with the duties imposed on Member States by the Treaty on the Functioning of the European Union, they are responsible for the effective implementation of this directive. They are free to choose the appropriate instruments according to their legal traditions and established structures, and, in particular, the form of their competent independent regulatory bodies, in order to be able to carry out their work in implementing this directive impartially and transparently. More specifically, the instruments chosen by Member States should contribute to the promotion of media pluralism
>
> (95) Close cooperation between competent regulatory bodies of the Member States and the Commission is necessary to ensure the correct application of this directive. Similarly close cooperation between Member States and between their regulatory bodies is particularly important with regard to the impact which broadcasters established in one Member State might have on another Member State. Where licensing procedures are provided for in national law and if more than one Member State is concerned, it is desirable that contacts between the respective bodies take place before such licences are granted. This cooperation should cover all fields coordinated by this directive.

The text of Art. 30 AVMS Directive and of these recitals reflects a sensitive compromise between the visions of the EU Parliament and the Commission (insisting on stricter rules on institutional design) on the one hand, and the Council (more concerned about national sovereignty) on the other. The sensitivity of the issue was explicitly mentioned by different institutions during the adoption process (Kleist 2006: 210–221). After the compromise on the current wording, the European Commission in its Communication of 18 October 2007 on the common position stated:

> With regard to the independence of regulatory authorities the Presidency proposed a reference in a recital referring to the faculty for Member States to create independent national regulatory bodies. These should be independent from national governments as well as from operators. The EP and the Commission found it necessary that the reference to such bodies be included in the operative part of the directive. The compromise in Article 23b, which is acceptable to the Commission, reads: 'Member States shall take appropriate measures to provide each other and the Commission with the information necessary for the application of the provisions of this directive, in particular Articles 2, 2a and 3 thereof, notably through their competent independent regulatory bodies.

As with most provisions which form a political compromise, several possible interpretations can be given with regard to the scope of Art. 30 AVMS Directive. In the discussions revolving around this Article, the following three dimensions can be distinguished:

1. the extent to which it entails an obligation for member states to create an audiovisual media services regulatory body,
2. the scope and requirements of the organization of independence of the audiovisual media regulatory bodies,
3. the powers, role and tasks to be assigned to the audiovisual media regulatory bodies.

For each dimension, the operative part of the directive does not necessarily reflect the same position as the recitals, as graphically indicated in Figure 4.1.

Obligation to create

Regarding the extent to which the AVMS Directive requires the creation of a regulatory body, there are basically three lines of interpretation:

1. The notion of independent regulatory bodies in the AVMS Directive is only declaratory and has no meaning as regards the obligations the member states have to fulfil.
2. If an audiovisual media regulatory body exists, member states have to ensure that it is sufficiently independent from government and industry, but if such a body does not exist, the AVMS Directive does not contain an obligation to create it, since the European Commission itself referred to the faculty for member states.
3. If an audiovisual media regulatory body exists, member states have to ensure that it is sufficiently independent from government and industry, and if such a body does not exist, the AVMS Directive obliges the member states to create it, as it presupposes its existence.

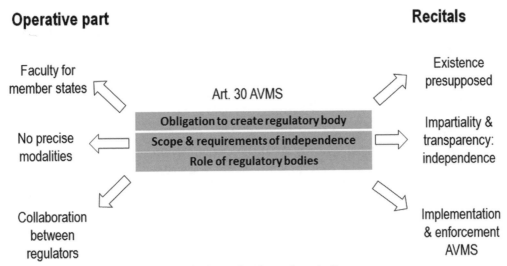

Figure 4.1: Dimensions of independence of audiovisual media regulatory bodies.

The controversial debate during the adoption process and the many amendments as they were suggested by the European Commission and Parliament make it highly unlikely that no requirement could be deduced from the reference to the concept of independent regulatory bodies in the AVMS Directive. Moreover, the recitals also clearly conflict with the first line of interpretation.

The third line of interpretation at first sight seems to be supported by the second part of Recital 94. However, it seems unreasonable to adhere to this interpretation, since during the adoption process there have been some amendments to the effect that the initial suggestion by the Commission and partly also the Parliament has at least been softened down when negotiating with the European Council. Based on the positions as they were expressed during the adoption process of the current text, it seems more correct to conclude that – although Art. 30 AVMS Directive presupposes 'independent regulatory bodies' in the member states – it in itself does not contain the obligation for member states to create such an independent regulatory body.

This interpretation is also put forward by Scheuer and Palzer (2008: 996), who write that:

> contrary to the initial proposal by the Commission, the legislative decision of the European Parliament in first reading, and the first amended proposal by the Commission, [the finally approved article] does not explicitly prescribe the establishment of independent regulatory bodies (previous phrasing: 'authorities'). Neither did the Council presidency take up dedicated requests by some delegations of member states to this effect.

They therefore conclude that the Article should be interpreted in such a way that it does not contain the obligation for member states to establish independent regulatory bodies, but that where regulatory bodies exist, they must be independent.

It should be noted that the importance of the distinction between the third and second line of interpretation is quite limited, since most member states already have established an audiovisual media regulatory body.

Requirements for independence

Regarding the institutional and organizational requirements of the independence of regulatory bodies under the AVMS Directive, one could argue that the directive does not prescribe any specific criterion. The preamble to the directive, however, indicates the objective for member states to guarantee the impartiality and transparency of the decisions of the regulatory bodies. Taking into account the specific characteristics of the audiovisual media sector (i.e. the objective for the regulatory bodies to guarantee not only a fair competition on the markets, but also the protection of fundamental rights such as the freedom of expression, see above),[4] one could argue that the regulatory body should not be subject to disproportionate influence either by the state or by market players. According to Scheuer and Palzer (2008: 997–998), Art. 30 AVMS Directive should be interpreted in such a way that it requires member states to guarantee that any existing regulatory body is independent (i) from state interference as well as (ii) from the industry. Regarding the further modalities of institutional design, they stress the responsibility of the member states to ensure a sufficient level of independence, taking different experiences and cultural factors into account. The authors then provide a wide range of possible instruments, such as constitutional law rules aiming at assuring the independence of the authority; legal provisions governing the appointment of the director general and/or the members of the board heading such an authority; rules on incompatibility; rules on transparency; rules on organizational and/or financial independence of persons involved as well as of the authority itself; and rules on the operational independence of the authority (Scheuer and Palzer 2008: 997–999).

Instructive in this regard is also the jurisprudence of the Court of Justice in relation to the eligibility of administrative bodies with supervisory tasks to refer preliminary questions to it. In *RTL Belgium* the Court concluded that the Belgian CSA (*Conseil Supérieur de l'Audiovisuel*) does not qualify as a national court or tribunal for the purposes of Art. 267 TFEU (ex-234 TEC), since it does not fulfil the necessary requirements for independence. According to the case law of the Court, these requirements are inherent to the task of adjudication and imply above all that the body in question acts as a third party in relation to the authority which adopted the contested decision (para. 38). The concept of independence in relation to courts or tribunals in the sense of Art. 267 TFEU entails an external and an internal aspect, the former entailing that the body is protected against external intervention or pressure liable to jeopardize the independent judgement of its members as regards proceedings before them; the latter being linked to impartiality and seeking to ensure a level playing field for the parties to the proceedings and their respective interests in relation to the subject matter of those proceedings (paras. 39–40). The main reason why the Court found that the Belgian CSA does not comply with these independence requirements was because the decision-making body responsible for ensuring compliance by the media broadcasters with the broadcasting rules and for punishing any infringements, the Licensing and Control Authority, is closely linked with the CSA as a whole, including with the Investigatory Office upon whose proposals it decides, since four of its ten members are also members of the 'Bureau' which manages the CSA. Hence, when it adopts a decision, the Licensing and Control Authority of the CSA is not distinct from the administrative monitoring body, which can act as a party to proceedings relating to broadcasting matters (para. 45).

Other cases involving regulatory authorities in other sectors led to a similar outcome. In *Syfait and others* the Court found that the Greek national competition authority did not qualify as a national court or tribunal. The Court noted that the authority was subject to the supervision of the Minister for Development and that, although the members of the Hellenic Competition Commission (*Epitropi Antagonismou*) enjoyed personal and operational independence and were bound in the exercise of their duties only by the law and their conscience, it nevertheless remained that there were no particular safeguards in respect of their dismissal or the termination of their appointment. According to the Court, such a system did not appear to constitute an effective safeguard against undue intervention or pressure from the executive on the members of the Hellenic Competition Commission (para. 31). With regard to regulatory authorities in the electronic communications sector, a similar conclusion was reached in the Order of the Court in *Telekom Austria AG, anciennement Post & Telekom Austria AG*. Finally, the same reasoning was also applied in *Bengtsson*, in which the Court excluded a local administrative commission – ruling on protection of the environment and public health, also in the case of non-ionizing radiation from mobile communications infrastructure – from the scope of Art. 267 TFEU.

Powers

Regarding the powers, role and tasks of the audiovisual media regulatory bodies, a large discrepancy exists between the text of the directive and the recitals as well. At first sight, the wording of Art. 30 AVMS Directive and its place in the directive seem to only oblige member states to take appropriate measures to share among them and with the European Commission the information necessary for the application of the directive. It should, however, be noted that the relevant recitals seem to presuppose a much more important role for the audiovisual media regulatory bodies, since they provide that these bodies should carry out their work in *implementing the AVMS Directive* impartially and transparently. A broader interpretation of the role of regulatory bodies therefore seems most plausible. Such interpretation also makes sense in view of another aspect of Art. 30 AVMS Directive. Through the requirements laid down in this provision, a network of information exchange and cooperation among the main regulatory bodies in the field of audiovisual media is envisaged. Even if the directive does not contain a very explicit obligation in that sense, it has the long-term policy aim to steer the process in a way that creates incentives for member states to establish such bodies and to participate in the described network. Further support for this interpretation can also be found in Art. 288 para. 3 TFEU, on the obligation for member states to effectively implement Directives into national law (Schulz, et al. 2011: 315–317). On the other hand, arguments indicating a more restricted role for the AVMS regulatory bodies can be found in its Art. 4, para. 6 which explicitly assigns the task to ensure compliance with the provisions of the directive to the member states, and does not mention the regulatory bodies. Moreover, this Article also repeats the freedom of member states to choose the appropriate means.

Electronic communications

Contrary to the AVMS Directive, the Electronic Communications Directives provide for a wide range of powers, responsibilities and tasks to be vested in national regulatory authorities (NRAs) in order to ensure, amongst other things, effective competition between market players. The NRAs play a central role in effectively implementing the regulatory framework, since many regulatory powers and tasks are directly assigned to them. Under the electronic communications framework, NRAs are required to deal with important and complex issues such as determining relevant markets, conducting market analyses and imposing obligations on operators with significant market power. They enjoy a significant level of independence, based on the principle of separation of regulatory and operational functions. The most important requirements relate to the independence vis-à-vis market players (subsection 1) and the obligation for NRAs to take all reasonable measures to achieve a limited number of policy objectives and regulatory principles[5] (subsection 2). Furthermore, the NRAs must comply with some broader requirements of institutional design, such as on collaboration and consultation with other relevant institutions (subsection 3) and a right of appeal against their decision (subsection 4). Some of these requirements were reinforced by the directives of 2009, which inter alia also aim at eliminating political interference in the NRA's day to day duties, as well as the protection against arbitrary dismissal of the head of the NRA.

As indicated, it is highly relevant to include the institutional design requirements in the electronic communications sector in the analysis of the independence of the audiovisual media regulatory authorities for three different reasons:

1. *The close relationship between the audiovisual media sector and the electronic communications sector, both at European and national level:* From a technological and economic perspective, the audiovisual media sector and the electronic communications sector are highly intertwined. This close relationship is also mirrored at the legal level: since 2002, the scope of the electronic communications regulatory framework is no longer limited to the traditional telecommunications sector, but also includes the transmission of electromagnetic signals used for distributing audiovisual broadcasting content (de Streel, et al. 2002; Geradin and Humpe 2002). Moreover, the electronic communications regulatory framework even contains a number of provisions which are

directly applicable (or even exclusively relevant) to the audiovisual media sector, such as provisions on must-carry, on conditional access systems, on application programme interfaces, on electronic programme guides and on standardization in the area of (digital, interactive) television.

2. *The functional definition of NRA:* The concept of NRAs as it is defined in the electronic communications regulatory framework itself is also an important justification. Art. 2(g) of the Framework Directive defines the national regulatory authority in a strictly functional way, as 'the body or bodies charged by a Member-State with any of the regulatory tasks assigned in this directive and the specific directives'. As a result, every institution that performs a task that – according to the specific articles of the directives – should be assigned to an NRA, has to be considered as an NRA and therefore has to comply with all relevant institutional requirements. So, whenever an audiovisual media regulatory authority is carrying out one of the electronic communications regulatory tasks (e.g. frequency allocation, analysing broadcasting transmission markets and imposing of obligations), it has to comply with the – much stricter – independence requirements of the electronic communications directives.

3. *The independence of NRAs in electronic communications sector as best practice:* In the electronic communications sector, the NRAs' role as merely policy advisory bodies has been revised as a result of their obligation to implement the EU liberalization and achieve the harmonization of the regulatory frameworks. Today, NRAs in this sector have to comply with a large number of requirements for independence and collaboration, while having wide discretionary powers in their decision-making processes.[6] The electronic communications sector is without any doubt one of the sectors in which the institutional design is most developed. These requirements have also been intensely debated in civil society – both at European and national level – and in the academic literature (see for example: de Streel 2005: 148–158, 2008; Stevens and Valcke 2003; Geradin 2000; Melody 1997, 1999), and have been interpreted throughout the case law of the Court of Justice (see below).

The following subsections provide a concise overview of these different aspects of the institutional design in the EU electronic communications sector.

Independence

Art. 3 Framework Directive

The requirement on independence of the NRAs is laid down in Art. 3 of the Framework Directive. The objective of this requirement is mainly to avoid the risk of conflicts of interests between the regulation of the sector and operational (or financial) interests (Framework Directive, Recital 11)[7] and to ensure the impartiality and transparency of the decisions of the NRAs, referred to as the 'principle of separation of regulatory and operational functions' (Recital 11).[8]

Further modalities are formulated by Art. 3, al. 2 of the Framework Directive. The first sentence of this provision obliges all member states to ensure that their NRAs are legally distinct from, and functionally independent of, market players. In practice, member states must ensure that every NRA is a legal person separate from any undertaking providing electronic communications networks or services. Assigning the least part of the regulatory tasks to an undertaking would constitute a breach of this requirement. Furthermore, beside a strictly legal separation, this sentence also requires a 'functional independence' of the NRA in its relationship with market players. Market players should not be able to interfere with or to influence the decisions of the regulatory body (Stevens and Valcke 2003: 166).

Where a member state retains ownership or control of a market player, Art. 3, al. 2 of the Framework Directive obliges it to ensure an effective structural separation of the regulatory function from activities associated with ownership or control. This Article reflects the – legitimate – concern that member states which retain part of the operational task are subject to an increased risk of conflicts of interest. The obligation to ensure such effective structural separation is stronger, because it compels member states to realize a stricter separation between the regulatory function – defined in a very general way – and the activities associated with ownership or control. In practice, member states are obliged to avoid as much as possible every conflict of interest between those different functions at every level of their administration (Schütz 2002: 25; Bender 2001: 509). Some lack of clarity still persists about the precise scope of the supervision of the NRAs. While some authors seem to defend the thesis that the directives do not require more than assigning the supervision over the NRA to another minister than the minister managing the state's share in its incumbent operator (Scherer 2002: 279–280; Geradin 2000), others stay closer to the text of the Commission's communication of 1995 (European Commission 1995), indicating that the control over both the regulatory and operational function can remain the competence of the one minister, as long as he cannot control more than the accounts and the legality of the decisions of NRAs. In a recent press release about the situation in Lithuania, the European Commission in its press release IP/11/412 of 4 April 2011 seems to adhere more to the former interpretation.

Following a number of cases initiated by the European Commission (Rizzuto 2009: 37 and 67), even stronger requirements for independence were put into place in the context of the 2009 directives. First, member states are now obliged to ensure that NRAs exercise their powers impartially, transparently and in a timely manner. Moreover, member states also have to ensure that NRAs have adequate financial and human resources to carry out the task assigned to them and that NRAs have separate annual budgets, which have to be made public.

A number of other requirements are also added to Art. 3 of the Framework Directive. The newly added al. 3a obliges NRAs responsible for ex-ante market regulation or for the resolution of disputes between undertakings to act independently, and prohibits them from seeking or taking instructions from any other body in relation to the exercise of these tasks, assigned to them under national law implementing Community law. However, the text explicitly mentions that these obligations shall not prevent supervision in accordance with national constitutional law. This obligation should be understood in such a way that only the appeal bodies set up in accordance with Art. 4 of the Framework Directive should have the power to suspend or overturn decisions by the NRAs.

Another new requirement relates to the dismissal of the head(s) of the regulatory body. In this respect, member states have to ensure that the head(s) of a national regulatory authority may only be dismissed if they no longer fulfil the conditions required for the performance of their duties. The decision to dismiss the head(s) has to be made public at the time of dismissal. The dismissed head(s) has to receive a statement of reasons and shall have the right to require its publication, where this would not otherwise take place, in which case it shall be published.

Finally, the 2009 directives contain a number of requirements in relation to the newly established Body of European Regulators for Electronic Communications (BEREC), the platform of European regulatory authorities in the electronic communications sectors. In order to support the activities of BEREC, member states have to ensure:

- that NRAs dispose of adequate financial and human resources to enable them to actively participate in and contribute to BEREC,
- that the goals of BEREC of promoting greater regulatory coordination and coherence are actively supported by the respective national regulatory authorities,
- that national regulatory authorities take utmost account of opinions and common positions adopted by BEREC when adopting their own decisions for their national markets.

Most of these institutional design requirements are also further elaborated in a working document of the Communications Committee.[9]

Ministries as NRAs?
Through a recent judgement of the Court of Justice, it has become clear that an NRA in the electronic communications sector is not necessarily limited to applying rules to individual cases. However, a ministry can only serve as NRA if it is able to comply with all the institutional requirements that are applicable to NRAs (e.g. independence, policy objectives, consultation and coordination and appeal).[10]

The Court of Justice thereby clarified one of the limits to the concept of independence, as already explicitly mentioned in the recitals to the Framework Directive, which state that the concept of independence is without prejudice to the institutional autonomy and the constitutional obligations of the member states, or to the principle of neutrality with regard to the property ownership. Therefore the obligation to avoid possible conflicts of interest does not require member states to disregard their own constitutional or administrative framework and does not require member states to privatize their incumbent operator further.

Legislators as NRAs?

Similarly, the functional definition of the concept of NRAs was also explicitly referred to by the Court of Justice in its judgement in case C-389/08 *Base NV and others vs Ministerraad* of 6 October 2010. Responding to the request for a preliminary ruling of the Belgian Constitutional Court, the Court evaluated to what extent the national legislator could assess the reasonableness of the cost of universal service, a task which the Universal Service Directive explicitly assigns to the regulatory authority. In its judgement the Court ruled that the directive in principle does not preclude the national legislature from acting as NRA provided that, in the exercise of that function, the legislator meets the requirements of Art. 3 of the Framework Directive. The Court therefore stresses that member states must, in particular, ensure that each of the tasks assigned to NRAs be undertaken by a competent body; guarantee the independence of such bodies by ensuring that they are legally distinct from and functionally independent of all organizations providing electronic communications networks, equipment or services; and ensure that they exercise their powers impartially and transparently.

Interesting to note is that the Court in its (earlier) judgement in case C-424/07 (*European Commission v Germany*) followed a slightly different approach. In this case, the European Commission acted against a provision in the German Law on Telecommunications which stated that 'new markets' (in the act defined as markets for services or products which are significantly different from currently available services or products in terms of their effectiveness, their range, their availability for a large number of users (mass-market capacity), their price or their quality from the point of view of a knowledgeable buyer, and which do not simply replace those products) would, in principle, not be subject to regulation by the NRA. In its judgement, the Court did not focus so much on the functional definition of the concept of NRAs, but instead followed the interpretation of the European Commission, and concluded that this provision encroaches on the wide powers of the NRA.[11] Moreover, the Court in paragraph 106 not only stated that the legislator cannot serve as an independent national regulatory authority, but also ruled that the strict institutional procedures for market definition, market analysis and the imposing of obligations were not applied correctly:

> In that connection, it has already been held that the principle of non-regulation of new markets provided for in Paragraph 9a(1) of the TKG limits the discretion of the NRA under Articles 15(3) and 16 of the Framework Directive. The limitation of the NRA's discretion to submit 'new markets' to a definition and to a market analysis necessarily involves a failure to comply in certain circumstances with the procedures provided for in Articles 6 and 7 of the Framework Directive.

Multiple NRAs

The Electronic Communications Directives do not require the member states to concentrate all tasks in one single NRA. Art. 3, al. 4 of the Framework Directive even explicitly mentions the possibility of establishing more than one NRA. In that case, the tasks assigned to the different NRAs have to be made public in an easily accessible form.[12]

Regulatory objectives and principles

Besides requirements on independence, the Framework Directive also requires member states to ensure that all decisions of the NRAs are aimed at achieving a limited number of (harmonized) policy objectives. In practice, every decision of an NRA should aim at realizing at least one of those objectives. Member states are in principle not allowed to impose other objectives or principles on their NRAs. Imposing such a harmonized set of objectives and principles to underpin the tasks of the NRAs was considered to be an essential tool to ensure that the increased flexibility of the material rules of the framework (e.g. in the area of market regulation) would not hamper the harmonization of market conditions throughout the European Union (Geradin and Petit 2004: 15). Supported in this interpretation by the jurisprudence of the Court of Justice,[13] the European Commission therefore attaches great value to these objectives and principles and to their correct implementation into national law. Moreover, Art. 19 of the Framework Directive empowers the European Commission to issue a recommendation or a decision on the harmonized application of the electronic communications framework under certain conditions, in order to further the achievement of those harmonized objectives and principles.

The objectives that are imposed on the NRAs by Art. 8 of the Framework Directive mainly fall into three categories:

- promoting competition in the provision of networks, services and associated facilities and services,
- contributing to the development of the internal EU market,
- promoting the interests of the citizens of the EU.

Art. 1 8) h) of the Better Regulation Directive of 2009 added to this list the obligation for NRAs to apply objective, transparent, non-discriminatory and proportionate regulatory principles in their pursuit of these policy objectives.

For all those high-level objectives, the directive provides extensive lists of more specific ways in which the NRAs should pursue them. Beside those three general principles, the directives also require the NRAs to make their decisions (especially those aiming at ensuring effective competition) as technologically neutral as possible. In practice, when taking a decision, NRAs should neither impose nor discriminate in favour of the use of a particular type of technology. Only in justified cases the NRAs can take proportionate measures to promote certain specific services (for example digital television as a means for increasing spectrum efficiency). Furthermore, Art. 8 of the Framework Directive explicitly mentions the possibility for NRAs to contribute to ensuring the implementation of policies aimed at the promotion of cultural and linguistic diversity, as well as media pluralism.

Broader institutional framework

The Electronic Communications Directives not only prescribe in detail the requirements regarding the legal position and the powers of the regulatory authorities themselves. Besides this, they also contain requirements on the broader institutional framework (e.g. issues such as information, consultation, collaboration and harmonization with other institutions) in the electronic communications sector (Larouche 2002: 145–148). The impact of these procedures has been perceived by some scholars as significant in that they describe the current regulatory model in the electronic communications sector as a model of 'managed decentralisation, or decentralisation with EU cooperation (or networking) mechanisms' (Geradin and Petit 2004: 15).

In practice, the different instruments relate to:

- obligations to publish certain information and/or notify concerned parties,
- obligations to consult other regulatory authorities,
- harmonization or cooperation procedures,
- requirements on collaboration with competition law authorities,
- the obligation to collaborate with BEREC.

Appeal

Finally, the electronic communications framework also contains provisions on the harmonization of the appeals against NRAs' decisions. Art. 4 of the Framework Directive assigns to any user and undertaking providing electronic communications networks and/or services, when affected by a decision of an NRA, a right of appeal to a body that is independent of the parties involved. This body, which may be a court, must have the appropriate expertise available for functioning effectively and has to be competent to take the merits of the case duly into account. Pending the outcome of any such appeal, the decision of the NRA should stand, unless interim measures are granted in accordance with national law. Furthermore, member states must collect information on the general subject matter of appeals, the number of requests for appeal, the duration of the appeal proceedings and the number of decisions to grant interim measures. After reasoned request of the European Commission or BEREC, member states must provide them with such information (Nihoul 2004: 629–641; Lasok 2005: 787–801).

In *Tele2 Telecommunications v Telekom-Control-Kommission*, the Court of Justice stated that Art. 4 is derived from the general principle of EU law of effective judicial protection, pursuant to which it is for the courts of the member states to ensure judicial protection of an individual's rights (para. 38). This vision was shortly after also confirmed in *Arcor v Germany*, where a similar provision on appeal against a decision on local loop unbundling was challenged (paras. 176–177). The Court of Justice held that an undertaking that is eligible for unbundled access to a local loop, but is not an addressee of an NRA's decision, is a party affected by the decision and may challenge it, when the decision potentially affects its rights by reason of its content and the activity exercised or envisaged by the party. In *Mobistar v BIPT* the Court of Justice confirmed that the appeal body must have at its disposal all the information necessary in order to decide on the merits of the appeal, including, if necessary, confidential information which the NRA has taken into account in reaching the decision under appeal (para. 43). Finally, in the area of competition law, the Grand Chamber of the ECJ in *VEBIC* has stated that Art. 35 of Regulation 1/2003 (on the designation of national competition authorities) should be interpreted in such a way that a national competition authority's obligation to ensure that Art. 101 TFEU and 102 TFEU are applied effectively requires that the authority should be entitled to participate, as a defendant or respondent, in proceedings before a national court which challenge a decision that the authority itself has taken.

State aid and public service broadcasting

Another set of requirements which the audiovisual media regulatory bodies might have to comply with are those applicable to regulatory authorities in the area of state aid and public service broadcasting. State aid regulation has been the starting point for debates revolving around the specific supervisory structure some member states have implemented for monitoring public broadcasting.

Valuable guidance on the dimensions and indicators used to evaluate the independence of supervisory bodies can be found in a recent communication of the European Commission on the application of state aid rules to public service broadcasting (European Commission 2009). Regarding the necessity of effective supervision of public service broadcasting, the Commission states that it is desirable that an appropriate authority or appointed body monitors the application of the agreement between the state and the operator entrusted with the public service remit in a transparent and effective manner. 'The need for such an appropriate authority or body in charge of supervision is apparent in the case of quality standards imposed on the entrusted operator', the communication specifies. Referring to the Amsterdam Protocol, the Commission recalls that it is within the competence of the member state to choose the mechanism to ensure effective supervision of the fulfilment of the public service obligations, therefore enabling the Commission to carry out its tasks under Art. 106(2) TFEU (ex-86(2) TEC). The Commission also indicates that supervision would only seem effective if carried out by a body which is effectively independent from the management of the public service broadcaster, has the powers and the necessary capacity and resources to carry out supervision regularly, and is able to impose appropriate remedies insofar it is necessary to ensure respect of the public service obligations.

The Commission expresses similar concerns in relation to the financial control mechanisms of public service broadcasters, stating that such control mechanisms would only seem effective if carried out by an external body, independent from the public service broadcaster, at regular intervals, preferably on a yearly basis. According to the Commission, evaluating the appropriateness of 'public service reserves' could only be objective if carried out by a body which is effectively independent from the management of the public service broadcaster, including with regard to the appointment and removal of its members, and which has sufficient capacity and resources to exercise its duties. Finally, the Commission explicitly mentions that such a procedure can be proportionate to the size of the market and the market position of the public service broadcaster.

Evaluating the Commission's interference in the supervision of state aid and public service broadcasting, Donders and Pauwels state that it:

> has created more awareness about not only the necessity of control but also the need for effective and credible control. Better and more accountable monitoring systems will benefit the legitimacy of public broadcasters expanding their activities to new media markets. This does not mean that Member States should accept each and every demand of the Commission concerning the monitoring of public broadcasters. It does, however, lead us to the conclusion that the European debate on control also fosters urgent national discussions about an appropriate organisation of control systems for public broadcasting.
>
> (Donders 2010: 125)

Data protection

The independence of regulatory agencies has also been highly debated in the field of data protection law. Analysing these requirements can be interesting for the media sector, since both involve fundamental rights, respectively the right to privacy and the freedom of expression.

Contrary to most of the other sectors, Art. 28 of Directive 95/46/EG requires a 'complete independence' of the supervisory authorities in the data protection area, stating that each member state has to provide that one or more public authorities are responsible for monitoring the application within its territory of the provisions adopted pursuant to the Data Protection Directive, and that these authorities shall act with complete independence in exercising the functions entrusted to them. The regulatory authorities have to be consulted when member states are drawing up administrative measures or regulations regarding data protection. The regulatory authority also has to be assigned a minimal set of powers (e.g. investigative powers, effective powers of intervention and the power to engage in legal proceedings).

Before the Court of Justice, the European Commission claimed that Germany had not correctly implemented this provision. For defining 'complete independence' the Commission referred to the criteria stated in Art. 1 para. 3 of the explanatory report to the Additional Protocol to the Convention for the Protection of Individuals with regard to Automatic Processing of Personal Data regarding supervisory authorities and transborder data flows, which also contains the notion of complete independence. The criteria described in this document relate to:

- the composition of the authority,
- the method for appointing its members,
- the duration of exercise and conditions of cessation of their functions,
- the allocation of sufficient resources to the authority,
- the adoption of decisions without being subject to external orders or injunctions.

In addition, the Commission also refers to Art. 44 para. 2 of Regulation (EC) No 45/2001, which regulates the independence of the European Data Protection Supervisor. According to this provision, the European Data Protection Supervisor shall, in the performance of his duties, neither seek nor take instructions from anybody.

The Commission particularly criticized the effect of dependence through state scrutiny in Germany as an incorrect implementation of the directive. German data protection authorities of the Länder are subject to legal, technical as well as administrative scrutiny. According to the Commission, all three types of supervision infringe upon the principle of complete independence.

In his opinion, the Advocate General Jàn Mazàk argued that the wording of the directive does not require an independent regulatory body as such, but rather a body having complete independence in carrying out its functions. In view of the functions of the directive, a legal, technical as well as administrative scrutiny would not conflict with the concept of complete independence as laid down by the directive (paras. 15 and 30).

In its judgement of 9 March 2010, the Court of Justice to a large extent follows the thesis of the European Commission, considering independence as necessary to create an equal level of protection of personal data and thereby contributing to the free movement of data, which is necessary for the establishment and functioning of the internal market (para. 37).

The Court's main argument revolves around two different lines, of which the first one relates to the actual wording of Art. 28 of the Directive. On this issue, the Court concludes that, because the words 'with complete independence' are not defined by the directive, it is necessary to take their usual meaning into account. The Court continues by stating that in relation to a public body, the term 'independence' normally means a status which ensures that the body concerned can act completely freely, without taking any instructions or being put under any pressure. Furthermore, it dismisses all the arguments of the Federal German Republic by explicitly stating that there is nothing to indicate that the requirement of independence concerns exclusively the relationship between the supervisory authorities and the bodies subject to that supervision. The Court states that the concept of 'independence' is complemented by the adjective 'complete', which implies a decision-making power independent of any direct or indirect external influence on the supervisory authority (paras 18–19).

The second argument of the Court is built around its interpretation of the objectives and the context of the Data Protection Directive, and of the requirement of independence. On the latter, the Court states that the guarantee of the independence of national supervisory authorities is intended to ensure the effectiveness and reliability of the supervision of compliance with the provisions on protection of individuals with regard to the processing of personal data. Therefore, when carrying out their duties, the supervisory authorities must act objectively and impartially. For that purpose, they must remain free from any external influence, including the direct or indirect influence of the state or the 'Länder', and not of the influence only of the supervised bodies (paras. 20–25).

The Court of Justice then turns to the analysis of whether the German state scrutiny over the data protection supervisory authorities is consistent with the requirement of complete independence. Although it recognizes that the state scrutiny *a priori* only seeks to guarantee that decisions of the authorities comply with the national and European legislation, and therefore does not aim to oblige those authorities to potentially pursue political objectives inconsistent with the protection of individuals with regard to the processing of personal data and with fundamental rights, the Court nevertheless concludes that the current organization of state scrutiny does not exclude the possibility that the scrutinizing authorities, which are part of the general administration and therefore under the control of the government of their respective Land, are not able to act objectively when they interpret and apply the provisions relating to the processing of personal data. Furthermore, the Court also rules that the mere risk that the scrutinizing authorities could exercise a political influence over the decisions of the supervisory authorities is enough to hinder the latter authorities' independent performance of their tasks. To support this finding, the Court refers to the possibility that there could be 'prior compliance' on the part of the data protection authorities, and to the necessity for the decisions of the regulatory authorities, and therefore for the authorities themselves, to remain above any suspicion of partiality (paras. 31–37).

Concluding, the Court also dismisses the argument that a broad interpretation of the requirement of independence would be contrary to various principles of European Community law and to the principle of democracy, stating in its paragraph 42:

That principle [of democracy] does not preclude the existence of public authorities outside the classic hierarchical administration and more or less independent of the government. The existence and conditions of operation of such authorities are, in the Member States, regulated by the law or even, in certain States, by the Constitution and those authorities are required to comply with the law subject to the review of the competent courts. Such independent administrative authorities, as exist moreover in the German judicial system, often have regulatory functions or carry out tasks which must be free from political influence, whilst still being required to comply with the law subject to the review of the competent courts. That is precisely the case with regard to the tasks of the supervisory authorities relating to the protection of data.

The Court, however, rules that the required balance between the necessity for independence and the principle of democracy does not oblige member states to abolish every possible form of state scrutiny. In this respect, the Court explicitly states that the management of the supervisory authorities may be appointed by the parliament or by the government, and that the legislator may define the powers of those authorities. Furthermore, the legislator may impose also an obligation on the supervisory authorities to report their activities to the parliament.

However, because of the much wider state scrutiny in Germany, the Court declares that, by making the authorities responsible for monitoring the processing of personal data by non-public bodies and undertakings governed by public law which compete on the market (*öffentlich-rechtliche Wettbewerbsunternehmen*) in the different Länder subject to state scrutiny, Germany has not correctly transposed the requirement that those authorities perform their functions 'with complete independence'. On 16 October 2012, the Court confirmed this strict interpretation in a similar case against Austria.

The direct impact of these judgements on the requirement of independence applicable to the audiovisual media regulatory authorities will most likely remain limited because, in most cases, the data protection regulatory authority will be separate from the audiovisual media regulatory body. Moreover, the data protection situation is also particular because the directive explicitly requires a 'complete independence'. The judgement nevertheless contains useful criteria on the dimensions and indicators that are used to evaluate the independence of the regulatory authority in its relationship with the government and/or state. Ongoing relevant developments which will have to be monitored include the discussions between the European Commission and the Hungarian government on the independence of the data protection authority (European Commission 2011) and the future provisions on institutional design in the data protection reform recently initiated by the European Commission.[14]

Closing observations

In this chapter, we analysed the legal framework with regard to the independence and effective functioning of regulatory bodies in the European audiovisual media sector. While the first section focused on the provisions of the AVMS Directive, the following sections examined the institutional design in a number of closely related sectors.

Although the text of the AVMS Directive is the result of a sensitive compromise and was to a large extent softened down during the adoption process, the objective of impartiality of the decisions of the regulatory bodies remained. This final objective is not only relevant in the relationship between the public and the private sector, but also needs to take into account the delicate relationship between the media and politics (i.e. when shaping the relationship between the regulatory body and the government). The obligation of impartiality is further elaborated in the AVMS Directive, in which Art. 30 formulates a minimum requirement of independence for existing regulatory bodies. However, if an independent regulatory body has not been established in the member state, Art. 30 AVMS Directive in itself cannot serve as a sufficient legal basis for the obligation to establish such a body. When a specific regulatory body exists, this body should be organized sufficiently independent from market players and government (e.g. requirements at the level of status and powers, financial autonomy, autonomy of decision-makers, knowledge, and accountability and transparency mechanisms) and dispose of the necessary powers to effectively implement the aims of the AVMS Directive. This conclusion is supported by the wording of the recitals of the directive, as well as the underlying long-term objective to establish a network of information exchange and cooperation among the main regulatory bodies in the field of audiovisual media. While member states have some leeway in deciding on the concrete way of implementing the AVMS Directive provisions into national law (e.g. with regard to the legal status, organizational layout and decision-making procedures), they nevertheless have to guarantee that the aims of the directive (i.e. impartiality of the decisions of the regulatory bodies) are effectively implemented.

Summarizing, it follows from the AVMS Directive that member states have to ensure a national regulatory framework which is capable of providing impartial and effective supervision of the audiovisual media sector, preventing undue influences both from the political sector and from the regulated sector. Therefore, with regard to the regulatory bodies competent for implementing the AVMS Directive, a functional rather than an organizational understanding of independence should be adopted. This functional approach is supported by the wording of the AVMS Directive, which links the notion of independent regulatory bodies to the action of carrying out specific duties and obligations imposed by the directive. In contrast to the sector of data protection, the directive does not, however, demand the 'complete independence' of audiovisual media regulatory bodies.

Besides the specific requirements of independence within the audiovisual sector, this chapter also analysed a number of related sectors in which EU legislation requires certain guarantees for the independence of the regulatory bodies (the electronic communications sector, state aid and public service broadcasting, and data protection). The analysis of these requirements is highly relevant, because in some cases the audiovisual media regulatory body will also perform functions in these other sectors, in which case it has to comply with these additional institutional requirements as well. Moreover, elements of the institutional design in these sectors could potentially also serve as best practices for the audiovisual media sector. Taking into account these different elements leads to the conclusion that even though the original wording of the AVMS Directive at first sight might seem rather weak, the requirements as they are applicable in a number of closely related information and communication technology sectors (e.g. electronic communications, public service broadcasting and data protection) are all likely to influence the concept of regulatory bodies in the audiovisual media sector, as they clearly indicate a trend towards more empowered and more independent regulatory authorities, centred around the objective to guarantee the impartiality of their decisions.

Notes

1 Already in 1994, M. Thatcher wrote about the rise of the regulatory state in Europe (see Thatcher 1994).

2 The AVMS Directive of 2010 has codified the original 'Television without Frontiers' Directive (89/552/EEC) which dates already from 1989 (Council Directive 89/552/EEC on the coordination of certain provisions laid down by law, regulation or administrative action in Member States concerning the pursuit of television broadcasting activities, Official Journal L 298, 17/10/1989, p. 23) as well as the two subsequent amending Directives: Directive 97/36/EC of the European Parliament and of the Council of 30 June 1997 amending Council Directive 89/552/EEC on the coordination of certain provisions laid down by law, regulation or administrative action in Member States concerning the pursuit of television broadcasting activities (Official Journal L 202, 30/7/1997, p. 60–70) and Directive 2007/65/EC of the European Parliament and of the Council of 11 December 2007 amending Council Directive 89/552/EEC on the coordination of certain provisions laid down by law, regulation or administrative action in Member States concerning the pursuit of television broadcasting activities (Official Journal L 332, 18/12/2007, p. 27–45).

3 Originally inserted as article 23b by the Audiovisual Media Services Directive of 2007, see note 2.

4 For the requirements in this area deriving from Art. 10 ECHR, see Chapter 3 in this book by Valcke, Voorhoof and Lievens.

5 Court of Justice of the European Union, Judgment of 3 December 2009, *European Commission v Germany*, case C-424/07, para. 59: 'In carrying out their tasks, the NRAs are required, pursuant to Article 7(1) of the Framework Directive, to take the utmost account of Article 8 thereof. In accordance with Article 8(1) of that Directive, Member States must ensure that the NRAs take all reasonable measures which are aimed at achieving the objectives set out in Article 8. Furthermore, that provision states that the measures taken by the NRA must be proportionate to those objectives.'

6 See: Court of Justice of the European Union, Judgment of 3 December 2009, *European Commission v Germany*, case C-424/07, para. 61: 'In carrying out those regulatory functions, the NRAs have a broad discretion in order to be able to determine the need to regulate a market according to each situation on a case-by-case basis (see, to that effect, Case C-55/06 Arcor [2008] ECR I-2931, paragraphs 153 to 156)'.

7 As it is also the case in the WTO Agreement on Basic Telecommunications, where many countries commit, among other things, to establish a regulator that is separate from the incumbent operator.

8 Recital 11 of the Framework Directive reads: 'In accordance with the principle of the separation of regulatory and operational functions, Member States should guarantee the independence of the national regulatory authority or authorities with a view to ensuring the impartiality of their decisions. This requirement of independence is without prejudice to the institutional autonomy and constitutional obligations of the Member States or to the principle of neutrality with regard to the rules in Member States governing the system of property ownership laid down in Article 295 of the Treaty. National regulatory authorities should be in possession

of all the necessary resources, in terms of staffing, expertise, and financial means, for the performance of their tasks.' See also Court of Justice of the European Union, Judgment of 3 December 2009, *European Commission v Germany*, case C-424/07, para. 54: 'Pursuant to Article 3(2) and (3) of the Framework Directive and recital 11 in its preamble, in accordance with the principle of the separation of regulatory and operational functions, Member States must guarantee the independence of the national regulatory authority or authorities with a view to ensuring the impartiality and transparency of their decisions.'

9   EU Communications Committee Working Document, Implementation of the revised Framework Directive – Independence of National Regulatory Authorities, COCOM10-16, 15 April 2010.

10 Court of Justice of the European Union, Judgment of 6 March 2008, *Comisión del Mercado de las Telecomunicaciones v Administración del Estado*, case C-82/07, para. 26: 'As a consequence, where those functions are to be discharged, even partially, by ministerial authorities, each Member State must ensure that those authorities are neither directly nor indirectly involved in 'operational functions' within the meaning of the Framework Directive'.

11 Court of Justice of the European Union, Judgment of 3 December 2009, *European Commission v Germany*, case C-424/07, para. 78: 'Therefore, by laying down a legal provision, according to which, as a general rule, the regulation of new markets by the NRA is excluded, Paragraph 9a of the TKG encroaches on the wide powers conferred on the NRA under the Community regulatory framework, preventing it from adopting regulatory measures appropriate to each particular case. As it is clear from point 54 in the Advocate General's Opinion, the German legislature cannot alter a decision of the Community legislature and cannot, as a general rule, exempt new markets from regulation.'

12 See also: Court of Justice of the European Union, Judgment of 6 March 2008, *Comisión del Mercado de las Telecomunicaciones v Administración del Estado*, case C-82/07, para. 25: 'Thus, in accordance with Article 3(2), (4) and (6) of the Framework Directive, the Member States must not only guarantee the functional independence of regulatory authorities in relation to the organisations providing electronic communications networks, equipment or services, but must also publish, in an easily accessible form, the tasks to be undertaken by the national regulatory authorities, and notify to the Commission the names of the regulatory authorities entrusted with carrying out those tasks, and their respective responsibilities.'

13 See: Court of Justice of the European Union, Judgment of 3 December 2009, *European Commission v Germany*, case C-424/07, para. 92; Court of Justice of the European Union, Judgment of 31 January 2008, *Centro Europa 7 Srl v Ministero delle Comunicazioni e Autorità per le garanzie nelle comunicazioni and Direzione generale per le concessioni e le autorizzazioni del Ministero delle Comunicazioni*, case C-380/05, para. 81; Court of Justice of the European Union, Judgment of 13 November 2008, *European Commission v Poland*, case C-227/07, paras 62–68; Court of Justice of the European Union, Judgment of 10 January 2008, *European Commission v Republic of Finland*, case C-387/06; Court of Justice of the European Union, Judgment of 12 November 2009, *TeliaSonera Finland*, Case C-192/08, para. 50.

14 See http://ec.europa.eu/justice/newsroom/data-protection/news/120125_en.htm.

References

Bender, G. (2001), 'Regulierungsbehörde quo vadis?', *Kommunikation und Recht*, 10, pp. 506–515.

Council of Europe (2001), ETS 181 of 28 November 2001, Additional Protocol to the Convention for the Protection of Individuals with regard to Automatic Processing of Personal Data regarding supervisory authorities and transborder data flows, http://conventions.coe.int/Treaty/EN/Reports/Html/181.htm. Accessed 25 May 2012.

Court of Justice of the European Union (2005a), Judgment of 31 May 2005, *Syfait and others*, case C-53/03.

Court of Justice of the European Union (2005b), Order of 6 October 2005, *Telekom Austria AG, anciennement Post & Telekom Austria AG*, case C-256/05.

Court of Justice of the European Union (2006), Judgment of 13 July 2006, *Mobistar*, case C-438/04.

Court of Justice of the European Union (2008a), Judgment of 21 February 2008, *Tele2 Telecommunication*, case C-426/05.

Court of Justice of the European Union (2008b), Judgment of 24 April 2008, *Arcor*, case C-55/06.

Court of Justice of the European Union (2010a), Judgment of 9 March 2010, *Commission of the European Communities v Federal Republic of Germany*, case C-518/07.

Court of Justice of the European Union (2010b), Judgment of 7 December 2010, *VEBIC*, case C-439/08.

Court of Justice of the European Union (2010c), Judgment of 22 December 2010, *RTL Belgium*, case C-517/09.

Court of Justice of the European Union (2011), Order of 24 March 2011, *Bengtsson*, case C-344/09.

Court of Justice of the European Union (2012), 16 October 2012, *Commission of the European Communities v Republic of Austria*, case C-640/10.

De Streel, A. (2005), 'A First Assessment of the New European Regulatory Framework for Electronic Communications', *Communications & Strategies*, 58: 2, pp. 141–170.

De Streel, A. (2008), 'The current and future European regulation of electronic communications: A critical assessment', *Telecommunications Policy*, 32: 11, pp. 722–734.

De Streel, A., Queck, R. and Vernet, P. (2002), 'Le nouveau cadre réglementaire européen des réseaux et services de communications électroniques', *CDE*, pp. 243–314.

Donders, K. and Pauwels, C. (2010), 'What if Competition Policy Assists the Transfer from Public Service Broadcasting to Public Service Media? An analysis of EU State aid control and its relevance for public service broadcasting', in J. Grisprud and H. Moe (eds.), *The Digital Public Sphere: Challenges for Media Policy*, Gothenburg: Nordicom, pp. 117–131.

European Commission (1995), Communication of the European Commission on the status and implementation of Directive 90/388/EEC on competition in the markets for telecommunications services, Official Journal of the European Union of 20.10.1995 C 275/2.

European Commission (2002), Commission Directive 2002/77/EC of 16 September 2002 on competition in the markets for electronic communications networks and services (Competition Directive, CD), Official Journal of the European Union of 17.09.2002 L 249/21.

European Commission (2009), Communication no. 2009/C 257/01 from the Commission on the application of State aid rules to public service broadcasting, Official Journal of the European Union of 27.10.2009 C 257/1.

European Commission (2011), *Digital Agenda: Latvia ensures independence of national telecoms regulators; Commission closes infringement case*, press release IP/11/412, 4 April 2011.

European Commission (2012), *Hungary – infringements: European Commission satisfied with changes to central bank statute, but refers Hungary to the Court of Justice on the independence of the data protection authority and measures affecting the judiciary*, press release IP/12/395, 25 April 2012.

European Parliament and the Council of the European Union (2000), Regulation (EC) 2001/45 of the European Parliament and the Council of 18 December 2000 on the protection of individuals with regard to the processing of personal data by the Community institutions and bodies and on the free movement of such data, Official Journal of the European Union of 12.01.2001 L8/1.

European Parliament and the Council of the European Union (2002a), Directive 2002/58/EC of the European Parliament and of the Council of 12 July 2002 concerning the processing of personal data and the protection of privacy in the electronic communications sector (Directive on privacy and electronic communications), Official Journal of the European Union of 31.07.2002 L 201/37.

European Parliament and the Council of the European Union (2002b), Directive 2002/22/EC of the European Parliament and of the Council of 7 March 2002 on universal service and users' rights relating to electronic communications networks and services (Universal Service Directive), Official Journal of the European Union of 24.04.2002 L 108/51.

European Parliament and the Council of the European Union (2002c), Directive 2002/19/EC of the European Parliament and of the Council of 7 March 2002 on access to, and interconnection of, electronic communications networks and associated facilities (Access Directive), Official Journal of the European Union of 24.04.2002 L 108/7.

European Parliament and the Council of the European Union (2002d), Directive 2002/20/EC of the European Parliament and of the Council of 7 March 2002 on the authorisation of electronic communications networks and services (Authorisation Directive), Official Journal of the European Union of 24.04.2002 L 108/21.

European Parliament and the Council of the European Union (2002e), Directive 2002/21/EC of the European Parliament and of the Council of 7 March 2002 on a common regulatory framework for electronic communications networks and services (Framework Directive), Official Journal of the European Union of 24.04.2002 L 108/33.

European Parliament and the Council of the European Union (2009a), Regulation (EC) No 1211/2009 of the European Parliament and of the Council of 25 November 2009 establishing the Body of European Regulators for Electronic Communications (BEREC) and the Office, Official Journal of the European Union of 18.12.2009 L 337/1.

European Parliament and the Council of the European Union (2009b), Directive 2009/136/EC of the European Parliament and of the Council of 25 November 2009 amending Directive 2002/22/EC on universal service and users' rights relating to electronic communications networks and services, Directive 2002/58/EC concerning the processing of personal data and the protection of privacy in the electronic communications sector and Regulation (EC) No 2006/2004 on cooperation between national authorities responsible for the enforcement of consumer protection laws, Official Journal of the European Union of 18.12.2009 L 337/11.

European Parliament and the Council of the European Union (2009c), Directive 2009/140/EC of the European Parliament and of the Council of 25 November 2009 amending Directives 2002/21/EC on a common regulatory framework for electronic communications networks and services, 2002/19/EC on access to, and interconnection of, electronic communications networks and associated facilities, and 2002/20/EC on the authorisation of electronic communications networks and services, Official Journal of the European Union of 18.12.2009 L 337/37.

European Parliament and the Council of the European Union (2010), Directive 2010/13/EU of the European Parliament and of the Council of 10 March 2010 on the coordination of certain provisions laid down by law, regulation or administrative action in Member States concerning the provision of audiovisual media services (Audiovisual Media Services Directive), Official Journal of the European Union of 15.4.2010 L 95/1.

European Union (2010), Treaty on the Functioning of the European Union, Official Journal of the European Union of 30.03.2010 C 83/47 (TFEU).

Geradin, D. (2000), 'Institutional Aspects of EU Regulatory Reforms in the Telecommunications sector: Analysis of the Role of National Regulatory Authorities', *Journal of Network Industries*, 1, pp. 5–32.

Geradin, D. and Humpe, C. (2002), 'Regulatory Issues in Establishment and Management of Communications Infrastructure: The Impact of Network Convergence', *Journal of Network Industries*, 3, pp. 99–127.

Geradin, D. and Petit, N. (2004), *The Development of Agencies at EU and National Levels: Conceptual Analysis and Proposals for Reform*, New York University: School of Law.

Hans Bredow Institute for Media Research, Interdisciplinary Centre for Law & ICT (ICRI), Katholieke Universiteit Leuven; Center for Media and Communication Studies (CMCS), Central European University; Cullen International; Perspective Associates (eds., 2011), *INDIREG. Indicators for independence and efficient functioning of audio-visual media services regulatory bodies for the purpose of enforcing the rules in the AVMS Directive*, Study conducted on behalf of the European Commission, Final Report. February 2011.

Kleist, T. and Scheuer, A. (2006), 'Neue Regelungen für audiovisuelle Mediendienste – Vorschriften zu Werbung und Jugendschutz und ihre Anwendung in den Mitgliedstaaten', *Multimedia und Recht*, 9: 4, pp. 206–12.

Larouche, P. (2002), 'A Closer Look at Some Assumptions Underlying EC Regulation of Electronic Communications', *Journal of Network Industries*, 3, pp. 145–148.

Lasok, K. (2005), 'Appeals Under the New Regulatory Framework in the Electronic Communications Sector', *European Business Law Review*, 16: 4, pp. 787–801.

Melody, W. H. (1997), 'On the Meaning and Importance of Independence in Telecoms Reform', *Telecommunications Policy*, 21: 3, pp. 195–199.

Melody, William H. (1999), 'Telecom Reform: Progress and Prospects', *Telecommunications Policy*, 23, pp. 7–34.

Nihoul, P. and Rodford, P. (2004), *EC Electronic Communications Law. Competition and Regulation in the European Telecommunications Market*, Oxford: Oxford University Press.

Scherer, J. (2002), 'Die Umgestaltung des europäischen und deutschen Telekommunikationsrechts durch das EU-Richtlinienpaket – Teil I', *Kommunikation & Recht*, 6, pp. 279–280.

Scheuer, A. and Palzer, C. (2008), 'Cooperation between Member States' Regulatory Bodies – Commentary of Article 23b', in O. Castendyk, E. Dommering and A. Scheuer (eds.), *European media law*, Alphen aan den Rijn: Kluwer Law International.

Schütz, R. and Attendorn, T. (2002), 'Das neue Kommunikationsrecht der Europäischen Union – Was muss Deutschland ändern? ', *MMR Beilage*, 4, pp. 1–56.

Stevens, D. and Valcke, P. (2003), 'NRAs (and NCAs?): Cornerstones for the Application of the New Electronic Communications Regulatory Framework', *Communications & Strategies*, 50, pp. 159–189.

Thatcher, M. (1994), 'Regulatory Reform in Britain and France: Organisational Structure and the Extension of Competition', *Journal of European Public Policy*, 1: 3, pp. 441–464.

Chapter 5

Locating a regulator in the governance structure: A theoretical framework for the operationalization of independence

Stephan Dreyer
Hans Bredow Institute for Media Research

Abstract

There is no such thing as an independent regulator, at least if that term refers to absolute independence. Every regulator builds its activities on power, financial resources and knowledge – none of which can be produced by the regulator autonomously. With this as a basic assumption, independence has to be an arm's-length relationship with all players that can influence at least one of these three resources: market players, politicians or political institutions and society. Independence in this perspective is about possible influences and their respective safeguards ensuring this arm's length from particular actors and interests.

In order to pursue this approach, it is necessary to position the regulator in governance structures which can display the possibilities that different actors have at their disposal to influence the decision making of the regulator. This mapping of governance structures can show the actual interaction distance between regulators and those actors likely to exercise influence.

This chapter develops a theoretical framework that is able to provide a starting point on how to assess, rank or measure independence of regulatory bodies. To operationalize independence, different dimensions and criteria have to be defined to make the outcome of any assessment significant, transparent and reasonable. The chapter develops a theoretical concept of independence, taking into account issues from recent literature. From here it identifies respective dimensions and concrete independence criteria within those dimensions.

Keywords: independence, governance structure, control theory, autonomy, impartiality, mapping independence, assessing independence, independence criteria

Introduction

A lot of research has been done on the subject of independence of agencies, regulators or non-majoritarian institutions. Most of the projects aimed at shedding light on the question whether the independence of bodies correlates with greater efficiency, a better regulation outcome or a more stable policy system. Hence the studies defined specific indicators for independence and related them to specific indicators for an outcome that should be examined. The result of this is that most of the research narrows down indicators for independence to a workable level, specifically tailored for the respective research question. Though this methodology is absolutely legitimate from a research-economic perspective, it means that many of these projects lack an encompassing theoretical framework for independence and its indicators.

There are few contributions that try to fill this gap by developing thorough criteria suitable to measure independence profoundly within different levels (Verhoest, et al. 2004: 101). Those proposals clearly revealed the multi-dimensionality of independence, the vast amount of possible indicators and – sometimes – their inter-relatedness. Coming from a theoretical perspective, this chapter tries to lay out a possible approach to identify and categorize indicators for independence, building a fundament for future research approaches and mediating between the different approaches already proposed.

Independence as a theoretical concept

Notions and definitions

In the meaning of the word, 'independence' first and foremost is the antonym of the word 'dependence', resulting in an understanding that independence means 'freedom from control or influence of another or others', 'no externally imposed constraints' or 'immunity from arbitrary exercise of authority'. Terms often – but not always – used synonymously are autonomy and, with a stronger focus on self-realization, freedom.

Independence has been the subject of thorough research activities since the rise of state agencies during the 1970s. Often, independence has been identified primarily as a requirement for other regulatory outcomes, such as efficiency, performance, quality, impartiality, more stable long-term policies and so forth, rather than as a regulatory aim in itself. Hence many studies have focused on the relation between independence and its indicated outcome in markets, in regulation quality and other framing criteria (e.g. Baudrier 2001; Cukierman, Webb and Neyapti 1992; Montoya and Trillas 2007). Against this background, notions of independence have been presented that often are shaped with regard to the context of the study's interest and/or focus.

On a more abstract level, independence is understood to connote self-determination, in the sense that actors can judge and follow their own interests and values (Dahl 1989: ch. 9). Here, independence looms as variant of (institutional) self-determination. According to this concept, a core characteristic of independence is the ability to transform self-set values into authoritative actions. This concept proceeds on the assumption that independence of political institutions can be assessed from the extent to which self-imposed goals and values can be distinguished from external determination, and already points at an understanding of independence as a descriptive variable in relation to various possible external influences.

Inspecting the field of regulators closer, the US has been the 'home' of regulatory agencies, long before their rise in Europe. Here, *independent* agencies have been understood as 'governments in miniature' (Jacobzone 2005: 72), as they combine legislative (e.g. rule-making), judicial (e.g. adjudication and dispute-settlement) and executive (e.g. enforcement) functions within their scope of competencies (cf. Majone 2005b: 133). In other words, they combine three state functions that are normally separated: rule making, rule application and litigation (Demarigny 1996: 162). This phenomenon already points at debates also referring to challenges when it comes to such agencies' democratic legitimacy.

Thatcher defines an independent regulatory body as 'a body with its own powers and responsibilities given under public law, which is organisationally separate from ministries and is neither directly elected nor managed by elected officials' (Thatcher 2002a: 125; Thatcher and Sweet 2002: 2; Gilardi 2008: 21). Meanwhile, Gilardi and Maggetti suggest a definition that combines characteristics which have been put forward by Majone and Thatcher. Independent regulatory authorities, they suggest, are commonly 'highly specialised organisations enjoying considerable autonomy in decision making as they are institutionally and organisationally disaggregated from the ordinary bureaucracy and constitutionally separated from elected politicians' (Gilardi and Maggetti 2011: 202). Both these views point at another pivotal aspect of independence, at least with regard to institutions carrying out official tasks: the risk of undue external influence is most likely to come from the direction of the state, as it is the lawmaker – usually the government – which establishes the regulator and shapes the institutional structures, standards and procedures. In the context of media regulation, a recent World Bank study, for instance, stated that: 'The regulation of broadcasting should be the responsibility of an independent regulatory body established on a statutory basis with powers and duties set out explicitly in law. The independence and institutional autonomy of the regulatory body should be adequately and explicitly protected from interference, particularly interference of a political or economic nature' (Buckley, et al. 2008: 160).

But the state is not the only source of potential influence from actors with particular interests. Fesler (1942: 22), too, proposes 'independence of control by the governor and legislature as well as independence of control by [utility] companies'. Fesler's definition stresses independence not only from government but also from regulated parties, ruling out traditional corporatist agreements. Or, as Geradin and Petit (2004: 49) state, independence can be understood as 'the absence of pressures from political and industry interests' – of course, the regulatees follow strategies to safeguard their interests, too.

One more potential source of external influence can be seen in the public, or more specifically, the consumers (Smith 1997: 1) benefiting from or being disadvantaged by the regulator. Smith, too, includes the consumer side. For him independence consists of three elements: (1) an arm's-length relationship with regulated firms, consumers and other private interests; (2) an arm's-length relationship with political authorities; (3) the attributes of organizational autonomy (Smith 1997: 1), also pointing at potential influence from industry and public. Here, Lamanauskas points out that independence from consumers might pose less of a threat to independence because 'it is unlikely that regulators would be captured by unreasonable consumer interests' (cf. Lamanauskas 2006: 73).

Absolute independence?

Research contributions point out that absolute independence neither is desirable nor possible for regulatory bodies (Lamanauskas 2006: 75). Regarding the former, democratic theory objects to situations of authorities being absolutely independent. Having a body that has no formal back links to societies' will, can undermine the democratic legitimacy of both the authority and its decisions (Majone 1997b: 152). Considering the hypothetical risk of such a regulator straying from its mandate, engaging in corrupt practices or just becoming mostly inefficient (Smith 1997: 3), accountability measures are regularly being implemented, with varying consequences for independence (see below).

What is even more important here, however, is that in institutional and/or social contexts it has been argued, both theoretically and empirically, that it is impossible to act in complete autonomy. As organizations are not self-referential autopoietic systems – but rather open systems (Kickert 1993: 272) – they influence other systems and are influenced by other systems, e.g. by the political or the economic system (cf. Gilardi and Maggetti 2011: 2). Preferences and behaviours of regulatory bodies (including the people working there) are always more or less shaped by social interaction with other systems, resulting in the insight that they are neither completely independent from nor fully dependent on external influences. Moreover, regulatory bodies need decisive power, financial resources and knowledge, none of which can be produced by the regulator autonomously. These are additional and maybe even wider gateways for external players to wield influence.

This has lead to the (accepted) conclusion that independence has to be understood as a relative and not an absolute concept (Smith 1997: 3; Gilardi and Maggetti 2011: 2; Thatcher 2005: 351; Gilardi 2008: 56). This perception of independence also has been supported by research on a practical-empirical level (cf. Majone 1996: 227; Hall, Scott and Hood 2000: 64), which concludes that the 'concept of a completely autonomous and absolute regulator may be very far from the practical reality of independent regulators' (cf. Johannsen 2003: 25).

The notion of independence as a relative concept first and foremost involves relativity in view of the relationships of a regulator with its 'partners' in the political system, in the market and on the consumer-side. The form and efficacy of external influences are different and can be described as a continuum between absolute independence (=complete autonomy) and absolute dependence (=no autonomy). Verhoest, et al. (2004: 105) describe this phenomenon as 'different degrees of involvement in the decision-making processes […] ranging from no involvement to high involvement'.

Second, relativity of independence also means context-relativity, e.g. with regard to the specific sector, its legal objectives as well as the functional role of the regulator within this sector. Here, independence refers to specific outcome-related effects, with impartiality of decisions being one of the most important goals. A regulatory body is established in an independent manner on purpose either to achieve something that a state-integrated authority could not or to follow constitutional provisions when it comes to preventing state

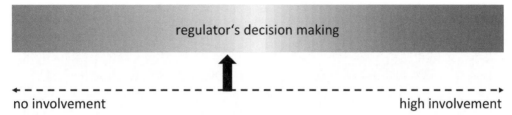

Figure 5.1: Continuum of involvment in a regulator's decision-making process.

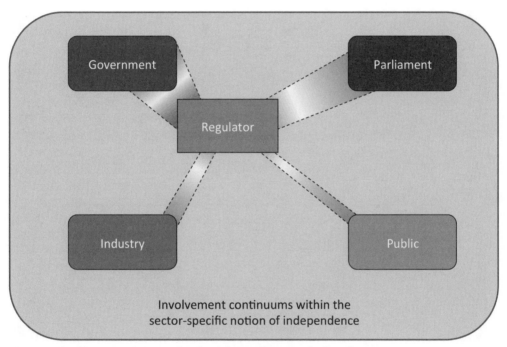

Figure 5.2: Involvement continuums within the sector-specific notion of independence.

influence on supervisory bodies (e.g. in the fields of data protection or media supervision). Hence a regulator is independent in this relative notion if it is able to exercise its powers in a way that corresponds to the reasons for its setup (cf. Han Bredow Institute, et al. 2011: 46). This definition also shows the complexity of measuring independence, since first identifying undue influences against the background of the features of the specific independence put in place and then assessing the existing due and undue interferences within the decision-making process is a rather difficult undertaking (cf. Melody 1997: 197).

Now, the objective of independence can be pursued first and foremost by reducing dependencies, i.e. reducing risks of improper external interference (Smith 1997: 3).

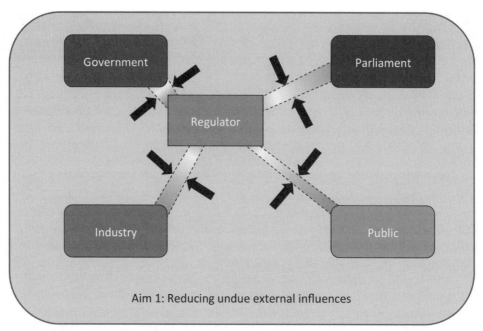

Figure 5.3: Aim 1 – Reducing dependencies.

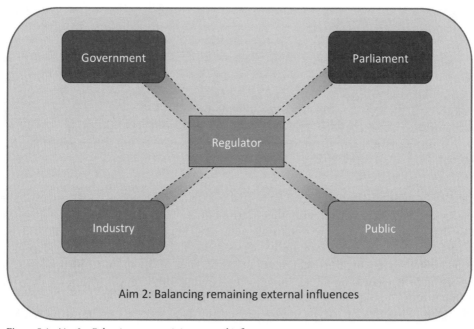

Figure 5.4: Aim 2 – Balancing out remaining external influences.

In case there are dependencies, the notion of independence in an interpretation that sees it as an instrument to ensure impartiality would lead to the necessity to balance out the remaining dependencies, so no external stakeholder has the dominance when it comes to influencing the regulatory body. Rather than aiming at a specific outcome of independence (cf. Johannsen 2003: 20), the balancing of different interests here concurrently serves as a theoretical, but necessary, precondition for independence.

Governance structure as a starting point for analysing relations

The problem in assessing the level of dependence of a regulator within the continuum between total autonomy and full subordination is the diversity of possible forms of control, influence, constraints and their respective countermeasures – and all of them in relation between the regulator and different external players, such as the government or parliament, the industry, the public and other stakeholders. Identifying and differentiating between distinct dimensions and directions can thus be helpful to break down the variety of dependence criteria. A theoretical-analytical approach that can be fruitful in this regard can be seen in the concept of 'governance structures'.

The factual complexity of institutional configurations accomplishing public tasks and their interdependent behaviour urged more and more legal scientists to change the way we think about 'the state' and the not-so distinct demarcation line with 'society' (Schuppert 2007: 37; Mayntz 1995: 163). Evolved from social sciences' steering theory, governance theory marks this change of perspective: it is the consequence of the insight that governing in response to societal pluralism, dynamism and complexity is taking place on different levels and by means of area-specific players and instruments, leading to the situation, nowadays, in which a formerly identifiable central control subject can consist of more than one protagonist using more than one form of control (Trute, Kühlers and Pilniok 2007: 240; Mayntz 2005: 13; Benz 2007: 17). Legal governance theory broadens the perspective on traditional control by means of law and administration, taking into account not only different settings and intrinsic logics of the players involved but also extending the scope of analysis on strategies, informal means and contexts (cf. Benz 2007: 18).

Here, the notion of 'governance structure' serves as an analytical framework that is able to capture those complex systems, including interdependencies, substitution and complementary effects between players, their norms, rules and instruments (Trute, Kühlers and Pilniok 2007: 245). What is new about legal science using the concept of governance structures is the analysis beyond individual, norm-driven (and/or constitutionally framed) actions, taking into account the wider internal and external configurations and negotiating spots: as the analytical framework encompasses instances with different underlying logics, it does not (solely) focus on the internally or externally set rules for concrete decisions ('legal steering as structural control' and 'cooperation-promoting infrastructure', Schuppert 2007: 43/45). Instead, it tries to comprehend the institutional structure that an instance is acting within, and how this is shaping decisions, procedures and behaviour of each entity (Trute 2007: 59). Moreover, analysing the governance structure not only consists of examining those overarching institutional configurations and norms, but also considers all legal (or: formal) and non-legal (or: informal) means forming the coordination between the instances comprised, as both frame the institutional setting within which the players act. Analysing informal aspects in this context (see below) is especially important, as the behaviour and institutional practice of the instances is shaping the setting in itself (Trute, Kühlers and Pilniok 2007: 246, 249).

By integrating formal and informal aspects, legal and non-legal norms, tools and instruments, the analysis of a governance structure also allows to examine the effects of the existing structures, determining whether the system accomplishes the purpose it has been put in place for, making it a perfect fit for the objective-relative, multi-dimensional notion of independence described above.

Mapping dependencies within the governance structure to assess independence

The governance structure approach described above can be fruitfully used for analysing the actual interaction distance between regulators and external actors and for pointing to intersections where it seems likely that they can exercise influence. By doing so, this approach is able to identify and operationalize criteria to assess the independence (or better: dependence) of a regulatory body, as it encompasses exactly those institutional settings and relations that are influencing and shaping its behaviour. More figuratively speaking, the governance structure in this sense can be seen as a map of the regulatory instance and its partners of interaction. To locate a regulator in its governance structure, dependence-wise, we can make use of vectors between the regulator and its counterparts, where specific criteria either pull the regulator towards one or more external players or push it away from them. This way the parallelogram of power becomes a parallelogram of dependencies.

Scientists have metaphorically described independence as operating 'at arm's length' of government and industry (Majone 1997a: 1; Lamanauskas 2006: 79; Pollit, et al. 2001: 274). Locating the regulator within its governance structure, and describing the different vectors of dependence between the regulating body and its opposites is building on this picture, while at the same time it uses the given analytical approach of governance structures. On this map, a regulator would be most independent if it can be located in an area where it keeps 'an equal distance from all possible interests in order to balance them impartially and aim at achieving long-term results benefiting all stakeholders as contrary to serving short term interests of various groups' (Lamanauskas 2006: 79).

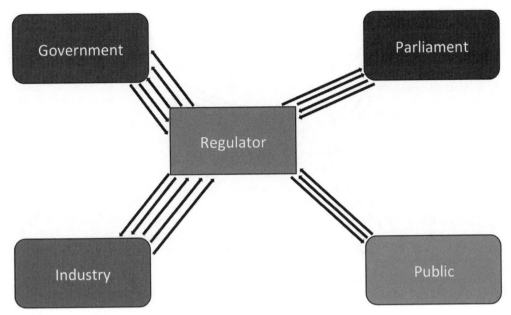

Figure 5.5: Parallelogram of dependencies.

Dependencies and their countermeasures: dependencers and autonomizers on formal and de facto levels

When mapping a body within its governance structures and (again metaphorically) drawing influences as vectors between regulator and interaction partners, the first differentiation of criteria for independence is to separate between those that pull the regulatory body towards an external player (making it more dependent) and those that push the regulator away from its counterpart (making it more independent). Both these forms can exist on their own and in parallel, without disturbing each other. However, to reach the goal of independence, we would have to strike out the 'dependencers', i.e. situations or cases where an aspect is detrimental to the regulator's autonomy. This can be achieved by either abolishing them (where possible) or putting in place 'autonomizers' that are actively working against dependencies, be it proactive or retroactive. This concept is vaguely comparable to Verhoest, et al. (2004: 104), who differentiate between two kinds of autonomy, namely autonomy 'as the level of decision-making competencies of the agency' and autonomy 'as the exemption of constraints on the actual use of decision-making competencies of the agency'.

As this approach follows a governance theoretical approach, 'dependencers' and 'autonomizers' have to be identified both on the formal as well as on the de facto level.

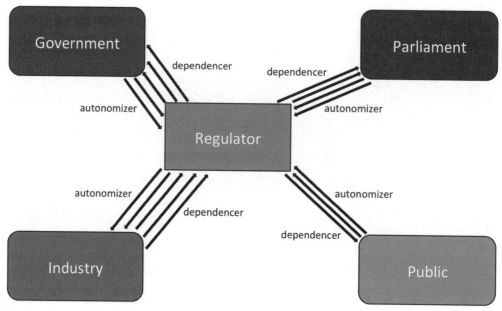

Figure 5.6: Dependencers and autonomizers as vectors.

This is in line with existing scientific approaches and assessments: they assume that formal and de facto independence (or better: dependence) in no way automatically coincide (cf. Gilardi and Maggetti 2011: 2; Baudrier 2001: 7). Formal criteria are all provisions, standards and procedures that are laid down in written laws, bylaws, regulations, decrees, codes, agreements, self-commitments etc.; due to their more tangible nature, they are the primary assets when assessing independence. However, the formal level of independence does in no way automatically lead to a comparable level of de facto independence (Gilardi and Maggetti 2011: 5; regarding a possible light association cf. Hanretty and Koop 2009: 15). First, there is scope for discretion within which a regulator can develop and perform its everyday activities, implementing its compliance with formal provisions; second, the above-mentioned 'effects of the relationships – less formalized – with other actors [...] possibly will affect the behaviour' of regulatory bodies (Gilardi 2008: 4). To fully analyse the dependencies of a regulator, we have to take into account the pulling and pushing vectors on the informal level, too.

Identifying and categorizing dependencies

A vector-like approach is able to display the direction of dependencies. However, we have to admit that it cannot show structural starting points and levers. For identifying criteria and – afterwards – grouping them within different 'dimensions of independence', we can make structural use of the governance perspective described above.

Influence by which means?

First of all, it is important to understand what forms external influence can have. Dependencies always rely on some kind of 'hook' to leverage actual influence on a regulator. Steering theory names three different instruments that can be used as means to control ('media to control', 'Steuerungsmedien'): power, money and knowledge (Wilke 2001: p. 151).

Power, in this sense, means all orders that are able to influence behaviour because they can be enforced by using either explicit or implicit violence. Especially in highly ordered structures like states, the power of higher organs is the standard medium to control lower hierarchies. By using formal or de facto power, external entities – usually state organs – are able to influence such entities that do not have or do not want to make use of power-limiting countermeasures. Formal forms of power can be identified rather easily, as control is the main objective of such norms. Forms of de facto power, in contrast, are rather difficult to identify, to prove – or both; the main reason for which is that threats of actually making use of power are either anticipated only by the regulator itself or are being uttered on an informal level only. Possibilities of influences by means of external power correlate with the level of power of the regulator itself; weak regulators are more vulnerable to external pressure than those that are equipped with more powers themselves.

Compared to power, money can be used not only by (legitimate) democratic bodies. Financial resources enable a regulator to become an entity that is capable of acting deliberately instead of passively relying on natural processes. It can buy resources that are able to strengthen its effectiveness and efficiency by raising the powers of the body itself and – where suitable – its level of knowledge. By making payments to a regulator subject to specific conditions, money can be seen as a very powerful instrument to take influence on an organization's behaviour.

Knowledge as a third resource to exert influence refers to the relative concept of information. Taking informed, conscious decisions is optimally suited to serve the regulator's objectives – information is of key importance in regulatory processes and can be 'source of resistance to improper influences' (Smith 1997: 3). However, usually information is not distributed equally among the players within a governance structure: regulators do not normally enjoy full access to all necessary information, partly as a consequence of the diverging interests of the regulatee and regulator. As the regulated stakeholders have more information about things the regulator needs to know, they want to keep them as an advantage for themselves. Regulatees are able to exert specific influence by granting the regulator (only) selected access to this information for their own benefit, handing over or especially not handing over information that the regulator would need to have to draw a decision that is based on all relevant facts (cf. Baudrier 2001: 7).

This trilogy of means to exert influence is applicable to regulators, since they cannot produce any of these resources by themselves. Where a regulator has to rely on or refer to a third party to produce or delegate the respective resource, risks for dependencies occur.

Target of influence impact

The described risks for dependencies occur in different locations within a regulator. They can affect either the institution as such (institutional level), one or more organs of a regulator (board/executive level) or single persons within these organs (individual level). Power, for instance, can be used to apply pressure on one of these three locations by different means (threatening to abolish the institution or to dismiss single board members or the board as whole). As regulators exert power especially by taking decisions, the decision-making organ within a regulatory body is of utmost importance in this category. In general, the location of the 'impact' of a dependency risk also can help to categorize criteria.

Influence by whom?

A third category of criteria – and probably the most evident one – can be identified in differentiating between the different directions of influence vectors: regulation systems are complex systems, consisting of several to many institutions, stakeholders and interaction partners. To identify which external institutions actually can exert influence – by a specific means and towards a specific location within the regulator – can show whether an influence can be seen as a unidirectional, a bidirectional or even a multidirectional vector within the governance structure. While power-related criteria regularly tend to point towards the state, money-based influences regularly can be seen as multidirectional influences, depending on the financing sources. Knowledge-based control, in contrast, often indicates industry-specific influence potentials.

Differentiating between the particular influence potentials of all institutions within the governance structure helps in giving the found vector its direction.

Installing wanted dependencies: Transparency and accountability mechanisms

Up to now, the approach sounds simple in theory. However, things get a little messy in practice, because sometimes, dependence is the objective of a formal provision and its practical implementation: those willingly established 'chains' like accountability and transparency mechanisms aim to ensure that a regulator sticks to its mandate. Hence their objective is to limit independence, making such instruments 'dependencers'. At the same time, transparency and accountability mechanisms serve as instruments that help the regulator to protect itself from improper external influences (Lamanauskas 2006: 78). These mechanisms enable the body to hint at a case of external pressure or publicize objectionable interference in internal decision making, increasing its ability to show undue constraints and to transparently fight against cases where external players try to use existing dependencers. Here, such measures can be categorized as 'autonomizers'. Both independence and accountability are – as Majone (2005a: 52) states – 'complementary objectives', especially when it comes to efficient functioning, but you cannot take transparency and accountability as yardsticks for independence; the two concepts are intertwined, but in no way causally connected. To assess dependencies, however, you have to bring mechanisms aimed at ensuring transparency and accountability into the equation – with the caveat that, here, the objective is not independence as such, but rather to steer a middle course between restraining accountability provisions and complete, democratically non-legitimized autonomy.

Dimensions of independence

This threefold categorization approach – means, impact and originator – is able to deliver a matrix-like overview of possible independence criteria. The following table combines the medium to control and the location of its impact; within each field, the different directions of influence can be tested. However, in most cases these are structurally comparable, regardless of the type of institution that exerts the influence.

Looking at the matrix, it seems already obvious in theory that overlapping will occur especially in the fields of money and knowledge. As both resources have structural and individual influence, it will be difficult in practice to differentiate between the targets. For example, insufficient money will always have consequences for all three targets, and so does insufficient knowledge. It seems the money and knowledge levels are meta-levels comparable to the procedural characteristics of transparency and accountability mechanisms. This leads to agglomerations of criteria within specific combinations, resulting in significantly larger criteria groups: 'dimensions of independence' (cf. Verhoest, et al. 2004: 107). In line with

Table 5.1: Control-theory based matrix for independence criteria.

Target of influence impact Medium to control	Institution as a whole	Decision-making organ	Individuals within that organ
Power	e.g. no third-party binding decisions; external rights to overturn decisions; external veto rights; threat to sanction regulator	e.g. nomination and appointment of board members	e.g. individual capture, revolving door
Money	e.g. existence, mid-term budgeting, staff resources	e.g. senior staff resources	e.g. salaries, bonuses
Knowledge	e.g. no information rights; withholding information or giving wrong information	e.g. no means for acquisition of external knowledge	e.g. marginal experience
Transparency and accountability mechanisms			

categories developed in research, we can find five major areas that – together – encompass nearly all criteria for independence that can be found today:

1. *'Status and powers'*: In this dimension, we collect criteria that show power-related, institution-wide influence potentials, especially exerted by lawmakers and governments. The general legal outline determining the legal status and powers of the regulators as well as the veto rights of external institutions are at the very core of the regulator's activities. Without competence there is no action, and without power to sanction there is no implementation of policies. Status and powers criteria may refer to the institution as a whole or the decision-making body, sometimes also to single persons within the regulator.

2. *'Autonomy of decision makers'*: The organ within a regulator that is actually taking the policy and supervisory decisions is the most probable 'hook' for influence exerted by external sources. Its composition, its members and their appointment, their tenures and salaries as well as dismissal procedures are able to point to theoretical or actual influences from the direction of lawmakers and governments, from industry or from societal groups. Criteria within this group usually are power-related influences that apply to the decision-making body as well as single persons within that body.

3. *'Financial autonomy'*: Where external parties – usually lawmakers and governments, sometimes industry actors – have legal influence on the source and the level of the budget of a regulator, they can either exert pressure to get interest-specific decisions from the body or undermine its operational capacity by inadequately financing it. The greater the influence of a single external institution on the budget level, the more probable it might be used to punish or reward the body in order to generate favourable decisions. Criteria in this dimension use money as a 'hook' and can apply to the regulator as a whole, the decision-making board or individuals within it.

4. *'Knowledge'*: Knowledge-related criteria refer to the expertise of the board members and/or the staff of the regulators as well as instruments to attain more knowledge. Knowledge in this perspective is able to both fight asymmetric access to information and to argue against undue or false arguments from the direction of lawmakers and governments as well as industry and societal groups.

5. *'Transparency and accountability mechanisms'*: The criteria in the area of transparency and accountability are two-faced when it comes to assess independence (see above). However, as they can have influence on both the formal and the de facto independence of a regulator, they have to be analysed, too. They usually are being implemented to draw legitimacy from the procedures being used ('procedural legitimacy'). Hence, transparency and accountability directly influence a body's independence, as a weakened transparency might undercut the regulator's support and reduce the respect it enjoys; without the goodwill and support of the industry and the public it will be more vulnerable

to political pressure. As transparency can be seen as a standard or a procedural meta-provision, it relates to all levels of the regulator's activity. Usually, transparency and accountability are more power- than knowledge-based and relate to the institution as a whole, its decision-making organ and the individuals within. Accountability often involves governments, parliaments and – sometimes – the public; these criteria usually refer to both state and public (and, indirectly, towards the industry).

A citation of a well-known practitioner, former FTC Chairman Powell, reflects these dimensions significantly: 'To be independent, not only should a regulator be physically and operationally separated from those it regulates, but also be empowered to carry out policy by making objective, well-reasoned, written decisions arrived at through transparent processes, and based on a complete, public record. Regulators should be free from undue political influence during this process, and impartial decisions based on the record should not be undermined for political reasons. Finally, the scope and substance of a regulator's jurisdiction should be clearly mandated by statute, and there should be adequate funding to carry out its responsibilities' (cited in Baudrier 2001: 5).

Collection of potential indicators with theoretical impact on a regulator's independence

On the basis of a thorough literature analysis, relevant criteria can be identified and categorized under the proposed five dimensions. What follows is an overview of these criteria, differentiated by formal and de facto situations.

Table 5.2: Status and powers.

Formal criteria	De facto criteria
General legal framework including source of recognition of independence	
– Legal/constitutional provisions naming independence as a value	– Incidents of political pressure in the form of threatened alteration of legal objectives
– Amendments or changes to the legal provisions formulating the tasks and objectives (and the respective motives)	
– Form of legal provisions that establish the regulatory body and specify its tasks and powers (parliamentary law, governmental bylaw, ministerial decree) (Jacobzone 2005: 89)	
– Clarity of legal provisions, especially regarding the objectives, powers and tasks assigned to the regulatory body (Gilardi 2005b: 149)	
– Type of audiovisual regulator (i.e. single 'converged' regulator (Gilardi 2002: 883), traditional sector-specific regulator), including scope of activities and sectors under the regulatory powers of the body	

Cont.

Formal criteria	De facto criteria

General legal framework including source of recognition of independence

- Exclusiveness of regulatory powers in the audiovisual media sector(i.e. one or more regulatory bodies competent in this sector) (Larsen, et al. 2006; Jacobzone 2005: 90)

Legal status of body

- Legal nature of the regulatory body (Thatcher 2002b: 130; Jacobzone 2005: 92)	- Geographical location of regulatory body (Vatiero 2008)

Regulatory powers criteria

- Possibility to give binding instructions to regulatory body (ECJ, C-518/07, 09/03/2010, No. 28) by state authority or industry body, also with regard to the form of such instructions, e.g. general policy or concrete decisions (Hanretty and Koop 2009; Gilardi 2005b: 149; Jacobzone 2005: 95) - Power to make rules that are legally binding to third parties or just limited consultative power (Larsen, et al. 2006) - Right to initiate legislative acts - Power to sanction and sanction instruments, e.g. warnings, fines, suspension or revocation of licences, where applicable - Powers to solve disputes between state institutions and regulatees, e.g. offering a board of complaints (Larsen, et al. 2006) or moderating debates - Scope of power to monitor compliance by regulatees, e.g. with regard to areas and forms of monitoring - Market entry: competence for issuing licenses and the supervision of the licence conditions - Margin of discretion (Larsen, et al. 2006: 7) - Ex-ante or ex-post regulation - Flexibility of the internal organization, Responsibility for personnel policy, e.g. hiring and firing staff, deciding on its allocation and composition (Gilardi 2002: 883; Jacobzone 2005: 97) - Possibility to use third party contractors - Possibility to determine staff salaries (Vatiero 2010; Lamanauskas 2006) - Possibility to decide on the regulator's internal organization (Gilardi 2002: 883)	- Possibilities to create long-term policies (Cukierman, Webb and Neyapti 1992: 363; Larsen, et al. 2006) - Application of a visible and important regulatory power (Thatcher 2002b) - Reported cases of arbitrary or inconsistent rule application or sanctioning - Reported accusations that sanctions have been too harsh, too lax or politically motivated - Legal or political conflicts, i.e. number of legal challenges to the decisions of the body (Thatcher 2002b) - Sufficient flexibility of body in managing own resources (Lamanauskas 2006) - Reported cases of actual use of powers of elected politicians to overturn decisions (Thatcher 2002b)

Table 5.3: Autonomy of decision makers.

Formal criteria	De facto criteria
Nature and composition of decision-making organ	
– Form of decision-making organ (board/director/ chambers) (Majone 1997a; Lamanauskas 2006; Döhler 2002: 110) – Composition of the board and total number of board members (Hanretty and Koop 2009)	– Factual party politicization of the highest decision-making organ
Appointment procedures	
– Procedure of nomination of director/board/chairman (Hanretty and Koop 2009; Gilardi 2002: 881) – Possibility for appointer(s) to ignore nomination (Hanretty and Koop 2009) – Procedure of appointment: who (Gilardi 2005b: 147; Gilardi 2002: 882) and how (Lamanauskas 2006; Oliveira, et al. 2005: 17; Gilardi 2005b: 147; Jacobzone 2005: 85 and 93; Thatcher 2002a: 130) – Independence of nominees as a formal requirement for the appointment (Gilardi 2005c: 147–149: Gilardi 2002: 881); political independence as a formal requirement for the appointment (Jacobzone 2005) – Renewability of appointment (Gilardi 2005b: 147–149; Gilardi 2002: 881; ECJ, C-518/07, 09/03/2010, No. 44) – Participation of regulator in the appointment process, e.g. proposal, right to vote (Gilardi 2005b: 147)	– Informal arrangements between appointing parties; collusive behaviour
Rules to prevent conflict of interest or capture	
– Legal provisions against conflicts of interest regarding head/board members (Gilardi 2005b: 147; Jacobzone 2005: 94) – Rules prohibiting holding other offices in the government at the same time (Gilardi 2005b: 147; Gilardi 2002: 881) – Rules prohibiting being under contract to, or associated with, a regulatee (Larsen, et al. 2006) – Rules prohibiting taking instructions from external persons or bodies (Council of Europe 2000) – Provisions against conflicts of interest regarding family members/relatives – Rules regarding cooling-off periods (Oliveira, et al. 2005; Larsen, et al. 2006) – If there are no provisions against conflicts of interests: behavioural rules that help to separate private interests from public ones (Lamanauskas 2006)	– Proportion of 'revolving-door' appointments and follow-up positions (Maggetti 2007; Thatcher 2002b: 'relational distance') – Frequency of ad hoc contacts such as internships, collaborations, and regular meetings (Maggetti 2007) – Actual independence of board members and/or staff from personal interests in the market players (Lamanauskas 2006) – Adequacy of internal organization (Thatcher 2002b) in relation to regulatory tasks and national context

Cont.

Formal criteria	De facto criteria
Tenure and salaries	
– Duration of the term of office (Thatcher 2002b; Gilardi 2005b: 147; Oliveira, et al. 2005; Gilardi 2002: 881; Jacobzone 2005: 85 and 93) – Staggered terms to ensure they do not coincide with election cycles (Smith 1997) – Legal provisions allowing an adequate level of salaries	– Average effective term length (Vatiero 2008) – Early resignations, e.g. because of informal agreement to resign after the election of a new government (Cukierman, Webb and Neyapti 1992: 363) – Degree to which the term of office of political decision-makers and the term of office of head/board of regulatory body de facto correspond with each other (Cukierman, Webb and Neyapti 1992: 366, 367) – (At least) constant levels of income of head/board members during the last years (Vatiero 2008)
Dismissal	
– Possibility of dismissal before the end of term of office (Gilardi 2005b: 147; Jacobzone 2005; Thatcher 2002b; Gilardi 2002: 881) – Reasons for dismissal (e.g. not obeying the rules of incompatibility, personal incapacity, violation of material law) – Scope of dismissal (e.g. board member as such or only whole board) – Competent body to dismiss – Dismissal procedures (Council of Europe 2000)	– Details and circumstances of personnel changes (notably dates of start and end of office) regarding the head/board of the regulator (Jacobzone 2005) – Reported cases of dismissals and their reasons – Departures (dismissals and resignation) of board members before the end of the term (Thatcher 2002b)

Table 5.4: Financial autonomy.

Formal criteria	De facto criteria
– Source(s) of the body's budget (Oliveira, et al. 2005: 17; Gilardi 2002: 883), their legal basis and their respective shares in percent, e.g. concession fees; licences; public funds; taxes (Gilardi 2005c: 149; Jacobzone 2005: 86 and 97) – Level of autonomy in allocating the budget; involvements of other actors in the budget allocation process (especially the supervisory body, cf. Jacobzone 2005: 97)	– Adequacy of the budget to perform delegated duties (Thatcher 2002b; Maggetti 2007) – Factual influence of third parties over the budget (Maggetti 2007) – Budget trends over time (Thatcher 2005: 361); (at least) constant budget during recent years (Vatiero 2008)

Formal criteria	De facto criteria
– Form of budget allocation procedures (Gilardi 2002: 883) – Margin of discretion of body in charge of external budget allocation	– Reported cases of supervisory authorities threatening to cut funding plans or to use funding decisions as leverage in political power struggles

Table 5.5: Knowledge.

Formal criteria	De facto criteria
Qualifications and professional expertise of decision-makers	
– Requirements of being an expert (in the respective sector) (Thatcher 2002b; Oliveira, et al. 2005: 17; Jacobzone 2005: 94) – Requirements of professional background (Oliveira, et al. 2005: 17)	– Board members actually being experts or having professional background
External advice	
– Legal requirement or possibility to gather external advice	– Factual use of requirement or possibility to gather external advice
Cooperation with other regulatory bodies	
– Legal requirements for cooperation with other regulatory bodies within the regulatory system – Legal requirements for cooperation with regulatory bodies in other states (cf. Majone 1997b)	– De facto cooperation with regulatory bodies in the same state – De facto cooperation with regulatory bodies in other states (cf. Majone 1997b) – Form and institutional level of cooperation, e.g. formalized network structures, systematic formal meetings, ad-hoc meetings (Majone 1997b) – Existence of informal cooperative arrangements

Table 5.6: Transparency and accountability mechanisms.

Formal criteria	De facto criteria
Transparency mechanisms	
– Specific vs. general provisions on transparency – General openness, e.g. regarding rule making, public decisions sessions (Oliveira, et al. 2005; Thatcher 2002b) or public hearings in important cases (Oliveira, et al. 2005)	– Actual transparency (especially when there is no statutory transparency rule) (Thatcher 2002b) – Disclosure of decision procedures (Jakubowicz 2007) and reasoning

Cont.

Formal criteria	De facto criteria
Transparency mechanisms	
– Requirements to give reasons for the decisions (Thatcher 2002b; Jacobzone 2005: 99)	– Indication or announcement of likely future actions
	– Publication of board meeting minutes
– Answerability, i.e. actions being openly discussed in public with members of board (Thatcher 2002b)	– Forms of dissemination (e.g. print, website, directly to parliament, official journal, magazine etc.)
– Publication of decisions (Oliveira, et al. 2005) and information, including models or guidelines on which decisions are based (Thatcher 2002b)	
– Dissemination of published information (Thatcher 2002b)	
– Prohibition of informal discussions of pending cases with any of the parties involved (Larsen, et al. 2006)	
– Transparent procedure regarding the issuing of licenses (Council of Europe 2008)	
– Developing models or guidelines, public doctrines and principles and conceptual frameworks for their actions (Thatcher 2002b)	
Consultation procedures	
– Legal framework for consultations (systematic/ad-hoc/mandatory/voluntarily) (Thatcher 2002b)	– Forms of external advice acquisition (scientific advisory board (Majone 1997b)/external studies/consultations/expert hearings etc.)
	– Public availability of the basic data relevant for the conduct of regulatory policy (Jacobzone 2005)
	– Disclosure of basic market data (Jacobzone 2005)
	– Actual consultations of stakeholders and/or the public (Jakubowicz 2007)
	– Number and nature of players involved in consultations (Oliveira, et al. 2005; Thatcher 2002b; Larsen, et al.2006; Lamanauskas 2006)
	– Actual consultation procedures for knowledge gain, e.g. white papers, consultation papers, invitation of comments on draft decisions (Thatcher 2002b)
	– Inclusion of consultation results in the decision-making process, reaction of the regulator to arguments or claims (cf. Jakubowicz 2007)
	– Stage of decision-making process where consultations have been integrated

Formal criteria	De facto criteria

Formal accountability and auditing mechanisms

- General requirement to produce periodic (i.e. annual) reports assessing the extent to which objectives have been achieved (Jacobzone 2005)
- Formal accountability obligations vis-à-vis the parliament (Gilardi 2002: 882; Gilardi 2005b: 147–149) or the government (Thatcher 2002b), e.g. no formal obligation
- Accountability requirements and objectives clearly defined in law (Jacobzone 2005)
- Presentation of an annual report for information only vs. presentation of an annual report that must be approved (Gilardi 2005b: 148; Jacobzone 2005: 98)
- Objectives of regulation clearly defined in law; formal pre-defined performance criteria (Lamanauskas 2006)
- External evaluation procedure (Jacobzone 2005), e.g. national audit offices, private consulting firms, independent academic research
- Prioritization of multiple objectives stipulated in law (Jacobzone 2005)
- Measurability of regulatory objectives in statutes or decrees (Jacobzone 2005)

- Periodic internal or external evaluation procedures assessing to what extent the regulatory objectives have been met (Jakubowicz 2007)
- Degree to which regulatory body explains rules or strategies that describe its policy (Jakubowicz 2007) and decision practices

Supervision of regulatory body

- Existence of legal provisions regarding supervision
- Form of supervision (systematically vs. ad hoc) (Döhler 2002: 112; Hanretty and Koop 2009)
- Competent body/bodies for supervision
- Competence of third party (other than a court) to overturn a body's decision (Gilardi 2005b: 147–149; Gilardi 2002: 883)

- Rights of co-determination regarding informal agreements or the publication of official documents by government/parliament (Döhler 2002: 116)

Cont.

Formal criteria	De facto criteria
Appeal procedures	
– Existence of appeal procedures that are open to review the body's decisions	– Number of legal challenges to the decisions of the body (Thatcher 2002b)
– Bodies/organs that are allowed to review decisions (internal appeals, organs from political branch, external commissions, judiciary branch i.e. courts) (Lamanauskas 2006; Oliveira, et al. 2005)	– Opportunities for legislator/government to overrule regulatory decisions through new legislation
– In the case of a non-judicial review (Lamanauskas 2006): possibility of the appeal decisions undergoing judicial review	
– Scope of judicial review, e.g. margin of discretion left to the regulator (Lamanauskas 2006; Jacobzone 2005: 89)	
– Groups of relevant appellants (consumer, market players, politicians/government)	

Outlook: Limits of a theoretical approach

This short presentation of a potential theoretical approach to identify and categorize criteria to assess the independence of a regulator shows two things: First, the notion of independence is relative. And second, because of this, independence is relatively complex when it comes to assessing it on a practical level. As promising as it might look, there are substantial caveats when applying the approach described in this chapter in practice. First, some criteria are not clearly working towards one of the two vector directions (e.g. accountability, transparency, revolving door phenomena or dismissals). Second, as stated above, the notion of independence always follows the interpretation of its originating reasons in a specific field. Depending on the rationality for installing autonomous regulators, the features of the specific notion of independence may very well vary (cf. Gilardi 2002: 889). This leads to practical difficulties when it comes to distinguishing between wanted dependencies and undue influences. And, thirdly, some of the collected criteria are not very workable when it comes to scientifically operationalizing them. Measuring the level of a context-related, changing concept like independence by using interpretative yardsticks – or at least criteria that are open to subjective assessments – is far from scientifically and hermeneutically perfect. And, last but not least, criteria are always subject to national context information (cf. Thatcher 2002a: 136). This knowledge about 'how things actually work over here' is something that is extremely difficult to put into the equation, making the 'culture of independence' as intangible as important when it comes to operationalizing indicators for independence.

However, even if independence as such is too complex to mathematically calculate or measure it, the approach presented here is able to constitute a structurally ordered methodology to show locations, situations and potentials for undue influence, interfering with, or even obstructing, the formal and/or the practical implementation of independence. In this way, it is a fruitful possibility to take notice of structures or circumstances that need closer attention.

Acknowledgements

This chapter builds on the approach and insights of the INDIREG study, which had as one of its objectives to operationalize the notion of independence in order to measure independence as such. The INDIREG study was carried out in 2009/2010 by a research consortium on behalf of the European Commission (Hans Bredow Institute, et al. 2011). My thanks go to the project team, in particular Wolfgang Schulz, Peggy Valcke, Kristina Irion, Michelle Ledger, Tim Suter, David Stevens, Szabolcs Koppányi, Regine Sprenger and Jannes Beeskow.

References

Baudrier, A. (2001), 'Independent Regulation and Telecommunications Performance in Developing Countries', in The International Society for New Institutional Economics, *Annual ISNIE Conference*, Berkeley, United States, 13–15 September.

Benz, A. (2007), 'Governance in Connected Arenas – Political Science Analysis of Coordination and Control in Complex Rule Systems', in D. Jansen (ed.), *New Forms of Governance in Research Organizations*, Dordrecht: Springer, pp. 3–22.

Buckley, S., Duerm, K., Mendel, T. and O Siocgru, S. (2008), *Broadcasting, Voice and Accountability. A Public Interest Approach to Policy, Law, and Regulation*, Washington D.C.: The World Bank Group.

Council of Europe (2000), *Recommendation Rec(2000)23 of the Committee of Ministers to member states on the independence and functions of regulatory authorities for the broadcasting sector*, 20 December 2000.

Council of Europe (2008), *Declaration of the Committee of Ministers on the independence and functions of regulatory authorities for the broadcasting sector*, 26 March 2008.

Cukierman, A., Webb, S., and Neyapti, B. (1992), 'Measuring the Independence of Central Banks and its Effect on Policy Outcomes', *The World Bank Economic Review*, 6: 3, pp. 353–398.

Dahl, R. A. (1989), *Democracy and its Critics*, New Haven: Yale University Press.

Demarigny, F. (1996), 'Independent Administrative Authorities in France and the Case of the French Council for Competition', in G. Majone (ed.), *Regulating Europe*, London and New York: Routledge, pp. 157–159.

Döhler, M. (2002), 'Institutional Choice and Bureaucratic Autonomy in Germany', *West European Politics*, 25: 1, pp. 101–124.

Fesler, J. W. (1942), *The Independence of State Regulatory Agencies*, Chicago: Public Administration Service.

Geradin, D. and Petit, N. (2004), *The Development of Agencies at EU and National Levels: Conceptual Analysis and Proposals for Reform*, New York: New York University School of Law.

Gilardi, F. (2002), 'Policy Credibility and Delegation to Independent Regulatory Agencies: a Comparative Empirical Analysis', *Journal of European Public Policy*, 9: 6, pp. 873–893.

Gilardi, F. (2005b), 'The Formal independence of Regulators: a Comparison of 17 Countries and 7 Sectors', *Swiss Political Science Review*, 11: 4, pp. 139–167.

Gilardi, F. (2005c), 'The Institutional Foundations of Regulatory Capitalism: The Diffusion of Independent Regulatory Agencies in Western Europe', *The ANNALS of the American Academy of Political and Social Science*, 598: 1, pp. 84–101.

Gilardi, F. (2008), *Delegation in the Regulatory State: Independent Regulatory Agencies in Western Europe*, Massachusetts: Edward Elgar Publishing.

Gilardi, F. and Maggetti, M. (2011), 'The Independence of Regulatory Authorities', in D. Levi-Faur (ed.), *Handbook on the Politics of Regulation*, Cheltenham: Edward Elgar.

Hall, C., Scott, C., and Hood, C. (2000), *Telecommunications Regulation*, London and New York: Routledge.

Hanretty, C. and Koop, C. (2009), *Comparing Regulatory Agencies: Report on the Results on a Worldwide Survey*, EUI Working Paper RSCAS 2009/63, http://cadmus.eui.eu/bitstream/

handle/1814/12877/RSCAS_2009_63.pdf;jsessionid=3274739824D3F734B7C57DA02024969E? sequence=1. Accessed 21 March 2012.

Hans Bredow Institute for Media Research; Interdisciplinary Centre for Law & ICT (ICRI), Katholieke Universiteit Leuven; Center for Media and Communication Studies (CMCS), Central European University; Cullen International; Perspective Associates (eds., 2011), *INDIREG. Indicators for independence and efficient functioning of audio-visual media services regulatory bodies for the purpose of enforcing the rules in the AVMS Directive*, Study conducted on behalf of the European Commission, Final Report. February 2011.

Huntington, S. P. (1968), *Political Order in Changing Societies*, New Haven: Yale University Press.

Jacobzone, S. (2005), 'Independent Regulatory Authorities in OECD countries: An overview', in Organisation for Economic Co-operation and Development(ed.), *Designing Independent and Accountable Regulatory Authorities for High Quality Regulation, Proceedings of an Expert Meeting in London, United Kingdom, 10–11 January 2005*, Paris: OECD, pp. 72–88.

Jakubowicz, K. (2007), Keynote Speech prepared for delivery at the plenary session 'The independence of regulatory authorities', 25th meeting of the European Platform of Regulatory Authorities (EPRA), 16–19 May 2007, pp. 3–6; available at http://epra3-production. s3.amazonaws.com/attachments/files/1380/original/EPRA_keynote_KJ.pdf?1323685662. Accessed 16 September 2013.

Johannsen, K. S. (2003), *Regulatory Independence in Theory and Practice – a Survey of Independent Energy Regulators in Eight European Countries*, AKF Forlaget, http://www.akf. dk/udgivelser/2003/pdf/regulatory_independence.pdf. Accessed 22 March 2012.

Kickert, W. J. M. (1993), 'Autopoiesis and the Science of (Public) Administration: Essence, Sense, and Nonsense', *Organisation Studies*, 14: 2, pp. 261–278.

Lamanauskas, T. (2006), 'The Key Features of Independence of National Telecommunication Regulatory Authorities and Securing them in Law', *Law*, 61, pp. 73–80.

Larsen, A., Pedersen, L. H., Sørensen, E. M. and Olsen, O. J. (2006), 'Independent Regulatory Authorities in European Electricity Markets', *Energy Policy*, 34: 17, pp. 2858–2870.

Maggetti, M. (2007), 'De Facto Independence after Delegation: A Fuzzy-set Analysis', *Regulation & Governance*, 4: 1, pp. 271–294.

Majone, G. (1996), *Regulating Europe*, London and New York: Routledge.

Majone, G. (1997a), 'The Agency Model: The Growth of Regulation and Regulatory Institutions in the European Union', *EIPASCOPE*, 1997: 3, pp. 1–6.

Majone, G. (1997b), 'From the Positive to the Regulatory State: Causes and Consequences of Changes in the Mode of Governance', *Journal of Public Policy*, 17, pp. 139–167.

Majone, G. (2005a), 'Agency Independence and Accountability', in Organisation for Economic Co-operation and Development (ed.), *Designing Independent and Accountable Regulatory Authorities for High Quality Regulation*, London, pp. 52–53, http://www.oecd.org/ dataoecd/15/28/35028836.pdf. Accessed March 2012.

Majone, G. (2005b), 'Strategy and Structure the Political Economy of Agency Independence and Accountability', in Organisation for Economic Co-operation and Development (ed.), *Designing Independent and Accountable Regulatory Authorities for High Quality Regulation*, London, pp. 126–155, http://www.oecd.org/dataoecd/15/28/35028836.pdf. Accessed March 2012.

Mayntz, R. (2005), 'Governance Theory als fortentwickelte Steuerungstheorie?', in G. F. Schuppert (ed.), *Governance Forschung. Vergewisserungüber Stand und Entwicklungslinien*, Baden-Baden: Nomos, pp. 11–20.

Melody, W. H. (1997), 'On the Meaning and Importance of "independence" in Telecom Reform', *Telecommunications Policy*, 21: 3, pp. 195–199.

Montoya, M. Á. and Trillas, F. (2007), 'The Measurement of the Independence of Telecommunications Regulatory Agencies in Latin America and the Caribbean', *Utilities Policy*, 15: 3, pp. 182–190.

Oliveira, G., Machado, E. L., Novaes, L. M. and Cardoso, M. R. (2005), *Aspects of the Independence of Regulatory Agencies and Competition Advocacy*, Rio de Janeiro: Getulio Vargas Foundation.

Pollit, C., et al. (2001), 'Agency fever? Analysis of an international policy fashion', *Journal of Comparative Policy Analysis*, 2001: 3, pp. 271–290.

Schuppert, G. F. (2007), 'Governance – A Legal Perspective', in D. Jansen (ed.), *New Forms of Governance in Research Organizations*, Dordrecht: Springer, pp. 31–52.

Smith, W. (1997), 'Utility Regulators – The Independence Debate', *Public Policy for the Private Sector*, 127, pp. 1–2.

Thatcher, M. (2002a), 'Delegation to Independent Regulatory Agencies: Pressures, Functions and Contextual Mediation', *West European Politics*, 25: 1, pp. 125–147.

Thatcher, M. (2002b), 'Regulation after Delegation: Independent Regulatory Agencies in Europe', *Journal of European Public Policy*, 9: 6, pp. 954–972.

Thatcher, M. (2005), 'The Third Force? Independent Regulatory Agencies and Elected Politicians', *Governance*, 18: 3, pp. 347–373.

Thatcher, M. and Stone Sweet, A. (2002), 'Theory and Practice of Delegation to Non-majoritarian Institutions', *West European Politics*, 25: 1, pp. 1–22.

Trute, H.-H. (2007), 'Governance: Interrelationships and Open Questions', in D. Jansen (ed.), *New Forms of Governance in Research Organizations*, Dordrecht: Springer, pp. 57–63.

Trute, H.-H., Kühlers, D. and Pilniok, A. (2007), 'Governance und Rechtswissenschaft', in U. Schimank, S. Lütz, A. Benz and G. Simonis (eds.), *Handbuch Governance*, Wiesbaden: VS Verlag.

Vatiero, M. (2008), *Measuring Independent Regulatory Authorities: A Review*, Working Paper (unpublished).

Verhoest, K., Peters, B. G., Bouckaert, G. and Verschuere, B. (2004), 'The Study of Organisational Autonomy: A Conceptual Review', *Public Administration and Development*, 24: 2, pp. 101–111.

Wilke, H. (2001), *Systemtheorie III. Steuerungstheorie*, Stuttgart: Lucius & Lucius.

Chapter 6

Measuring independence: Approaches, limitations,
and a new ranking tool

Kristina Irion
Central European University

Michele Ledger
Cullen International

Abstract

It is the starting point of this chapter that there is no accepted methodology to measure the formal and de facto independence of independent regulatory authorities, even if some progress has been made in this field, and that empirical research on the subject, consequently, is scarce and very fragmented. To the extent that they exist at all, studies tend to concentrate on measuring formal independence, since specific legal provisions can be identified and assessed much more easily than the de facto expression of independence. This chapter will introduce the different approaches to measuring formal and de facto independence that have been proposed and critically reflect their potential and limitations, especially for comparative research. Two aspects specific to the audiovisual media sector are particularly relevant in this respect:

1. *the objective of regulation in the media sector to guarantee media freedoms and,*
2. *the specific and sometimes sensitive relationship between the media sector and elected as well as non-elected politicians (i.e. the media as 'fourth state power').*

Subsequently, this chapter introduces a ranking tool which has been developed specifically to measure the risk of influence by external players, rather than one to measure the level of independence of the regulators themselves. This enables a more objective method for ranking the indicators. The ranking approach follows the overall distinction between formal and de facto indicators. The methodology will be described and the use of the ranking tool will be illustrated.

Keywords: independent regulatory authorities, independence, formal independence, de facto independence, composite index, ranking tool

Introduction

Measuring complex social systems via composite indices is at full-cycle. These efforts are characterized by the desire to devise a methodology that combines the virtues of qualitative and quantitative research. The UN Human Development Index (HDI) provides a harmonized statistical approach to measure countries' human and economic development. A point of reference in the field of media is the IREX Media Sustainability Index (MSI) which offers a methodology 'to assess the development of media systems over time and across countries' (IREX 2013). Both HDI and MSI have excelled in their field and became commonly accepted as useful tools although they have nevertheless been criticized for some of their underlying assumptions and weightings (e.g. CIMA 2010). Another example of a composite index in the media sector at the EU level is the Media Pluralism Monitor, which offers a holistic methodology to assess a country's performance at various dimensions that contribute to a pluralistic media environment (ICRI, et al. 2009).

In the light of the popularity of such indices, it should not come as a surprise that the INDIREG study on which this chapter is based (Hans Bredow Institute for Media Research, et al. 2011) was tasked with identifying key characteristics for a functioning 'independent regulatory body' as referred to in the Audiovisual Media Services (AVMS) Directive and, where possible, formulating criteria with which these characteristics could be measured. This task poses the dilemma of measuring a quality, i.e. the independence of a supervisory authority, and when doing so involves a multi-layered analytical approach. The first of these layers, which concerns how regulatory independence relates to the wider governance system and how it conditions the functioning of regulatory supervision, is tackled in Chapter 1 by Wolfgang Schulz and Chapter 5 by Stephan Dreyer. The second layer, which involves the question of what the meaningful dimensions and indicators are that would best describe regulatory independence in relation to its functions, is introduced in Chapter 5 by Stephan Dreyer. This chapter introduces the third layer involved in measuring regulatory independence and will describe the so-called Ranking Tool, which was one of the central outcomes of the work in the INDIREG research to operationalize the measuring approach.[1]

It is the point of departure of this chapter that there is no accepted methodology to measure the formal and de facto independence of independent regulatory authorities (IRAs), even if some progress has been made in this field, and that empirical research on the subject, consequently, is scarce and very fragmented. To the extent that they exist at all, studies tend to concentrate on measuring formal independence, since specific legal provisions can be identified and assessed much more easily than the de facto expression of independence. In the following, this chapter reviews the different approaches to measuring formal and de facto independence that have been proposed, and critically reflect their potential and limitations, especially for comparative research. Two aspects specific to the audiovisual media sector are particularly relevant in this respect:

1. the objective of regulation in the media sector to guarantee media freedoms and,
2. the specific and at times sensitive relationship between the media sector and elected as well as non-elected politicians (i.e. the media as 'fourth state power').

The INDIREG Ranking Tool integrates existing approaches, but inverts their logic by measuring the risk of influence by external players (rather than measuring the level of independence of the regulators). This risk-centred logic enables a more objective method for ranking the indicators and weighting them according to their significance. The ranking approach follows the overall distinction between indicators for formal and de facto independence that are allocated on five dimensions: (1) status and powers, (2) financial autonomy, (3) autonomy of decision makers, (4) knowledge and (5) accountability and transparency. It is one of the achievements that the Ranking Tool's method goes beyond the state-of-the-art in proposing a coherent set of indicators to measure de facto independence, which complements and corresponds with the measurement of formal independence. The methodology will be described and the use of the Ranking Tool will be illustrated.

This chapter is structured as follows: The first section provides an overview of the literature which has attempted to measure certain aspects of regulatory independence, in various sectors and for different purposes; the second section describes the INDIREG study's approach to measuring formal and de facto independence, and introduces the Ranking Tool, its methodology and how it can be applied; followed by the conclusions. The entire INDIREG Ranking Tool is published in the Annex to this chapter.

Measuring regulatory independence

For some time already, significant research has been devoted to measuring the quality of regulatory independence in different sectors and in relation to different purposes. For about a decade, this type of research has been primarily occupied with the independence of regulators of central banks and network industries, but recently independent regulators in other sectors have moved into focus too (Hans Bredow Institute for Media Research, et al. 2011). This is not coincidental, given that supervision by IRAs has become the standard governance mechanism in regulated sectors – a tendency which is amplified in Europe by EU harmonization legislation and other Europeanization processes (see Chapter 2 in this book by Irion and Radu). After all, IRAs are one of the central lynchpins of the regulatory state (Majone 1997). As Hanretty and Koop (2012) put it:

> for independence to lead to better policy outcomes, a complex causal chain needs to operate, leading from statutory provisions granting independence to behavioral patterns demonstrating independence, to policy decisions, and, ultimately, to policy outcomes.

Research to date has yielded many notable achievements, but no generally accepted methodology to measure the formal and de facto independence and efficient functioning of IRAs. Aside from matters of prescriptive legislation, it is particularly challenging to identify and collect relevant data about the different aspects of independence. This section revisits the research community's efforts to measure regulatory independence regardless of the sector of regulation concerned. Empirical approaches are selected and presented in relation to which of the major strands they belong to:

- measuring formal independence,
- measuring actual or de facto independence,
- measuring efficient functioning.

It is important to note that methodologies presented rarely follow this division but rather tend to combine indicators from various strands. Moreover, the different concepts of independence (or autonomy for that matter) which contemporary research relies on are already bound to significantly influence the research outcomes (Verhoest, et al. 2004). Empirical research has also not stopped short at measuring independence for its own sake and instead, more often than not, seeks to investigate a direct relation or correlation with sectoral policy outcomes or the economic performance of a specific sector.

Measuring formal independence

The bulk of available research concentrates on the measurement of formal or de jure independence of different regulatory agencies. As explained in Chapter 5 in this book by Dreyer, due to their tangible nature, formal criteria are primary assets when assessing regulatory independence. Concrete legal provisions can be identified and measured much more easily than any other form (actual or de facto) of independence. However, early research on the independence of central banks already points to the inconclusive results of focusing solely on the formal aspects (Cukierman, Webb, and Neyapti 1992).

Originating from methodologies developed to assess central banks, formal independence is coded with indicators that are clustered around dimensions and weighted according to their presumed influence (Cukierman, Webb and Neyapti 1992; Gilardi 2001). Cukierman, Webb and Neyapti (1992) use sixteen different legal variables, which are then combined with one additional indicator for actual independence, i.e. turnover of directors/presidents of the central bank. The authors weight each variable and use weighted averages as indicators (Cukierman, Webb and Neyapti 1992) in addition to survey of monetary policy experts to appraise the level of independence of the institution.

Subsequent empirical studies adapted this methodology for the assessment of regulatory independence in deregulated network industries, more specifically in telecommunications (Gutiérrez 2003; Edwards and Waverman 2006; Gual and Trillas 2004, 2006; Montoya and Trillas 2007) and energy (Pedersen and Sørensen 2004; Larsen, et al. 2006). The following survey omits research in which the formal independence of a regulator was but one variable among a number of regulatory aspects being reviewed in relation to the performance of the sector after deregulation (e.g. Bortolotti, et al. 2002; Fink, Mattoo and Rathindran 2002). Edwards and Waverman (2006), Gual and Trillas (2004, 2006) and Gutiérrez (2003) build multi-component indices concerning regulatory agencies in the telecommunications sector after liberalization, and correlate with regulatory policy and market performance. With some variation in the detail, the indicators they use concern relevant sector-specific powers, financial independence, appointment and dismissal rules, highest decision-making body, and turnover of decision-makers (for an overview see Montoya and Trillas 2007).

Some authors follow a more generalized approach, by developing universal independence indices (Gilardi 2001; Hanretty, Larouche and Reindl 2012; Olivera, et al. 2005). Although there are many uncontested formal independence requirements, some authors recognize that there is no general blueprint for what makes an independent regulator. For instance, Hanretty, Larouche and Reindl (2012) notice that their index cannot adequately capture the unique governance structure of certain regulators surveyed. This is the reason why a standardized composite index would benefit from a research approach that allows for a context-sensitive interpretation of the results.

Gilardi's (2001, 2002, 2005a; 2005b, 2008) extensive research emphasizes the link between the credibility of a regulator and its formal independence. He draws on the model of Cukierman, Webb and Neyapti (1992) to construct an extensive index capable of appraising various dimensions of formal independence:

- status of the head of the agency,
- status of the management board,
- relationship with the government and legislative,
- financial and organizational autonomy.

Each indicator is appraised on a scale of zero to one which is then aggregated for each dimension. However, Gilardi (2005b: 58) recognizes the difficulty of drawing conclusions from this measurement about the degree of credibility. In his words: 'Like beauty, credibility is in the eyes of the beholder' (Gilardi 2008: 134).

Whether sector-specific or universal, the different indices proposed have in common that they ascribe value to the factors that would ensure, on the one hand, organizational autonomy (formal status, regulatory powers, financial resources) and, on the other hand, the independence of its highest decision-making body and senior executive management (rules regarding appointment, dismissal and re-election, term of office, rules to prevent conflict of interest, etc.). The role of transparency of regulatory processes has been sporadically recognized as well (Gutiérrez 2003; Pedersen and Sørensen 2004). Authors generally concede that formal independence alone does not equal the absence of political interference (Cukierman, Webb and Neyapti 1992; Gilardi 2005, 2008; Pedersen and Sørensen 2004).

Although there is no generally accepted standard in terms of methodology, the state-of-the-art of measuring formal independence is by now fairly established. Most recent research slightly modifies composite indices to fit its purpose, and there is some fundamental debate about the validity and weighting of certain indicators (e.g. the length of tenure of members of the highest decision-making organ), but newer works are actually more inclined to applying them. It is interesting to observe that research in sectors characterized by the presence of strong stakeholder-interests also stresses the need for formal safeguards to preserve regulatory independence from stakeholders (Pedersen and Sørensen 2004; Larsen, et al. 2006).

Measuring de facto independence

When investigating regulatory independence the most straightforward research question concerns the level of de facto (or actual, for that matter) independence of the regulatory body. While there is an abundance of literature which is suspicious of de facto independence, research is often not substantiated by empirical evidence. The literature review reveals that it is particularly challenging to find meaningful ways to interrogate regulatory independence in practice. Such research is not only hampered by a lack of computable data about IRAs but also a lack of objective and verifiable information in a domain that is predominantly characterized by informal means of influence.

The assessment of de facto independence relies to a large extent on qualitative social science research methods. For instance, Cukierman, Webb and Neyapti (1992) incorporated an expert survey into their research design, whereas Pedersen and Sørensen (2004) conducted semi-structured interviews and Maggetti (2007) suggests using media content analysis to assess a regulator's reputation. In the literature, the reputation (Maggetti 2007) or credibility (Gilardi 2002) of the regulatory body is considered a function of its de facto independence, which is arguably hard to measure objectively. Outside the formative influence of systemic parallelism, Cukierman, Webb and Neyapti (1992) and Jakubowicz (see Preface in this book) emphasize the influence of the personalities of the members of the highest decision-making body. This would point towards a potentially fruitful contribution of anthropological and sociological methodologies in examining how individual characteristics of decision-makers of independent regulators play a role in supporting and defending the independence of their organizations.

Empirical research often proceeds via suitable proxies as indicators of de facto independence, but input data and assumptions vary widely. Only very few indicators are commonly accepted in relation to the use of formal controls by elected politicians; for example the politicization of appointments, the years a regulatory body is in operation, the extent to which the IRA's decisions have been reversed and the turnover of the members of the highest decision-making organ (Cukierman, Webb and Neyapti 1992; Gilardi 2008; Gual and Trillas 2004, 2006; Gutiérrez 2003; Hanretty and Koop 2012; Thatcher 2005). Considering the turnover of a regulator's presidents and directors is based on the assumption that a greater turnover indicates a lower level of independence. In addition, Hanretty and Koop (2012) operationalize political vulnerability, i.e. changes of members of the regulator's highest decision-making organ within the first six months of a change in government. This can be a regular event, when terms are designed to coincide with election cycles, or irregular through early resignation, dismissal or the change of constituting legislation which affects the composition of the highest decision-making body.

Maggetti (2006: 4 ff.) observed that formal independence alone cannot explain the variations in de facto independence. He developed a framework of two distinct dimensions of de facto independence, i.e. one concerning the relationship with the political decision-makers and one concerning the relationship with the regulatees.[2] The indicators explore, respectively, individual career paths (e.g. frequency of 'revolving door' appointments, partisan membership and political vulnerability) and tenets of institutional autonomy (e.g. power to determine budget and internal organization). Maggetti (2006: 15) uses fuzzy-set analyses that show some statistically significant correlations. According to his findings agencies show high de facto independence when

- they have been recently established and correspond to very high standards of formal independence, such as in the telecommunications sector,
- they are mature agencies which have been going through a process of autonomization, such as banking and financial supervisory authorities.

The three following conditions appear to correlate with de facto independence: (1) an institutional context where many veto players exist,[3] (2) the age of the regulator, (3) in conjunction with high formal independence (Gilardi 2008: 135; Maggetti 2006: 4 ff.; Gilardi and Maggetti 2011). Thatcher (2005) points to the legislator's power to reform the constituting legislation of a regulatory authority, which may result in fewer or more powers and independence. It is important to recognize that it may not even be necessary to resort to this *ultima ratio* but that the mere possibility of such legislative changes may already discipline an independent regulator. Thatcher (2005: 364 ff.) argues that when the exercise of formal controls is a ready option, IRAs could be prompted to comply with political preferences voluntarily (see also Tsebelis 2002; Gilardi and Maggetti 2011). There are a few other factors cited in the literature, although not proven empirically; for example, the participation in networks of agencies at the European level has been described as conducive to de facto independence (Gilardi and Maggetti 2011).

The literature review reveals that de facto independence has at least three general defining features:

1. the implementation of normative rules from the realm of formal independence,
2. the delegation of relevant powers as well as organizational autonomy,
3. the absence of undue external influence on the regulator, in particular on the members of its highest decision-making organ.

First, reviewing the implementation of legislative rules into practice should be a comparatively straightforward exercise, but research nevertheless often stops short at the normative level when appraising the regulator's constituting legislation. Going beyond that level, however, might find – to name just one example – that a regulator's independent status may be conferred by statute, but in practice appointments are politicized (Hanretty and Koop 2012).

Second, following principal-agent theory, the type and degree of powers that are delegated to regulators matter as these powers strengthen the independence of the agency from elected politicians. It is plausible to find agencies that are formally independent, but with so little power, resulting in a practically non-existing regulatory role (Gilardi 2005a; 2005b; see also Gual and Trillas 2004, 2006). This feature also ascribes key elements of an IRA's organizational autonomy, such as budget authority and the power to determine internal organization. Arguably, an IRA which cannot command its own resources is de facto less independent.

The third and last feature, i.e. the absence of undue external influence, is probably the most difficult to come to terms with empirically. The use of formal controls by elected politicians can be both formally legitimate and an interference with the regulator's independence. Nonetheless, a few objective indicators are available (e.g. the regulatory body's years of operation, politicization of appointments and political vulnerability, as well as frequency of revolving door appointments), which are best triangulated with qualitative research to be interpreted adequately.

Measuring efficient functioning

Most empirical research is interested in the performance of a given regulated market and whether this correlates with certain regulatory arrangements, among which the type of regulatory governance is one variable (see for a conceptual critique Hanretty, Larouche, and Reindl 2012). This approach has also been inverted, in research which evaluated independent regulators according to their impact on the performance of the markets they regulate. Doing so is very reasonable in the context of economic regulation, which is designed to produce economic efficiencies. It may be less appropriate to assess regulators' performance against market indicators in fields of general public interest regulation, such as non-discrimination, audiovisual media and data protection, among others. Other authors take into consideration the capacity of regulators to strike a balance between conflicting policy objectives and interests, the quality of their regulatory output and their respect for accountability standards (Gilardi 2005b: 58; Hanretty, Larouche and Reindl 2012; Nicolaïdes 2006: 33). In this approach, however, the availability of appropriate and/ or objective data is likely an issue.

There is great variation with regards to the methodologies proposed and deployed. Without testing his assumptions empirically, Nicolaïdes (2005) recommends carrying out 'ex post impact assessments of the effects of regulation on the economy and consumers' as well as process-tracking regarding the outcomes of regulators' decisions, especially 'how quickly individual decisions translate into action and what their specific effect may be'. Gilardi (2005a) meanwhile recommends assessing the performance of IRAs by looking at their output using econometric analyses. For the more complicated situations in which regulators have to balance conflicting goals, he maps out an econometric analysis that would be capable of exploring the interaction between the two conflicting goals in relation to regulatory independence. In this situation independent regulators would outperform traditional bureaucracies if they are better in dealing with such trade-offs.

Hanretty, Larouche and Reindl (2012) empirically study the links between formal independence, accountability and quality across multiple sectors in five different countries. For measuring the effective functioning of IRAs the authors rely on peer review of the regulators' perceived quality by other regulators, regulatees and academics, and statistically account for various biases. When exploring the empirical links between formal independence, accountability and perceived quality, they find all three positively related to each other. The study concludes that '[a] sustainable and fruitful trade-off between independence and accountability is possible' without detriment to the regulator's perceived quality (Hanretty, Larouche, and Reindl 2012). Likewise, Gilardi (2005a; 2005b) argues that independent regulators have to observe procedural legitimacy which underpins accountability.

To sum up the research into the effective functioning of IRAs, there is a strong tendency towards equating the effective functioning of the regulator with the performance of the regulated sector. This perspective may however not be borne out by reality, since a given sector can thrive or suffer economically due to various other influences. In any case, this concept falls short by definition when regulators have to balance conflicting goals that cannot be described in economic performance indicators alone. Most research does not answer conclusively what effective functioning means, but aside from economic performance there is a strong inclination to read it as referring to the quality of regulation. What characterizes regulatory quality can also be disputed, but it certainly involves looking at the efficiency and impact of the regulators' decision making as well as other principles of good regulation that have 'general currency' (see Baldwin, Cave and Lodge 2012: 6). Here, in particular, the adherence to public accountability standards is considered important, understood broadly as measures that hold a regulator accountable towards its constituency (as opposed to political accountability[4]).

Conclusion on methodologies of measuring regulatory independence

A summary review of the state-of-the-art measuring of independence and effective functioning of IRAs reveals a multitude of possible approaches and methodologies. Both independence and effective functioning are complex notions which are best approached as multi-dimensional concepts. This is the reason why most research commonly proceeds with composite indices grouped along various dimensions. However, in the theory there is no common understanding what the defining elements of a regulators' independence are, despite some recent convergence concerning the operationalization of formal independence. Often the underlying notion of what is to be measured differs and most methodologies cannot be transplanted outside of their specific context and research question (Verhoest, et al. 2004). Aside from the methodological challenges there are practical challenges that are not easy to overcome, notably with regards to the lack of objective and empirical data concerning indicators of de facto independence and effective functioning.

Empirical approaches to measure formal independence are most advanced (e.g. Gilardi 2008; Hanretty, Larouche and Reindl 2012). However, in order to obtain a full assessment of regulatory independence, aside from criteria on formal independence, the level of de facto independence and efficient functioning (or regulatory quality, for that matter) also need to be taken into account. For one, criteria for de facto independence cannot be fully separated from formal independence criteria, as they are – to a certain degree – in a complementary relationship with each other, at least where they concern the degree to which the real situation complies with the legal provisions. However, de facto independence is not limited to such compliance, but requires, in addition, the delegation of relevant powers, organizational autonomy, as well as the absence of external constraints or influence. With respect to measuring de facto independence, it must be noted that, despite a number of fruitful contributions, this research still lacks a comprehensive concept and methodology that could be used as an initial framework. The methodological and empirical basis for measuring regulatory quality or efficient functioning of the regulators has evolved significantly over the recent years as well, but a number of aspects only sometimes overlap, and are sometimes different from those involved in measuring independence, as shown above.

As almost all available empirical studies and approaches concern other sectors, rather than the media sector, both assumptions and methodologies need to be evaluated and transposed with a certain caution. Although the banking and financial, telecommunications and energy sectors more or less share the same institution of independent regulators, they are different from the media regulators in their goals and means.[5] Organizational customs, for instance, vary between sectors, e.g. IRAs in utility sectors are often headed by a single decision-maker, e.g. a president or director, whereas collective decision-making organs, such as a board or a council, prevail in the media regulatory bodies (Hans Bredow Institute for Media Research, et al. 2011: 221). Caution is required both when relying on a standardized approach for comparative research across different sectors and, equally, when relying on a standardized approach for a single sector but across different countries, because national configurations of IRAs differ and any assessment should be highly contextualized (Hanretty, Larouche and Reindl 2012).

Moreover, two aspects that are specific to the media sector deserve particular attention when devising any approach to the measurement of IRAs' independence and effective functioning:

1. the double objectives of legislation and regulation in the media sector, which not only aims at guaranteeing fair competition on the market, but also at the protection of fundamental rights, notably freedom of expression and media freedoms,
2. the specific and at times sensitive relationship between the media sector and elected as well as non-elected politicians (i.e. the media as 'the fourth estate').

As a consequence of the former aspect, transparency, accountability and impartiality are central virtues for any media regulatory body vis-à-vis its constituencies. What follows from the latter, however, is a constant tension between especially the mass media and the political sphere. For this reason, it appears that the institutional design and legal endowment of the media regulatory body holds equal political salience as with IRAs in the economically more potent utility sectors. In other words, certain modes of appointment politicization and political vulnerability of IRAs in the audiovisual media sector are not alone the signature of democratic legitimization of media regulatory bodies.

Ranking Tool for the self-assessment of IRAs' independence and efficient functioning

This section introduces the so-called Ranking Tool as one of the central outcomes of the INDIREG research (Hans Bredow Institute for Media Research, et al. 2011), whereas a copy of the entire Ranking Tool from the INDIREG study can be found in the Annex to this chapter.[6] It is grounded in the understanding that regulatory independence should be measured separately for formal and de facto independence, while preserving the complimentary relationship between both sides. Another novelty is that the Ranking Tool integrates existing approaches but inverts their logic, measuring the risk of influence by external players rather than the level of independence of the regulators.[7] The output of the ranking tool is a graphical visualization that separately charts formal and de facto independence.

The Ranking Tool's methodology

In a nutshell, this Ranking Tool is a new composite index that operationalizes the measuring of IRAs' independence for the audiovisual media sector. However, its scope of application is potentially wider, since there are only a few indicators that are truly media-specific. The approach follows the overall distinction between formal and de facto independence, which are separated but need to be interpreted as a whole. For each division, i.e. formal and de facto independence, relevant indicators are allocated on five dimensions:[8]

1. status and powers,
2. financial autonomy,
3. autonomy of decision-makers,
4. knowledge,
5. transparency and accountability.[9]

The organization of indicators in different dimensions is also an advantage in the interpretation stage of using the Ranking Tool.

When devising a workable set of indicators, only those indicators are included in the Ranking Tool that would give a clearer, and probably more objective, result in terms of influence. Since the Ranking Tool has been conceived to measure the risk of influence by external actors, for each dimension, only indicators that were associated with the power to protect the regulator against potential influence (especially from politics and industry) were used. Therefore, each indicator can be either perceived as a safeguard against undue interference ('autonomizers') or, conversely, as a negative factor that increases the risk of undue interference ('dependencers') (see Chapter 5 in this book by Dreyer). If an indicator's role is ambiguous in that it could be interpreted as being a route for influence, while at the same time being a source of autonomy, it was not included as an indicator.

The justification for each indicator invokes relevant European standards and/or research. The indicators on formal independence were formulated on the basis of EU legislation and jurisprudence of the European Court of Justice, which address IRAs in the broadcasting sector but also in other sectors (see Chapter 4 in this book by Stevens). Recommendation (2000)23 of the Council of Europe on the independence and functions of regulatory authorities for the broadcasting sector was one of the prime sources used for this exercise (see Chapter 3 in this book by Valcke, Voorhoof and Lievens). The weighting and ranking with regard to potential risks of influence is based on the assumptions derived from the key characteristics and the analysis conducted during the INDIREG research, and builds exclusively on that.

The indicators which determine de facto independence are far less established in the available research, whereas legal texts do not address the actual situation either. Corresponding with the theory, the indicators pertaining to de facto independence consist of different tiers: on the one hand, they correlate compliance indicators and, on the other hand, they measure further perceivable effects or phenomena that might indicate influence being exerted or a de facto increased risk of influence. Where indicators were designed as the de facto counterparts of formal indicators, they measure the extent to which formal requirements are implemented and powers and competences granted by law are exercised in practice. Other indicators of de facto independence enquire into the politicization of appointments and incidents that signify political vulnerability, which are recognized in the empirical literature on IRAs. Therefore, describing the de facto situation is not seen merely in terms of the implementation of formal requirements, but as a way to draw attention to further potential avenues and attempts to influence the independent regulatory body.

Table 6.1: INDIREG indicators to assess formal and de facto independence before weighting.

Formal independence	Dimension	De facto independence*
1. Legal structure 2. Legal recognition of independence 3. Type of regulatory powers 4. Legal definition of powers 5. Supervision powers 6. Information collection powers 7. Formal right of being instructed (except courts) 8. Formal right of being overturned (except court) 9. Type of enforcement powers 10. Organizational autonomy (internal organization and human resources)	**Status and powers**	1. Legislative modifications that reduced mandate and powers 2. Modifications of the governing law to influence a particular case/conflict 3. Actual use of the formally granted powers 4. Supervision and monitoring of implementation 5. Instructions by a body other than a court in individual cases/decisions or in relation to its policy-implementing powers 6. Decisions of the regulatory body having been overturned by a body other than a court/administrative tribunal 7. Adequate use of enforcement powers in cases of a material breach 8. Adequate enforcement in case of a continued breach 9. Even-handed/comparable measures concerning all regulatees 10. Effective autonomy regarding internal organization and human resources 11. Sufficient number of staff to fulfil tasks and duties
11. Determination of budget 12. Legal clarity regarding budget-setting and approval procedure 13. Sources of income 14. Legal clarity concerning sources of funding	**Financial autonomy**	12. Sufficient budget to carry out tasks and duties 13. Budget stability over time 14. Sufficient autonomy regarding internal budget allocation 15. Any pressure to compensate a lack of stable funding from the state or from the market

Cont.

Formal independence	Dimension	De facto independence*
15. Nature of the highest decision-making organ 16. Decision-making rights about nominations and appointments 17. Term of office of the chairman/board members 18. Concurrence of term of office and election cycle 19. Staggered appointments 20. Renewals of board members'/chairman's terms of office 21. Rules on incompatibility at the stage of nomination/appointment 22. Extension of incompatibility rules to relatives 23. Requirement to act in an independent capacity 24. Rules preventing conflicts of interest of chairman/board members during term of office 25. Cooling-off period after term of office 26. Rules on the dismissal of the chairman and/or individual board members 27. Rules on the possibility of dismissing the entire board	Autonomy of decision-makers	16. Any reflection of political majorities or political power structures in the composition of the highest decision-making organ 17. Cases where the appointer failed to appoint the nominated candidate 18. Resignations before the end of term of office due to political pressures 19. Dismissal of board member/s on non-objective grounds 20. Dismissal of entire board or replacement otherwise before the end of term
28. Legal requirements specifying professional expertise for chairman/board members 29. Legal requirements specifying professional expertise for senior staff 30. Legal requirements for qualifications for chairman/board members 31. Legal requirements for qualifications for senior staff 32. Legal option to seek external advice 33. Legal mandate to cooperate with other national or foreign regulators	Knowledge	21. Adequacy of qualifications and professional expertise of board members/chairman 22. Adequacy of qualifications and professional expertise of senior staff 23. Seeking of external advice when necessary 24. Cooperation with other national/foreign regulators
34. Legal obligation to publish decisions 35. Legal obligation to justify decisions 36. Legal requirement to organize consultations 37. Nature of the consultations (open or closed)		25. Proactive publication of decisions together with motivations 26. Publication outlet 27. Organization of consultations 28. Nature of consultations organized (open or closed)

38. Legal reporting obligations 39. Legal mechanism of ex-post control by a democratically elected body 40. Right of appeal against decisions 41. Accepted grounds for appeal 42. Legal requirement on external audit of the financial situation	Accountability and transparency	29. Publication of responses to consultation 30. Explanation to which extent responses are taken into account 31. Publication of periodical activity reports 32. Assessment or control by a democratically elected body 33. Incidents of the activity report (or other forms of approval) being refused 34. Decisions of the regulatory body having been overturned by a court/administrative tribunal in a significant number of cases 35. Periodic external financial auditing 36. Revelation of serious financial malpractices during any audit

*Where a retroactive assessment is required, the last five years are to be considered.

Indicators are framed as questions with either a binary answer option or a drop-down menu of answer options, which render the Ranking Tool easy to apply (see example in Box 6.1). Every possible answer to an indicator has been ranked on a scale between 0 and 1, with '0' signifying the likelihood of a risk of the exertion of influence and '1' representing a strong safeguard against potential influences. Where there are non-binary answers for an indicator, the scale has been adjusted to represent and rank all different possibilities in a graduated way. Where there are different answer options they have been informed by the literature review, a comparative analysis of media regulatory bodies in 43 different countries, and a stakeholder survey (Hans Bredow Institute for Media Research, et al. 2011).

Since not all indicators have the same relevance, the Ranking Tool incorporates a weighted approach. It means that all indicators within one dimension were weighted on the basis of their likeliness to be routes for potential influence. The relative weight of individual indicators is determined by their weighting factor, which can be low, medium or high. The

Box 6.1: Example of survey question (Formal Indicator 26).

How can the chairman/individual board members be dismissed?
- Dismissal not possible
- Dismissal possible only for objective grounds listed in the law (no discretion)
- Objective grounds listed in law, but margin of discretion. Power of dismissal given to the regulator/the judiciary
- Objective grounds listed in the law, but margin for discretion. Power of dismissal not given to the regulator/the judiciary
- Dismissal possible but grounds not listed in the law, or no rules on dismissal

weighting is achieved by multiplying the points of an indicator with its weighting factor. It is not be possible to change the weighting associated with each of the indicators. Within every dimension the total of all achievable points adds up to 100. The INDIREG study provides explanations on the ranking of answer options and the weighting associated with each indicator (Hans Bredow Institute for Media Research, et al. 2011: 370). The entire Ranking Tool is published in the Annex to this chapter.

This approach is consistent except for three caveats: first, for the fifth dimension, transparency and accountability, a different logic was adopted, because the more a regulatory authority adheres to transparency and accountability mechanisms, the better the situation. As a rule, best practices would achieve higher points as compared to arrangements that increase the risk of exerting undue influence on the regulatory body. Second, because certain indicators correlate with answers given to other indicators, they are not applicable in all cases. This is taken into account by offering the additional option 'not applicable'. Where this answer is chosen, the points attributed to the indicator will not be taken into account within the dimension, leading to a reduction of the overall achievable points within that dimension. Third and finally, due to the varying number of indicators within each dimension, the fewer indicators there are in a dimension, the more significant their relative weight. For example, the de facto dimension of financial autonomy is composed of only two indicators, whereas the formal dimension includes four differently weighted indicators, therefore allowing a more granular approach to assessing the risk of influence.

After applying the Ranking Tool, the results are calculated according to the methodology and translated into a graphical representation (see Figure 6.1). The five dimensions define the axes of a spider web chart, and the graphical visualization charts formal and de facto independence separately, and overlays them. The results for each dimension derive from the calculation of the total points awarded as a proportion of the total of possible points. If all possible points have been awarded, the result is a full extension of the 'spider web'. Correspondingly, if no points are awarded, the 'spider web' collapses for the relevant dimension at the centre of the web.

As with other composite indices there will be scope for contestation. The weighted approach is internally consistent, but the relative weighting reflects the judgment of the INDIREG study team. The reasons for the decision on the point values and on the respective weightings of the indicators have been made fully transparent in the INDIREG study, both for the formal and de facto set of indicators (Hans Bredow Institute for Media Research, et al. 2011).

Application and interpretation of the Ranking Tool

The Ranking Tool has been published as a self-assessment instrument that offers interested parties a structured method to appraise the situation of a media regulatory body with a view to the risk potential for the influence of external players. With the necessary information on the governing law, institutional design and operational activities of the IRA in hand, interested parties can apply the Ranking Tool by answering the survey and selecting the most appropriate answer for each question. While the use of the Ranking Tool is intuitive, its accurate implementation nonetheless requires substantial background knowledge of law and practice as well as a knowledgeable interpretation of local arrangements. Indicators that interrogate the compliance with formal requirements or the impartiality of the IRA's decision making inevitably invite a certain degree of subjectivity. This is the reason why the results concerning a specific media regulatory body can vary when different interested parties apply the Ranking Tool individually. In order to account for subjective bias, it is recommended to form an expert panel that combines various interests and perspectives and jointly applies the Ranking Tool.

The following restrictions condition a successful self-assessment with the Ranking Tool. It is only possible to use the tool to assess the risk potentials for a single regulatory body. In countries where there are several regulatory bodies active in the audiovisual media sector, such as in the federal states Germany and Belgium (see Chapter 9 in this book by Docquir, Gusy and Müller), the assessment has to be repeated for each authority. The Ranking Tool has been designed with an independent regulatory authority in mind and cannot be transposed to assess self-regulatory bodies, such as self-governing public service media or industry bodies. Finally, the tool represents the current situation, based on the answers given by the evaluator, and should not be used to predict future trends. In order to analyse a trend, however, it would be possible to repeat the self-assessment in intervals.

The graphical representation provides added value by presenting the results in a very intuitive way: it helps to focus the interpretation on dimensions that are underperforming and spot significant divergences between formal and de facto independence which would require contextual interpretation. The so-called spider web chart should be interpreted taking into account that, within the spheres of status and powers, financial autonomy, autonomy of decision-makers and knowledge, the further outwards the position of the point along the relevant axis, the more the regulator can resist external influence. As explained above, regarding the dimension of accountability and transparency mechanisms, the assumption is different in the sense that accountability and transparency are legally foreseen routes for influence, and therefore tools to counterbalance the powers and autonomy given to

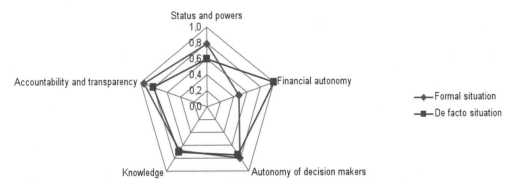

Figure 6.1: Example of the Ranking Tool's graphical representation when applied.

regulators. The reading is therefore different for this dimension, in the sense that 'the fuller the web', the more effective transparency and accountability mechanisms are in place.

It is important to note that the Ranking Tool does not deliver a ready 'verdict' but that it highlights potential attention points that would require interpretation against the local context. It would be impossible to develop a standardized method that is flexible enough to account for highly customized local governance structures. What the tool can reveal are discrepancies between the status quo and best practice characteristics for independent media regulatory bodies, and between formal and de facto independence of these bodies. Only an informed interpretation of such attention points will reveal whether the risk potential can be refuted by taking into account contextual information (see the section on piloting the Ranking Tool below). The contextual interpretation of the results may, for example, refute concerns over potential undue influence on the media regulatory authority because there are local characteristics that counterbalance the potential risks identified by this standardized method. Moreover, the Ranking Tool might also pinpoint potential risks which, depending on the national context, a contextual interpretation may prove unlikely to actually materialize.

Piloting the Ranking Tool

In order to validate the methodological approach and the relevance of the Ranking Tool, the INDIREG study conducted an in-depth analysis of eight countries. The cases were selected with a view to obtaining a representative sample of approaches and configurations of regulatory bodies, as well as different regulatory practices and national context factors (see table below). It must be stressed that the case studies were mainly motivated by the need to pilot the methodology of the Ranking Tool and not to obtain the results of the measurement of the respective regulators. It was also an attempt to discover possible relationships between formal and de facto independence as well as the influence of the socio-political context on IRAs' operations. This is also the reason why the following description summarizes the findings without going into detail about the in-depth country reports (for details please refer to Hans Bredow Institute for Media Research, et al. 2011: 277 ff.).

The in-depth case studies started with the application of the prototype of the Ranking Tool by the INDIREG team and the assigned country correspondent, a role fulfilled by a local expert who contributed to the study by compiling a country report and tabulating information on the IRA's situation. The results of the Ranking Tool were then jointly interpreted, and those areas where the application had notable results were marked as attention points that merited further contextual interpretation. For each country, three to four additional experts were identified and the attention points were discussed with them in semi-standardized phone interviews. Finally, the expert interviews were analysed with regards to the indications of the Ranking Tool, as well as with a view to the validity and practicability of the Ranking Tool.

The regulatory structure for the media sector differs significantly from country to country – a fact vividly underlined by the INDIREG research's inability to identify common structures (Hans Bredow Institute for Media Research, et al. 2011: 245). It further appears

Table 6.2: Countries selected for the application of the INDIREG methodology (see Hans Bredow Institute for Media Research, et al. 2011: 278).

	Name of the country	Regulatory body/bodies
EU Member States	Estonia	Ministry of Culture of the Republic of Estonia
	Hungary	• National Radio and Television Board (ORTT) • Hungarian National Communications Authority (NMHH)
	Italy	AGCOM
	Netherlands	Commissariaat voor de Media (CvdM)
	Slovenia	• APEK • Broadcasting Council • Ministry of Culture • Inspectorate for Culture and Media – Media Inspector
	United Kingdom	Office for Communication (Ofcom)
Candidate country	Former Yugoslav Republic of Macedonia	Broadcasting Council
Potential candidate country	Bosnia and Herzegovina	National Communications Authority (CRA)

that the relationship between formal and de facto independence rarely overlaps completely, and that in most cases the formal framework outperforms the de facto situation with respect to regulatory independence. However, there were also cases in which it was observed that the media regulatory body is acting more independently than the legal framework for its operation would suggest. Whereas the first situation provokes concerns over undue interference on an independent media regulatory body, the second situation does not raise similar concerns from the point of view of regulatory independence. However, it should not be forgotten that it is not always necessary to apply formal controls, because where they exist the independent regulator may anticipate them and adjust its actions accordingly.

Box 6.2: Example of the context-sensitive interpretation of an attention point.

After applying the Ranking Tool to UK's Office of Communications (Ofcom), which has regulatory competences in the field of audiovisual media services, a number of attention points concerning Ofcom's formal independence emerged. As an example, on the dimension of the autonomy of decision-makers, the board members of Ofcom are appointed by the Secretary of State for Culture, Media and Sport. The Ranking Tool's logic considers that an appointment by the government holds a higher risk of appointment politicization. However, a context-sensitive interpretation of this attention point reveals that such appointments are governed by the 'Nolan principles' which provide additional safeguards against political instrumentalization of public appointments in the UK, and the experts agreed that there is effectively no concern about the autonomy of decision-makers.[10]

The in-depth analysis of the country case studies supports the assumption from theory-based analysis that the de facto independence of a regulator depends on many external factors, which vary considerably from country to country and which are – at least partly – not measurable structurally. In line with the findings of comparative media systems research, the pilot confirmed that socio-political factors and local cultural influence both formal and de facto independence of national media regulatory bodies. Actions within an organization and between organizations are to a high degree structured not only by formal law and its implementation but by social norms that reflect the social fabric of society (see also Chapter 7 in this book by Klimkievicz and Chapter 8 by Psychogiopoulou, Casarosa and Kandyla). Assessing the de facto independence of a regulatory body may reflect the influence of such external factors to some extent, but may not be capable of internalizing them fully. As is generally the case with 'soft' factors, empirical validation is notoriously difficult. Thus, in order to avoid producing statistical artefacts, the Ranking Tool must be applied and interpreted in the light of the country-specific circumstances.

Conclusion

Aside from being a sector of economic activity, the audiovisual media sector never ceased to display all characteristics of political salience. Media regulatory bodies have a double function, which consists of the supervision of economic regulations while ensuring the impartial governance of the sector. In other words, IRAs function as a buffer by moving audiovisual media out from the sphere of direct influence by elected politicians or other vested interests. With only four exceptions, the European audiovisual media sector is governed by independent regulatory bodies, which underlines the importance of understanding the indispensable tenets of independence and how to assess its quality. It is a precondition for recognizing potential spheres of influence and discovering shortcomings with respect to independence or discrepancies between the formal framework and the actual practice.

A review of the empirical and theoretical literature reveals that, in spite of significant progress being made, there is no generally accepted methodology to measure formal and de facto independence of such bodies. Yet in parts a common understanding has evolved of the multiple factors that have a positive or negative influence on IRAs, on which the INDIREG study could build when devising the Ranking Tool. This tool advances methodology development in several respects:

- It reverses the logic of previous approaches, by measuring the risk of influence by external players rather than the level of independence of the regulators.
- It neatly separates the methodologies to assess formal independence and de facto independence, while preserving the complementary relationship between these dimensions in the assessment.
- It proposes a coherent set of indicators, and with regards to assessing de facto independence the method goes beyond the state-of-the-art.

- Within a given indicator, alternative answer options (accounting for the variety of formal structures and de facto actions) are ranked and indicators are weighted with a view to their relative potential to create avenues for exerting influence on the regulator.
- Results of the applied Ranking Tool are represented graphically, offering a very intuitive way to identify possible attention points which should be the focus of contextual interpretation.

It was the objective of the INDIREG study to develop a scientifically validated methodology to assess the independence of media regulatory bodies that can be used as a self-assessment tool. Provided that evaluators are acquainted with a handful of recommendations on how to use the Ranking Tool, its application is relatively straightforward and user-friendly. The online version of the tool is fully automated and evaluators can proceed step by step and export the results (see endnote 6). However, the approach nonetheless recognizes that the regulatory structure in the audiovisual media sector differs significantly from country to country, which limits the possibilities for standardized assessment methods. It is important to account for this variety across countries, which is why the Ranking Tool delivers only attention points that require further contextual interpretation to if they are to yield firmer evidence on a regulator's independence.

While the Ranking Tool offers a coherent methodology to measure various aspects of regulatory independence, it could be contested what can be inferred from this approach. As has been aptly reported and captured by numerous case studies, similar institutional arrangements for audiovisual media supervision and governance play out differently in different national contexts (Hallin and Mancini 2004; Hans Bredow Institute for Media Research, et al. 2011; Larsen, et al. 2005: 3). Moreover, what Jakubowicz refers to as 'systemic parallelism', 'whereby media systems are shaped by the socio-political and cultural features of the countries in which they operate' (see the Preface of this book) actually undermines any understanding based on a linear relationship between institutional design and regulatory outcomes. Yet, if measured separately, the level of formal and de facto independence (or dependence for that matter) can reveal attention points that in turn can be examined more closely to understand the possible nature of an issue. For example, large discrepancies between formal and de facto independence that are not only an issue of implementation failure may signify systemic parallelism.

After two years the INDIREG study's impact is now unfolding. A survey among media regulatory bodies in Europe in March 2013 that was facilitated by the European Platform of Regulatory Authorities (EPRA) revealed that the study is well known among regulators, with the Ranking Tool being the most prominent output. All sixteen regulators which responded to the survey were acquainted with the Ranking Tool, twelve of them had applied it to themselves, and in almost half of these cases this was followed by informal discussions at an external or at least internal level (Dreyer 2013). What is remarkable is that several regulatory authorities invoked the study's results as an argumentative shield against possible future intrusions into their independence (Dreyer 2013). However, none of the respondents was aware of instances where external parties applied the tool to a regulatory body (Dreyer 2013). Quoting the INDIREG study, European policy-makers and experts have called for better safeguards of regulatory independence in the AVMS Directive; but in order for such safeguards to be really effective de facto independence has to receive adequate attention. The Ranking Tool can be a foundation of such an effort to regularly monitor the formal and de facto independence of media regulatory bodies.

Notes

1   The INDIREG Ranking Tool is a product of collective research to which the whole INDIREG study team has contributed; however, we would like to acknowledge significant contributions from Jannes Beeskow, Regine Sprenger, Stephan Dreyer, as well as Nathalie Vereecke.
2   Maggetti's findings also suggest that, with regard to young regulatory agencies, high de facto independence from regulatees can also be a consequence of low de facto independence from politicians (Maggetti 2006: 15). It follows that an agency that acts as an intermediary between politicians and industry cannot serve both masters (Gilardi and Maggetti 2012).
3   Building on Tsebelis' influential concept, veto players are individual or collective actors who have to agree for the legislative status quo to change. The more veto players a political system has, the higher policy stability is; the fewer veto players, the higher the likelihood for policy change.
4   Note that democratic accountability of independent regulatory authorities already features under formal and de facto independence above.
5   Not to mention the significantly smaller impact on the overall economic sector-performance.
6   The INDIREG Ranking Tool is also accessible as an online application here: http://www.indireg.eu/?page_id=329.
7   This risk-centred logic, which is founded on the reasoning in Chapter 1 in this book by Wolfgang Schulz and Chapter 4 by Stephan Dreyer, enables a more objective method for ranking the indicators and weighting them according their significance.
8   Dreyer in Chapter 5 of this book explains the theoretical basis for these five dimensions, which are derived from the role of a given IRA in the overall governance system and the different spheres of potential influence.
9   Gilardi (2008) introduced a similar approach to assessing the level of formal independence of regulators (in the competition, electricity, environment, financial markets, food safety, pharmaceuticals and telecoms sectors). He proposed a ranking of between 0 and 1 to measure the independence of regulators according to five dimensions (status of the agency head, status of the members of the management board, relationship with government and parliament, financial and organizational autonomy, and regulatory competences).
10 The Nolan Principles are a list of recommendations on public appointment, set out in the report by Lord Nolan of 1995 to which the government adheres. These principles are intended to ensure that public appointments are based on merits and fairly governed. See http://www.archive.official-documents.co.uk/document/parlment/nolan/nolan.htm.

References

Baldwin, R., Cave, M. and Lodge, M. (2012), *Understanding Regulation: Theory, Strategy and Practice*, 2nd ed., Oxford: Oxford University Press.

Bortolotti, B., D'Souza, J., Fantinie, M. and Megginson, W. (2002), 'Privatization and the Sources of Performance Improvement in the Global Telecommunications Industry', *Telecommunications Policy*, 26: 5–6, pp. 243–268.

Center for International Media Assistance (CIMA) (2010), *Evaluating the Evaluators: Media Freedom Indexes and What They Measure*, Washington, D.C.: National Endowment for Democracy.

Cukierman, A., Webb, S. and Neyapti, B. (1992), 'Measuring the Independence of Central Banks and its Effect On policy outcomes', *The World Bank Economic Review*, 6: 3, pp. 353–398.

Dreyer, Stephan (2013), *INDIREG Follow-up Survey: Results*, internal project communication, on file with the authors.

Edwards, G. and Waverman, L. (2006), 'The Effect of Public Ownership and Regulatory Independence on Regulatory Outcomes: A Study of Interconnect Rates in EU Telecommunications', *Journal of Regulatory Economics*, 29: 1, pp. 23–67.

European Parliament and the Council of the European Union (2010), Directive 2010/13/EU of the European Parliament and of the Council of 10 March 2010 on the coordination of certain provisions laid down by law, regulation or administrative action in Member States concerning the provision of audiovisual media services (Audiovisual Media Services Directive), Official Journal of the European Union of 15.4.2010 L 95/1.

Fink, C., Mattoo, A. and Rathindran, R. (2002), 'An Assessment of Telecommunication Reform in Developing Countries', *World Bank Policy Research Working Paper 2909*, Washington, D.C.: World Bank.

Gilardi, F. (2001), 'Policy Credibility and Delegation of Regulatory Competencies to Independent Agencies: a Comparative Empirical Consideration', University of Siena, Centre for the Study of Political Change (CIRCaP), *First YEN Research Meeting on Europeanization*, Siena, Italy, 2–3 November.

Gilardi, F. (2002), 'Policy Credibility and Delegation to Independent Regulatory Agencies. A Comparative Empirical Analysis', *Western European Journal of European Public Policy*, 9: 6, pp. 873–893.

Gilardi, F. (2005a), 'Evaluating Independent Regulators', in OECD Working Party on Regulatory Management and Reform, *Designing Independent and Accountable Regulatory Authorities for High Quality Regulation: Proceedings of an Expert Meeting in London, United Kingdom, 10–11 January 2005*, Organisation for Economic Co-operation and Development (OECD) pp. 101–125.

Gilardi, F. (2005b), 'Assessing the Performance of Independent Regulatory Authorities', in OECD Working Party on Regulatory Management and Reform, *Designing Independent and Accountable Regulatory Authorities for High Quality Regulation, Proceedings of an Expert Meeting in London, United Kingdom, 10–11 January 2005*, Organisation for Economic Co-operation and Development (OECD), pp. 58–59.

Gilardi, F. (2008), *Delegation in the Regulatory State: Independent Regulatory Agencies in Western Europe*, Cheltenham: Edward Elgar.

Gilardi, F. and Maggetti, M. (2011), 'The Independence of Regulatory Authorities', in D. Levi-Faur (ed.), *Handbook on the Politics of Regulation*, Cheltenham: Edward Elgar.

Gual, J. and Trillas, F. (2004), 'Telecommunications Policies: Determinants and Impacts', *CEPR Discussion Paper 4578*.

Gual, J. and Trillas, F. (2006), 'Telecommunications Policies: Measurement and Determinants', *Review of Network Economics*, 5: 2, pp. 249–272.

Gutiérrez, L. (2003), 'The Effect of Endogenous Regulation on Telecommunications Expansions and Efficiency in Latin America', *Journal of Regulatory Economics*, 23: 3, pp. 228–257.

Hallin, D. C. and Mancini, P. (2004), *Comparing Media Systems: Three Models of Media and Politics*, Cambridge: Cambridge University Press.

Hanretty, C., Larouche, P. and Reindl, A. (2012), *Independence, Accountability and Perceived Quality of Regulators: A CERRE study*, Brussels: Centre on Regulation in Europe, 6 March.

Hanretty, C, and Koop, Ch. (2012), 'Shall the Law Set Them Free: The Formal and Actual Independence of Regulatory Agencies', *Regulation and Governance*, 2012, pp. 195–214.

Hans Bredow Institute for Media Research; Interdisciplinary Centre for Law & ICT (ICRI), Katholieke Universiteit Leuven; Center for Media and Communication Studies (CMCS), Central European University; Cullen International; Perspective Associates (eds., 2011), *INDIREG. Indicators for independence and efficient functioning of audio-visual media services regulatory bodies for the purpose of enforcing the rules in the AVMS Directive*, Study conducted on behalf of the European Commission, Final Report. February 2011.

Interdisciplinary Centre for Law & ICT (ICRI), Katholieke Universiteit Leuven; Center for Media and Communication Studies (CMCS), Central European University; Jönköping International Business School – MMTC; and Ernst & Young Consultancy Belgium (2009), *Independent Study on Indicators for Media Pluralism in the Member States – Towards a Risk-Based Approach*, Study conducted on behalf of the European Commission, Final Report. July 2009.

IREX (2013), *Media Sustainability Index (MSI) Methodology*, http://www.irex.org/resource/media-sustainability-index-msi-methodology.

Larsen, A., Pedersen, L. H., Sørensen, E. M. and Olsen, O. J. (2006), 'Independent regulatory authorities in European electricity markets', *Energy Policy*, 34: 17, pp. 2858–2870.

Maggetti, M. (2006), 'Between Control and Autonomy: Implementing Independent Regulatory Agencies', In ECPR, Standing Group on Regulatory Governance, *Frontiers of regulation: Assessing scholarly debates and policy challenges*, , Bath, United Kingdom, 7–8 September.

Maggetti, M. (2007), 'De Facto Independence after Delegation: A Fuzzy-set Analysis', *Regulation & Governance*, 4: 1, pp. 271–294.

Majone, G. (1997), From the Positive to the Regulatory State: Causes and Consequences of Changes in Government, *Journal of Public Policy*, 17: 2, pp. 139–167.

Montoya, M. Á. and Trillas, F. (2007), 'The measurement of the independence of telecommunications regulatory agencies in Latin America and the Caribbean', *Utilities Policy*, 15: 3, pp. 182–190.

Nicolaïdes, P. (2005), 'Regulation of Liberalised Markets: A New Role for the State?', D. Geradin, R. Muñoz and N. Petit (eds.), *Regulation through Agencies in the EU – A New Paradigm of*

European Governance, Cheltenham and Northampton: Edward Elgar Publishing Inc, pp. 23–42.

Olivera, G. et al. (2005), *Aspects of the Independence of Regulatory Agencies and Competition Advocacy*, Rio de Janeiro: Getulio Vargas Foundation.

Pedersen, L. and Sørensen, E. (2004), 'Transfer and Transformation in Process of Europeanization', In EPGA (European Group of Public Administration), *EPGA Annual Conference*, September.

Thatcher, M. (2005), 'The Third Force? Independent Regulatory Agencies and Elected Politicians', *Governance*, 18: 3, pp. 347–373.

Tsebelis, G. (2002), *Vetoplayers: How Political Institutions Work*, Princeton: Princeton University Press.

Verhoest, K., Peters, B. G., Bouckaert, G. and Verschuere, B. (2004), 'The Study of Organisational Autonomy: A Conceptual Review', *Public Administration and Development*, 24: 2, pp. 101–111.

Annex INDIREG Ranking Tool

(Country)

(Body)

(Evaluator)

(Date)

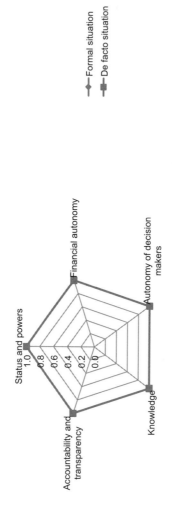

◆— Formal situation
■— De facto situation

	Formal situation	De facto situation
Status and powers	1.000	1.000
Financial autonomy	1.000	1.000
Autonomy of decision makers	1.000	1.000
Knowledge	1.000	1.000
Accountability and transparency	1.000	1.000

Formal situation

Status and powers

points (out of): 100 100 100

What is the legal structure of the regulatory body? — 1 / 12 / 12

- ● A separate legal entity/autonomous body — 12
- ○ Not a separate legal entity/autonomous body but existence of sufficient safeguards (Chinese walls) — 6
- ○ Not a separate legal entity/autonomous body and no Chinese walls — 0

How is independence of the regulatory body guaranteed? — 1 / 9 / 9

- ● In the constitution / high court decision — 9
- ○ In an act of Parliament — 7
- ○ In a secondary act — 5
- ○ It is not recognised — 0

What type of regulatory powers does the body have? — 1 / 9 / 9

- ● Policy implementing powers and third party decision making powers — 9
- ○ Third party decision making powers only — 3
- ○ Consultative powers only / No third party decision making powers — 0

Are these regulatory powers sufficiently defined in the law? — 1 / 3 / 3

- ● Yes — 3
- ○ No — 0

Does the regulatory body have supervision powers? — 1 / 13 / 13

- ● Yes — 13
- ○ No — 0

Status and powers

	points (out of):	100	100

Does the regulatory body have information collection powers towards regulatees (eg. regarding quotas)?

	points (out of):	100	100
● Yes	1	6	6
○ No	6		
	0		

Can the regulatory body be instructed (other than by a court) in individual cases/decisions or in relation to its policy implementing powers (notwithstanding possible democratic control mechanisms by government or parliament)?

	points (out of):	100	100
● No	1	13	13
	13		
○ Yes, by the parliament	4		
○ Yes, by the government/minister in limited cases	3		
○ Yes, by the government/minister in many cases	0		

Can the regulatory body's decision be overturned (other than by a court/administrative tribunal)?

	points (out of):	100	100
● No	1	13	13
	13		
○ Yes, by the parliament	4		
○ Yes, by the government/minister in limited cases	3		
○ Yes, by the government/minister in many cases	0		

What type of enforcement powers does the regulatory body have?

	points (out of):	100	100
● Availability of a range of proportional enforcement powers (warnings, deterrent fines, suspension/revocation of licence)	1	13	13
	13		
○ Not all range of enforcement powers available, but power to impose deterrent fines	10		
○ No power to impose deterrent fines	0		

Does the regulatory body have sufficient legal power to decide on internal organisation and human resources?

	points (out of):	100	100
● Yes	1	9	9
○ No	9		
	0		

Financial autonomy

points (out of):   100   100

How is the budget of the regulatory body determined?

| | | 1 | 40 | 40 |

- ● By the authority only — 40
- ○ By the parliament with involvement of regulator — 29
- ○ By the government/minister with involvement of regulator — 26
- ○ No involvement of regulator — 0

Does the law clearly specify the budget setting and approval procedure?

| | | 1 | 17 | 17 |

- ● Yes — 17
- ○ No — 0

What are the sources of income of the regulatory body?

| | | 1 | 30 | 30 |

- ● Fees levied from industry - own funds, spectrum fees — 30
- ○ Mixed fees (industry and government funding) — 20
- ○ Government funding only — 0

Does the law clearly specify the source of funding?

| | | 1 | 13 | 13 |

- ● Yes — 13
- ○ No — 0

Autonomy of decision makers

	points (out of):	100	100

What is the nature of the highest decision making organ of the regulatory body?

		1
● A board		10
○ An individual		0

Who has a decisive say in nomination/appointment of the regulatory body's highest decision making organ?

	1	13	13
● Mix between parliament / government / civil society / professional associations	13		
○ Ruling and opposition parties involved	12		
○ Parliament and government	11		
○ Parliament and prime minister/president	9		
○ Parliament and political parties	8		
○ Parliament only	7		
○ Government only	3		
○ President/prime minister/minister only	0		
○ Not applicable/other procedures	0		

What is the term of office of the chairman/board members?

	1	7	7
● A fixed term of office of a certain duration (above the election cycle)	7		
○ A fixed term of office (lower or equal to the election cycle)	3		
○ Not specified	0		

Does the term of office coincide with the election cycle?

	1	10	10
● No	10		
○ Yes/not specified	0		

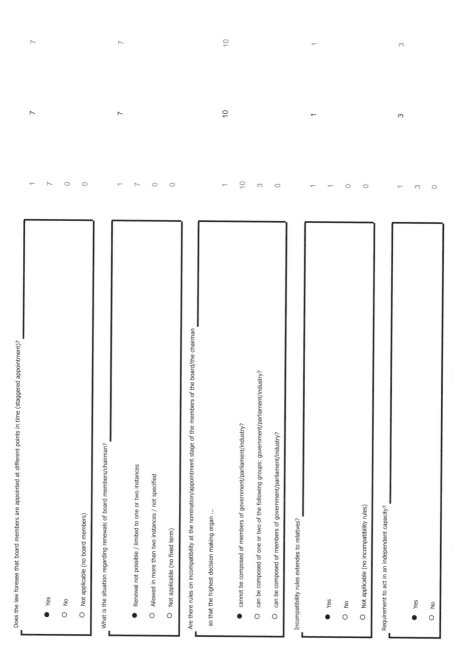

Does the law foresee that board members are appointed at different points in time (staggered appointment)?

- ● Yes — 1
- ○ No — 7
- ○ Not applicable (no board members) — 0

7   7

What is the situation regarding renewals of board members/chairman?

- ● Renewal not possible / limited to one or two instances — 1
- ○ Allowed in more than two instances / not specified — 7
- ○ Not applicable (no fixed term) — 0

7   7

Are there rules on incompatibility at the nomination/appointment stage of the members of the board/the chairman

so that the highest decision making organ …

- ● cannot be composed of members of government/parliament/industry? — 1
- ○ can be composed of one or two of the following groups: government/parliament/industry? — 10
- ○ can be composed of members of government/parliament/industry? — 3

10   10

Incompatibility rules extends to relatives?

- ● Yes — 1
- ○ No — 1
- ○ Not applicable (no incompatibility rules) — 0

1   1

Requirement to act in an independent capacity?

- ● Yes — 1
- ○ No — 3

3   3

Autonomy of decision makers

	points (out of):	100	100

Are there rules preventing conflicts of interest of chairman/board members during their term of office?

- ● Yes — 1 — 3 — 3
- ○ No — 3
- 0

Is there a period during which former board members are limited to work for the regulatees (so called cooling-off period)?

- ● Yes — 1 — 3 — 3
- ○ No — 3
- 0

How can the chairman / individual board members be dismissed?

- ● Dismissal not possible — 1 — 13 — 13
- ○ Dismissal possible only for objective grounds listed in the law (no discretion) — 13
- ○ Objective grounds listed in the law, but margin of discretion. Power of dismissal given to the regulator / the judiciary. — 13
- ○ Objective grounds listed in the law, but margin of discretion. Power of dismissal not given to the regulator / the judiciary. — 9
- ○ Dismissal possible, but grounds not listed in the law, or no rules on dismissal — 7
- 0

Dismissal of entire board

- ● Not possible to dismiss entire board — 1 — 13 — 13
- ○ Entire board can be dismissed — 13
- ○ Not applicable (no board) — 0
- 0

Knowledge

points (out of):   100   100

Are requirements for professional expertise (i.e. knowledge/experience) specified in the law? For board members/chairman?

- ● Yes   1   19   19
- ○ No   19
-    0

Are requirements for professional expertise specified in the law? For senior staff?

- ● Yes   1   19   19
- ○ No   19
- ○ Not applicable (no senior staff)   0   0

Are requirements for qualifications (eg. education, diploma requirements) specified in the law? For board members/chairman?

- ● Yes   1   19   19
- ○ No   19
-    0

Are requirements for qualifications specified in the law? For senior staff?

- ● Yes   1   19   19
- ○ No   19
- ○ Not applicable (no senior staff)   0   0

Does the law foresee that the regulatory body can seek external advice?

- ● Yes   1   12   12
- ○ No   12
-    0

Is the regulatory body legally obliged to cooperate with other national or foreign regulators and does it have the required mandate to do so?

- ● Yes   1   12   12
- ○ No   12
-    0

Accountability and transparency

points (out of):   100   100

Does the law specify that the regulatory body's decisions need to be published? — 1 — 12 — 12

- ● Yes — 12
- ○ No — 0

Does the law specify that the regulatory body's decisions need to be motivated? — 1 — 12 — 12

- ● Yes — 12
- ○ No — 0

Is the regulatory body required by law to organise consultations? — 1 — 8 — 8

- ● Yes, in all cases (which have a direct or indirect impact on more than one stakeholder) — 8
- ○ Yes, but only in cases specified by law — 4
- ○ No — 0
- ○ Not applicable — 0

Is the regulatory body required to organise these consultations as open or closed consultations? — 1 — 8 — 8

- ● Open consultations — 8
- ○ Closed consultations — 4
- ○ No consultations required — 0

Is the regulatory body subject to a reporting obligation and is it specified in law? — 1 — 12 — 12

- ● Yes, the reporting obligation is specified in law and to the public at large (including public bodies) — 12
- ○ Yes, the reporting obligation is specified in law and is limited to public bodies only (e.g. Parliament and/or government) — 9
- ○ No — 0

Does the law specify a mechanism of ex-post control by a democratically elected body

(e.g. approval of annual report by the parliament or a political/public debate with participation of the body)?

	1	16	16
● Yes	16		
○ No	0		

Is an appeal procedure against the decisions of the regulatory body foreseen in the law?

	1	12	12
● Yes, in all circumstances and before an external court	12		
○ Yes, in all circumstances, but only before an independent body (with no further appeal before a court)	9		
○ Yes, but in some circumstances only and before an external court	6		
○ Yes, but in some circumstances only, and only before an independent body (with no further appeal before a court)	4		
○ No	0		

What are the accepted grounds for appeal?

	1	8	8
● Errors of fact and errors of law (ie. the merits)	8		
○ Errors in law only	5		
○ Errors in fact only	3		
○ Not applicable (no appeal procedure exists)	0		

Is external auditing of the financial situation foreseen in the law?

	1	12	12
● Yes	12		
○ No	0		

De facto situation

Status and powers

points (out of):

Has the act on the status of the regulatory body been modified in a way that has reduced the tasks and powers of the regulatory body?

- ● No — 1
- ○ Yes — 9
- ○ Not applicable (not set up as separate body) — 0

	100	100
	9	9

Has the governing law of the regulatory body been modified to influence a particular case/conflict?

- ● No — 1
- ○ Yes — 9

	100	100
	9	9

Have the formally granted powers (policy implementing powers and third party decision making powers, excluding sanctions) been used?

- ● Yes, for all types of powers and in all instances — 1
- ○ Yes, but not for all types of powers or in all instances — 10
- ○ No — 5
- — 0

	100	100
	10	10

How does the regulatory body supervise whether the rules are correctly applied by the regulatees?

- ● Through monitoring according to a set strategy and/or methodology — 1
- ○ Through adhoc monitoring/monitoring after complaints, with concrete procedures to follow complaints — 9
- ○ Through adhoc monitoring/monitoring after complaints, without concrete procedures to follow complaints — 5
- — 0

	100	100
	9	9

Has the regulatory body received instructions by a body other than a court in individual cases/decisions or in relation to its policy implementing powers in the last 5 years?

● No   1   9   9

○ Yes   0

Have the decisions of the regulatory body been overturned by a body other than a court/administrative tribunal in the last 5 years?

● No   1   9   9

○ Yes   0

Has the regulatory body taken adequate measures in case of material breach by an AVMS/TVwF provider?

● Yes   1   9   9

○ No   9

○ Not applicable (no material breach has occured)   0

Has the regulatory body taken adequate sanctions in case of continued breach by an AVMS/TVwF provider?

● Yes   1   9   9

○ No   9

○ Not applicable (no continued breach has occured)   0

Status and powers

points (out of):   100   100

In case of several breaches by different AVMS/TVwF providers: Have even-handed/comparable measures been taken against all providers?

- ● Yes   1   9   9
- ○ No   9
- ○ Not applicable (no breaches by different providers has occured)   0

Does the regulatory body effectively decide on internal organisation and human resources?

- ● Yes   1   9   9
- ○ No   9
    0

Does the regulatory body have a sufficient number of staff to fulfill its tasks and duties?

- ● Yes   1   9   9
- ○ No   9
    0

Financial autonomy

points (out of): | 100 | 100

Is the regulatory body's budget sufficient for the regulatory body to carry out its tasks and duties?

- ● Yes   1   40   40
- ○ No   0

Is the regulatory body's budget sufficiently stable over time?

- ● Yes   1   20   20
- ○ No   0

Does the regulatory body have sufficient autonomy to decide for which tasks it spends its budget?

- ● Yes   1   20   20
- ○ No   0

Is the regulatory body under pressure to compensate a lack of stable funding from the state or from the market, by imposing fines or requesting ad-hoc financial contributions from the state?

- ● No   1   20   20
- ○ Yes   20   0
- ○ Not applicable   0

Autonomy of decision makers

Composition of the highest decision making organ (board or council) of the regulatory body

	points (out of):	100	100

Are political majorities or political power structures reflected in the composition of the highest decision making organ?

			19	19
●	No	1		
○	Yes	19		
○	Impossible to say	0		
		0		

Have there been cases where the appointer failed to appoint the nominated candidate?

			12	12
●	No	1		
○	Yes	12		
○	Not applicable (no nomination stage)	0		
		0		

Have board members/chairman resigned before their term of office due to internal/political conflicts?

			19	19
●	No	1		
○	Yes	19		
		0		

Have one or more board members been dismissed for non-objective grounds in the past 5 years?

			25	25
●	No	1		
○	Yes	25		
		0		

Has the entire board been dismissed or otherwise replaced before the end of term in the last 5 years?

			25	25
●	No	1		
○	Yes	25		
○	Not applicable (not possible)	0		
		0		

Knowledge

points (out of):

		100	100	100

Do board members/chairman have adequate qualifications and professional expertise to fulfill the duties of the regulatory body?

		points (out of):		
● Yes, all	1	30	30	
○ Yes, a majority	30			
○ No	15			
	0			

Does senior staff have adequate qualifications and professional expertise to fulfill the duties of the regulatory body?

● Yes, all	1	30	30	
○ Yes, a majority	30			
○ No	15			
○ Not applicable (no senior staff)	0			
	0			

Does the regulatory body seek external advice when needed?

● Yes	1	20	20	
○ No	20			
	0			

Does the regulatory body cooperate with other national/foreign regulators in charge of audio-visual media regulation?

● Yes	1	20	20	
○ No	20			
	0			

Accountability and transparency

	points (out of):	100	100

Does the regulatory body publish its decisions (together with motivations)?

	1	9	9
● Yes, all decisions (and motivations) are published	9
○ Yes, but only some decisions are published	5
○ No	0

Where are the decisions published?

	1	6	6
● On the website (and eventually other official channels)	6
○ In the official journal or other official channels (but not on the website)	0
○ Not applicable (decisions are not published)	0

Does the regulatory body organise consultations?

	1	8	8
● Yes, in all cases (which have a direct or indirect impact on more than one stakeholder)	8
○ Yes, but only in cases specified by law	4
○ No	0

Does the regulatory body organise these consultations as open or closed consultations?

	1	8	8
● Open consultations	8
○ Closed consultations	4
○ No consultations	0

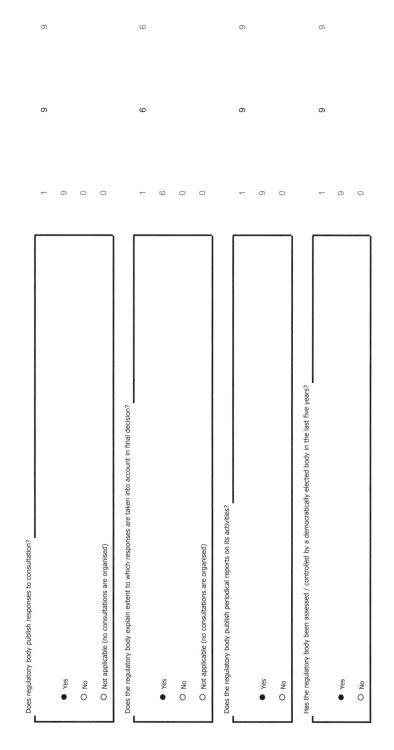

Does regulatory body publish responses to consultation?

- ● Yes
- ○ No
- ○ Not applicable (no consultations are organised)

1 9 0 0   9 9

Does the regulatory body explain extent to which responses are taken into account in final decision?

- ● Yes
- ○ No
- ○ Not applicable (no consultations are organised)

1 6 0 0   6 6

Does the regulatory body publish periodical reports on its activities?

- ● Yes
- ○ No

1 9 0   9 9

Has the regulatory body been assessed / controlled by a democratically elected body in the last five years?

- ● Yes
- ○ No

1 9 0   9 9

Accountability and transparency

	points (out of):	100	100

Have there been cases where the report (or other form of approval by a democratically elected body) has been refused in the last 5 years?

● No	1	9	9
○ Yes	9		
○ Not applicable (no requirement to have a report approved by an external body)	0		
	0		

Have the decisions of the regulatory body been overturned by a court/administrative tribunal in a significant number of cases?

● No	1	9	9
○ Yes	9		
○ Not applicable (not possible)	0		
	0		

Is the regulatory body subject to periodic external financial auditing?

● Yes	1	9	9
○ No	9		
	0		

Has auditing revealed serious financial malpractices?

● No	1	9	9
○ Yes	9		
○ Not applicable (not subject to periodic external auditing)	0		
	0		

Part II

Media systems and the culture of independence

Chapter 7

Independence or balance of dependencies? Critical remarks on studying conditions of media regulators and public service media in Poland

Beata Klimkiewicz
Jagiellonian University

Abstract

The concept of 'independence' plays a crucial role in justifying an operational role of Media Regulatory Agencies (MRA) and a special status of Public Service Media (PSM). This contribution analyses a dynamic relationship between autonomy *and* external dependency *of MRA and PSM. The chapter argues that neither autonomy nor external dependency can ever be absolute, but have to constitute themselves against the limits set by many factors including socio-cultural, economic and political factors. Both MRA and PSM accommodate manifold interests in society, and therefore they would hardly achieve factual independence from individually or collectively formulated values. In empirical terms, the chapter focuses on the case of Poland. It applies an analytical assessment of the conditions and constraints of* autonomy *and* external dependency *under which MRA and PSM operate in a given geographical, cultural and political context. Thus the analytical framework integrates specific historical/cultural dimensions as well as more technical dimensions such as appointment procedures and management, accountability, financing mechanisms and performance.*

Keywords: public service media, media regulatory agencies, independence

Autonomy and external dependency: Two sides of a mirror

Media Regulatory Authorities (MRA) and Public Service Media (PSM) constitute important 'defining centres' in the infrastructure of public communication. In normative terms, MRAs are perceived as 'operational' or 'assisting' in a process of developing an autonomous media system that gains independence from its social environments, and thus can facilitate a deliberative legitimation process (Habermas 2006). PSM are expected to provide universal access, a diversity of perspectives in which the common world presents itself and a space of constant bargaining over the definition and common understanding of social reality (Arendt 1958; Keane 1991). The concept of 'independence' (interchangeably used with autonomy) plays a crucial role in this respect: it serves as a principal rationale for a specific status of MRA and PSM. The principle of 'independence' ensures that influence of the state and market, as well as their institutions (including e.g. government, parliament, commercial entities), is reduced to the minimum so that both PSM and regulatory agencies are allowed to fulfil their mission in full professional autonomy.

Thus, the concept of autonomy[1] can be seen as a form of independence from external control, influence, sources, support etc. More precisely, *autonomy* would refer to a capacity of MRA and PSM to achieve their goals regardless of the influence and resources of the external domains, including the political realm, the media market (with a special role of advertising) and the socio-cultural environment (in particular articulated through claims and support of various social groups). On the contrary, *external dependency* would define conditions under which the capacity of MRA and PSM to achieve their goals is contingent upon the influence and resources of the external domains. *Autonomy* and *external dependency* present two sides of a mirror: there is a constant, dynamic and bipolar relation between the two due to the fact that their meaning is associated with both value-ridden and value-free qualities. As value-free categories, *autonomy* and *external dependency* describe relational settings of observed phenomena with external domains. Such descriptions would be technical in a sense that they do not entail a simultaneous evaluation of these relations. In the media policy field, however, 'impartial' or 'technical' readings of the phenomena and problem areas in question often lean toward evaluations, offering justifying or criticizing perspectives. These may be associated with attributing 'positive' and 'negative' evaluations to e.g. determinants of *autonomy* and *external dependency*. For example, PSM are perceived as institutions that are *best* equipped to fulfil their mission when they are professionally autonomous. In other words, autonomy *justifying* PSM status is associated with *good* performance. Positive determinants of autonomy include, quite obviously, editorial independence from political or economic influences. Vice versa, political and economic influences are seen as negative determinants of PSM' external dependency. At the same time, not all determinants of external dependency are perceived as 'negative'. PSM are highly dependent on the support from audiences – both in terms of their viewership and their financial contribution to the very existence of the PSM where licence fee-based systems are in place. The table below summarizes some determinants of *autonomy* and *external dependency* that are associated with positive and negative values. Some of these examples refer to MRA, the others to PSM.

Table 7.1: Examples of 'positive' and 'negative' determinants of *autonomy* and *external dependency*.

	Autonomy	External Dependency
Positive	*Professional:* editorial independence (especially from political and commercial pressures) *Legal:* guarantees of an impartial and professionally-determined composition of relevant bodies	*Audience-related:* influence of the audience on programming *Citizenship and community-related:* accommodation of manifold interests in a society
Negative	*Democratic deficit:* lack of accountability to external institutions	*Economic:* dependency on commercial sources of financing *Political:* politicization of appointments to decision-making bodies and management structures

MRA and PSM do not operate in a cultural vacuum, and therefore the way how *autonomy* and *external dependency* function in a given society does not only depend on technical dimensions (appointment procedures and management, accountability and financing mechanisms and performance), but also on cultural precepts: these include collective perceptions, attitudes and behaviour. In other words, actual fulfilment of MRA and PSM autonomy is strongly shaped by cultural values and practices, including political culture (Humphreys 1996). However, global media and policy flows generate some commonalities and interdependencies in the normative understanding of *autonomy* and *external dependency* of MRA and PSM, especially in a pan-European context. There is, de facto, less national sovereignty now over PSM and MRA operations, especially in terms of perceived standards and solutions which extend over an area wider than the nation state (McQuail 1994).[2] This can be illustrated by the standard-setting initiatives of the Council of Europe (Council of Europe 1996, 2007, 2008, 2009a, 2009b) or the legal recognition of MRA independence by the AVMS Directive (European Parliament and the Council of the European Union 2010).

Limits of independence

Autonomy of MRAs implies that they – as devices of media governance – are created and given responsibilities by legitimate public institutions proportionally representing a given society. At the same time, their status should be defined in such a way that it guarantees independence from governments and other political institutions (for example parties) as well as media and communication entities (such as AVMS providers). MRAs are expected to carry out their work in full autonomy, impartially and transparently, in accordance with their professional remit (defined by their administrative, supervisory, rule-making and monitoring functions), in order to eliminate a potential risk of political or economic interference.

There are several potential inconsistencies embedded in these requirements. First of all, autonomy and independence can never be absolute, but have to constitute themselves against the limits set by e.g. socio-cultural factors (Hans Bredow Institute for Media Research, et al. 2011). MRAs accommodate manifold interests in society, and therefore would hardly be able to achieve factual independence from individually or collectively formulated values. For example, when deciding about possible programming sanctions to be imposed on the grounds of a broadcast having ridiculed certain religious practices, MRAs have to take into account two conflicting rights – a right to freedom of speech and expression, and a right not to be discriminated against on grounds of religious feelings. A decision on such a matter will, in most cases, also reflect such socio-cultural factors as the religious composition of a society and cultural traditions.

We can observe similar inconsistencies and tensions between *autonomy* and *external dependency* in the case of PSM. The special status of PSM might be conceptualized through their competitive and complementary relationship with other actors in a media landscape

(Blumler and Hoffmann-Reim 2002). The competitive function arises with respect to size and share of viewership, but also to other dimensions such as quality, innovation, professionalism, standards, social relevance, ability to serve a variety of interests, etc. (Blumler and Hoffmann-Reim 2002). In a competitive relationship autonomy is compromised by *what is expected by audiences*, but also by the extent to which PSM have to attract mass audiences (when they are e.g. co-financed from advertising). The complementary function arises on the one hand from the narrowing imperatives of the market, and on the other hand from the importance for a society at large of preserving values that other actors (commercial broadcasters in particular) tend to neglect (Blumler and Hoffmann-Reim 2002). In other words, a side-effect of the operation of media markets under profitability considerations is that they fail to produce and offer the overall quality and diversity of media services that audiences would desire. The two most important reasons why this happens are, first, that broadcasting can have adverse 'external effects' (e.g. amplifying violence in society), and second, that good broadcasting is a 'merit' good (just as education) (Graham 1999: 19).

In addition, an important complementary dimension stems from a basic principle of democracy. The creation and sustenance of 'common knowledge' is a vital element of the functioning of democracy. In order to meet with agreement, solutions have to be derived from a common understanding (Graham 1999: 6), as well as an 'enlarged' opinion-forming which involves the careful consideration of other people's points of view and imagination of their preferences, and thus, ultimately, representativeness and impartiality (Arendt 1969). In a complementary relationship, autonomy is compromised by this 'enlarged mentality' that validates the opinion, and consequently also the representation, of collective interests. Organized pressure groups are only one aspect of these limits; others might be illustrated by the indirect formulation of claims, interests and preferences of various identity groups defined by e.g. ethnicity, gender, language, social position etc.

Methodological design

The main argument of this contribution is that studying conditions under which MRAs and PSM operate should not focus on the assessment of 'independence' broadly defined, but rather on understanding the dynamic relationship between *autonomy* and *external dependency* over a longer period of time and in a given cultural and geographical context. In other words, the crucial questions should revolve around the following considerations: What is the vector of the *autonomy/external dependency* relationship? How it can be operationalized and described?

Figure 9 offers a conceptualization of four 'technical' dimensions of the autonomy/external dependency relationship that will be used for the description of the Polish case, namely: appointment procedures and management, accountability, financing mechanisms and performance – dimensions which are discussed in more detail in Chapter 5 in this book by Dreyer.

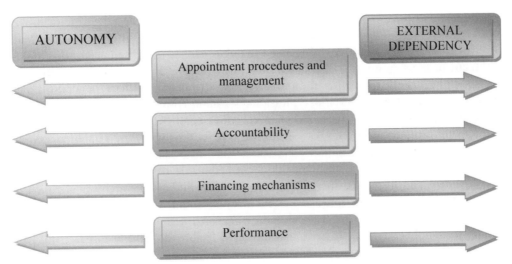

Figure 7.1: Four dimensions of *autonomy* and *external dependency* in studying the conditions of operation of MRAs and PSM.

Appointment procedures and management present a crucial dimension, because they condition the performance and financing activities of both MRAs and PSM. Ideally, the appointment procedures of MRAs should guarantee a composition of membership that will be at arms' length from political and business interests, and at the same time, will 'represent collectively the interests of society in general' (Council of Europe 1996). Thus, on the one hand, the MRA membership mandate requires *autonomy*, on the other hand *external dependency* in terms of the pluralistic representation of social interests. The composition of the management and governing boards of PSM is expected to gravitate more towards professional requirements, thus sanctioning *autonomy* more than *external dependency*.

Yet the normative prerequisites and functioning of appointment procedures and management of MRAs and PSM are related with the dimension of accountability, and more specifically with the question: to whom are they accountable? What kind of accountability (administrative, legal, political, social) plays a leading role? Does this role in turn define specific features of the appointment procedures and management of MRAs/PSM? Administrative accountability involves answerability to superiors; it is related with auditing, evaluation, oversight mechanisms and other obligations meant to measure the fulfilment of management or performance requirements imposed by law, agreement or regulation (Blind 2011). Legal accountability is directly linked to the rule of law, not efficiency; it is the judiciary, not politicians, which checks whether officials and managers act within the mandates of their legally prescribed competences (Goetz and Gaventa 2001: 7). Political accountability can be defined as the obligation of elected officials to answer to the public, and of public servants to answer to the elected officials. It is generally ensured through elections and the legislative system, and is supported by a well-functioning political party system and a healthy executive division of labour (Blind 2011: 7). Social accountability is generally seen as a bottom-up process, encapsulated in a variety of initiatives of direct and indirect civil society and citizen engagement in public affairs (Ackerman 2005: 16).

Financing mechanisms of MRAs and PSM – in particular – should reflect independence from the political environment and especially the government, as well as the market. They should guarantee managerial and professional autonomy accordingly. As regards PSM, longstanding practice in various European countries contributed to a broad acceptance (though not without controversy) of various forms of funding including a flat broadcasting licence fee, taxation, state subsidies, subscription fees, advertising and sponsoring revenue, specialized pay-per-view or on-demand services, the sale of related products such as books, videos and films, and the exploitation of PSM's audiovisual archives (Council of Europe 2009b). At the same time, as a public institution in law and governance, PSM are seen to best preserve their managerial and professional autonomy if they are primarily funded from public sources – in particular through a flat broadcasting license fee. This type of funding does not only prevent a dependency on government in terms of a direct amount that is transferred in the form of subsidies, grants or other similar financial mechanisms, it also secures a long-term approach to the future planning of PSM which annual funding from state budgetary sources would not allow.

Financing mechanisms significantly determine quality and autonomy of performance. MRAs are expected to carry out their work impartially and transparently, in line with their legally defined competences. PSM, integrating competitive and complementary functions, are to offer a set of qualitative priorities which differ from those of market-driven media. This difference is not so much congruent with genres and areas of programming as with functions, financing, standards and quality, as well as with their reputation for accessibility to public concerns and responsiveness to public needs (Blumler and Hoffmann-Reim 2002). In addition to genre provisions (information, entertainment, education), qualitative priorities should reflect such important social and cultural functions as cultural self-determination, innovation, transnational appeal, imaginativeness, an ability to illuminate controversy, authenticity, social relevance, expressive richness and integrity (Blumler and Hoffmann-Reim 2002: 207).

The four dimensions (appointment procedures and management, accountability, financing mechanisms, performance) described above will be further studied through the following indicators:

- legal measures,
- social practices,
- quantitative indicators (such as proportions of funding from different sources).

The sections below will focus on the implementation of this analytical frame in the case of Poland. The Polish MRA and PSM will not be analysed separately in their entirety, but mainly as institutions related to each other through a network of power dependencies. It should be mentioned in this context that the PSM in Poland are supervised by a media regulatory agency – the National Broadcasting Council (*Krajowa Rada Radiofoniii Telewizji*, KRRiT). Thus, KRRiT will be studied in its relation to PSM, not as a complex institution performing a number of complementary functions including the regulation of private broadcasting, content monitoring etc. This kind of relational structure is certainly specific in a given geographical context, although it cannot be easily extracted from its historical, cultural and geopolitical roots. Thus, an analytical assessment of the conditions and constraints of *autonomy* and *external dependency* under which KRRiT and PSM operate will integrate both – specific – historical/cultural dimensions and – more general – technical dimensions (appointment procedures and management, accountability, financing mechanisms, performance).

Historical and geopolitical background

The current position of the MRA and PSM in Poland has been shaped by specific historical currents and the growing importance of shared regulatory trends in Europe. Recently, these trends have accentuated a decline in normative certainties, especially regarding the function of PSM in a new communication environment. Moreover, new challenges have arisen in the light of increasing regulatory pressure from the European Commission in terms of clarifying PSM remit in relation to financial mechanisms (Meier 2003; Bardoel and d'Haenens 2008; Ward 2008) as well as new political decisions motivated by commercial incentives (removal of advertising in Spain and France) or populist considerations (abolition of licence fee in Hungary and policy debate about similar solutions in Poland and the Czech Republic). How does this new – technological, economic and, most importantly, political – constellation affect the perception and shaping of the regulatory mechanisms within which MRA and PSM have operated so far?

Poland seems well suited as a case study in this matter: within the last 20 years, PSM were created through a far-reaching media system reform and then experienced subsequent regulatory changes. This phenomenon could be described as 'compressed' time. In other words, phases of PSM development – introduction, growth, maturity – are marked by a different length and intensity than in other European countries or regions. In particular, the process of 'inventing' and 'reinventing' PSM appeared to coincide with the development of commercial broadcasters, which imposed their own commercial logic and way of action. Thus, PSM were exposed relatively early in their development to competition with their private counterparts. Moreover, a new understanding and conceptualization of media (less as institutionalized entities and more as services and applications available online) has created a new discursive space where the justification of a centralized institution offering a public service seems even more difficult.

In Poland, PSM were born as a product of a profound media system change, starting in 1989. Normative expectations revolved around two prerequisites. One aimed at achieving a full independence both from the state and party politics. The second assumed a partial independence from the market forces through a dual financing system, in which PSM could obtain sponsorship and advertising and also receive revenues from a licence fee for fulfilling their public service mission. These aspirations met many practical difficulties (Klimkiewicz 2007).

At the general level, at least three limitations can be identified. First, 'new' PSM preserved an institutional continuity with the former state media. Polish Radio was established as a private joint stock company already in 1925; it was nationalized in 1935 and transposed into the supervisory competence of the Ministry of Post and Telegraph. After World War II, Polish Radio was integrated, both structurally and ideologically, with communist rule. Polish Television started to broadcast its programmes in 1953, at the end of the Stalinist era. Unlike radio, TV from its very beginning was instrumentally located in the discursive and ideological universe of the communist regime. Its remit and programming obligations were adjusted according to the cultural and political goals of the communist propaganda. Consequently, the later attempt to formally convert the state media into newly formed PSM (including the introduction of corresponding financing and programming obligations) was burdened with institutional links to the former communist past.

Second, although there was, in 1989, a chance for a domestic, locally-conceived, three-level broadcasting system composed of public, private/commercial and social/civic media, eventually a solution prevailed that was inspired by the wish to copy the legal and institutional framework of the West-European dual model (Ociepka 2003). As a result, not only the dual system was 'borrowed' from the Western European media landscape and policy tradition, but the PSM and regulatory authorities were also modelled after West-European institutional patterns.

Third, the institutional birth of PSM in Poland and other Central European countries (1990–1995) coincided with a time of crisis and pronounced criticism for PSM in the Western part of Europe. Jakubowicz (2004) argues that the internal reform and adoption of the normative West European PSM model in Central Europe has been put into question even before it was successfully completed, and before an alternative option of self-regeneration was conceived. In the given historical circumstances, the West-European pattern appears obsolete, born in a completely different historical time and altogether different social, political, cultural and technological conditions – and now in acute need of a redefinition of its rationale and purpose (Jakubowicz 2004: 67).

Taken together, these three circumstances determined a quite specific course of action, in which PSM have not developed as a formally autonomous system (as in the case of a professional model described by Humphreys 1996: 155–58), but as a more inclusive system that combines a 'Western' normative model as a point of reference with political control (mainly via appointments in decision-making and management structures), legal norms granting professional autonomy and commercial prerequisites.

The National Broadcasting Council KRRiT was established by the 1992 Broadcasting Act, adopted by the Polish Parliament on 29 December 1992. The Act was intended to revamp the regulatory structure, most importantly through a decomposition of former dependencies and relations of control between institutions of political power, regulatory units and the media. The National Broadcasting Council was designed according to the French model of the *Conseil supérieur de l' audiovisuel* in order to reflect the institutional components of representative democracy: four of KRRiT's nine members were to be appointed by the Sejm (the Lower House of the Polish Parliament), two by the Senate and three by the President. This composition has since changed. The KRRiT's competences can be divided into four basic groups: granting and revoking broadcasting licences, supervision of PSM management and performance (mainly through operations of the Supervisory and Program Councils who oversee the activities of PSM), participating in broadcasting policy formation, and scrutinizing the activity of broadcasters (content and audience in particular). In the Polish Constitution enacted in 1997, the KRRiT was recognized as one of the organs of state control and protection of rights (The Constitution of the Republic of Poland 1997, Arts. 213–15). The constitution defined tasks and competences of the KRRiT in general terms, and also outlined its composition (without providing a precise number of KRRiT members to be appointed by the Sejm, Senate and the President) and incompatibility rules. Thus any potential future change in law would have to respect and be adjusted to constitutional provisions.

Appointment procedures and management

The issue of *autonomy* and *external dependency* of both the regulatory body (KRRiT) and PSM (interrelated with the regulator especially through the appointment and supervisory procedures) has long been on the political and public agenda in Poland. Many experts argue that the legal measures and regulatory framework in Poland are satisfactory, but that the political culture and the way rules are used and implemented in practice generate a whole set of political dependencies both regarding KRRiT membership and the PSM. In other words, the same legal and procedural safeguards of *autonomy* may yield different results depending on political culture, the level of democratic consolidation, and political manners. Thus, when it comes to the direct implications of the development of rational-legal authority[3] for PSM in Poland and their regulatory supervision, one has to emphasize a relatively low *autonomy* of both the regulatory body and PSM. This form of autonomy might be also defined as 'shadow' autonomy: the PSM and the media regulator potentially enjoy formal independence, but it seems substantially diminished in the course of political actions.

Seen from a legal perspective, the independence of the KRRiT and PSM has not been recognized as a value to be explicitly protected by constitutional or media law provisions. However, there have been some rules in force that counterbalance external dependencies and stimulate professional autonomy. First, these include the constitutional provisions that prevent members of political parties from being nominated to the KRRiT (The Sejm and Senate of the Republic of Poland 1997), and thus also from having a direct influence on the appointment of PSM management and the supervision of their performance. Second, the nomination of the KRRiT members by the parliament and President, both elected in general elections, potentially creates a representative balance of powers (The Sejm and Senate of the Republic of Poland 1993). Nevertheless, Figure 10 illustrates a fairly complex governance structure, indicating a whole set of dependencies between political representation in parliament, Presidential Office, regulatory body and PSM.

Appointment decisions relating to the regulatory body have always raised turbulent disputes. A relatively fast circulation of political power in Poland and successive changes in central administration proved to bring about an appetite for a more direct control over the composition of the regulator. Although the constitutional provisions protect representative composition of KRRiT and eliminate party membership of KRRiT's members, the constitution does not sharply define the number of KRRiT members and the length of

SEJM		SENATE		PRESIDENT	
nominates 2 members of KRRiT		nominates 1 member of KRRiT		nominates 2 members of KRRiT	

NATIONAL BROADCASTING COUNCIL (KRRiT) 5 members (term of office: 6 years)					
appoints 15 members of the Television Program Council; 10 members represent parliamentary groups, 5 members are experts in culture and mass media fields. (term of office: 4 years)	appoints 15 members of the Radio Program Council; 10 members represent parliamentary groups, 5 members are experts in culture and mass media fields. (term of office: 4 years)	selects, through a competition, 5 of the 7 members[4] of the Supervisory Board of Polish Television (TVP). Candidates for the competition are nominated by collegial bodies of university-type higher education institutions.	selects, through a competition 5 of the 7 members[5] of the Supervisory Board of Polish Radio (PR). Candidates for the competition are nominated by collegial bodies of university-type higher education institutions.	selects, through a competition, 4 of the 5 members[6] of the Supervisory Boards of regional broadcasting companies. Candidates for the competition are nominated by collegial bodies of university-type higher education institutions, operating in the relevant region.	

SUPERVISORY BOARDOF POLISH TELEVISION 7 members	SUPERVISORY BOARDOF POLISH RADIO 7 members
issues a motion and approves the appointment of one to three members of the Board of Management of Polish Television by the National Broadcasting Council	issues a motion and approves the appointment of one to three members of the Board of Management of Polish Radio by the National Broadcasting Council

Sources: 1992 Broadcasting Act, as amended.

Figure 7.2: The structure of PSM governance.

their terms. Both the number of members and their length of terms are regulated by the 1992 Broadcasting Act. This legal gap has been used by politicians not only to change the number of the KRRiT members, but also its composition.

For example, in December 2005, the newly elected right-wing government prepared the Act on Transformations and Modifications to the Division of Tasks and Powers of State Bodies Competent for Communications and Broadcasting (The Sejm and Senate of the Republic of Poland 2005), which reduced the number of KRRiT members from nine to five. Although the given rationale behind the Act was the establishment of a new super-regulatory body – the Office of Electronic Communications (*Urząd Komunikacji Elektronicznej*, UKE), most critics of the project pointed out that the Law merely changed the composition of the National Broadcasting Council KRRiT, the Supervisory Councils of Polish Television and Radio, and in consequence, the management boards of both PSM institutions. In fact, the law passed by the Sejm at a great speed on 29 December 2005 stipulated that the term of office of the current nine members would expire on the day the law was enacted (14 January 2006). Five new members were to be nominated by the new Sejm (2), Senate (1) and President (2), all linked to the governing Law and Justice Party and its coalition allies. The Constitutional Court openly criticized the shortening of KRRiT terms, pointing out that legislative argumentation was lacking and that the appropriate stabilization of the mandate of KRRiT members was not secured (judgement K 4/06).

A history of nominations to the KRRiT proves that many of its members did not meet the legal requirement of 'a distinguished record of knowledge and experience in mass media' (The Sejm and Senate of the Republic of Poland 1993). A vast number of KRRiT members were politically active before or after their term in the regulatory body. These include active politicians as well as members of political parties. Many other members did not qualify for membership because of their knowledge or professional experience in the media, but because of political recommendations. It happened several times in the course of KRRiT's short history that a former KRRiT member returned back to active politics or media-related businesses. In some other cases, lawyers or experts advising commercial broadcasters became KRRiT members or former KRRiT members returned to consultancy business. This record proves that despite legal safeguards of *autonomy*, including conflict of interest regulations, appointment procedures and management structures externally depend on political choices.

Accountability

The accountability dimension refers to the questions of whom the MRA and PSM are accountable to, and what the proportions between administrative, legal, political and social accountability are. In the case of Poland, legal accountability is directly linked to the provisions and implementation of the 1992 Broadcasting Act. An important frame for legal accountability is set by constitutional provisions aimed at rendering impossible arbitrary law changes. In practice, however, such arbitrary and instrumental legal changes have been repeatedly performed by politicians of different political orientations. The 2005 law change has not been the only case that raised broad criticism in recent years. Rywingate – the disclosure of a corruption scandal – caused far-reaching consequences and ended ultimately with the resignation of left-wing Leszek Miller's government in 2004. In 2002, KRRiT and the Ministry of Culture in Poland proposed a Draft Amendment to the 1992 Broadcasting Act that was publicly advertised as a set of measures to protect media pluralism and limit cross-media concentration. The crucial roles in this legislative procedure were played by Włodzimierz Czarzasty, the KRRiT member appointed by former President Aleksander Kwaśniewski for the term 1999–2005, Robert Kwiatkowski, the director of Polish Television (TVP) and Aleksandra Jakubowska, the former deputy Minister of Culture. A main political rationale behind the regulatory change had been given as creating a legal environment that would facilitate prioritizing the needs of some media actors and controlling functional and property redistribution in the audiovisual media sector (i.e. a prospective privatization of TVP's channel 2). However, as the scandal later revealed, the main logic behind the law was clientelistic and instrumental. In 2002, the Agora company[7] was approached by the film producer Lew Rywin (representing interests of the 'group in power') and asked to pay a bribe in order to induce changes in the draft amendment that would be advantageous to Agora. The revealing of the scandal (by the Agora's daily *Gazeta Wyborcza*) induced investigation by the Sejm Investigation Committee and the courts, which disclosed several serious irregularities and manipulations concerning the legislative work on the draft amendment.

In the case of Poland administrative accountability, which mainly involves answerability to superiors, is strongly dominated by political accountability. While PSM are accountable to the KRRiT, the KRRiT is accountable to the parliament and the President. Each year, the KRRiT has an obligation to submit an annual report to the Sejm, Senate and President on its activities during the preceding year, as well as information concerning key issues in radio and television broadcasting. In case of rejection of the report by both the Sejm and the Senate, the term of office of KRRiT members expires, but only if this decision is approved by the President. In Polish political practice, with its relatively fast pace of exchange of political power, the political affiliation of the President often differed from the parliamentarian majority. In June 2010, however, for the first time since the KRRiT's establishment, its annual report was rejected by the Sejm, Senate and the President and, as a result, the term of office of the KRRiT members expired. President Bronislaw Komorowski, affiliated with the Civic Platform[8] party, nominated two new candidates for the KRRiT, the Senate nominated one person who was proposed by the Civic Platform party and, finally, the Sejm nominated two candidates who were proposed in agreement between the Civic Platform party and the oppositional Democratic Left Alliance[9] party. The new KRRiT started to operate on 10 August 2010. In parallel with these developments, the Sejm passed the renewal of the 1992 Broadcasting Act, called also 'small renewal.' The renewal stipulated that the terms of office of the top managers of Polish Television and Polish Radio would expire fourteen days after the enactment of the renewal. 'The small renewal' was one of the first parliamentary acts signed by President Bronislaw Komorowski at the beginning of his presidential term.

The instrumentalization of legislative powers and the abuse of KRRiT's accountability mechanisms were widely criticized by independent experts. First, the replacement of PSM's management and KRRiT's members before the end of their terms was politically motivated. Second, the governing party decided to prompt this 'small renewal' of the current media law despite the fact that a more complex change of the law had been prepared simultaneously in consultation with producers, artists and the academic community. To sum up: political parties representing the whole political spectrum, from the left-wing Democratic Left Alliance, which was involved in the 'Rywingate' scandal, to the right-wing Law and Justice party, have tended to enforce the political accountability of KRRiT and PSM by instrumentalizing the media law. A normative trajectory towards a greater autonomy has been re-directed in political practice towards a stronger structure of political dependencies.

Why has there been such a strong pressure for political, rather than legal, administrative or social accountability? Referring mainly to the developments in a Western part of Europe, Bardoel and d'Haenens (2008) describe a growing critical attitude among governments and politicians towards PSM, resulting from frustration about the inability to build a more clientelistic partnership. 'The forced tango that national politics and public broadcasters have danced for many decades' is being discreetly replaced by a partnership with private media promising 'to be less critical and cynical towards politics than PSB' (Bardoel and d'Haenens 2008: 339). The Polish experience, however, shows that politicians were relatively successful in building clientelistic relationships with PSM. Despite constitutional and legal safeguards of representative balance and institutional autonomy, political practice was aimed at restoring a form of control that would facilitate the exchange of political support targeting PSM (manifested through different 'sluice-gates' in the form of appointment procedures, supervision of PSM's performance etc.) for access to social resources.[10] This would probably not be the case if PSM would not have such a significant audience share in Poland. The popular appeal of PSM has become an important resource that politicians have sought to use to build 'safe' discursive environments that reinforce rather than question their political choices.

Financing mechanisms

Financing mechanisms play a crucial role in ensuring professional autonomy and counterbalancing external dependencies. Financing of PSM solely from licence fees appeared unaffordable in Poland. During the last fifteen years, licence fee revenue has oscillated between 13 per cent and 34 per cent of the total revenues of Polish Television (TVP). Thus most of TVP's activities were financed from advertising, sponsoring and other commercially related sources. Given the strong position of the TVP in national audience share and the national TV advertising market, it seems obvious that commercial competitiveness strongly influenced its performance and fulfilment of public service remit.

Table 7.2: Sources of financing of public service broadcasters over the years 1995–2010.

	1995	1996	1997	1998	1999	2000	2001	2002	2003	2004	2006	2007	2008	2009	2010
Polish television															
Advertising and sponsoring (%)	58.1	60.5	58.3	60.6	67.0	62.3	61.9	59.0	58.3	60.8	62.7	60.2	66.9	68.2	68.0
Licence fee (%)	34.9	33.8	34.0	32.0	29.2	29.9	30.7	31.3	33.6	31.9	28.3	24.7	20.5	17.4	13.1
Others (%)	7.0	5.6	7.7	7.4	3.8	7.8	7.4	9.7	8.1	7.3	8.9	14.9	12.6	13.5	18.9
All units of public radio															
Advertising (%)	13.9	14.6	16.2	16.2	17.2	14.7	12.1	10.4	11.3	13.3	14.5	14.5	17.5	13.2	14.7
Licence fee (%)	75.4	75.1	74.3	72.2	71.3	73.4	76.5	77.5	77.4	76.0	72.3	71.9	66.3	73.5	67.9
Others (%)	10.7	10.3	9.5	11.6	11.5	11.9	14.6	12.1	11.3	10.7	13.2	13.6	16.2	13.3	17.4

Sources: KRRiT 1997; KRRiT n.d.

A debate about advertising as a primary source of PSM revenues has indicated that the downside of such a system is that the value of performance only depends on the number of viewers, or in other words on a strategy 'to attract all people all of the time' instead of the BBC parable 'all people some of the time.' So advertising funding encourages PSM to spend only the minimum required to keep the largest possible audience watching and to successfully compete with private commercial counterparts (Graham, et al. 1999).

In the case of Poland, the result has been a vicious circle: on the one hand, viewers have not opted for paying licence fees, because the PSM have spent too much of their broadcasting time on advertising and programmes similar to those the commercial broadcasters offer; on the other hand, the PSM have not succeeded in collecting substantial revenues from licence fees to make themselves independent from advertising sources. In consequence, the pure pressure to achieve ratings has eroded an ability of PSM to secure their professional autonomy.

As can be seen in Table 7.2, the collection of licence fees has significantly dropped since 2007, when the Civic Platform party and its leaders started to announce new plans for financing PSM in Poland.[11] Some institutions and experts have argued that the lack of control mechanisms is responsible for this situation; others have insisted that, in fact, the long-term state policy killed the licence fee and only some form of a fixed allocation from the state budget can serve as a remedy (See: KRRiT 2009: 30; Kublik 2009).

Commercial dependence has primarily affected public television, not radio. It is Polish Television which has become a cardinal player in the national advertising market and leader in television audience share, thus positioning itself as the main rival of commercial channels. This superior position has ensued from two reasons. First, the public (formerly state) broadcaster monopolized the TV landscape for 40 years before the first private commercial channels appeared on the scene, thus securing a high audience loyalty. Second, unlike in the case of the press, broadcasting regulation imposed limits and control on the broadcasting market. Until 2004, foreign investors were allowed to hold only minority shares (up to 33 per cent) in the Polish broadcasting media. As a consequence, the absence of influential foreign investors contributed to a division of the television market into two parts: one covered by the strong Polish public service television TVP and the other dominated by two strong private companies – Polsat and TVN, each owning several channels. In recent years however, the share of other companies (offering mostly thematic channels) significantly increased (see Table 7.3).

Paradoxically, the viewer loyalty and high advertising shares enjoyed by public service television has not been accompanied by a wide public consensus over its role and a willingness to pay licence fees. According to a survey conducted by PBS DGA (July 2009), 46 per cent of respondents declared that PSM in Poland should not obtain financing from the state budget and their activities should be covered solely from advertising. 37 per cent claimed that PSM should be financed from the state budget and only 17 per cent favoured licence fees.

Table 7.3: Audience shares of dominant television actors over the years 1997–2010.

	1997	1998	1999	2000	2001	2002	2003	2004	2005	2008	2009	2010
TVP 1	32.3	30.0	27.5	25.7	24.4	26.5	26.5	24.9	24.5	22.6	20.9	19.4
TVP 2	18.9	18.3	18.0	19.1	19.7	20.6	21.4	21.4	21.6	16.8	15.4	14.5
TVP 3 Regional/ TVP3	5.6	5.0	4.1	2.9	3.5	4.4	5.3	4.7	4.5	4.3	4.4	4.9
All Polish Television channels	**58.1**	**54.7**	**51.1**	**49.2**	**48.9**	**53.0**	**54.5**	**52.2**	**51.7**	**43.7**	**40.7**	**38.8**
POLSAT	25.7	25.2	23.4	25.3	22.6	18.5	17.5	17.4	17.0	15.4	14.8	13.8
TVN	1.3	6.4	10.7	11.4	13.9	13.8	13.4	14.2	14.6	16.7	15.9	15.2
TV4	–	1.6	1.5	2.8	3.7	3.9	4.1	3.1	2.7	1.8	2.1	2.1
TVN Siedem/ RTL7	2.7	3.4	3.6	2.9	2.4	2.2	2.2	–	1.4	1.6	1.7	1.6
TVN24	–	–	–	–	–	–	–	–	–	–	2.7	3.5
Others	12.3	8.7	9.7	8.4	8.5	8.6	8.3	13.1	12.6	20.8	22.1	25.0

Sources: AGB Polska, TNS-OBOP.

Performance

Quality and autonomy of performance is determined by all remaining dimensions, including financing, appointment and accountability. In the case of the MRA, autonomy in performance may be assessed through the level of impartiality, transparency and fulfilment of legal competencies. The KRRiT's long-term performance encompasses various fields of activity including licence-granting issues, sanctioning, content monitoring, PSM supervision, advising and contributing to the development of media policy etc. A primary concern among political and academic observers has been that these fields have not attracted proportionate attention from KRRiT's members. Some areas, in particular PSM supervision and appointment procedures have absorbed a greater focus from KRRiT members than other fields. As concerns cases of arbitrary and inconsistent rule application, the KRRiT has most often been publicly criticized for using sanction powers especially in the case of controversial programming contents. These were sometimes perceived as politically or ideologically motivated, mainly in cases where programmes were deemed to 'have not respected the Christian system of values' as stipulated under the 1992 Broadcasting Act.[12] A 2006 content penalty illustrates this practice. The commercial broadcaster Telewizja Polsat was sanctioned with a penalty of 500,000 PLN (EUR 125,628) for broadcasting a programme in which a disabled journalist working for Radio Maryja[13] was ridiculed and satirized by the host of the channel's talk show and his guests. Polsat appealed against the KRRiT decision to the Appellate Court and subsequently the Supreme Court. On 14 January 2010 the Supreme Court supported the KRRiT's decision (KRRiT 2010: 12). The KRRiT's sanction decision has not been generally questioned in terms of its substance but rather non-proportionality of the high penalty. On the positive site, it is worth mentioning that many everyday monitoring and regulatory practices carried out by the KRRiT are not directly affected by the political affiliation of the KRRiT members. These are part of an administrative and analytical routine.

PSM performance has been guided by a relatively broad and institutionally defined public service remit. Thus 'public service mission' (*misja publiczna*) is directly linked to Polish Television (TVP) and Polish Radio (PR), assuming that other services provided by alternative platforms (e.g. IPTV) should be institutionally connected with TVP and PR. Art. 21(1) of the 1992 Broadcasting Law states:

> *Public radio and television* shall carry out their *public mission* by providing [...] the entire society and its individual groups with diversified programme services and other services in the area of information, journalism, culture, entertainment, education and sports which shall be pluralistic, impartial, well balanced, independent and innovative, marked by high quality and integrity of broadcast. (emphasis added)

This very general formulation is accompanied by a list of ten tasks to be carried out by the public radio and television. The law also lists nine attributes that should characterize programme services of the public radio and public television. These seem to be formulated in equally general terms (Broadcasting Act 1992, Art. 21).

Over the last fifteen years, the implementation of this public service mission and production of public service contents has been increasingly criticized in Poland. In particular, public television has been seen as a medium that abandons its high-quality programming profile and employs a strategy of imitation of commercially popular programmes in order to defend its high market shares. In other words, editorial autonomy has become externally depended on commercial incentives. A consideration of programming output and genre structure shows, however, that in comparison with commercial channels, public channels do offer higher proportions of certain programme types and genres, especially news and current affairs, documentary films, drama and children and youth-oriented programmes (Table 7.4 below). Also, advertising and paid-types of contents have composed a smaller portion of programming of the PSM than of private channels. Public service television has offered a higher proportion of European and independently produced programming than commercial channels.

Yet another aspect of influence has been political. TVP's management and journalists have generally lacked the ethos of independence characteristic of revered PSM institutions such as the BBC. The recent history of TVP's journalistic performance has been marked by many cases of biased news representation. One of the most recent cases met a reaction from the KRRiT. On 29 November 2010, the regulator issued a decision in which the TVP was called to cease practices breaching Art. 21.1. of the 1992 Broadcasting Act, in response to the broadcaster's portrayal of events related to the removal of a cross from by the Presidential Palace to the St. Anna's Church. The cross was placed in a front of the Presidential Palace after the crash of the presidential airplane on 10 April 2010. The place served as a space where commemorative meetings of supporters of the former President Kaczynski were organized. The newly elected President Komorowski decided to relocate the

Table 7.4: TV output in hours of programme, share of programme genres, European production, programming produced originally in Polish and independent production in 2004 and 2008.

	News, current affairs and documentary (%)		Entertainment, music and sports (%)		Movies (%)		Advertising, sponsoring and other paid contents (%)		Production in Polish (%)	European production (%)
	2004	2008	2004	2008	2004	2008	2004	2008	2004	2004
POLSAT	8.8	4.5	32	29	33.4	43.6	14.7	15.9	45	53
TVN	8.2	17.4	36.9	30.6	26.7	25.8	16.5	19.9	45.9	47.3
TVP1	29.9	22.8	11.1	9.8	42.5	46.8	7.6	11.4	51.3*	67.7*
TVP2	22.1	19.5	21.5	17.6	34.8	44.3	6.7	13.6	–	–

*The data refer to January–March 2004, July–September 2004 and October–December 2004.

Sources: KRRiT: Information about basic issues of radio and television broadcasting, 2005; 2008.

cross to the St Anna's Church. Some TVP journalists at that time not only reported events in an overly favourable way to the right-wing Law and Justice party led by Lech Kaczynski's brother Jaroslaw, but were actively engaged in organizing political protests largely contesting government investigation activities.

One of the greatest challenges for PSM performance in the future will be the issue of social cohesion and a cumulative social change that produces, and is also impacted by, fragmentation. The 'participatory architecture' of new media activities and communities does not necessarily support cohesion. Many web communities instead engage individuals with activities that reinforce fragmentation and not by all means build bridges between users with different political preferences, cultural identities, and interests. This poses another external pressure on the issue of autonomy. Moreover, the relations between PSM and audiences in Poland have been characterized by significant asymmetry. Part of the problem lies in the fact that relations between PSM and society could hardly be institutionalized and that society is not an established actor as such (Jarren et al. 2001; Bardoel and d'Haenens 2008). The argument of the PSM's detachment from the audiences has been used during the legislative debates about the 2009 draft Act on Public Tasks in the Area of Audiovisual Services. Supporters of the 2009 draft Act agreed with critics that PSM, and in particular television, have been conveniently detached from their audiences and, despite relatively high viewing rates, were not able to build stable relations with their users and generate a common understanding of the public value of PSM. In this sense, a dominant dependence on commercial and political externalities has not been counterbalanced with audience or societal influence.

A new policy initiative: What future?

An alternative legal project was initiated by a group of journalists, film directors, artists and media producers with the primary aim to redistribute controlling power over the PSM in Poland. The draft Act on Public Service Media, submitted to the Ministry of Culture and National Heritage in the spring of 2010, substantially redefines the position of the Polish PSM in the broadcasting and regulatory environment. The law emphasizes the cultural role of PSM and opts for a replacement of political control with control by civil society and producers. The draft Act foresees the establishment of a specific regulator for the PSM, a Public Service Media Council (*Rada Mediów Publicznych*), which is to be nominated by a Public Service Media Committee (*Komitet Mediów Publicznych*) representing producers' and journalists' associations, universities and non-governmental organizations, but not politicians. This is an interesting bottom-up initiative – the first since 1989 – that addresses two issues important for the redefinition of the public service remit: cultural excellence and accountability to civil society rather than representative politics.

The future of PSM in Poland, however, remains uncertain. An eventual success of the 'civic draft act' would require some modifications concerning representative procedures and membership in relevant bodies. It will also heavily depend on political support, or a more prominent support of extra-political actors, including various social, professional and cultural organizations.

Conclusions

Basic-Hrvatin and Thompson (2008) observe that PSM take their shape and ethos from the states that sustain them. This is the case with MRAs too, and more specifically with the way how both domestic PSM and MRAs accommodate conditions of *autonomy* and *external dependency*. Some paradoxes and specificities that characterize the state of the evolving MRA and PSM in Poland are certainly also reflected in the operation of the state and the political system and in cultural and historical contexts. The table below summarizes some conditions and features of the four 'technical' dimensions of *autonomy* and *external dependency*.

As regards appointment procedures and management, the autonomy of both the KRRiT and PSM has, theoretically, benefited from legal safeguards. In practice, however, the KRRiT and PSM are interwoven into a complex set of relations with the political system, determined by political culture, democratic consolidation and political manners. The accountability dimension has been heavily dominated by instituting political dependencies through which the MRA's political accountability is ensured, not providing parity or stability

Table 7.5: Summary of autonomy and external dependency in the case of Poland.

	Autonomy	**External Dependency**
Appointment procedures and management (refers to both MRA and PSM)	– legal safeguards of autonomy	– high external dependency on political parties in power
Accountability (refers to both MRA and PSM)	– legal safeguards of administrative, political and legal accountability – lack of legal safeguards of social accountability	– high dominance of political accountability over administrative, legal and social accountability – external dependency on supervision by political institutions (especially the parliament and President)
Financial mechanisms (refers to PSM)	– legal safeguards of financing from licence fees	– high external dependency on commercial sources
Performance (refers to MRA and PSM)	– legal safeguards of autonomy at very general level	– political interferences into managerial and journalistic performance – programming dependence on commercial sources of funding

between administrative, legal and social accountability. In terms of financial mechanisms, over-reliance on advertising as source of financing has created tensions with the fulfilment of public service provision. The viewer loyalty and high advertising shares enjoyed by public service television has not been accompanied by a wide public consensus over its role or a willingness to contribute to its maintenance through the licence fees. This makes an important point about redirecting the considerations on PSM towards new normative suggestions, especially in terms of regaining the symbolic capital of the PSM and their relative weight in the entire media environment. Finally, the performance dimension has been characterized, on the one hand, by legal safeguards of autonomy, and on the other hand, by political interferences and programming dependence on commercial sources of funding.

The vibrant relation between *autonomy* and *external dependency* will determine the future of the MRA and PSM in Poland: this seems to be a point in time when critical decisions have to be made. The digital switchover and move of PSM into a new area of Internet services is likely to increase tensions between PSM and commercial media, and expose new external dependencies. These are likely to be pronounced more frequently at the EU level. An ostensible status quo can soon be challenged by those with whom PSM have tended to build a fragile equilibrium. Without a clear strategy seeking support and alliance with PSM users, considerable changes which PSM will have to undergo can bring an unpredictable result. The role of the political system will be crucial in this process, especially as regards the questions of PSM and MRA autonomy. There is certainly a demand for more autonomous PSM and, equally, a more autonomous MRA in Poland in the near future. The question would be: is this really a new demand or a demand centred on those aspects of public service provision and regulatory expectations that have long been neglected for financial or other reasons? 'Classical' public service purposes and regulatory expectations seem to be still valid. But they have to be filtered through new social conditions including among others increasing mobility and migration, virtual networking, social fragmentation, uncertainty and a lack of stabilization and global competitiveness, including competitiveness in the realm of cultures and ideas. These certainly pose new external dependencies, but also create competing forces that have a capacity to hold each other in check (especially when counterposing or reinforcing political realm, market and 'traditional' socio-cultural dependences), thus providing the very-much sought structural equilibrium between autonomy and external dependencies.

Notes

1   On conceptualization of 'autonomy' and 'independence' see also Chapter 1 in this book by Schulz.
2   See Chapter 2 in this book by Irion and Radu.
3   More on the application of the Weberian concept of rational-legal authority for the media system in Hallin and Mancini 2004.

4   The two remaining members are appointed as follows: one member is appointed by the Minister of Culture and National Heritage and one member is appointed by the Minister of State Treasury.

5   The two remaining members are appointed as follows: one member is appointed by the Minister of Culture and National Heritage and one member is appointed by the Minister of State Treasury.

6   One remaining member is appointed by the Minister of State Treasury acting in agreement with the Minister of Culture and National Heritage.

7   One of the largest multimedia corporations in Poland, which owns the flagship title *Gazeta Wyborcza*.

8   The Civic Platform party is a liberal conservative party, governing in Poland since the 2007 general election.

9   The Democratic Left Alliance is a left-wing social-democratic party.

10   More on clientelism in: Halin and Mancini 2004: 37.

11   In 2009, the work on a Draft Act on Public Tasks in the Area of Audiovisual Media Services was completed. The Act stipulated that the licence fee will be withdrawn and public service activities will be covered directly from the state budget (Art. 17.2). Despite protests by international organizations (including a reaction by Miklos Haraszti, the then OSCE Representative on Freedom of the Media) and a highly polarized discussion with involved parties in Poland, the draft Act was passed by the Parliament (24 June 2009). However, the former President Lech Kaczyński vetoed the Act (17 July 2009), and the governing party (Civic Platform) was not able to gather the 2/3s of MPs necessary to overturn the President's veto in September 2009. As a result, the whole policy initiative failed.

12   Article 18 (2) of the 1992 Broadcasting Act stipulates that: 'Programmes or other broadcasts shall respect the religious beliefs of the public and the Christian system of values.'

13   Radio Maryja has been part of a Catholic media network led by a Redemptorist Order.

References

Ackerman, J. M. (2005), 'Social Accountability in the Public Sector: A Conceptual Discussion' in *Social Development Papers, Participation and Civic Engagement*, No. 82.

Arendt, H. (1958), *The Human Condition*, Chicago: The University of Chicago Press.

Bardoel, J. and d'Haenens, L. (2008), 'Reinventing Public Service Broadcasting in Europe: Prospects, Promises and Problems', *Media, Culture and Society*, 30: 3, pp. 337–55.

Basic-Hrvatin, S. and Thompson, M. (2008), 'Public Service Broadcasting in Plural and Divided Societies', in S. Basic-Hrvatin, M. Thompson and T. Jusić (eds.), *Divided They Fall: Public Service Broadcasting in Multiethnic States*, Sarajevo: Mediacentar, pp. 8–40.

Blind, P. K. (2011), 'Accountability in Public Service Delivery: A Multidisciplinary Review of the Concept', in DMB/DPADM/UNDESA, *Expert Group Meeting Engaging Citizens to Enhance Public Service Accountability and Prevent Corruption in the Delivery of Public Services*, 7–8 and 11–13 July, Vienna.

Blumler, J. G. and Hoffmann-Reim, W. (2002), 'New Roles for Public Service Television', in D. McQuail (ed.) *McQuail's Reader in Mass Communication Theory*, London: Sage Publications, pp. 201–10.

Castells, M. (2009), *Communication Power*, Oxford: Oxford University Press.

Council of Europe (1996), *Recommendation No. R (96) 10 of the Committee of Ministers to Member States on the Guarantee of the Independence of Public Service Broadcasting*, 11 September 1996.

Council of Europe (2007), *Recommendation Rec (2007)3 of the Committee of Ministers to Member States on the Remit of Public Service Media in Information Society*, 31 January 2007.

Council of Europe (2008), *Resolution 1636 (2008) of the Parliamentary Assembly on Indicators for Media in a Democracy*, 3 October 2008.

Council of Europe (2009a), *Recommendation 1855 (2009) of the Parliamentary Assembly on the Regulation of Audiovisual Media Services*, 27 January 2009.

Council of Europe (2009b), *Recommendation 1878 (2009) of the Parliamentary Assembly on Funding of Public Service Broadcasting*, 25 June 2009.

European Parliament and the Council of the European Union (2010), Directive 2010/13/EU of 10 March 2010 on the coordination of certain provisions laid down by law, regulation or administrative action in Member States concerning the provision of audiovisual media services (Audiovisual Media Services Directive), Official Journal of the European Union of 18.12.2007 L 95/1.

Goetz, A. M. and Gaventa, J. (2001), 'Bringing Citizen Voice and Client Focus into Service Delivery', *Working Paper 138, Institute of Development Studies (IDS)*.

Graham, A., et al. (1999), *Public Purposes in Broadcasting: Funding the BBC*, Luton: University of Luton Press.

Habermas, J. (2006), 'Political Communication in Media Society: Does Democracy Still Enjoy and Epistemic Dimension? The Impact of Normative Theory on Empirical Research', *Communication Theory*, 16, pp. 411–26.

Hallin, D. C. and Mancini, P. (2004), *Comparing Media Systems: Three Models of Media and Politics*, Cambridge: Cambridge University Press.

Hans Bredow Institute for Media Research, Interdisciplinary Centre for Law & ICT (ICRI), Katholieke Universiteit Leuven; Center for Media and Communication Studies (CMCS), Central European University; Cullen International; Perspective Associates (eds., 2011), *INDIREG. Indicators for independence and efficient functioning of audio-visual media services regulatory bodies for the purpose of enforcing the rules in the AVMS Directive*, Study conducted on behalf of the European Commission, Final Report. February 2011.

Jakubowicz, K. (2004), 'Ideas in Our Heads: Introduction of PSB as Part of Media System Change in Central and Eastern Europe', *European Journal of Communication*, 19: 1, pp. 53–74.

Keane, J. (1991), *The Media and Democracy*, London: Polity.

Klimkiewicz, B. (2007), 'Poland', in L. d' Haenens and F. Saeys (eds.), *Western Broadcast Models: Structure, Conduct and Performance*, Berlin: Mouton de Gruyter, pp. 293–318.

KRRiT (1997), *Sprawozdanie KRRiT z rocznego okresu działalności/Annual Report*, http://www.krrit.gov.pl/bip/LinkClick.aspx?fileticket=KiOm0rcrJo0%3d&tabid=61. Accessed 28 May 2011.

KRRiT (2009), *Informacja o podstawowych problemach radiofonii i telewizjiw 2008 roku/ Information about basic issues of radio and television broadcasting 2008*, http://www.krrit.gov.pl/Data/Files/_public/Portals/0/sprawozdania/spr2009/informacja_za_2008.pdf. Accessed 7 September 2012.

KRRiT (2010), *Sprawozdanie KRRiT z działalności w 2010 roku/Annual Report 2010*, http://www.krrit.gov.pl/bip/LinkClick.aspx?fileticket=KiOm0rcrJo0%3d&tabid=61. Accessed 28 May 2011.

KRRiT (n.d.), *Informacja o podstawowych problemach radiofonii i telewizji w 1997, 1998, 1999, 2000, 2001, 2002, 2003, 2004, 2005, 2008, 2011 roku/Information about basic issues of radio and television broadcasting 1997, 1998, 1999, 2000, 2001, 2002, 2003, 2004, 2005, 2008, 2011*, http://www.krrit.gov.pl/krrit/informacje-o-krrit/sprawozdania. Accessed 28 May 2011.

Kublik, A. (2009), 'Abonament w dawnej formie został zabity. Już nigdy ludzie nie będą go płacić', *Gazeta Wyborcza*, Interview with Karol Jakubowicz, 29 July, p. 3.

McQuail, D. (1994), 'Mass Communication and the Public Interest: Towards Social Theory for Media Structure and Performance', in D. Crowley and D. Mitchell (eds.), *Communication Theory Today*, Stanford: Stanford University Press, pp. 235–53.

Meier, H. E. (2003), 'Beyond Convergence: Understanding Programming Strategies of Public Broadcasters in Competitive Environments', *European Journal of Communication*, 18, pp. 337–65.

Ociepka, B. (2003), *Dla kogo telewizja? Model publiczny w postkomunistycznej Europie Środkowej/ Who gets the television? The model of PSB in post-communist Central Europe*, Wrocław: Wydawnictwo Uniwersytetu Wrocławskiego.

The Sejm and Senate of the Republic of Poland (1993), Broadcasting Act (Ustawa o Radiofoniii Telewizji) adopted on 29 December 1992, Official Journal 1993, No 7, item 34, 1993, as amended, http://www.krrit.gov.pl/Data/Files/_public/pliki/office/broadcasting-act_10-08-2011.pdf. Accessed 5 January 2012.

The Sejm and Senate of the Republic of Poland (1997), The Constitution of the Republic of Poland (Konstytucja Rzeczypospolitej Polskiej) adopted on 2 April 1997, Official Journal 1997, No 78, item 483, Arts. 213–15, http://www.sejm.gov.pl/prawo/konst/angielski/kon1.htm. Accessed 5 January 2012.

The Sejm and Senate of the Republic of Poland (2005), Act on transformations and modifications to the division of tasks and powers of state bodies competent for communications and broadcasting (Ustawa o przekształceniach i zmianach w podziale zadań i kompetencji organów państwowych właściwych w sprawach łączności, radiofonii i telewizji) adopted on 29 December 2005, Official Journal 2005, No 267, item 2258.

Ward, D. (2008), 'The European Commission's State Aid Regime and Public Service Broadcasting', in D. Ward (ed.), *The European Union and the Culture Industries: Regulation and the Public Interest*, Aldershot: Ashgate, pp. 59–80.

Chapter 8

The independence of media regulatory authorities and the impact of the socio-political context: A comparative analysis of Greece and Italy

Evangelia Psychogiopoulou
Hellenic Foundation for European and Foreign Policy

Federica Casarosa
European University Institute

Anna Kandyla
Hellenic Foundation for European and Foreign Policy

Abstract

This chapter examines the independence of the media regulatory authorities in Greece and Italy from a comparative perspective. First, it focuses on the two country cases respectively, distinguishing between the formal and the actual independence of the regulators under study. Then it discusses in a comparative fashion the ways in which the regulators' formal and actual independence interrelate. The analysis shows that the legal frameworks governing the regulators under examination display significant variance. Despite such differences, however, there are ample opportunities, both in Greece and in Italy, for political forces to exert influence on the regulators. Regulatory independence has been undermined in both countries by the persistence of an essentially centralized model of regulation. This is characterized by robust state intervention in the field of the media, marked by highly politicized procedures, testifying to the central features of the polarized pluralist media system model defined by Hallin and Mancini (2004).

Keywords: independence, media regulatory authorities, status and powers, autonomy in decision making and knowledge, financial autonomy, transparency and accountability, formal and actual independence

Introduction

The increasing emphasis placed by the European Union (EU) on regulatory independence has revitalized debates on media governance in general and the independence of media regulatory authorities in particular. By recognizing the importance of national independent regulators for the impartial and transparent application of its provisions, the Audiovisual Media Services (AVMS) Directive has moved the issue of regulatory autonomy to the top of the media governance and policy agenda (European Parliament and the Council of the European Union 2010, recitals 94–95 and Art. 30). Although the AVMS Directive has simply confirmed the progressive recognition of independent regulators as a quasi-natural component of the institutional structures in most EU Member States for media regulation, its enactment has intensified discussion on the characteristics and principal features that render independent media authorities actually autonomous.

Independent media authorities have spread across Europe as the result of a growing consensus that media regulation needs to be firmly based on decisions that are insulated from external influence and control. As part of the research carried out for the MEDIADEM project, which is dedicated to the study of the media policy processes, institutional arrangements and regulatory tools that can best support free and independent media in Europe,[1] the purpose of this chapter is to investigate the independence of media regulatory authorities in Greece and Italy from a comparative perspective. Media regulation involves complex rule-making, rule-monitoring and enforcement functions, largely aimed at rendering effective the rights and freedoms inherent in media activity, namely freedom of expression and the right to information, upon which media freedom is founded. Prescriptions concerning the values and normative principles that the media should serve in the public interest are also to be embedded in media regulatory choices. Independent regulators are assumed to make a substantive contribution in this regard by ensuring that the regulatory process is freed from political, industry and other private interference, thus promoting 'better' regulation.

Drawing from the influential work of Hallin and Mancini, *Comparing Media Systems: Three Models of Media and Politics* (2004), Greece and Italy fall under the *Mediterranean model*, also known as the *polarized pluralist model*. According to Hallin and Mancini (2004), the two countries share a wide set of common characteristics, including media politicization and instrumentalization, low journalistic professionalization and strong state intervention in the development of the media and media regulation. Perhaps the principal shared feature of the media systems in Greece and Italy is the close ties of the media to the world of politics and the use of the media by both politicians and business interests in the pursuit of political or other particularistic ends (Psychogiopoulou, Anagnostou, and Kandyla 2011; Casarosa and Brogi 2011). Such a context presents a clear challenge for media regulation and regulatory independence more broadly. In a media system characterized by a wide range of political and business actors competing for influence, regulatory independence might not be a value that is fully endorsed in law and forcefully defended in practice. Political elites and business interests may indeed have both the incentives and the means to resist regulatory independence, so as to steer the operation of the media in ways that suit their purposes.

With a view to examining whether regulatory independence is a principle embedded in law and respected in reality, this chapter engages in a study of both the formal (*de jure*) and the actual (*de facto*) independence of the media regulators in the two countries reviewed.[2] In order to identify similarities but also possible differences across the countries under examination, the analysis builds on the findings of the INDIREG study and the key dimensions that it has identified for evaluating the 'risk of influence' on the workings of regulators (Hans Bredow Institute for Media Research, et al. 2011). In particular, the analysis addresses (1) the legal status of the authorities and their regulatory powers; (2) their autonomy in decision making and the knowledge they enjoy in the areas falling within their competence; (3) the funding arrangements made to support their activity; and (4) the transparency and accountability mechanisms that define their action, as elements of regulatory design and practice that have a bearing on the authorities' ability to fulfil their remit in an independent manner. The objective is not to measure the actual level of independence of the regulators, nor to engage in a ranking exercise of the two countries examined. Rather the purpose of this chapter is to verify whether the commonalities that the Greek and Italian media systems arguably display are also reflected in the ways in which their independent regulatory authorities are structured and operate in practice.

The analysis is structured as follows: before embarking on a discussion of the organization and actual performance of the media regulators under study, the basic structures for media regulation in Greece and Italy are presented, so as to position the independent regulators in the domestic institutional setting. The next sections focus on the two country cases respectively, distinguishing between the formal and the actual independence of the regulators reviewed. Findings feed the comparative analysis that follows. The chapter concludes with some remarks concerning the effects of the polarized pluralist features of the two media systems investigated on the ability of the regulators to secure themselves against potential influence.

Regulatory structures

Greece

The design of the Greek media policy is in the hands of the Secretariat General of Information and Communication – Secretariat General of Mass Media, currently under the auspices of the Minister of State, though technical issues pertaining to the electronic communications sector are addressed by the Ministry of Infrastructure, Transport and Networks. Contrary to the press, whose freedom is explicitly recognized in the Greek Constitution, the broadcast media are under the 'direct control of the state' (Art. 15(2) Const.). The exercise of this control, which inter alia targets 'the objective transmission, on equal terms, of information and news reports as well as works of literature and art' (Art. 15(2) Const.), is under the exclusive competence of the National Council for Radio and Television (Εθνικό Συμβούλιο Ραδιοτηλεόρασης, ESR). An independent administrative authority explicitly recognized by the Constitution (Art. 15(2) Const.), ESR has the mandate to ensure that both public and private television and radio broadcasters comply with domestic legislation and it can impose sanctions in case of violations. A set of regulatory powers for the electronic communications and media sectors have further been assigned to the National Telecommunications and Post Commission (Εθνική Επιτροπή Τηλεπικοινωνιών και Ταχυδρομείων) and the Hellenic Competition Commission (Επιτροπή Ανταγωνισμού). Although both bodies enjoy the status of an independent authority, albeit not constitutionally protected, the analysis focuses on ESR as the principal independent authority in charge of the audiovisual media sector.

Italy

The media policy agenda in Italy has traditionally been mostly in the hands of the Ministry of Economic Development, where the Department of Communications is located. The leading role played by the ministry has resulted in various legislative interventions, which however have not led to a comprehensive regulatory framework that is apt to properly coordinate the different media sectors (i.e. the press, broadcasting and online media). Only a few years ago did the Italian legislator succeed in codifying the patchwork of media legislation in a unique code, the Code of Audiovisual and Radio Media Services (*Testo unico dei servizi media audiovisivi e radiofonici*, Legislative decree 177/2005), but without making any modifications that would improve its coherence.

The previous stratification of regulatory intervention has been reflected in the existence of a number of regulatory bodies responsible for the implementation of the adopted rules. Efforts to re-organize and define their competences more clearly were made in the late 1990s, resulting in the creation of a 'converged' regulator. This new body, however, did not eliminate the pre-existing ones, which retained strategic, if limited, competences. Presently, the constellation of regulatory actors in the Italian framework includes the National Communications Authority (*Autorità Garante delle Comunicazioni*, AGCOM); the Parliamentary Committee for the general guidance and monitoring of radio and television broadcasting services (*Commissione Parlamentare per l'indirizzo generale e la vigilanza dei servizi radiotelevisivi*); the Regional Committees for Communication, which have delegated competences for monitoring audiovisual media programmes and updating the register of electronic and audiovisual communications operators; and the National Competition Authority (*Autorità Garante per la concorrenza*). Although all these bodies have competences in the field of communications, the analysis centres on AGCOM, which was created in 1997 as an independent body expressly recognized in law in order to ensure fair competition and to protect consumer rights in the electronic communications and audiovisual media sector (Art. 1(1), Law 249/1997 and Art. 2(3), Law 481/1995). For the purpose of this chapter the focus is on AGCOM's functions with regard to the Italian audiovisual media sector. Reference to other bodies is made only in the case of overlapping competences.

The Greek National Council for Radio and Television

Formal independence

Status and powers

The establishment of ESR as an independent body was brought about by the liberalization of the broadcasting market in the late 1980s (Law 1866/1989). Following the constitutional revision of 2001, ESR was one of five authorities[3] whose status as independent authorities was enshrined in the constitution. The constitution laid down common rules for their establishment and operation. It also rendered the authorities subject to parliamentary control (Art. 101A Const.), thus establishing a direct link with popular sovereignty, in accordance with the classic democratic principle that requires all bodies exercising state power to bear responsibility for their actions (Kamtsidou 2003: 144).

The constitutional provisions concerning the Greek independent authorities in general were specified by Law 3051/2002, whereas the powers and organizational features of ESR in particular were set out in several laws governing the audiovisual media sector. Domestic legislation makes clear that ESR is not subject to supervision, hierarchical control (whether preventive or repressive) or any monitoring by organs of the executive branch (Spyropoulos and Fortsakis 2009: 149). The authority enjoys legal personality and its decisions constitute executable administrative acts that are not subject to preceding control of legality (Kozyris 2003: 36), prior governmental intervention of any form, or overturn. They are only subject to judicial scrutiny by the Council of State (Art. 2(8), Law 3051/2002 and Art. 5(8), Law 2863/2000), the supreme administrative court in Greece.

In terms of competences, the current mandate of ESR includes the supervision of the broadcasters' compliance with domestic legislation regarding the pursuit of broadcast activities in general and the monitoring of compliance with broadcast content regulation in particular either *ex officio* or on the basis of alleged breaches. The authority is also charged with keeping records on media ownership (Art. 10(1)(a), Presidential Decree 213/1995 as inserted in Art. 1, Presidential Decree 310/1996 and Art. 8(1) and (2), Law 2644/1998), including for press undertakings and online news media enterprises (Art. 2(4)(d), Law 3310/2005 as amended), and examining compliance with media ownership legislation in the case of acquisitions (Art. 1(13) and 6(11), Law 2328/1995) and changes in broadcast media shareholding, which inter alia involves scrutiny of the operators' financial means. It should be noted that, while ESR is mandated to supervise compliance with media ownership legislation, the responsibility for the application of competition law in the electronic communications sector (including the assignment of obligations to operators with significant market power) has been bestowed to the National Telecommunications and Post Commission (Art. 12(a) and (f), Law 4070/2012). The Hellenic Competition Commission, for its part, applies competition rules in the media sector, through a sector-specific department (Art. 3(10), Law 3592/2007).

ESR is also responsible for licensing the radio and television channels transmitted by terrestrial and satellite networks in accordance with pre-defined criteria, as well as for renewing and revoking the licences.[4] It enjoys quasi-judicial powers through the imposition of sanctions on broadcast operators that violate the legislation pertaining to the operation of the broadcast media, or the codes of conduct adopted for programmes and advertisements and intellectual property rules (Art 4, Law 2328/1995 as in force and Art. 12, Law 2644/1998). The legislation allows the authority to decide among several types of sanctions and defines in broad terms the criteria upon which its decisions should be based: the severity of the infraction, the viewer or listener ratings of the programme concerned and the existence of previous infractions, among others. The various sanction instruments comprise, in degrees of severity: moral sanctions, including demands to broadcast specific announcements; recommendations to comply with domestic rules; fines; programme suspension and temporary suspension or revocation of licence. The authority also examines applications for redress in the case of offences against the protection of one's personality and human dignity (Art. 4(1)(f), Law 2863/2000), which are submitted to it in accordance with the procedure laid down in Art. 27 of Presidential Decree 109/2010 that transposed the AVMS Directive.[5]

ESR's rule-making competences focus on the drafting of codes of conduct for news and entertainment programmes and advertising spots in the broadcast media. The authority retains a consultative role by issuing directives, recommendations and expert opinions towards public and private bodies on the implementation of the laws and decrees relating to the broadcasting sector (Art. 4(2), Law 2863/2000). It is also entrusted with the task of delivering an opinion on the composition of the board of directors of the Greek public service broadcaster ERT (Art. 3(4), Law 1866/1989 as amended by Art. 1(2), Law 2173/1993) and concerning the coverage of national election campaigns in the broadcast media and the access of political parties and their candidates to them (Art. 5(2), Law 2173/1993). Furthermore, it is under duty to deliver an opinion on the Presidential Decree that regulates procedures and the applicable criteria for the licensing of content operators providing digital terrestrial television services in the context of the digital switchover, and the Presidential Decree determining the number of related licences available per type of reception (free-to-air or not), geographical reach (nationwide or regional) and programme content (informational or not) (Art. 13(4)-(5), Law 3592/2007 as amended by Art. 80, Law 4070/2012) (both pending).

Moreover, ESR enjoys the power to regulate its internal procedures by means of its own internal Rule. The internal Rule is drafted by the authority and ratified by ministerial act (Art. 5(1), Law 2863/2000 and Art. 2(7), Law 3051/2002). However, the power of the regulator to decide on its human resources and the organization of its services is rather limited. For such issues, the law stipulates that ESR has to submit a proposal to the Minister of Economy, who then decides accordingly, after having consulted the Minister of Interior, Decentralization and Electronic Governance (Art. (5), Law 3051/2002).

In the exercise of its duties, ESR may address questions to any public or private body. It may also request any kind of information related to the operation, administration and management of television and radio broadcasters (Arts. 1(17) and 6(16), Law 2328/1995, Art. 2(2)-(8), Law 2644/1998), and ask broadcasters for proof on payment of intellectual property royalties (Art. 6(6), Law 1866/1989, as replaced by Art. 1(24), Law 2328/1995).

Autonomy of decision making and knowledge
ESR is governed by a plenary (or board), consisting of a president, a vice-president and five members. Decisions are taken by majority. The constitution provides that the members of the ESR board are appointed for a fixed tenure (Art. 101A Const.), specified in law as of four years (Art. 3(2), Law 3051/2002), which can be renewed once, consecutively or not (Art. 101A Const. and Art. 2, Law 2863/2000). The selection of members is made by decision

of the Conference of Presidents of the Hellenic Parliament, a cross-party parliamentary college,[6] seeking unanimity or in any case the increased majority of 4/5 of its members. The appointment decision is then issued by the minister responsible for the media (presently the Minister of State) and published in the Official Journal of the Hellenic Republic. Pursuant to Art. 56(3)(b) of the constitution, the members of the ESR board may not stand for election, nor be elected to parliament. Law 2863/2000 further stipulates that the duties of a member of the ESR board and that of an administrative or scientific staff member are incompatible with a whole range of duties in government, parliament, political parties and the industry that is monitored by the authority (Arts. 3(3)–(4) and 6(4), Law 2863/2000). These incompatibility rules also apply for three years after completion of the term in office (Art. 3(4), Law 2863/2000).

The autonomy of ESR board members is also safeguarded by a set of provisions that offer protection against dismissal. The president, vice-president and other ESR board members can only be dismissed if they are found guilty in court for crimes against property, service or morals or any type of felony, if they are found in breach of duty, or in case of violation of the rules preventing conflicts of interest (Art. 3(2), Law 2863/2000 and Art. 3(4) and (6), Law 3051/2002). Dismissal lies with the competence of a disciplinary council, which is instituted by decision of the minister in charge of the media (Art. 3(5), Law 2863/2000). The law refers to individual members and does not specify whether dismissal of the whole board is possible.

The authority's internal Rule asserts that the members of the ESR board, in the exercise of their duties, shall be bound only by the law and their conscience (Art. 1, Ministerial Decision 20291/2002). With the exception of the president and the vice-president, who are both appointed for a fixed four-year term, the length of term of the remaining five members is chosen by a lot: three members are appointed for a three-year term, while the remaining two members are appointed for a four-year term (Art. 2(4), Law 2863/2000). For those members of the board who are appointed for a four-year term, no legal requirements are set to preclude the term of office from coinciding with the four-year election cycle. Membership is extended *ex officio* until the official publication of the appointment decision of new members. The president and vice-president are appointed full-time and on an exclusive basis (Art. 3(1), Law 2863/2000). During their term of office, the exercise of any other public service duty is suspended, and they are not allowed to engage in any professional activity, with or without payment, in either the public or the private sector. The remaining five members are employed full-time, though not on an exclusive basis, and are required to participate regularly in the work of ESR (Art. 3(1), Law 2863/2000).

Expert knowledge of the regulated industry enhances the ability of the board members and senior staff to resist external influence. As regards membership of the ESR board, the law determines in broad and general terms the professional expertise and qualifications required: ESR members must be distinguished scientists, professionals or public figures, coming mainly from sectors which are related in a direct or indirect manner to the authority's mission and powers (Art. 2(3), Law 2863/2000). For the scientific staff, the law does not set any such requirements; rather it delegates to the authority the power to decide on the necessary qualifications and experience required (Art. 6(3)(a), Law 2863/2000). The law foresees that, for matters that fall within the ESR's areas of competence, if the need arises to address issues that concern specific or wider social and professional groups, the authority may seek an opinion by the representative and collective bodies of these groups (Art. 4(3), Law 2863/2000). In the execution of its functions, ESR may also request the cooperation and assistance of any other, domestic or foreign, administrative or judicial authority (Art. 4(2), Law 2863/2000).

Financial autonomy

As regards its financial resources, ESR is exclusively funded by the state. The ESR president submits to the Minister of Economy an annual budget plan for approval (Art. 2(2), Law 3051/2002). The authority enjoys responsibility for the management of its budget, in line with a specific regulation that it drafts for that purpose and which needs to be approved by the Minister of Economy (Art. 2(2), Law 2863/2000 and Art. 2(3), Law 3051/2002).

Transparency and accountability

In order to establish a certain level of accountability towards political institutions, domestic legislation provides that the ESR's activities must be presented on an annual basis to parliament and also be communicated to the minister in charge of the media (Art. 4(4), Law 2863/2000). The authority's annual activity reports are subject to the approval of the parliament's plenary assembly. The Special Permanent Committee on Institutions and Transparency, a cross-party parliamentary committee working on issues of transparency in public life, reserves the right to invite the president or the members of the authority for a hearing on an ad hoc basis (Art. 43A of the Standing Orders of the Parliament). Domestic legislation also specifies that the decisions of the ESR board, adopted through open, nominative vote (Art. 5(6), Law 2863/2000), must be fully justified (Art. 5(7), Law 2863/2000) and be made available through the ESR website (as prescribed by Law 3861/2010).

One aspect of accountability concerns the actual scope of the parliamentary control to which ESR is subject. Due to the personal and functional independence safeguards enacted for the ESR board members, the parliament may only ask the authority to provide explanations for its acts before the competent parliamentary committee, without further consequences (Chrysogonos 2000).

Actual independence

Status and powers

The aforementioned constitutional and legal provisions seek to provide safeguards for the independence of ESR from the turbulence of everyday politics, and distance it from the industry it supervises. Nonetheless, the actual independence of the authority has been strongly challenged by the domestic socio-political conditions that have surrounded the development of Greek audiovisual media policy. Since the liberalization of the broadcasting market, the evolution of domestic audiovisual media policy has been marked by strong politicization and an interweaving of interests between the political elites and powerful media moguls (Psychogiopoulou, Anagnostou and Kandyla 2011: 8). In this context, the dominant political forces in the country have proven unwilling to release the broadcasting sector from their control and consequently, to strengthen ESR's position in the regulatory system. This is evidenced in several areas pertaining to ESR's structure and operation but is particularly reflected in the limited delegation of norm-setting powers to the authority.

In order to better understand the nature and effects of the limited rule-setting powers of ESR, it is essential to present some of the basic features of the domestic audiovisual media policy context. The liberalization of the domestic broadcasting market in the late 1980s was not only the outcome of international trends towards market liberalization, associated with the country's membership to the then European Economic Community; it was also the result of a major internal political crisis between the political parties Nea Dimokratia and PASOK (Papathanassopoulos 1997: 354), which also extended to the audiovisual media field. The inability of the government to respond promptly to the establishment and operation of illegal radio stations by local mayors that belonged to the opposition led to the de facto liberalization of the broadcasting market (Papathanassopoulos 1997: 355–356). Against this background, the establishment of ESR as an independent authority with the mandate to supervise the operation of the newly liberated sector and the public service broadcaster ERT was seen by many as aimed at surpassing the mutual distrust that had developed between the government and the opposition (Kamtsidou 1996: 650).

For some, the initial reluctance of the legislator to delegate norm-setting competences to ESR could be justified on the basis of the arguments advanced against the regulatory model of independent regulatory authorities in general, namely that the exercise of regulatory power by institutions which are not subject to administrative control is not consistent with the principles underpinning a democratic polity and in particular the principle of popular sovereignty (Karakostas 2005: 97). It seems, however, that the limited will of the Greek political elites to grant ESR norm-setting powers has largely stemmed from their particularistic attitude towards the broadcasting sector. Although ESR's task of carrying out 'direct state control over broadcasting' may be construed as involving the exercise of rule-making powers (Manitakis 2003), the role of ESR has been confined for the most part to the implementation of the broadcasting rules that the legislator adopts, that is, their application and monitoring (Karakostas 2005: 99). One of the consequences of this framework is that ESR has been unable, for instance, to license analogue broadcasters from 1995 until today (Anagnostou, Psychogiopoulou and Kandyla 2010: 263–264). The government has retained competences for determining the licensing requirements and procedures, and has enacted ambiguous, rather confusing rules, which have prevented ESR from fulfilling the licensing task. As it has been aptly explained in literature, the bad drafting of the rules was motivated by the desire of successive Greek governments to control the licensing process and hopefully secure positive coverage by the operators anticipating the award of a licence (Charalambis 2006: 131).

In the field of policy implementation, there are no instances of bodies other than courts having overturned the authority's decisions. Also there is no evidence to ascertain that political elites have sought to influence the decision-making practice of the authority. This is so despite the fact that strong ties between political party mechanisms and the public administration in general have traditionally developed in the country (Mouzelis 2003). What seems, however, to challenge the ability of ESR to act in an independent manner is the inconsistency of the rules pertaining to the broadcasting sector overall. The incoherence and complexity of the legal framework is a clear impediment to the ESR's operation and frequently undermines the authority's ability to fulfil its remit. Exemplifying this is that ESR does not engage in proper control of compliance with media ownership regulation (in case of acquisitions and changes in the composition of electronic media shareholding). This is because the legal acts that would have enabled the authority to investigate media ownership structures are either pending or remain inapplicable due to conflict with other legal provisions (such as the rules pertaining to tax secrecy), or because there are no international and bilateral agreements that would have enabled the collection of the necessary information from foreign authorities (ESR 2011: 16).

The limited powers ESR enjoys in deciding on its human resources and the organization of its services are another 'inhibiting factor' in its activity.[7] The lack of sufficient staff and information technology equipment challenges the authority's operational capacity, particularly due to the great number of audiovisual operators in the market, and renders it prone to regulatory capture due to information asymmetries. Although the issue has been continuously raised by ESR in its annual activity reports (ESR 2011: 12–13; 2010: 11–12), so far no action has been taken on behalf of the government. As a result, fundamental competences enjoyed by ESR cannot be properly exercised. For example, the authority is not able to develop a systematic strategy concerning the monitoring of the content aired by radio and TV channels, especially those operating at the regional/local level (Psychogiopoulou and Kandyla 2011a). Rather, the supervision of content requirements is carried out on an ad hoc basis, solely through the investigation of alleged breaches.

Autonomy in decision making and knowledge

Another important point relates to the mode of appointment of the ESR board members. The increased majority voting requirements set in law essentially mean that an agreement between the political party (or parties) in power and those in opposition is required. Such an agreement is expected to safeguard the board's independence from the government. In reality, however, the ability of the political parties in opposition to veto the nominations of their counterparts poses two kinds of challenges. First it enables the successive exclusion of the most suitable candidates, which usually have some kind of political affiliation (Koulouris 2007), thus limiting the pool of available candidates to persons with fewer qualifications. Second, appointments can be totally blocked (Koulouris 2007). The significant delays in the renewal and/or replacement of the ESR board members, whose term of office had long expired, brought the issue of the authority's independence centre stage in the late 2000s, when the then two dominant political parties, Nea Dimokratia and PASOK, criticized each other for inertia while at the same time engaging in lengthy back-door negotiations about the composition of the board (Galanis 2008; Chaimanta 2008). Notably, a recent decision of the Council of State ruled that the statutory provisions extending the board members' term of office beyond a reasonable period of time after the end of their term are unconstitutional (Council of State, decision no. 1098/2011). Unsurprisingly, such a decision raises much concern about the legality of the ESR decisions, as a significant number of them have been adopted during this 'interim', 'unreasonable' period and could therefore in principle be annulled (Oikonomou 2011). Elements that can further strengthen the politicization of the appointment procedure are the lack of transparency in the process of nomination. For instance, there is no public call for nominations, no hearing and no short-listing of candidates, all of which precludes a public deliberation on the nominees.

Moreover, as the qualifications required for membership are determined in broad and general terms, nominators can select individuals primarily on the basis of political criteria and affiliations. The importance of the board members' expertise for protecting their personal independence, especially from pressures from the regulated industry, is generally accepted. In Greece, however, while the law requires the fulfilment of certain qualifications and experience, it provides that these can be related in an *indirect* manner to ESR's mission, or even, be completely unrelated to ESR's mandate (Oikonomou 2004: 186).[8] In fact, an overview of the professional background of the persons who have served, or currently serve, as members of the ESR board shows that, with the exception of journalists, the presence of experienced professionals from the broadcasting sector has been minimal (187). It is also important to mention that although the law prescribes 'exclusivity' in employment for the president and the vice-president of ESR, it *omits* to do so for the other members of the board. So, in practice, these other members of the board can continue to exercise another profession in parallel (Oikonomou 2011), which might even involve engagement with the media sector. Bearing in mind that the disciplinary procedures for securing respect of the incompatibility rules described above lack efficiency, and that no standardized procedures for the required checks exist (Oikonomou 2004: 187), non-exclusivity can undermine the personal independence of the board members from the industry they supervise. The unavailability of public information as to whether ESR members are employed elsewhere in parallel undermines transparency and raises further concerns about their independence.

Financial autonomy

The independence of regulatory authorities is directly related to the autonomy they enjoy in determining and controlling their financial resources. Unlike other independent authorities in Greece whose financial autonomy is ensured through the collection of fees from the regulatees (the National Telecommunications and Post Commission, for instance), ESR is exclusively dependent on the state. The adequacy of its financing is actually reliant on the government's budget plan. Under the current severe economic crisis, cutbacks have been introduced, which have negatively affected the ESR's equipment infrastructure and software resources (ESR 2012: 36). Of relevance is also the fact that the authority cannot compensate the lack of adequate funding either through ad hoc state contributions or through funds from the fines imposed on broadcast operators that violate the legislation; the latter constitute state revenue and form part of the state budget.

Transparency and accountability

To counterbalance the lack of democratic legitimacy of independent regulators, independent authorities should apply enhanced accountability and transparency mechanisms in their decision making and overall activity. Concerning ESR's openness toward the public and stakeholders, the authority makes its annual activity reports and its decisions available through its website in a timely manner. However, its decisions usually do not contain any proper justification or analysis, although this is prescribed by law. Consultation procedures, which could promote transparency in ESR's activity, are not generally encouraged and applied, at least in the last five years or so (Psychogiopoulou and Kandyla, 2011b). Only recently, in January 2012, did the authority hold an open consultation, inviting stakeholders and the general public to submit their views on the appropriate labelling of music videos aired on television.

In terms of financial accountability, the lawfulness of the authority's expenditure is subject to an a priori and a posteriori audit by the Greek Court of Auditors (Art. 2(2), Law 2863/2000). So far, no instances of financial malpractice have been detected.

The Italian Communications Authority

Formal independence

Status and powers

Italy was one of the few EU countries without an independent authority, neither in communications nor in the broadcasting sector, up to the 1990s.[9] This absence allowed Italy, when it became necessary to implement EU law,[10] to be the forerunner in Europe by introducing a 'single' or 'converged' regulator for communications and the media. AGCOM is a powerful body with a remit for the whole communications sector. It was created by Law 249/1997 and is responsible for monitoring the press, broadcasting, new media and telecommunications. However, such a wide competence is not exclusively exercised, as many other bodies hold related competences, in particular the Department of Communications within the Ministry of Economic Development.

The independence and autonomy of AGCOM is recognized in legislation. Law 249/1997 provides that the authority will 'work with full autonomy and independence in its decisions and assessments' (Art. 1(1), Law 249/1997). This implies that there must be no interference by the political authorities in either the activity of AGCOM or its decisions. The fact that AGCOM is accountable to parliament also shows that the authority is linked to popular sovereignty and not to the executive. AGCOM's Ethical Code extends the requirement of independence, along with impartiality, privacy, diligence and loyalty, to the staff of the regulatory body as well (Art. 3(1), Delibera n. 577/10/cons).

AGCOM has legal personality and therefore can be declared responsible for its own acts and decisions. The law provides that AGCOM's decisions can be appealed before administrative courts, and in particular before the Regional Administrative Tribunal of Lazio, which enjoys exclusive and mandatory competence in this regard (Art. 1(26), Law 249/1997). Legislation has reduced procedural time-limits, allowing for the delivery of judgments with their motivations in an abridged form.[11] This applies also in the case of further appeals to the upper court, the Council of State.

AGCOM is required by law to carry out two distinct missions: to ensure fair competition in the market and to protect consumer rights. These two broad missions entail specific functions and responsibilities: monitoring the shift towards digital terrestrial television, applying antitrust laws to the communications sector (Montella 2004: 189), and monitoring broadcasting services in terms of quality and their compliance with the rules on advertising, political pluralism and the protection of minors.

AGCOM's remit covers both the electronic communications sector and the audiovisual media services sector. However, its internal governance system does not directly reflect this distinction. The legislator wanted to 'internalize' it and created two internal committees operating across sectors: the Infrastructures and Networks Committee and the Products and Services Committee. The two committees address the entire communications sector but have distinct powers. The Infrastructure and Networks Committee makes rather technical decisions. It is in charge of all operations relating to frequencies and interconnection: spectrum management, regulation and control over interconnection and access to telecommunications infrastructure, and definition of the subjective and objective elements of universal service (Art. 1(6)(a), Law 249/1997). The Products and Services Committee is more concerned with content quality. Its role is to ensure compliance with the rules concerning advertising limits, minors' protection, rectification and European quotas. Moreover, it is in charge of providing information about the audience rates of different media (Art. 1(6)(b), Law 249/1997). Both of these committees seek to protect users and operators alike.

Looking at the powers of AGCOM in terms of rule-making, monitoring and sanctioning, these depend on the existence of a delegation clause provided by a legislative act; otherwise AGCOM (as any other independent authority in Italy) would act *ultra vires*. AGCOM enjoys an autonomous rule-making power in relation to its internal organization (Art. 1(9), Law 249/1997). Its acts can address the committees' activities and functioning, as well as budgetary issues and cost management. Independent decision-making power is attributed to AGCOM in two other cases: first, with regard to the creation of an alternative dispute resolution system for conflicts between viewers and licensed operators or between different licensed operators; second, in relation to the rules regarding telecommunications and broadcasting licences (Art. 1(5)(c)(5), Law 249/1997). In this case, the regulations adopted by AGCOM must define the requirements and the procedures for the attribution of licences and authorizations, their duration, and the obligations regarding interconnection, access and provision of universal services, endorsing the principles defined by law, namely objectivity, transparency, non-discrimination and proportionality (Art. 1(2), Law Decree 545/1996, converted into Law 650/1996). Such regulations are proposed to the Department of Communications, which presents them to the Chambers of the Parliament, and if no opinion is provided within the time limit set by law by the parliament they are enacted and implemented by the Department of Communications.

In several cases, AGCOM implements acts enacted by other bodies by adopting practical rules. Concerning radio spectrum management, for instance, AGCOM must provide an opinion on the general frequencies distribution scheme defined by the Department of Communications. As soon as such a scheme is approved by the department, AGCOM must draft and approve the frequencies allocation plan. This requires international coordination in order to harmonize and have a compatible use of resources with neighbouring countries.

With regard to technological innovations, AGCOM provides consulting and advice services to the government (Art. 1(6)(c)(3), Law 249/1997). It can also promote research and studies that might form the basis of legislative intervention, especially in the communications sector or for the development of new media services. Moreover, AGCOM provides mandatory but not binding opinions on competition and misleading advertising in the electronic communications sector to the National Competition Authority.

Concerning its monitoring powers, AGCOM is in charge of verifying compliance with antitrust rules and has a specific mandate over conflict of interest legislation regarding cases of incompatibility between the role of public officer and other positions in the media market (Law 215/2005 in relation to the Delibera n. 220/08/Cons). Competition powers are exercised in collaboration with the National Competition Authority. This authority enjoys the power to start competition proceedings, while AGCOM has only consultative powers in such proceedings. Of greater importance, in terms of (both *ex ante* and *ex post*) monitoring and potential sanctioning powers, is AGCOM's function of defining markets in the telecommunications sector. AGCOM has not only defined various markets, i.e. the access and interconnection markets, but has also imposed asymmetrical obligations concerning transparency, non-discrimination, prices, etc. on major operators, so as to improve the competitive level in the defined sub-markets. A recent addition to its competences is the possibility for AGCOM to accept commitments made by companies under its scrutiny with the objective of enhancing competition in network provision and in electronic communication services (Law decree 223/2006, converted into Law 248/2006, Art. 14-*bis*. and Delibera n. 645/06/Cons, modified by delibera n. 131/08/Cons), following the similar practice of the National Competition Authority.

Another monitoring function of AGCOM that requires attention concerns the public service broadcaster RAI. Each year AGCOM provides a report on RAI's compliance with its contractual obligations, as set out in the service contract negotiated between the

Department of Communications and RAI's Board of Directors. This includes general and specific provisions regarding programme type and quality. AGCOM also monitors compliance with the annual objectives set for RAI by the Parliamentary Committee for the general guidance and monitoring of radio and television broadcasting services,[12] which, however, are not particularly detailed and therefore leave AGCOM much leeway to evaluate their achievement.

AGCOM also holds wide-ranging sanctioning powers (Delibera n. 136/06/Cons, modified by delibera n. 130/08/Cons). The sanctions applied are proportional to the gravity of the violation, and range from administrative sanctions of a financial nature to more severe sanctions such as the withdrawal of telecommunications and broadcasting licences for up to ten days.[13]

As regards its internal organization, AGCOM, as mentioned above, enjoys delegated powers to decide on the issue (Delibera n. 453/03/Cons).[14] In 1998, it issued the *Regulation on the organization and management* (hereinafter ROM), in order to define its internal governance structure. The regulation, which has been regularly updated, has a wide scope. It clarifies the internal AGCOM directorates, their competences and budget allocation, cost management issues, hiring procedures and the allocation of staff activities, as well as the rules applicable to proceedings before AGCOM.

Autonomy in decision making and knowledge
The internal structure of AGCOM consists of four main bodies: the President, the Council (composed by the President and four Commissioners), and the two committees mentioned above, the Infrastructures and Networks Committee, and the Products and Services Committee (composed respectively by the President and two Commissioners).

The selection process is different for the President and the Commissioners. The President of AGCOM is nominated by the President of the Republic upon suggestion of the Head of Government, with the approval of the Ministry of Development. The parliamentary committees that are competent in the communication sector must also give their consent with a 2/3 majority vote of their members. The Commissioners are selected by the two Chambers of the Parliament (two each) and appointed by presidential decree. Each member of the parliament must put forward two names, one for each of the AGCOM committees. This process was purposely devised to keep an even distribution between the members selected from the majority and the opposition in parliament. Given that the AGCOM members are appointed for seven-year terms, their appointment does not coincide with the election cycle.

The law does not provide for staggered appointments or for the renewal of the mandate of any member of AGCOM. Regarding dismissal, the President of AGCOM can be substituted upon decision of the President of the Republic, and individual Commissioners can be substituted upon decision of the President of the respective Chambers of the Parliament (Art. 1(3), Law 249/1997). A dismissal of the entire board is not envisaged by law. Dismissal can be justified on the basis of the incompatibility clauses provided by law: both the President and the Commissioners cannot exercise any other professional activity or institutional function for the duration of their term of office. In addition, they cannot enjoy any representative role in political parties (Art. 2(9), Law 481/1995). Potential conflicts of interest with stakeholders are more strictly regulated, as the law requires the President and the Commissioners to refrain from collaborating, consulting or establishing a working relationship with companies operating in their field of competence during their term of office but also for four years after its termination. In the latter case, if breaches occur, financial sanctions can be imposed both on the Commissioners and on the President and the media company.[15]

All AGCOM bodies have autonomous decision-making power. In the case of the President, this is an extraordinary decision-making function, and any decision must be ratified by the Council (Art. 3(3), ROM, Delibera n. 17/98/Cons). The President also convenes the meetings of the other AGCOM bodies, sets the agenda, directs their work and supervises the implementation of the decisions taken (Art. 3(1), ROM). The President's important role is also reflected in the decision-making rules. Any decision of the Council and the two committees must be based on a majority vote (abstentions do not count), with no secret voting, except for exceptional and justified cases. In the case of an equal number of votes, the vote of the President prevails. The Council is the main reference body for appointing AGCOM's personnel and monitoring its activity. Appointments take place for a limited duration of two years (with possible renewal up to the end of the Council's term of office).

The criteria set by law for the appointment of the President and the Commissioners generally refer to a 'person with high professional reputation and expertise in the field' (Art. 2(8), Law 481/1995). The law does not provide further specifications or required qualifications and does not explain how the necessary expertise is to be verified. The same criteria are also required for AGCOM's internal staff. The law is again vague regarding the specific qualifications that are 'needed to exercise each task' (Art. 1 (20), Law 249/1997).

In the exercise of its duties, AGCOM may cooperate with other bodies, either at the national or the international level. At the national level, the law provides for specific cases of cooperation, in particular with other independent regulatory authorities, namely the National Competition Authority and the Data Protection Authority. At the international level, the law encourages cooperation (Art. 33 ROM).

Financial autonomy

Concerning the finances of AGCOM, the law initially provided for public funding of its management costs. However, the situation changed in 2006 when funding was extremely reduced and the cost burden shifted to the stakeholders, i.e. the media and electronic communication companies. Each year, AGCOM defines the amount of private funding, with a maximum ceiling set at 2‰ of the revenues of the last approved budget of the companies concerned. The amount of private contribution is determined by a decision of the authority, respecting the limits provided by law. The law does not provide any obligations of cost orientation (Art. 1(65), (66) and (68), Law 266/2005).

Transparency and accountability

AGCOM is bound by the ROM to observe the principles of transparency, participation and adversarial procedure (Art. 29, ROM). All AGCOM decisions must therefore be justified (Art. 3, Law n. 241/1990) and any administrative act by AGCOM, including regulations and decisions, must become publicly available through publication in the Official Gazette and also on AGCOM's website (Art. 10-bis, ROM). AGCOM also issues a bimonthly bulletin (in electronic and paper form) in order to provide information about its most recent activities. Hearings take place as a general rule behind closed doors but the ROM allows for the conduct of public hearings subject to prior decision (Art. 10(2), ROM).

All AGCOM activities are presented on an annual basis to parliament. These include regulatory, monitoring and enforcement activities, as well as administrative and management actions. However, reporting on AGCOM's activities does not involve any approval or the possibility for parliament to require any revisions or modifications. Financial auditing is foreseen (Art. 2, n. 26, L. 481/1990), and it is carried out by an auditing committee composed of judges and university professors. The final balance is subject to the control of the Court of Auditors.

Actual independence

Status and powers

In order to understand the socio-political environment in which AGCOM functions it is important to present some of the features that characterize Italian media policy. First, it should be emphasized that the development of the national media system has always had a political connotation (Casarosa 2010: 274; Hanretty 2010: 86; Hibberd 2006), both in the press and then in the broadcasting sectors. In recent years, the interaction between media corporations and political authorities has become particularly pronounced, as the former Head of Government was the media tycoon Silvio Berlusconi, who still owns – yet no longer runs directly – a large corporation involved in each stage of media production and distribution (Balbi and Prario 2010: 893). In such a framework, the creation of an independent authority was viewed as a way to depart from the existing enmeshment of political authorities and the media industry, attributing to the new body the power to regulate and control sensitive issues in the communications sector without interference from politics or the industry. However, although AGCOM's independence is clearly declared by law, actual independence is not fully achieved. Various aspects indeed demonstrate this.

As regards AGCOM's regulatory powers, the law provides specific powers to AGCOM which are clearly defined but in some cases lack a coherent structure. This is due to the fact that a limited number of competences are shared between AGCOM and other bodies. Although the trend is to increase the tasks and powers allocated to AGCOM, the current distribution of competences may hamper the independence of AGCOM in its decision-making power. This is because, in most cases, the concurrent competent bodies are clearly politically biased. With regard to frequency spectrum allocation, for example, or the monitoring of RAI, the implicated bodies are the Department of Communications and the Parliamentary Committee for the general guidance and monitoring of radio and television broadcasting services. The objectives pursued by AGCOM and these bodies, though in theory converging, could be conflicting in practice, leaving AGCOM a limited space to decide autonomously on sensitive issues. One example of a possible deadlock of competences is provided by the recent case decided by the Court of Justice of the European Union[16] and also by the European Court of Human Rights,[17] involving a media outlet, Centro Europa 7, which in spite of obtaining a licence had never had the opportunity to broadcast due to lack of radio frequencies. The Department of Communications had opened a bid for national television concessions. Centro Europa 7 was successful, but the concession granted by the Department of Communications was not followed by the allocation of the required radio frequencies, which AGCOM was responsible for, as the frequencies were being used by another broadcaster, Rete4 within the RTL-Mediaset group. AGCOM, which was also in charge of defining the time at which the frequencies would be withdrawn from Rete4, as the operator's activity exceeded the anti-concentration cap established by domestic legislation,[18] delayed the transfer of frequencies up to the end of 2003. This allowed the legislator to intervene with the adoption of Law 112/2004, which provided for a further delay in view of the forthcoming switch-over from analogue to digital terrestrial broadcasting (Mazzoleni and Vigevani 2005: p. 893).

Another example sheds light on the importance of providing a system of checks and balances in relation to AGCOM's regulatory activity. The regulatory powers of AGCOM over audiovisual media services are based on Art. 1(8) of the Code of Audiovisual and Radio Media Services, as amended by legislative decree 44/2010, which implemented the AVMS Directive in Italy. This article covers expressly the audiovisual media service providers, as defined by the EU directive. However, AGCOM's regulatory proposal concerning copyright protection has extended its scope to ISPs as well,[19] and has provided for an alternative 'notice and take-down' procedure focused on copyright violations. AGCOM initially asserted that it enjoyed the competence for such a proposal on the basis of the *combinato disposto* of the national legislative implementation of the E-Commerce Directive,[20] the AVMS Directive and the domestic law on collecting societies, and thus sought to bypass the role of the legislator. In the end, however, it acknowledged the need for a legislative intervention that would provide it with a clear delegation of regulatory power over ISPs (Nicotra and Ventriglia 2011: 116; Calabrò 2012: 24).

It is clear that independence from political powers should in principle allow AGCOM to pursue its objectives without undue influence. However, such independence should not be detached from a certain level of accountability, given that AGCOM, as any other independent authority, is not directly responsible to either citizens or elected officials (Gilardi 2008). The introduction of specific limits to the regulatory power of AGCOM serves to overcome this democratic deficit. Relevant limits take the form of a specific delegation of regulatory power to AGCOM. It is only through such delegation that the intervention of AGCOM in the communications sector can be justified.

Generally speaking, the powers allocated to AGCOM by law have been used, and no instances of AGCOM decisions being overturned by a body other than court have occurred. Criticism, however, has been raised regarding the exercise of AGCOM's supervisory powers, in particular as regards the monitoring over politicians' presence on television (Zaccaria 2011: 215). Here the problem is not the absence of control, but the absence of systematic organization of the data gathered. This would have enabled the verification of possible breaches of the principle of internal pluralism in public and commercial broadcasting, which may justify the adoption of sanctioning measures.

In terms of internal organization and human resources, AGCOM enjoys a sufficient number of people to fulfil its tasks and duties. No concerns whatsoever have been raised in this respect.

Autonomy in decision making and knowledge

Much criticism has been expressed in relation to the organizational structure of AGCOM, in particular as regards appointment procedures. The procedures as provided by law can, in fact, impair the functioning of the independent authority. This can occur through the reproduction of existing conflicts between the political parties in parliament within the authority, especially since AGCOM's members are appointed in a way that seeks to keep an even distribution between the members selected from the majority and those selected by the opposition in parliament.[21] As a consequence of this, there is a risk of tied votes, in which case a decisive role lies with the AGCOM President, who is appointed on the basis of a joint proposal of the Head of Government and the Ministry of Economic Development and thus represents the government (Mazzoleni and Vigevani 2005: 888). A concurrent problem of political involvement is raised by the direct contacts that exist between the members of AGCOM and the political parties that proposed them (Perez 2002: passim; Marino 2007: 140), although some claim that the appointment procedure strengthens the ability of AGCOM to take into account all the positions of the political debate in its decisions (Carlassare 1999). Moreover, given that potential candidates are not disclosed in advance, the process lacks transparency.[22]

Academics have proposed changes to the appointment procedure aimed at countering the dependence on politics. In particular, it has been suggested to reduce the number of Commissioners and to place responsibility for the selection of Commissioners with the President of the Republic, the Presidents of the two Chambers of the Parliament, the President of the Constitutional Court and the Labour and Economy National Committee, while leaving the selection of the AGCOM President to AGCOM's members (Bruno and Nava 2006: 149).

While there has been no case in AGCOM's recent history of a single member being dismissed for non-objective grounds or the entire board being dismissed, a recent case confirms that a revision of the legal framework is needed, as the link between the executive power and AGCOM is far from hypothetical. The case involved former Head of Government, Silvio Berlusconi, and one of the members of the Council of AGCOM (selected by the majority party). Silvio Berlusconi repeatedly called this member of the Council, asking him to intervene and eventually close down a television show, which allegedly contested the activity of the executive power and the Head of Government – i.e. Berlusconi himself. As soon as the content of the telephone calls was made public, the member of AGCOM resigned, before the start of any disciplinary proceedings, and he was substituted by a new member of the same political orientation (Il Fatto quotidiano 2011). In the aftermath of this case, the current president of AGCOM underlined the need for a revision of the rules governing the appointment procedure, together with those provided by the third EU Electronic Communication package,[23] so as to exclude any further attempt to undermine the authority's independence (AGCOM 2011b).

The criteria concerning the expertise required of the AGCOM members can also conflict with the objective of ensuring their personal independence. Expertise is a requirement that is set by law in order to select individuals that have a wide knowledge and experience, and are therefore able to identify and address the most relevant issues raised in the communications sector. However, the requirement of expertise can have possible side-effects on the independence of members, as expertise is mostly acquired when engaging with the sector, which – apart from academic research – is usually based on a working relationship with the relevant market players (either as a consultant or as an employee). Thus any individual chosen could have a personal background that relates him/her with media corporations and this could influence perceptions, though no cases of clear misbehaviour have been acknowledged up to now.[24] The alternative option of mandating an external body to verify the level of expertise of the selected members could be given consideration but again it is of limited practical significance; such a solution would only duplicate the need of having to verify the independence and autonomy of those who control the controllers (Donati 2007: 56).

Financial autonomy

Given that AGCOM determines most of its budget on a yearly basis itself, the funds are usually commensurate to the needs of the authority. The financial autonomy AGCOM enjoys enables financial stability over time and protects the authority from financial pressures.

Transparency and accountability

As regards transparency and accountability, it should be acknowledged that AGCOM has always complied with the obligation to publish motivated decisions,[25] a periodical bulletin and annual reports. External auditing control has never revealed any financial malpractice. However, the consultation practice of the authority might provide some reason for concern. The following example is particularly relevant. Exercising its authority to organize public consultations, AGCOM recently drafted a market study which involved over fifty market actors, which it invited to provide comments in order to present their needs in terms of online content distribution. The result of this study was the publication of a White Paper (AGCOM 2011a), which was coordinated with another market study on the related issue of copyright protection in the online environment (AGCOM 2010). AGCOM excluded civil society organizations from the consultation process, taking into account only the views of content producers and ISPs. The uneven balance in attention paid to the interests of stakeholders and the interests of citizens, which AGCOM must also protect in accordance with its remit, might be explained by the fact that the authority is mainly funded by media and telecommunications companies. Subsequently, AGCOM adopted a more participative approach, launching a public consultation on the content of the proposed regulatory intervention. However, the timing of the consultation did not enhance participation, and the consultation was based on strict criteria regarding the bodies that could submit observations.

Independent media regulatory authorities in Greece and Italy: An assessment

Status and powers

It is the government and, naturally, national parliaments that retain the power to draft legislation and set the statutory framework concerning the organizational design and competences of domestic independent media authorities. Legislation conditions the nature and degree of the authorities' independent behaviour, as independent performance largely depends on how much power the government and the political parties represented in parliament are willing to delegate, in what issue areas, and for what reasons, and on the ways in which these powers will be put in use. Admittedly, even when the legal framework abides by standards of genuine independence, governments, political elites and private interests may still try to pursue their partisan goals by interfering in the authorities' activity via use of informal means. From this perspective, it is clear that formal and actual independence must not be confounded; the latter is only partly determined by the former (Hans Bredow Institute for Media Research, et al. 2011: 48).

The preceding analysis reveals that both the Greek ESR and the Italian AGCOM are formally recognized as independent authorities. Their independence is affirmed in legislation, and extends to both functional independence and the personal independence of the authorities' members. Clearly, the constitutional recognition of ESR as an independent authority provides a higher level of protection, as it ensures that abolishment or changes in ESR's independent status require a complex constitutional amendment rather than the parliamentary majority that would be sufficient to pass a statutory law (Flessas 2007: 5).

Both ESR and AGCOM enjoy a wide set of competences, including rule-monitoring, enforcement, consultative and to some extent rule-setting functions. The responsibilities of AGCOM are more extensive, as the Italian authority is a 'converged' regulator, responsible for the communications sector in its entirety. AGCOM enjoys a broad mission, which incorporates a variety of tasks in the pursuit of two principal objectives: guaranteeing fair competition and protecting citizens' and consumers' rights. ESR is more constrained in its activity. It has no anti-trust functions, it does not regulate the electronic communications sector and it is not driven by a general aim of catering to citizens' and consumers' needs. Its activity is primarily restricted to monitoring compliance of operators with domestic broadcasting legislation and imposing sanctions in case of violations. Such differences in remit due to convergence, however, are not strictly related to, and do not appear to have a bearing on, the ability of regulators to perform in an autonomous manner as regards the regulation and oversight of audiovisual media services.

Delegated rule-setting powers that enable the adoption of general rules, that is, the adoption of rules that do not principally serve to simply specify the rules enacted by the legislator but rather engage in genuine decision making, are for the most part limited for both authorities. For instance, ESR is responsible for licensing the audiovisual sector, but in doing so it must respect the pre-defined criteria set by domestic legislation, both regarding the conditions that licensees need to fulfil and relevant licence allocation procedures, and regarding the number of licences available. ESR enjoys mere consultative powers on these aspects and final decision rests with the executive: the President of the Hellenic Republic through the adoption of a presidential decree and the minister responsible for the media through the adoption of a ministerial act, respectively (Art. 13, Law 3592/2007 as amended by Art. 80, Law 4070/2012). AGCOM enjoys the power to adopt regulations defining the requirements and procedures for the licensing of audiovisual media services providers. However, such regulations need to be proposed to the Department of Communications, which enacts and implements them if no changes are suggested in parliament within a specific period of time. The constrained delegation of norm-setting powers points to the unwillingness of the legislator to reinforce the authorities' mandate by handing over substantive decision-making functions. This arguably testifies to the resolve of the political elites in power to maintain a more or less centralized model of regulation regarding crucial audiovisual media policy decisions.

The preference for a centralized regulatory model can be explained by the fact that the media systems in both countries have been strongly marked by politicization and the development of robust ties between major media corporations and political elites. Independent authorities have been partly created to break with this tradition but have not been particularly successful in coping with the determination of successive governments to keep the audiovisual media market (or parts thereof) under control. In the case of Greece, the strong interconnection of the political forces with the world of the media has resulted in an incomprehensible legal framework that has substantially complicated the functioning of ESR. Successive political majorities in parliament have adopted incoherent, essentially contradictory rules – an attempt to keep the media in check and at the same time satisfy their media favourites – which has undermined the ability of ESR to properly discharge its duties. The limited powers assigned to ESR as regards the organization of its services and human resources, coupled with the excessive number of audiovisual media services providers under its purview, have exacerbated the situation. In the case of Italy, AGCOM has been established as an independent regulator with the power to determine autonomously its organizational structure but it has been required to coordinate with the executive or other politicized bodies (i.e. the Department of Communications under the auspices of the Ministry of Economic Development and the Parliamentary Committee for the general guidance and monitoring of radio and television broadcasting services) in order to fulfil its duties. The issue is not only one of a deadlock of competences that can thwart autonomous behaviour; it is also about being systematically exposed to potential political pressure, which could increase vulnerability to political interference. The analysis also shows that AGCOM has occasionally sought to expand its remit, transgressing the scope of its activities and sidelining the legislator. Whether this was driven by political motivation, resistance to political pressure for the adoption (or non-adoption) of a specific regulatory approach, regulatory capture or simply AGCOM's willingness to address regulatory challenges posed by convergence is nonetheless unclear.

Autonomy of decision making and knowledge

The legal framework governing the authorities' composition displays variance with implications for the level of independence they formally enjoy. Appointment, which takes place for a fixed tenure in both countries reviewed, generally rests on solid parliamentary majorities, in order to preclude an excessive influence being exerted by a single political party (commonly the party in power) over the selection. However, there are instances where the legislator has allowed the executive a wide margin of manoeuvring. For instance, the procedure for the nomination of the president of AGCOM is clearly driven by the executive. In Greece, a practice of staggered appointments is followed, which is not the case in Italy. On the other hand, in Italy, the term of office of the members of the regulator is longer but cannot be renewed. Despite these differences, what both countries seem to share are the limited checks built into the system in order to ensure transparent processes: there is no public hearing of candidates, no requirements for the competent bodies to justify the selection made and in the case of Italy, not even *ex ante* disclosure of the candidates' identity. This facilitates the politicization of appointments and undermines public scrutiny.

With a view to shielding the authorities' behaviour from political, executive or industry influence, various incompatibility provisions have been enacted in both countries, which, in fact, exceed the term of office of the individuals concerned. Moreover, a series of legislative provisions seek to protect the authorities' members from unwarranted removal. Besides resignation or expiry of remit, grounds for removal in the case of Greece range from the member being found guilty of a crime to violation of the rules preventing conflicts of interest or breach of duty. Breach of duty raises particular concerns in terms of the procedural safeguards in place to preclude arbitrary use. To guarantee an independent assessment, dismissal requires a decision by a disciplinary council that consists of high-ranked judges and public law university professors.

Notwithstanding the legal safeguards enacted, opportunities for the exercise of undue influence on the authorities' decision-making practice exist. Of relevance is the distinction drawn between the president and the vice-president of ESR on the one hand, and the regulator's other board members on the other. Contrary to the former, the latter are not employed on an exclusive basis. Simultaneous professional activity is thus possible and may jeopardise the independent performance of the tasks and duties assigned by law. True, the incompatibility provisions set by domestic legislation seek to break any links with the regulated sector, prohibiting board membership for the owners, shareholders, members of the management board or the employees of an enterprise falling directly or indirectly under the competences of ESR. However, supervisory procedures are lax and not systematized, while ways to circumvent the law exist. Moreover, in both countries, the loose definition of requirements regarding expertise and professional background can undermine resistance against improper influence, though the argument has equally been made that the requirement of expertise itself might work to the detriment of regulatory independence, since expertise is usually acquired through engagement with the sector.

The stance of the political elites towards the regulators has been controversial. In Greece, the replacement and/or renewal of the mandate of ESR board members encountered significant delays, due to the inability of the dominant political parties in parliament to reach agreement on the individuals that should become members of the authority. Not only should the persons selected enjoy the mutual support of the government and the main political party in opposition – a venture which proved extremely complex – but in addition, ESR board members who had been highly critical of the government for past media policy decisions needed to be removed. In the absence of an easy compromise, the political forces opted to postpone the selection of new members. This was a strategic move, largely aimed at impairing ESR's position in the regulatory system in general. The authority had to function for more than 20 months (June 2006 – February 2008) with a semi-legal composition, which devalued its activity, damaged its public profile and, quite importantly, placed the legitimacy of its decisions under significant strain.

In Italy, on most occasions, the nomination and appointment of AGCOM board members led to highly politicized procedures, with targeted efforts deployed by the political parties involved to select members that could represent their political positions within the authority. This has served to reproduce the party structures in parliament within AGCOM's Council and Committees, creating fertile ground for the establishment of direct contacts between the selected individuals and the political parties that supported their selection. The press has widely reported instances in which AGCOM was 'offered' sanctioning directions by politicians, including former Head of Government Silvio Berlusconi, who repeatedly called on the authority to intervene in cases of negative media coverage of his government.

Financial autonomy

Turning to funding, ESR is exclusively funded by the state. This contrasts with the funding arrangements made for AGCOM, which relies on both public finances and contributions from the electronic communications and audiovisual media services providers. The annual budget of ESR requires the executive's approval, which might serve as a means to reward the authority for politically motivated decisions or penalize it for their absence. Conversely, AGCOM, whose budget stems from different sources of income, with annual contributions from operators of different regulated sectors representing the main source of its revenues, enjoys financial independence. Financial autonomy is further strengthened by the ability of AGCOM to decide on its internal organization and ensuing budget allocation.

Perhaps a major concern regarding the regulators' financial independence presently derives from the harsh economic conditions affecting both countries reviewed. The economic crisis plaguing Greece and the austerity measures the government has recently adopted all but ensure that ESR will suffer substantive cutbacks in its finances. The government's efforts to diminish public spending might not only seriously undermine the authority's operational capacity, but also render it particularly vulnerable to political pressure in return for financial backup and support. A similar scenario might apply in Italy, which also experiences the effects of the economic crisis, though in a milder way. The AGCOM budget is calculated on the basis of the revenues of the last approved budget of media and electronic communication undertakings, which could be negatively affected by the economic downturn.

Transparency and accountability

Competence assignment goes hand in hand with the introduction of accountability and transparency mechanisms in both countries. Requirements include publishing decisions and their reasoning, making available other informational material in a periodic manner and reporting to parliament. Financial discipline must also be respected. AGCOM generally fulfils its transparency obligations, providing wide-ranging information on its activities, though hearings usually take place behind closed doors. ESR respects its publication requirements both offline and online but its decisions often lack sufficient reasoning and adequate analysis. In both countries, parliamentary control does not entail parliamentary interference in the activities of the authorities in terms of overturning decisions or requiring changes in decision making. Financial scrutiny has not disclosed any instances of maladministration.

AGCOM has a developed practice of organizing consultations, yet has shown a predisposition towards prioritizing the interests of the regulatees over those of citizens that also need to be protected in line with its remit. This might indicate a risk of regulatory capture by the industry, which might be explained by the fact that the authority's funding primarily stems from the industry. ESR has so far refrained from using consultations as a tool, either for information collection purposes or for strengthening its accountability towards the regulatees and citizens more broadly.

Conclusion

Given the strong interconnection between politics, business and the media, and the need to guarantee the effective exercise of fundamental rights such as freedom of expression and the right to information through the media, the creation and safeguarding of an independent media regulatory environment has been essential in both Greece and Italy. Institutional structures for media regulation have therefore been enriched with the establishment of ESR and AGCOM, whose independence has been affirmed in law, reaching constitutional rank in the case of Greece. Concurrently, various measures have been enacted to ensure that relevant bodies keep distance from the political elites and the industry they regulate. On this basis, it would be fair to conclude that independence has been recognized as an overarching principle that should guide the activities of the regulators.

Despite the fact that formal independence has been a value expressly recognized in law, the legal framework pertaining to the institutional and organizational set-up of ESR and AGCOM varies considerably. Italy has instituted a 'converged' regulator, taking due consideration of the regulatory challenges in the increasingly converged media environment, whereas Greece has preferred an audiovisual media-focused regulator. Besides differences in the definition and delineation of the authorities' missions, different institutional and decision-making structures have been mandated, different funding models have been followed, and different degrees of autonomy in internal organization have been granted, though both regulators have been required to be transparent in their activity and make use of a variety of accountability mechanisms to ensure good governance and respect of their remit. Procedures for the appointment of the authorities' members have also differed, although in both countries insufficient safeguards with respect to the transparency of the nomination and appointment process and the required expertise and qualifications of the individuals selected are creating conditions encouraging the politicization of appointments.

Despite the differences between the legal frameworks, the analysis has shown that there are many ways in the two countries examined, especially for the political forces, to exert influence on the regulators. Impediments to the autonomous behaviour of ESR and AGCOM do not only arise on account of the shortcomings of the legal frameworks, important as these may be. They are also the result of the prevailing domestic style of government and administration, with strong state intervention in the field of the media (as in other sectors of the economy) and media regulation, marked by highly politicized procedures. A central feature of the polarized pluralist media system model defined by Hallin and Mancini (2004) is indeed the important role of the state in the media's organization. Polarized pluralist systems are characterized by a tradition of state intervention in matters of media ownership, media funding and media regulation, which is further associated with the development of clientelist relationships and the instrumentalization of the media by the government, the political parties and industrialists with political ties. In such systems, regulatory independence and the establishment of independent regulatory authorities in particular, present a clear challenge to the role of the state as the 'primary definer' of the media system, a role that the state, in both Greece and Italy, has not been willing to let wither. This explains the resistance to delegate substantive norm-setting powers to the regulators and the willingness to maintain a more or less centralized model of decision making in both countries, including by requiring the cooperation and coordination of the regulators with the executive and parliamentary bodies, as the case of Italy shows.

The determination of the state to keep its central role in media regulation has also been reflected in appointment procedures and the ways in which these have been carried out. In Greece, marked politicization eventually led to the marginalization of the regulator in the domestic media policy setting. ESR has been progressively assigned new duties and competences but political parties, unable to reach an agreement on its composition, delayed the renewal and/or replacement of its members, constraining the authority to operate with a semi-legal composition for a considerable period of time. This has not only placed the legality of the authority's decisions under risk but has also damaged its public profile. In Italy, the unwillingness of the state to relinquish its grip over the media has also been reflected in highly politicized appointment procedures, which have allowed political parties to duplicate the parliament's composition within the authority, so as to maintain in an indirect way their prominent role in media regulation. This has allowed political elites in the country, including the Head of Government himself, to seek to direct AGCOM's activities, providing guidelines concerning the way in which things should be done.

To mitigate politicization, it is evident that careful attention must be given to introducing, through appropriate legal amendments, more transparent and open nomination and appointment procedures, encouraging increased public scrutiny. Of course, resistance to pressure ultimately depends on the professional ethos and formation of all those staffing the regulators, efficient management and strict respect for impartiality: all the virtues hailed as an internal culture of independence. Autonomous behaviour can be bolstered through appropriate training and managerial practices that resiliently reject biased behaviour. Counteracting risks to regulatory independence indeed needs to be a continuous, uninterrupted task that, first and foremost, enjoys the firm commitment of the regulators themselves.

Notes

1 See Chapter 1 by Schulz for an introduction of the MEDIADEM research project.
2 The differentiation between formal and actual independence is explained in detail in Chapter 5 in this book by Dreyer.

3   The other four are the Authority for the Protection of Personal Data, the Ombudsman, the Authority for the Protection of Communication Security and Privacy and the Higher Council for the Selection of Personnel.

4   Greece is presently undergoing a transitional phase preceding the definitive switchover to digital terrestrial television. During this period, the TV operators already established on the market were allowed to transmit their programmes in both analogue and digital mode. National broadcasters were required to submit a declaration to ESR for that purpose whilst regional and local operators had to have their programmes checked by ESR. ESR also approves the programme of broadband broadcasters.

5   The provisions of Presidential Decree 109/2010 pertain to TV broadcasting only. Similar provisions in relation to radio broadcasting were incorporated in Presidential Decree 100/2000, which was repealed by Presidential Decree 109/2010. According to ESR, the relevant provisions of Presidential Decree 100/2000 continue to apply until the enactment of new rules concerning the exercise of the right of redress with regard to radio broadcasting. See ESR, Directive 1/12.7.2011, point 46.

6   The Conference of Presidents of the Hellenic Parliament consists of the Speaker of Parliament, the Deputy Speakers, former Speakers (who retain a seat), the presidents of the Parliamentary Standing Committees, the president of the Special Permanent Committee on Institutions and Transparency, the presidents of each of the parliament's political parties and a representative of independent MPs.

7   Note for instance that the ministerial decision concerning the organization of ESR's services (specified by Art. 2(5), Law 3052/2002) was issued with significant delay in 2009 (Ministerial Decision 2/95354/0021). ESR had submitted its proposal as early as the beginning of 2003 (Oikonomou 2004).

8   Note the use of the adverb 'mainly' in Article 2(3) Law 2863/2000.

9   Monitoring functions were originally assigned to the Parliamentary Monitoring Committee, which subsequently became the Parliamentary Committee for the general guidance and monitoring of radio and television broadcasting services. In 1990 a first, yet unsuccessful, attempt was made to create an independent authority: the Guarantor for Broadcasting and Publication (Mazzoleni and Vigevani 2004: 884).

10 Since the end of the 1980s, the EU institutions introduced a set of directives where legislative power was delegated to independent authorities in different fields. In the communications sector, it was Directive 97/13/EC which provided for the creation of a national independent authority that would be competent for the attribution and monitoring of broadcasting licences, whereas Directive 2002/21/EC [the Framework Directive] clarified the criteria to assess the independence as well as the role and competences of the relevant authority. Although the requirements of autonomy and independence were emphasised, they were not expressly defined in legislation (Ottow 2011).

11 Judgments generally consist of the judges' decision and their motivation. In Italian proceedings, a judicial decision may not immediately provide the reasoning of the judges, which can follow several weeks later.

12 The Parliamentary Committee for the general guidance and monitoring of radio and television broadcasting services was created by Law 103/1975 in order to define and monitor compliance

with public broadcasting principles, such as pluralism, fairness, completeness and impartiality of information. It only focuses on the public service broadcaster, RAI. It does not provide a detailed definition of the objectives to be met by RAI on an annual basis, so as not to limit freedom of expression, and enhance competition with private broadcasters (Casarosa 2010).

13 Note that in general, AGCOM's sanctions concerning breaches of antitrust regulation have been limited and have rather sought to safeguard the *status quo*, particularly in the broadcasting sector.

14 In relation to its organization, AGCOM is not bound by the *ex ante* control of the Council of State and the *ex post* legitimacy control.

15 Domestic legislation also provides for confidentiality in the exercise of the authority's activity given the status of members as public officials (Art. 1 (10) Law 249/1997).

16 European Court of Justice, Case C-380/05, *Centro Europa 7 Srl v Ministero delle Comunicazioni e Autorità per le garanzie nelle comunicazioni and Direzione generale per le concessioni e le autorizzazioni del Ministero delle Comunicazioni*, 31 August 2008, ERC 2008 I-00349.

17 European Court of Human Rights (Grand Chamber), *Centro Europa 7 and Di Stefano v Italy*, 7 June 2012, judgment no. 38433/09.

18 Art. 2 (6) of Law 249/1997 provided that any media company could own no more than 20 per cent of the analogue television channels available, in other words no more than two channels.

19 See in the same sense the extension of scope to radio service providers that have editorial control over the content that is broadcast, despite the fact that no mention of these providers is made in the Code of Audiovisual and Radio Media Services or in the EU directive that were the bases of AGCOM's proposal.

20 Directive 2000/31/EC of the European Parliament and of the Council of 8 June 2000 on certain legal aspects of information society services, in particular electronic commerce, in the internal market (Directive on electronic commerce), Official Journal L 178, 17/7/2001, p. 1.

21 This is usually referred to as a form of 'lottizzazione'. This term was first applied to Italian public service broadcasting, indicating the attribution of managerial positions in each broadcasting channel to individuals belonging to a specific political party. The use of the term was then extended to any case of clientelist forms of political patronage (Mancini 2009).

22 It should be mentioned that this is not an issue limited to AGCOM, as other independent authorities are also subject to similar rules. Recently, the issue has also been addressed by a citizens' coalition (the Open Media coalition). The coalition advocated a more transparent process of selection that does not move the power of designation away from the members of parliament but requires them to disclose the identity of the proposed members, informing citizens about their competences and their views and approaches on the most critical issues in each sector.

23 Directive 2009/140/EC of the European Parliament and of the Council of 25 November 2009 amending Directives 2002/21/EC on a common regulatory framework for electronic communications networks and services, 2002/19/EC on access to, and interconnection of, electronic communications networks and associated facilities, and 2002/20/EC on the authorisation of electronic communications networks and services, Official Journal L 337, 18/12/2009, p. 37.

24 Although in general expertise is an element that strengthens independence (Thatcher 2002), in the Italian framework, in view of the strong interconnection between political and media representatives, the criterion of expertise could be exploited for the selection of members that share the views of the designating political party.

25 Art. 10-bis (5) ROM provides that after five years, sanctioning decisions should be only available through a specific section of the AGCOM website, which should not be accessible by means of external search engines.

References

AGCOM (2010), *Indagine conoscitiva – Il diritto d'autore sulle reti di comunicazione elettronica/ Survey – Copyright in electronic communication networks*, 12 February 2010, http://www. agcom.it/default.aspx?DocID=3790. Accessed 12 March 2012.

AGCOM (2011a), *Libro Bianco sui contenuti/White book on contents*, 21 January 2011, http:// www.agcom.it/default.aspx?DocID=5558. Accessed 12 March 2012.

AGCOM (2011b), *Speech of the AGCOM president*, http://www.agcom.it/Default.aspx?message= downloadpdf&DocID=125. Accessed 12 March 2012.

Anagnostou, D., Psychogiopoulou, E. and Kandyla, A. (2010), *Media policies and regulatory practices in a selected set of European countries, the EU and the Council of Europe: The case of Greece*, Background information report for the Mediadem project, http://www.mediadem. eliamep.gr/wp-content/uploads/2010/05/Greece.pdf, p. 237. Accessed 12 March 2012.

Balbi, G. and Prario, B. (2010), 'The History of Fininvest/Mediaset's Media Strategy: 30 Years of Politics, the Market, Technology and Italian Society', *Media, Culture and Society*, 32: 3, pp. 391–409.

Bruno, F. and Nava, G. (2006), *Il nuovo ordinamento delle comunicazioni. Radiotelevisione, comunicazioni elettroniche, editoria/The New Communications Regulation. Broadcasting, Electronic Communications, the Press*, Milano: Giuffrè.

Calabrò, A. (2012), *Bilancio di mandato 2005–2012 – Presentazione del Presidente dell'Autorità Corrado Calabrò/Report for the mandate 2005–2012 – Presentation of the Agcom President Corrado Calabrò*, 2 May 2012, Roma: AGCOM, http://www.agcom.it/Default.aspx?message= visualizzadocument&DocID=8612. Accessed 7 August 2012.

Carlassare, R. (1999), 'Gli organi di governo del sistema/The Governing Bodies of the System', in R. Zaccaria (ed.), *Informazione e telecomunicazioni/Information and telecommunications*, Padova: Cedam, pp. 119–146.

Casarosa, F. (2010), 'The case of Italy', in *Media Policies and Regulatory Practices in a Selected Set of European Countries, the EU and the Council of Europe*, Background information report for the MEDIADEM project, http://www.mediadem.eliamep.gr/wp-content/uploads/2010/05/ BIR.pdf. Accessed 12 March 2012.

Casarosa, F., and Brogi, E. (2011), *Does media policy promote media freedom and independence? The case of Italy*, Case study report for the MEDIADEM project. http://www.mediadem. eliamep.gr/wp-content/uploads/2012/01/Italy.pdf. Accessed 5 March 2012.

Chaimanta, S. (2008), 'Νέο ΕΣΡ με τον ίδιο πρόεδρο/New ESR with the Same President', *Έθνος/ Ethnos*, 15 February, http://www.ethnos.gr/article.asp?catid=22733&subid=2&pubid=47646 7. Accessed 5 March 2012.

Charalambis, D. (2006), 'Ελευθερία της έκφρασης, πλουραλισμός και διαφάνεια στον χώρο των ηλεκτρονικών ΜΜΕ – Η ελληνική εμπειρία/Freedom of Expression, Pluralism and Transparency in the Field of Electronic Mass Media – The Greek Experience', in A. D. Tsevas (ed.), *Διασφάλιση του πλουραλισμού και έλεγχος της συγκέντρωσης στα μέσα ενημέρωσης/Ensuring pluralism and controlling concentration in the media*, Athens: Nomiki Vivliothiki, pp. 129–138.

Chrysogonos. K. (2000), 'Οι ανεξάρτητες αρχές στο σχέδιο της επιτροπής αναθεώρησης του Συντάγματος/The Independent Authorities in the Draft of the Constitution Revision

Committee', *To Σύνταγμα/The Constitution*, 2, http://tosyntagma.ant-sakkoulas.gr/afieromata/ item.php?id=123. Accessed 5 March 2012.

Donati, F. (2007), *L'ordinamento amministrativo delle comunicazioni/The Administrative Regulation of Communications*, Torino: Giappichelli.

ESR (2012), *Έκθεση πεπραγμένων 2011/Annual Report 2011*, http://www.esr.gr. Accessed 5 March 2012.

ESR (2011), *Έκθεση πεπραγμένων 2010/Annual Report 2010*, http://www.esr.gr. Accessed 5 March 2012.

ESR (2010), *Έκθεση πεπραγμένων 2009/Annual Report 2009*, http://www.esr.gr. Accessed 5 March 2012.

European Parliament and the Council of the European Union (2010), Directive 2010/13/EU of the European Parliament and of the Council of 10 March 2010 on the coordination of certain provisions laid down by law, regulation or administrative action in Member States concerning the provision of audiovisual media services (Audiovisual Media Services Directive), *Official Journal of the European Union* of 15.4.2010 L 95/1.

Il Fatto quotidiano (2011), 'Pressioni di Berlusconi per chiudere Annozero, la procura chiede l'archiviazione/Pressures by Berlusconi to Close Down Annozero, the Attorney Asks for Dismissal', *Il Fatto quotidiano*, 27 October, http://www.ilfattoquotidiano.it/2011/10/27/ pressioni-di-berlusconi-per-chiudere-annozero-la-procura-chiede-larchiviazione/166797/. Accessed 12 March 2012.

Flessas, P.G. (2007), 'From New to Better Governance? Practical Considerations of Independence with Regard to Certain Greek Independent Authorities', in Association of Greek Constitutionalists, *VIIth World Congress of the International Association of Constitutional Law*, Athens, Greece, 11–15 June, http://www.enelsyn.gr/papers/w16/Paper%20by%20 Panagiotis%20G.%20Flessas.pdf. Accessed 5 March 2012.

Galanis, D. (2008), 'Στα όρια της νομιμότητας το ΕΣΡ/ESR reaches the limits of legality', *To Βήμα/ To Vima*, 13 January, http://www.tovima.gr/relatedarticles/article/?aid=186183. Accessed 5 March 2012.

Gilardi, F. (2008), *Delegation in the Regulatory State: Independent Regulatory Agencies in Western Europe*, Northampton, MA: Edward Elgar.

Hallin, D.C. and Mancini, P. (2004), *Comparing Media Systems: Three Models of Media and Politics*, Cambridge: Cambridge University Press.

Hanretty, C. (2010), 'The Italian Media between Market and Politics', in A. Mammone and G. A. Veltri (eds.), *Italy Today: The Sick Man of Europe*, London: Routledge, pp. 85–98.

Hans Bredow Institute for Media Research; Interdisciplinary Centre for Law & ICT (ICRI), Katholieke Universiteit Leuven; Center for Media and Communication Studies (CMCS), Central European University; Cullen International; Perspective Associates (eds., 2011), *INDIREG. Indicators for independence and efficient functioning of audio-visual media services regulatory bodies for the purpose of enforcing the rules in the AVMS Directive*, Study conducted on behalf of the European Commission, Final Report. February 2011.

Hibberd, M. (2006), 'Silvio Berlusconi and the Media in Italy: Conflicts of Interest', *West European Politics*, 30: 4, pp. 881–902.

Kamtsidou, I. (2003), 'Σκέψεις σχετικά με τις θεσμικές και πολιτικές διαστάσεις της ανεξαρτησίας των ανεξάρτητων αρχών/Thoughts on the Institutional and Political Aspects of the Independence of Independent Authorities', in P.I Kozyris and S. Meglidou (eds.), *Η ανεξαρτησία των ανεξάρτητων αρχών. Προβληματισμοί και ελπίδες ενός νέου θεσμού/The independence of independent authorities. Reflections and hopes for a new institution*, Athens: N. Sakkoulas, pp. 141–147.

Kamtsidou, I. (1996), 'Η αναζήτηση του θεμελίου της ρυθμιστικής εξουσίας του Εθνικού Συμβουλίου Ραδιοτηλεόρασης μεταξύ των άρθρων 43 παρ. 2 και 15 του Συντάγματος/The search for the foundation of the regulatory power of the National Council for Radio and Television between Articles 43(2) and 15 of the Constitution', Το Σύνταγμα/*The Constitution*, 3, pp. 645–666.

Karakostas, I. (2005), *Το δίκαιο των ΜΜΕ/Mass Media Law*, 3rd ed., Athens: Ant. Sakkoulas.

Koulouris, N.D. (2007), 'Μην χαϊδεύετε αλλά και μην πυροβολείτε τις ανεξάρτητες αρχές/Do not pat but do not shoot the independent authorities', *Καθημερινή/Kathimerini*, 12 August, http://news.kathimerini.gr/4dcgi/_w_articles_economy_2_12/08/2007_237480. Accessed 5 March 2012.

Kozyris. P. I. (2003), 'Η "ανεξαρτησία" των ανεξάρτητων αρχών στην Ελλάδα – Προβλήματα και προοπτικές/The 'independence' of independent authorities in Greece – Problems and prospects', in P.I Kozyris and S. Meglidou (eds.), *Η ανεξαρτησία των ανεξάρτητων αρχών. Προβληματισμοί και ελπίδες ενός νέου θεσμού/The independence of independent authorities. Reflections and hopes for a new institution*, Athens: N. Sakkoulas, pp. 25–40.

Mancini, P. (2009), *Elogio della lottizzazione – La via italiana al pluralismo/Praise to lottizzazione – The Italian way to pluralism*, Roma: Laterza.

Manitakis, A. (2003), 'Ο άμεσος έλεγχος του κράτους στη ραδιο-τηλεόραση δια του ΕΣΡ μπορεί να συνεπάγεται και άσκηση κανονιστικών αρμοδιοτήτων/The exercise of state control over radio and television by ESR may entail the exercise of regulatory competences', Το Σύνταγμα/ *The Constitution*, 29: 3, pp. 573–582, http://tosyntagma.ant-sakkoulas.gr/theoria/print.php? id=884. Accessed 5 March 2012.

Marino, G. M. (2007), 'Gli organismi di controllo/The Monitoring Bodies', in S. Sica and V. Zeno-Zencovich, *Manuale di diritto dell'informazione e della comunicazione/Manual of Information and Communications Law*, Padova: Cedam, pp. 136–47.

Mazzoleni, G., and Vigevani, G. (2005), 'Italy', in Open Society Institute (ed.), *Television Across Europe: Regulation, Policy and Independence*, Vol. 2, Budapest: Open Society Institute, pp. 865–954.

Montella, G. (2004), 'La collaborazione dell'Autorità per le garanzie nelle comunicazioni all'attuazione della disciplina comunitaria/The Cooperation of Agcom in the Implementation of Community Law', in M. Manetti (ed.), *Europa e Informazione – Quaderni della Rassegna di diritto pubblico europeo/ /Europe and Information – Notes on the Review of European Public Law*, Napoli: ESI, pp. 189–200.

Mouzelis, N. (2003), 'Γιατί αποτυγχάνουν οι μεταρρυθμίσεις/Why all reforms fail', Το Βήμα/*To Vima*, 29 June, http://www.tovima.gr/opinions/article/?aid=152249. Accessed 5 March 2012.

Nicotra, L., and Ventriglia, F. (2011), 'Agcom, il rischio di *regulatory capture* e il ruolo del Parlamento italiano nella regolamentazione del diritto d'autore/Agcom, the Risk of Regulatory Capture and the Role of the Italian Parliament in Copyright Regulation', in F. Sarzana di

Sant'Ippolito (ed.), *Libro bianco su diritti d'autore e diritti fondamentali nella rete internet/ White book on copyright and fundamental rights online*, Roma: Fakepress, pp. 114–152, http://www.fulviosarzana.it/wp-content/uploads/2011/06/libro_bianco_fakepress.pdf. Accessed 12 March 2012.

Oikonomou, A. (2011), 'Το ΕΣΡ στο επίκεντρο κρίσιμων αποφάσεων/ESR at the Centre of Crucial Decisions', *Καθημερινή/Kathimerini*, 15 May 2011.

Oikonomou, A. (2004), 'Εθνικό Συμβούλιο Ραδιοτηλεόρασης: Τρείς ανεκπλήρωτες προϋποθέσεις για την αποτελεσματική λειτουργία του ως ανεξάρτητης αρχής/National Council for Radio and Television: Three unfulfilled requirements for its effective functioning as an independent authority', 2, pp. 185–191.

Ottow, A. (2011), 'The independence of regulatory authorities', in European University Institute, *Mediadem conference – Pluralism and competition*, Florence, Italy, 10–11 November 2011.

Papathanassopoulos, S. (1997), 'The Politics and the Effects of the Deregulation of the Greek Television', *European Journal of Communication*, 12: 3, pp. 351–368.

Perez, R. (2002), *Telecomunicazioni e concorrenza/Telecommunications and Competition*, Milan: Giuffre

Psychogiopoulou, E., Anagnostou D. and Kandyla, A. (2011), *Does media policy promote media freedom and independence? The case of Greece*, Case study report for the MEDIADEM project, http://www.mediadem.eliamep.gr/wp-content/uploads/2012/01/Greece.pdf. Accessed 5 March 2012.

Psychogiopoulou, E, and Kandyla, A. (2011a), *Interview with Officer at the National Council for Radio and Television on the Role and Functions of the National Council of Radio and Television*, 18 May 2011.

Psychogiopoulou, E, and Kandyla, A. (2011b), *Interview with Officer at the National Council for Radio and Television on the Activity of the National Council of Radio and Television*, 14 September 2011.

Spyropoulos, P.C., and Fortsakis, T. (2009), *Constitutional Law in Greece*, Kluwer Law International/Ant N. Sakkoulas: Alphen aan den Rijn.

Thatcher, M. (2002), 'Regulation after Delegation: Independent Regulatory Agencies in Europe', *Journal of European Public Policy*, 9: 6, pp. 954–972.

Zaccaria, R., and Valastro, A. (2011), *Il diritto dell'informazione e della comunicazione/Information and Communications Law*, Padova: Cedam.

Chapter 9

Does the complexity of institutional structures in federal states influence the independence of AVM regulatory authorities? A review of the cases of Germany and Belgium

Pierre-François Docquir[1], Sebastian Müller[2] and Christoph Gusy
University of Bielefeld

Abstract

This chapter looks into the formal and actual independence of the audiovisual media regulatory authorities in Germany and Belgium. A description and critical analysis of national situations precedes a comparative analysis. The choice of these two countries allows an investigation into the consequences that the federal institutional structure of both States may exert over the actual independence of media regulatory bodies. In the current state of scientific research, however, we conclude that it remains hard to tell whether or how the complexity of a federal state weighs on the issue of the independence of its regulatory authorities. We also look into the effectiveness of the independence of the regulatory bodies. In that respect, the relative scarcity of existing research has to be acknowledged. In such context, we endeavour to advance critical suggestions that, we hope, will help carve further research questions.

Keywords: Audiovisual Media Services Directive, Belgium, commercial broadcasting, European Commission, Germany, public service broadcasting, regulatory authority, three-step-test

Introduction

In the lexical field of television series and soap operas, this chapter would be called a 'crossover', something that happens when characters belonging to one fictional universe make appearances in a different show. Crossovers – such at least is generally the wish of the writers – increase the amusement of the audience by widening the background setting of the show, thus extending the range of possible interactions between characters and plots from both universes. To be sure, the present text would belong to the genre of 'scientific crossover', as its authors are partners in the FP-7 MEDIADEM research project who have been invited to contribute to a volume that derives from the INDIREG research programme (Hans Bredow Institute for Media Research, et al. 2011). These research projects and their objectives and approach are introduced in Chapter 1 of this book by Schulz. Most grateful for the invitation to tackle the issue of the independence of media regulatory authorities, we endeavour to broach the topic from the perspective and existing results of MEDIADEM.[3] Looking into the independence of the regulators thus constitutes an extension of our ongoing work, and joins the core preoccupations of INDIREG (Hans Bredow Institute for Media Research, et al. 2011).

In this chapter, we present the existing framework regarding the independence of audiovisual media regulatory authorities in two countries and then attempt to draw lessons from a comparative analysis. At first sight, there is little doubt that Germany and Belgium appear to be very different countries, if only in the size of their respective media landscapes. However, as we observed from research during the preparation of MEDIADEM reports, two characteristics of these countries justify a comparison between the neighbouring states. In the first place, their federal structure[4] appears generally to be a complicating factor in the development of media policy. In the second place, more specifically, both countries have a number of regulatory authorities that exert jurisdiction over regional media landscapes, and such a situation paves the way for coordination issues as soon as a consistent policy needs to be designed or implemented at the national level. It thus seems relevant to ask whether this shared characteristic of constitutional fragmentation somehow reverberates in the way the independence of the regulatory authorities is devised and applied.

This chapter looks into the formal and actual independence of the audiovisual media regulatory authorities in Germany and Belgium respectively before entering into a comparative analysis. We begin with a short introduction of both national contexts in order to better explain the position of the regulatory authorities, followed by an analysis of formal independence that led us to look at the following questions: the existence of legal provisions that safeguard the autonomy of the regulators; the organization of the regulatory authorities, their funding and the clarity of their mandate; and the existence of transparency and accountability mechanisms. We then turn to the examination of the actual independence of the regulation of media landscapes. Assessing the concrete, effective degree of autonomy enjoyed by the regulatory authorities is a tricky task. Any practice of undue influence obviously tends to happen in a fashion as discrete as possible and the persons involved have little desire to expose their behaviour to the light of public criticism. We also found that literature on the topic is not abundant. It was far beyond the reach of this contribution to conduct an in-depth investigation covering both practices and perceptions of all the regulatory authorities covered. However, relying on existing work, the INDIREG Final Report (Hans Bredow Institute for Media Research, et al. 2011), and findings from existing MEDIADEM results, we advance a number of observations as to the actual limits of the regulatory authorities' independence. Not all of these comments will appear equally scientifically solid to the readers, but we nevertheless claim that they are the actual points of tension when it comes to testing the effectiveness of a generally well-safeguarded formal independence.

After much thought, we chose to present the material for each country separately. While this may appear slightly less dynamic to the reader, we found it necessary to proceed in that fashion in order to be able to provide a clear presentation of the specificities of both national contexts. This choice also provides another benefit: it makes it possible to present some elements of internal (i.e., national) comparison, a precious dimension in the case of federal states, where there are numerous non-identical regulatory bodies.

Next we identify four areas in which we can examine the effectiveness of independence from a comparative perspective. We start with examining the cooperative relationships between bodies pertaining to different entities of the federal state, since their very existence was decisive in designing this chapter. We first assess the weight of legal constraints on the autonomy of the regulatory authorities, before turning to the fact that technological convergence induces further cooperation between media regulators and the regulatory authority for the telecommunication sector: here, cooperation might not be fully voluntary, but it constitutes an unavoidable strategy for the regulators if they are to maintain an effective impact over the fast-evolving Internet media landscape. The second step of the comparative analysis looks into the specific situation of the regulation of the public service media, which is the sphere where the amount of political influence over both the media and their regulator is the highest. Our comparison continues with the appointment processes of the members of the decision-making bodies in the regulatory authorities. Reflection here dwells on the respective influences that political forces and civil society organizations manage to exert upon the decision-making processes in the regulatory bodies. Finally, the amount and stability of the financing of the regulatory authorities is examined.

We conclude that even if the federal structure of a state renders the daily operation of regulatory authorities more complex (since they have to take into account the federal level in addition to the European sphere and to the actors of the media landscape where they are active – as well as a certain need for cooperation with their national counterparts), it remains hard to tell whether or how this increased complexity weighs on the issue of the independence of these regulatory authorities. The research presented in this chapter also allows for the advancement of some critical thoughts regarding the analysis of the effective ('actual') independence, which we hope may help nurture future research on that issue.

The national contexts of the media regulatory authorities' independence

A review of the media landscapes of Germany and Belgium

The media landscapes in Germany

Germany is a federal state that comprises sixteen states (*Länder*). The states vary greatly in size and number of inhabitants, from city states such as Bremen with some 660,000 inhabitants to the state of North Rhine-Westphalia, which more than 17.8 million people call home. Each state, as well as the federal state itself, is a legal entity with its own parliament, government and judicial system, and the Basic Law, the German constitution, ascribes the respective legislative competences to each tier (state or federal).

Historical, political and legal developments have led to a diverse media landscape, a system of multi-level legislative competences and a comprehensive media regulatory authority structure in Germany.[5] After the Second World War, the Allied Forces introduced public service broadcasting organizations in their respective areas of jurisdiction, which have shaped the public service broadcasting idea and the structure of public service broadcasting in Germany until now. Besides the national broadcasters *Deutschlandradio* and Second German Television (ZDF), nine state broadcasting stations and their working coalition, the Consortium of Public-law Broadcasting Institutions of the Federal Republic of Germany (*Arbeitsgemeinschaft der öffentlich-rechtlichen Rundfunkanstalten der Bundesrepublik Deutschland*, ARD) provides public service broadcasting outlets. The Allied Forces thus laid the basis for the strong position of the *Länder* in broadcasting and now audiovisual services. Traditionally, technical questions concerning cable transmissions of broadcasting signals or, more recently, Internet broadband infrastructure are decided by the federal legislature, the German Federal Parliament, while broadcasting issues on content and structure fall into the remit of the states. This distinction stems from the federal state's competence in telecommunication matters as well as from a dispute which arose from the planned inauguration of a national television channel in 1960. The Federal Government sought to establish a countrywide broadcaster (*Deutschland-Fernsehen-GmbH*), which the Federal Constitutional Court found in violation of the Basic Law. The Court underpinned its judgment with the argumentation that, in a democratic society, broadcasting had to be independent from the state. Simultaneously, it stipulated that the state legislatures, not federal-level entities, were vested with the competences regarding broadcasting legislation. Thus structural and content regulation of audiovisual media services, such as television broadcasting, falls in the remit of the state legislatures, i.e. the state parliaments. As a result, sixteen states are vested with the legislative power to enact regulation on public service broadcasting, commercial broadcasting, press, and online content linked to the traditional media outlets (press, radio and television broadcasting) as well as sole editorial online work, whereas the federal state focuses on technical issues of communications infrastructure and the transmission of electronic signals. This raises the question whether the independence of media is protected throughout all states in the same way. It was also the state governments which paved the way for commercial broadcasting services, as several state governments planned cable projects in distinct areas in Germany in order to investigate the technical advancements of cable networks for transmissions. In 1984, the first commercial television channel began to air via cable network and state parliaments began, rather hastily in some cases, to adopt media legislation to regulate commercial broadcasting (Eifert and Hoffmann-Riem 1999: 60).

The clear distinction between state and federal level, as well as national and European level, has become blurred with the Europeanization of audiovisual media services' regulation and the advent of the Internet. The Audiovisual Media Services (AVMS) Directive (European Parliament and the Council of Europe 2010) and the state aid control procedure of the European Commission against Germany regarding its funding regime of the public service broadcasters (European Commission 2007) testify to the European influence.

The developments outlined above influenced the existence, the composition and the competences of the audiovisual media regulatory authorities in Germany significantly. Premised on the idea of independent public service broadcasting, the organizational design of all nine regional broadcasting stations, Second German Television (ZDF) as well as *Deutschlandradio*, with its radio and online outlets, share the same underlying structure: legislation provides for an independent organization under public law, and all stations have a Broadcasting Council serving as internal regulatory authority (in the case of ZDF, the Television Council, and in the case of *Deutschlandradio*, the Radio Council), which governs the station in basic matters while a General-Director is responsible for the programming schedule and the content.

Commercial broadcasting is subject to external supervision by the state media authorities. Currently, fourteen state media authorities licence commercial broadcasters and supervise the programme performance of more than 300 commercial television channels and more than 500 radio channels. Established by state law as independent state bodies, Directors or Presidents generally constitute the executive organ of the state media authorities, while assemblies of representatives of societal groups – or, in some cases, a smaller body of experts – decide on licensing and supervision. Thus state media authorities have a bifurcated governing structure. Except for the states of Berlin, Brandenburg, Hamburg and Schleswig-Holstein, which each have one unified state media authority, each state has established and maintained a dedicated audiovisual media regulatory authority. Over the last two decades, state legislatures have developed several cooperative structures of the country's state media authorities with regard to specific issues stemming from their remit. In 1996, they introduced the Commission on Concentration in the Media (*Kommission zur Ermittlung der Konzentration im Medienbereich*, KEK), in 2003 the Commission for the Protection of Minors in the Media (*Kommission für Jugendmedienschutz*, KJM) and finally in 2008 the Commission on Licensing and Supervision (*Kommission für Zulassung und Aufsicht*, ZAK). Regarding national broadcasting, the legislatures' objective has been to harmonize the regulatory means in the areas of media concentration, the protection of minors as well as licensing and programme supervision.

The media landscapes in Belgium

Initiated in the 1970s, the federalization process from a unitary kingdom to contemporary Belgium has resulted in the distribution of political power between the federal state, three language-based Communities (the French Community, the Flemish Community and the German-speaking Community) and three territory-based Regions (the Region of Brussels, the Walloon Region and the Flemish Region). While the state initially created a National Institute for Radio-diffusion in 1930, which later evolved to become the public service radio and television broadcaster, this organization split into two separate entities owned by the Communities. The emergence of commercial radio and television followed a similar linguistic divide. The media market appears to be essentially split into two separate segments, the French-speaking South and the Dutch-speaking North, with the small German-speaking community (circa 75,000 inhabitants) as a third, notably smaller component.[6] The absence of any actual common media sphere at the national level must be noted: as a consequence, it is more appropriate to think of the Belgian media as constituting neighbouring media landscapes with common features, one of them being that they inherited some of the legal and regulatory framework from the formerly unitary state.

Communities hold responsibility for culture-related matters, and audiovisual media have constituted an important dimension of their activity. They can be described as the main level for the elaboration of media policy. It is for instance in their power to define the remit of the public service media and to fund them: to that end, the Communities negotiate management contracts with the autonomous public companies charged with operating the public service of audiovisual broadcasting. To be sure, their competence is in no way limited to the public sector: for instance, Communities also manage the allocation of radio frequencies to private radio operators. Generally, it can be affirmed that each Community operates independently from its counterparts. In the event of a dispute relating to the extent of the Communities' respective competences, the Constitutional Court will arbitrate.[7]

Even though they were partly inherited from the unitary state, media laws and policies may thus diverge from one Community to the other, within the limits of what the centripetal forces of federal legislation and European law will allow. The evolution of the regulators' powers and statuses – or their establishment in the case of the Medienrat – has been brought about by European Law. Another factor that has driven the three regulators to work together was the case law of the Constitutional Court, which induced the Communities and the federal state to cooperate in the field of electronic communications, a matter which technological convergence brought under the combined responsibility of all concerned components of the state. In 2006, said parties entered into a cooperation agreement that instituted an Interministerial Committee and a Conference of Regulators for the Sector of Electronic Communications (CRC) (Cooperation Agreement, 2006). The Committee serves the purpose of facilitating cooperation between the governments, while the CRC provides regulators with a consultative and collective decision-making forum. The effectiveness of the CRC has recently been illustrated by its capacity to coordinate a complex market analysis of audiovisual media distribution and broadband Internet access which led the regulators to adopt regulatory measures on the relevant markets.[8]

The regulatory authorities for audiovisual media have been created by the Communities. The High Council for the Audiovisual Sector (*Conseil supérieur de l'audiovisuel*, CSA) was first instituted by the French Community in 1987 as a merely consultative body and acquired its current status following legislative reforms in 1997 and 2003; the Media Council (*Medienrat*) was established by the German Community in 2005 and the Flemish Regulator of the Media (*Vlaamse Regulator voor de Medias*, VRM) came into being in the Flemish Community in 2006, replacing the former Vlaamse Commissariat voor de Media. In the course of the transposition of the revised European Community's Directive Television Without Borders, all three have become autonomous public bodies with full legal capacity (French Community Act, 2009; German Community Act, 2005; Flemish Community Act, 2009). The three Belgian regulators are members of the European platform of regulatory authorities (EPRA).[9]

The formal independence of regulatory authorities

The case of Germany
Over the last decades, Germany has developed a system of formal independence regarding the different types of media outlets, meaning that different regulatory mechanisms exist for the respective media types. As the German regulatory approach is shaped by the traditional distinction between broadcasting and press, 'original' online media (i.e. media solely published online, which excludes the online services of public service broadcasting and press entities) have not been addressed by the legislature in a comparable manner. Other than protection of minors regulations, such original online media are comparatively unregulated.

The legal guarantee of independence
It was the Federal Constitutional Court which stipulated in its landmark judgment in 1961 – nullifying the attempt of the Federal Government to establish a national broadcaster – the basic principle of the independence of broadcasting in a democratic society. In its interpretation of Art. 5 of the Basic Law, the court concluded that it established a constitutional safeguard for broadcasting as mass communication that must be guaranteed *institutionally* as means of shaping public opinion. Resulting from this, broadcasting has to be independent from the state and from particular interests of single groups *as well* (Federal Constitutional Court 1961: 262).

The principle of independence from the state and the pluralistic governing structure were the starting point for the legislatures. Thus, state legislatures have assumed the role of guaranteeing, as state organs, a public communicative sphere *free of state influence*, by adopting legislation prepared solely by state governments. What might sound paradoxical, in fact engenders public communicative discourse if implemented properly. The Interstate Broadcasting Treaty (2010), the legal backbone of the national broadcasting system prepared by the state governments and adopted by all sixteen state parliaments, contains provisions to ensure independence from the state. Each state enacted legislation for commercial broadcasters as well as for public service broadcasters. Essentially, all existing state legislation provides for regulation seeking to ensure independence from the state.

Supervision of audiovisual online content follows the standards of traditional offline regulation: public service broadcasters' online outlets are highly regulated and thus subject to the regulatory regimes of the broadcasting stations, while the liberal regulatory approach of print media was extended to their online outlets as well. The applicable regulation excludes editorial or journalistic online content from the state supervision of content (Art. 59 para. 3 Interstate Broadcasting Treaty) and thus leaves the field to the self-regulatory and state-independent press council system.

In summary, backed by the constitutional law, the statutory law of the states (*Länder*) seeks to ensure the independence of media regulatory authorities.

Organizational independence

Given the fact that public service broadcasters between them account for a 41.9 per cent television audience share (Schwotzer 2011: 39), the incentive for state actors (representatives of governments, the legislature or political parties) to exert influence on the council's decisions is obvious. As the external options of state influence are limited, the internal composition of governing bodies and any state influence on them merit attention. The independence of the broadcasting regulatory authorities constitutes a prerequisite in this regard. The governing and management structures are the same in all public service broadcasters and comprise the Broadcasting Council, the Administrative Council and the General-Director. The Broadcasting Council's remit lies with programme matters, while the Administrative Council reviews the management activities of the General-Director. He or she acts as executive organ and is responsible for the programmes. The main supervisory organ is, however, the Broadcasting Council, on which we will focus.

The Bavarian Broadcasting Act exemplifies in Art. 6 the basic function of the Broadcasting Council to act for the common good: 'The Broadcasting Council represents the interests of the general public in the field of broadcasting,' and thus has to act independently. Other broadcasting acts include comparable provisions. Furthermore, the state legislatures have transposed the requirements of the Federal Constitutional Court into state laws that determine the composition of the Broadcasting Council, modes of nomination, appointment and dismissal procedures as well as the adoption of programme guidelines and the regulation of online concepts to ensure the authorities' independence. Party or state representatives are not to be given decisive representation in broadcasters' regulatory bodies, i.e. the Broadcasting Councils, as composition rules in state broadcasting acts seek to prevent governments and political parties from gaining control over the governing bodies. All state broadcasting laws provide for a majoritarian position of societal groups, like unions, churches, sports or science associations and cultural groups. The Interstate Broadcasting Treaty and the interpretation of the Basic Law by the Federal Constitutional Court, however, do not provide any clear definition or concrete number of state representatives in the Broadcasting Councils to ensure independence. As a result of the federal approach, the different state broadcasting laws concede state and party representatives different degrees of influence on the public service broadcasting's governing bodies.

The broadcasting law seeks to ensure independence from the state for the representatives of societal groups by only prescribing which societal associations and groups can delegate a member to the council, while leaving the process of nomination and appointment to the societal groups and associations themselves. Once member of the Broadcasting Council, it is only the delegating organization which has the authority to withdraw the representative, for instance if the person leaves the association (Art. 15 para. 10 WDR-Broadcasting Act); neither the broadcasting station, nor the state government can act in this regard. The interstate treaty on the Second German Television (ZDF) presents the sole exception, as the members of the Television Council are nominated by the respective societal group, but appointed by the heads of the state governments.

Legislation formally ensures the independent position of council members, as it provides that members of the Broadcasting Councils are not bound by any instruction (e.g., Art. 21 para. 9 Interstate Treaty on Second German Television), and incompatibility requirements aimed at preventing any conflict of interest exclude Broadcasting Council members from regular employment by public or commercial broadcasters – or even state media authorities.

It is also the state legislatures' task to safeguard the independence of the regulatory authorities for commercial broadcasters: the state media authorities. Comparable to the margin of discretion afforded to state legislatures in enacting the legal framework for the independence of public service broadcasting, the Federal Constitutional Court and the Interstate Broadcasting Treaty only prescribe basic framework conditions for the independence of state media authorities and thus provide a significant degree of organizational freedom. Consequently, the states have enacted, alongside similar basic structures, different governing models to ensure the independence of media authorities.

Besides the fourteen state media authorities, the state legislatures have established three independent bodies to manage the cooperation among them and address federal questions: the Commission on Licensing and Supervision (ZAK), the Commission on the Concentration in the Media (KEK) and the Commission for the Protection of Minors (KJM). Especially in the case of the ZAK, the state lawmakers face the difficulties of a federal system. Since a single countrywide responsible media authority would violate the German Constitution, the legislatures as well as the individual state media authorities are compelled to seek efficient ways of cooperation without denying the organizational principle of independence in a federal system. State media authorities act as independent bodies with the right of self-administration, which means that state media authorities enjoy a broad discretionary power to organize their administrative work in accordance to their specific needs. It is in line with this role that other state authorities or state organs cannot devolve tasks to the state media authority.

The pluralistically composed assembly – or in some cases smaller expert councils – and the executive organ, in most cases the Director, form the governing and management bodies of state media authorities. Comparable to Broadcasting Councils in public service broadcasters, the state media authority's assembly comprises state representatives (of parliaments, and in some case governments) and, always in a majoritarian position, representatives of societal groups. In general, representatives of societal groups are nominated and delegated to the assembly by the legally prescribed institutions. Among them are – as Art. 40 of the State Media Law of Rhineland-Palatinate exemplifies – church, journalists', unions' and artists' representatives as well as representatives of employer or publisher organizations. Furthermore, incompatibility requirements exist to prevent conflicts of interest, as state government representatives, operators or employers of commercial broadcasters as well as representatives of public service broadcasters are barred from becoming a member of the state media authorities. Two state media authorities, in Berlin-Brandenburg and Hamburg/ Schleswig-Holstein, follow the council model and complement the governing position of the Director with a board of experts. They also deviate from the appointment model, as it is the respective state parliaments that elect their members.

The Commission on Licensing and Supervision (ZAK) is the joint body of the state media authorities regarding countrywide applicable licences and supervision. It consists of fourteen members – the Directors of the state media authorities – and adopts final decisions which have to be enacted by the respective state media authorities. This system puts into question the position and importance of the pluralistic governing bodies, because competence has been devolved to the ZAK. On the other hand, it can guarantee that decisions are less influenced by a single commercial operator, which in the end bolsters the state media authorities' independence.

The Commission on Concentration in the Media (KEK), the joint body of state media authorities on media concentration, consists of twelve members: six of them are appointed by the heads of the state governments in consent and six of them are delegated by the state media authorities, generally their Directors. Once elected, the members of the Commission enjoy an independent position from any state organ (Art. 35 para. 8 Interstate Broadcasting Treaty) and cannot be dismissed during their five-year term.

The Commission for the Protection of Minors (KJM) illustrates the cooperation of state authorities, in this case representatives of state governmental departments for the protection of minors, with media regulatory bodies, because the Commission's composition includes state authorities' representatives. Accounting for this is the remit of the applicable law, the Interstate Treaty on the Protection of Minors, which seeks to create a consistent approach in minors' protection and which the legislators deem an important task for the states. The law provides for the Commission's composition a board of twelve experts, of which six are appointed by state media authorities, four by state government authorities for the protection of minors and two by federal state authorities.

Financial independence

The question of budget autonomy poses another threat to the independence of public service broadcasters and thus the independence of their regulatory bodies (Federal Constitutional Court 1994: 1946f. and 2007: 773f.). The financing regime of German public service broadcasting comprises a three-step procedure with the aim of minimizing state influence (Art. 14 Interstate Broadcasting Treaty and Interstate Treaty on Broadcasting Financing). An independent body of sixteen experts (appointed by the states), the Commission to Determine the Financial Needs of the Broadcasters (*Kommission zur Ermittlung des Finanzbedarfs der Rundfunkanstalten*, KEF), scrutinizes the submissions of financial needs of all public service broadcasters and determines what the licence fee should be for the next four years, which subsequently has to be adopted in an interstate legislative act. The Federal Constitutional Court even curtails the discretionary power of the state parliaments in this regard, by allowing only a limited revision of the KEF's conclusions (Federal Constitutional Court 2007: 775).

The financing of state media authorities is linked to the public service broadcasting licence fee. It essentially guarantees the financial independence of each state media authority, since statutory law ascribes, as general rule, almost two per cent of the total licence fee revenues to the state media authorities. This income source accounts for an average of 90 per cent of the respective state media authority budgets and ranges from €2.5 million (state media authority Mecklenburg-Vorpommern) to €15.5 million (North-Rhine Westphalia) per annum, depending on the size of the state (Arbeitsgemeinschaft der Landesmedienanstalten 2011: 391 and 431). However, state legislators are entitled to reduce this amount and allocate only part of the licence fee revenues to state media authorities (Art. 40 para. 2 Interstate Broadcasting Treaty), which raises concerns for an independent financial budgetary organization.

Mandate
The Broadcasting Councils hold a decisive position in public service broadcasting. The Broadcasting Council adopts programme guidelines, scrutinizes after the airing of programmes whether the station adhered to general legal obligations and the programme guidelines, and gives advice to the General-Director. It reviews the online services of the broadcasting stations with regard to their journalistic benefit and the implications for commercial online outlets (the so called three-step-test) and adopts the comprehensive online concept of the stations prescribing the audiovisual online content. Furthermore, it is the Broadcasting Councils' task to appoint the General-Director and, in most cases, the senior positions within the station.

Established by state legislatures, state media authorities enjoy discretionary power to grant operation licences, control mergers, and supervise programme performances in the commercial audiovisual sector. They are also entitled to issue fines, in cases where private operators violate statuary law. Whereas licensing and programme supervision of regional broadcasting fall solely in the mandate of individual state media authorities, nationally broadcast outlets require the state media authorities to act commonly. Here, the state legislatures have chosen to adopt a cooperative model between the state authorities and established three cooperative bodies: the Commission on Licensing and Supervision (ZAK), the Commission on Concentration in the Media (KEK) and the Commission for the Protection of Minors in the Media (KJM). The Commission on Licensing and Supervision (ZAK) subjects national commercial broadcasting to licence and programme supervision requirements, the Commission on Concentration in the Media (KEK) scrutinizes plurality requirements of nationally distributed broadcasting, while the Commission for the Protection of Minors (KJM) pursues legal violations in national commercial broadcasting as well as in online content in general. Complementing KJM's work, the protection of minors authorities, i.e. state departments of state governments and the Federal Government, maintain a joint body to scrutinize online content (jugendschutz.net). Besides the statutory protection of minors by the KJM, co-regulatory mechanisms exist as well. However, the statutory regulatory procedure has proven to be indispensible as it can impose sanctions in cooperation with state media authorities.

Transparency and accountability
The websites of the public service broadcasters provide information about the respective regulatory authority's composition. It is thus possible to see which societal group or party sent its representative to the Broadcasting Council.

Depending on the issue, the degree of transparency of the Broadcasting Councils' work differs. The three-step procedures in which the Broadcasting Councils assess the online concepts have been transparent, including public hearings, publication of the online concept itself and publication of the Broadcasting Councils' decisions. Other processes are, however, less transparent.

The process of funding the public service broadcasters and thus also the Broadcasting Councils follows an elaborate transparency policy, because the KEF publishes comprehensively the figures on the basis of which it calculates and proposes the monthly licence fee (KEF 2009) and the Central Fee Collection Authority publishes which amount of money will be allocated to which public service broadcaster.

State media authorities publish annually a comprehensive report (see Arbeitsgemeinschaft der Landesmedienanstalten 2011). This report contains information on the state media authorities' funding, main media policy developments and also the main decisions of their governing bodies. The composition of the state media authorities' governing bodies can be accessed through the respective authorities' website. The joint bodies, the ZAK and the KEK, publish timely online their decisions regarding pending cases of supervision.

The publications of the Commission on Concentration in the Media (KEK) illustrate a good example of transparency, as their reports on media concentration, their composition and their decisions are publicly available (KEK 2011).

The case of Belgium

The legal guarantee of independence

As the parliaments of the Communities by themselves have no power to modify the constitution, giving constitutional dignity to their respective independent administrative authorities would remain beyond their reach. To be sure, neither the federal telecommunication regulator (BIPT) nor the regulatory authorities for other sectors have emerged in the constitution. By way of comparison, the constitution provides a number of guarantees relating to the judiciary, and it could thus be argued that the constitutional absence of the regulators may *per se* say a lot about the relative novelty and remaining margin of progression of independent regulatory authorities in terms of law. However, it must be acknowledged that nowadays the independence of the three regulatory bodies in charge of audiovisual media is anchored in ordinary law, as we detail hereafter.

The French Community Act on Audiovisual Media Services formally establishes the CSA as the independent administrative authority whose remit consists in the regulation of the audiovisual sector in the French Community (French Community Act 2009, Art. 133). The same disposition provides for the acknowledgement of the full legal capacity of the CSA, with the limitation that it cannot operate commercial activities. According to Art. 215 of the Flemish Act on Radio and Television Broadcasting, the VRM is an '*external independent agency with a legal personality under public law*'. The full legal capacity of the Medienrat is acknowledged by its instituting Act, the German Community Act of 27 June 2005; although the act does not explicitly refer to independence, it provides for a number of guarantees in that sense.

Organizational independence

The CSA and VRM are autonomous organizations that are entirely separated from the general administration and the corresponding ministries; they are responsible for the recruitment and management of their own staff. The smaller Medienrat relies for its operation on two delegated staff members from the Ministry of the German-speaking Community, where it is hosted. It is generally the governments that appoint the members of the decision-making organs of the three regulators, and there are a number of rules that render these positions incompatible with political functions or links with the industry. Additionally, the CSA has included rules on conflicts of interest in its internal regulation. When the position is not a full-time employment, members of decision-making bodies benefit from fees as arranged in accordance with government-adopted rules.

The Medienrat comprises two chambers: the ruling chamber and the advisory chamber. Only the former exercises decision-making power. It is composed of three members, the president and two vice-presidents (interestingly, one of the vice-presidents is currently the chairman of the German regulator *Landesanstalt für Medien Nordrhein-Westfalen*). The members of both chambers are appointed by the Government of the German-speaking Community for the length of the legislature. By law, it is requested that the decision-makers of the ruling chamber be knowledgeable in 'the sciences, law, economics or technologies in the field of media' or 'experts in the sector of electronic communications' (German Community Act 2005, Art. 91). The same disposition renders their position incompatible with both political functions (legislative or executive) and the possession of direct or indirect interests in the business of electronic communication. The government may dismiss the members if they fail to meet the mentioned requirements, if they are absent at more than half of the meetings (on a yearly basis), or if they fail to preserve the secrecy of trade and business information they come to learn in the course of their mission. The members of the consultative chamber are chosen on the basis of suggestions advanced by the industry, the stakeholders and the political parties represented at the Parliament of the German-speaking Community. Members of the advisory chamber cannot hold a political mandate, be it in the legislative or the executive. They may be dismissed if they fail to meet this requirement, if they are absent too often, or if the body that suggested their appointment withdraws its support and wishes them to be replaced.

The Flemish regulatory authority comprises two chambers. The general chamber has five members, two of whom have to be magistrates with at least five years of experience in the courts (including the chairman), whereas the other three need to be experts in the field of media, a concept defined either by a five-year educational or scientific experience in the Flemish higher education system or a five-year experience in the media sector. The second organ is the chamber for impartiality and the protection of minors. It brings together four professional journalists (with at least five years of experience) and five other members who come either from the magistracy or higher education (with the same five-year experience requirement).[10] Members of both chambers are prohibited from having any link with companies in the sector (as far as the four journalists are concerned, this requirement is specified as not holding a mandate in the board of a media or advertising business). In addition, members of the chambers cannot hold a political mandate in a legislative assembly or be the minister or member of the staff of the minister in charge of the audiovisual sector (Flemish Community Framework Act on Administrative Policy, Art. 21). The Government appoints the members of both chambers for a five-year renewable term (the length of the legislature is five years, too). It may dismiss them notably in case an incompatibility arises or in case of frequent absences. The Government also appoints the board of directors that is in charge of operating the Flemish regulatory authority and of concluding its management contract with the government. Directors may not be members of any of the two chambers, but the managing director sits as observer in both chambers. The position of the director is incompatible with a political mandate in legislative bodies or as minister in charge of the audiovisual media, or member of the minister's staff. When a director has a direct or indirect proprietary interest that would be affected by a decision made by the board of directors of the VRM, (s)he should abstain from partaking in the related deliberation and vote (Flemish Community Framework Act on Administrative Policy, Art. 19).

The CSA is managed by a four-member Board (*Bureau*) composed by the chairman (a full-time position) and three vice-presidents. The Government of the French Community appoints members of the Board for a five-year renewable term. The Licensing and Control Authority (*Collège d'autorisation et contrôle*, CAC) is the main decision-making organ and is composed of the members of the Board and six other members, who are appointed for a four-year renewable term. Out of those six members, three are appointed by the parliament and the three others by the Government. All ten members of the College are chosen on the basis of their 'competence in law, audiovisual media or communication' (French Community Act, Art. 139). All positions are incompatible with political functions (either legislative or executive) and with 'any position which, by its nature, creates a personal or functional conflict of interest' (French Community Act, Art. 139), e.g. a position with the public service broadcaster or a proprietary interest in the commercial audiovisual media sector. The chairman may dismiss a member who is absent six times in a row. Either at its own initiative or by request of one College, the Government may dismiss a member in case of an incompatibility or in case of breach of professional ethics. Additionally, the members are submitted to the same disciplinary measures as professional magistrates. The CSA also hosts an Advisory College (*Collège d'avis*) whose thirty members[11] are appointed by the Government in order to represent a certain number of identified stakeholders of the audiovisual sector. Members of the advisory college may not hold a political function.[12] The law also requires that the internal regulation of the CSA describe rules of professional ethics applicable to members and staff: it notably provides a duty of abstention when a conflict of interest arises. It is worth noting that the CSA has a Secretariat of Investigation (*secrétariat d'instruction*, SI) that operates under the authority of the Board and is responsible for initiating procedures before the CAC either at its own initiative or after a complaint has been lodged by the general public. While their function is somewhat similar to that of an investigation magistrate (*juge d'instruction*), the staff of the SI has no special status.[13]

Financial independence

The regulators mainly rely on public funding, and VRM draws part of its income from spectrum fees. Budgets are prepared by the regulators, submitted to the government, and included in the general budget that is voted on by parliament. The public financing is secured through a management contract that runs until a new government is sworn in (in the case of VRM) or a five-year financing agreement (in the case of CSA). The Communities fund their respective regulatory authority in a manner that is generally considered sufficient (Hans Bredow Institute for Media Research, et al. 2011: 99; Dumont 2010).

Mandate

The remit and powers of the regulatory authorities are accurately described by law. Generally, their mission can be described as the implementation of policy along the lines decided by the parliament and government. In the context of their advisory missions, the regulators may also influence the evolution of future policy. Their jurisdiction extends from audiovisual media services to network operators (terrestrial broadcast, cable, IPTV, satellite, mobile). Their powers range from monitoring the sector to imposing binding decisions upon the operators, be it in the allocation of frequencies or in the repression of breaches of the law (with sanctions ranging from a warning to a fine or the removal of authorization). They have investigative powers to obtain information from the operators. Their fields of activity range from content regulation (on such issues as quotas, advertising, or protection of minors) to the defence of pluralism and the promotion of competition. Following the conclusion of a cooperation agreement between the federal state and the Communities in 2006, the three regulatory authorities have to cooperate with BIPT for the regulation of electronic communications. They also maintain cooperation relationships with other public and private bodies and partake in European and international cooperation. Another important dimension of their remit lies in the defence of the general interest and in the corresponding relationship with the general public.

Transparency and accountability

The regulatory authorities are obliged to publish an annual report that is submitted to their respective Community's parliament and made available to the public at large. Beyond the legal obligations, the fairly rich content of the websites of the regulatory authorities may bear testimony to their dedication to communicating about their mission and their activities.[14] Administrative decisions must be published and duly motivated, but the preparatory process remains undisclosed. The regulatory authorities may and do organize public consultations and seminars prior to the adoption of decisions or recommendations. When the CAC acts in its capacity of imposing administrative sanctions, its hearings are accessible to the public (French Community Act, Art. 161).

The internal regulations of the regulators need to be approved by their respective Community's government before they enter into force. Governments may review decisions that concern the management of the administrative authorities but not their regulatory activities.

As for all administrative authorities, the decisions made by the three regulators are subject to judicial review by the Council of State (*Conseil d'Etat*), i.e. the supreme administrative tribunal. The Council of State will notably control the respect of the rights of the defence and the fairness of the proceedings. If it finds a decision to be in breach of the law, the Council of State has the power to quash it but not to reverse it: instead, the case is returned to the regulatory authority, which then has to make a new decision that complies with the decision of the Council of State. Unless the Council of State grants a suspense order, administrative decisions remain in force until the final judgment.

A look into the actual independence of regulatory authorities

The case of Germany

To identify the actual independence of the regulatory authorities proves to be challenging in the case of Germany. The number of regulatory bodies in the public service and commercial broadcasting sectors (eleven Broadcasting Councils and fourteen state media authorities) alone points to the desideratum of thorough and comprehensive social science studies. The work of mass communication scientists would be necessary to come to sound conclusions.[15] The last study on the work of German regulatory authorities was published in 2000 by Brosius, Rössler, and Schulte, which analysed and discussed the results of a questionnaire sent to all 940 members of the German public service Broadcasting Councils and state media authorities (Brosius, Rössler, and Schulte zur Hausen 2011: 426). The study focused on the quality of regulatory decisions, based on self-assessments by the members and not on their independence. Even so, the socio-political environment in which media authorities work may obstruct a clear view of whether the regulatory authority can function independently or not. In other words: it is unlikely that a regulator will tell in an interview that he or she cannot work independently.

The following outline of regulatory actual independence is based on the research work carried out in Germany for the MEDIADEM project. The project seeks to analyse media policies that impede or, conversely, promote media freedom and independence, and the reports on Germany are based on 26 interviews with experts and an analysis of parliamentary motions, media coverage and decisions pertaining to the situation in Germany. Part of the project also covered regulatory authorities and their independence, and the research results can help to understand the complexity of a federal state's media authorities better. But as the project covered regulatory authorities among other issues of media freedom, only general conclusions, derived from the structural framework and the respective regulator's composition as well as individual incidents, shall be presented succinctly to denote their actual independence.

The independence of Broadcasting Councils from state influence

The regulatory framework as well as the public service broadcasters' role in public debates renders their regulatory authorities prone to possible political influence. In general, state legislatures have been aware of the possible conflict of interests in the Broadcasting Council and thus have established legislation to ensure the regulatory bodies' independence from the state: the public service broadcasters are independent legal bodies under public law. Furthermore, the legislation always provides for a majority for the representatives of societal groups in Broadcasting Councils. In addition, these societal groups enjoy the right to appoint their representatives to the Broadcasting Council on their own account, without any possibility for the state government or parliament to intervene as long as the appointee fulfils the basic requirements stipulated in law (essentially incompatibility rules in cases of a conflict of interest). However, studies assert a discussion culture shaped by groups of interests (so called 'circles of friends') on Broadcasting Councils (Hahn 2010: 162), mainly reflecting political affiliations to the two large parties in Germany, the social democratic and conservative parties. Such a culture might give precedence to party political opinion. Furthermore, it occurs that representatives of governmental political parties consider their role in the Broadcasting Council as members of the party, and thus espouse only party positions vigorously, instead of acting as one societal group among others, as the Council was intended to function. The actual discussion culture in the Broadcasting Councils, i.e. the way the different members interact in debates, may however temper the approach of state and party representatives in order to rectify the systemic deficit. The body's composition encompassing different groups and various societal representatives in general thwarts the domination of state or party representatives in the Broadcasting Council, if they seek to influence the whole Broadcasting Council. In addition, legislation can provide for a justified number of party representatives as members of societal groups that cannot influence the council unduly.

For historical reasons, the regulatory system of the public service broadcaster Second German Television (ZDF) displays some peculiarities. The Television Council (as the Broadcasting Council is named) of the Second German Television (ZDF) illustrates this, as more than 40 per cent of all Council members belong to the group of representatives of political parties, federal and state governments and city representatives (see Art. 21 para. 1 Interstate Treaty on Second German Television). The heads of the state governments also appoint the remaining members (excluding those of religious institutions), whereas the Broadcasting Councils of the nine regional public service broadcasting stations generally allow the member to be delegated by the respective societal group itself.[16] The question arises whether this has negative repercussions for the station's daily operation. This is difficult to ascertain. However, undue state influence was evident in the case of the contested prolongation of the then chief-editor's contract in 2009. The Administrative Council denied its consent regarding this senior editorial position for political reasons (Dörr 2009). This internal conflict resulted in a constitutional application with the Federal Constitutional Court being lodged by the Rhineland-Palatinate state government, contesting the constitutionality of the ZDF's governing bodies' composition. On the other hand, attempts by political actors to influence the appointment procedure of senior positions – presumably for political reasons – have also been rejected. In 2011, the candidate for the position of

Director-General of the public service broadcaster MDR was not elected by the responsible Broadcasting Council, even though the nominating Administrative Council, influenced by the three state governments of Saxony, Saxony-Anhalt and Thuringia, had favoured and openly supported the candidate (MDR 2011).

The Broadcasting Council's independence within the system of public service broadcasting
The independence of the public service broadcasters' regulatory bodies has to be understood in the context of the relationship between the particular broadcaster and Broadcasting Council. This addresses the question whether the members of the Broadcasting Council act independently when scrutinizing the station's performance. From a practical point of view, the Broadcasting Councils meet in the building of the broadcaster, and are dependent on the broadcaster's infrastructure. It is argued that because of this close relationship, the objective and independent supervision might be in question, since the supervisory organ may identify itself with the object of supervision and relies on the information and infrastructure of the supervisee (Jarren, et al. 2001: 191–192; Hans Bredow Institute for Media Research, et al. 2011: 358).

Even though the basic assumption of the capture theory contains some truth, it is difficult to verify, in the German case, the existence of an overarching or systemic problem based on its premise. External authorities such as the state media authorities are prone to a prejudicial position that impedes their supervision as well. Moreover, through the necessary supervisory procedure regarding the online outlets of the public service broadcasters (three-step-test), the Broadcasting Councils have increased their supervisory position against the broadcasting stations, considering they have to approve the underlying online concept. The legislation obliges all public service broadcasters to present the respective Broadcasting Council (or Television Council in the case of the ZDF) with a concept of how the stations seek to ensure, regarding their online outlets (like online news websites), that they comply with the legal framework and the restrictions set out in the Interstate Broadcasting Treaty. This is a decisive position, especially in the growing online environment.

The governing bodies of the nine regional public service broadcasters need to work together in cases in which they supervise the cooperative tasks of all nine regional public service broadcasters. This is done in a joint body of the Broadcasting Councils' chairmen. The federal structure of the broadcasters poses challenges to this joint body, as each station seeks to secure its own area of influence. Essentially, the joint body of the chairmen does not have any legally binding right to exert discretionary power, since this authority remains with each station's governing bodies. Depending on the issue, it can occur that the joint body adopts a clear stance which puts into question the right balance between its position within the federal structure and each public service broadcaster's remit. That was the case in 2011, when broadcasting rights for boxing events exceeded the justifiable limit. Whether the federal structure enhances or impedes efficient supervision and whether the cooperative governing structure between the joint body of chairmen and the Broadcasting Councils themselves fosters their independence is an open question.

Independence from political and economic considerations: a look at the structures of commercial broadcasting supervision

An observation of the factual independence of the regulatory authorities has to take into account their diverse and federal structure. Alongside the important joint bodies that ensure countrywide regulatory cooperation (ZAK, KEK and KJM), fourteen state media authorities have to be covered as well. The historical developments of this structure as well as the underlying political and economic interests that might impede independent regulatory activities shall be addressed here first.

Political and economic considerations have influenced and eventually shaped the existing regulatory mechanisms for commercial broadcasting. During the 1980s, this was the case when the state governments were seeking to convince commercial broadcasting operators to establish their seat in their respective states. Essentially, state governments intended to gain influence over the commercial broadcaster and to ensure work opportunities. Concurrently, state legislators enacted distinct state media laws applicable to each of the states and, consequently, the state media authorities. While regional broadcasters airing only in one state were supervised by the respective state authority, national broadcasters were subject to a differentiated regulatory scheme depending on the means of transmission (Gersdorf 2003: 176–177). In this regard, the question arose (Schuler-Harms 1995: 56) whether state media authorities acted in competition to each other and gave precedence to the economic interests of the commercial broadcasters under licence over the exercise of lawful supervision (including fines). For instance, state media authorities reluctantly imposed fines regarding programme requirements such as personal rights (Landesanstalt für Medien NRW: 2010), although being aware of the possible adverse influence of some of the programmes aired (Schneider 2011; Klass 2011: 52 and 125). Here, the independence to act might be impeded by the specific environment and the relationship between state media authorities and commercial broadcasters. Based on the idea to harmonize supervision of countrywide commercial broadcasting, state legislatures introduced in 2008 a joint body, the ZAK. One objective was to reduce competition among state media authorities, improve the coordination between the regulators and, presumably, prevent single interest decisions by one of the state media authorities. In this case, the federal structure of the commercial broadcasters' supervision system had allowed private operators to act more freely, but concurrently had impeded the overarching implementation of applicable legal standards. Thus the federal system rendered independent supervision less efficient, a realization which led, as said already, to the creation of a joint body, the ZAK.

State influence also occurred when the state governments decided to change the composition of the Commission on Concentration in the Media (KEK), allegedly to mitigate the Commission's strict approach in merger control cases (Gounalakis and Zagouras 2008: 212; Westphal 2008). This development may raise the question of structural undue state influence on regulatory bodies. State bodies, like parliaments, can change the 'rules of the game', as the INDIREG-report pointedly stated, and may interfere thus directly (Hans Bredow Institute for Media Research, et al. 2011: 262f.). Preceding the Commission's re-organization, it had denied its legally required consent to the intended acquisition by Axel Springer AG of commercial broadcaster ProSiebenSat1 Media AG. In the Commission's view, the merger would have amounted to a dominant market position (KEK 2006), and the decision has impeded the largest cross-media merger in German history. Not surprisingly, the Commission's decisions and its methodology to gauge the percentage of viewers were criticized, and the Commission's composition came under revision. Until 2008, the Commission had comprised a board of media experts who had been appointed by the heads of states, already giving them considerable influence on the composition, which prompted critics to question whether this system adhered to the principle of freedom from the state (Westphal 2007: 458ff.). Since the new legislation came into force, the Commission is composed of twelve members, six of whom are media experts and the other six representatives of state media authorities (generally the directors).

Composition and nomination
Besides these very structural considerations, the composition of the state media authorities and their joint bodies merit attention. In some cases state participation in appointment procedures raises questions regarding the principle of independence from the state: for example, the senior executive of the state media authority of Baden-Württemberg (whose position is comparable to that of a Director) is elected by the state parliament of Baden-Württemberg and then appointed by the head of the state government. In Saxony, alongside the assembly, there is a media council with five members who are elected by the state parliament, whose role as a governing organ is comparable to that of a Director. The state parliament of Saarland elects the Saarland state media authority's Director, who is nominated by the parties in the state parliament. Out of the 47 members of the assembly of the Bavarian regulatory authority, twelve are representatives of the Bavarian state parliament and one represents the state government (Art. 13 para. 1 no. 1 and 2 Bavarian Media Act), giving those an influential position. Furthermore, in the case of two state media authorities, Berlin-Brandenburg and Hamburg/Schleswig-Holstein, state parliaments nominate and appoint the members of an expert council. With regard to the national cooperation bodies, state governments (i.e. the heads of the states) appoint six experts to the Commission on Concentration in the Media (KEK) and state representatives are members of the Commission for the Protection of Minors (KJM). Given the fact that the regulatory authorities exert influence on commercial broadcasting, the question arises (Westphal 2007: 456) to what extent the Federal Constitutional Court's stipulated requirement of independence from the state is respected, which obliges the state to avoid political and thus instrumental use of the media (Federal Constitutional Court 1994: 1944). The potential threat exists that state representatives decide about the appointment tactically and thus exert indirect influence (Bumke 1995: 155). The nomination and election procedure does not clearly violate constitutional requirements, but concerns remain (Dörr 2004: 182; Stock 1997: 76).

It only remains for us to raise this question at this stage. In-depth mass communication research would be necessary to verify or falsify the hypothesis that undue state influence is exerted via the appointment procedures.

The case of Belgium

The framework that has been described above provides accurate and detailed guarantees that would apparently allow the regulatory authorities to operate in effective autonomy and to efficiently achieve their goals. Nevertheless, however satisfactory the picture may seem, it would be necessary to try to uncover the processes of actual interaction between the regulators, the political forces, the industrial sector and civil society, to be able to assess the actual independence of regulatory intervention. Such a task is not easy because of the relative novelty of independent regulatory authorities in the Belgian political and legal landscape, the relatively scarce available research on the topic, and the discreet nature of influent forces that would aim at diminishing the independence of regulators. Nevertheless, a number of observations are worth advancing. They rely on research conducted in the framework of MEDIADEM, notably 21 interviews with experts, policy-makers and industry actors. The role and behaviour of the regulatory authorities, while not the sole focus of this research, was one of the issues covered (see Van Besien 2011 for details).

The gradual emergence of independent regulatory authorities

The judicial review of the regulatory authorities' decisions has been discussed above, and a mention must now be made of another branch of the Council of State (i.e., its legislative section, *section de législation*), whose role consists of providing high-level legal advice on projected legislation before discussion in parliament. The legislative section had traditionally opposed all projects of law that would entrust administrative authorities with a discretionary power of decision while not providing the relevant government with a sufficient capacity to control that decision. Its reasoning relied on the idea that the powers vested by the constitution could neither be renounced nor delegated: the government, as the only body accountable to the parliament, could not relinquish its responsibility to the benefit of an autonomous entity with no claim to democratic legitimacy. In other words, in its consultative capacity, the Council of State would not readily admit that an independent administrative authority be granted the power to exercise a great margin of appreciation in an autonomous manner (Delvax 2008; Renson 2011). This position, however, needs to be contrasted with the case law of the Constitutional Court. In a 2010 decision on a request for a preliminary ruling, the Court held that the absence of hierarchical control over an independent administrative authority did not violate the constitution (Cour constitutionnelle, 2010).[17] Taking into account the requirements of European law in sectors that have been submitted to a liberalization process, the constitutional judges confirmed that the legislator could entrust autonomous bodies with broad powers of appreciation when it pursued the aim of removing a field of activity from the domain of competence of the government. This seems to have confirmed the constitutional legitimacy of independent regulatory authorities (Renson 2011).

The status of members

The members of decision-making organs are appointed by the government, which means in practice that they are appointed by the political parties, generally proportional to the respective importance of each political force in the current legislature. Indeed, it has become almost a tradition in Belgian political life to organize the management of cultural institutions to mirror the composition of each community's parliament (following on a 1973 law 'ensuring the protection of ideological and philosophical leanings', known as the 'Cultural Pact'). As a consequence, the political leaning of each member of the authority is known publicly or may be found.[18] In terms of internal organization, this may lead members of the same political colour to act collectively to weigh in on the regulatory body's decisions, or to reflect the political agenda of their appointing party. Instead of depending on individual experts exerting their personal judgements, decisions may depend on similar dynamics of political opposition as occur in parliament. By contrast, Dumont (2010: 83) relies on interviews to indicate that personal sensitivity and convictions – rather than political leaning – play the decisive role in determining the attitudes of individual members of the CAC during the decision-making process. This shows that questions remain open in the present state of research.

A second possible consequence is an increased risk of influence peddling: industry lobbyists as well as politicians may tend to concentrate their attempts at influencing a decision on the few members who are of the same political colour as them. Additionally, as members may find themselves dependent on the elite of one political party for the renewal of their mandate, this situation increases their susceptibility to influence. No matter the existence of actual pressure, the non-renewal of a member may be interpreted as a sanction from the political party against an overly independent member. Finally, this situation may induce the general public to extend its feelings of distrust from politicians to the regulatory authorities. Both in terms of actual practice and of appearances, the independence of members of decision-making organs vis-à-vis the political parties could be increased.

One solution could possibly lie in the verification of the competences and personal independence of candidates before the parliament or a parliamentary committee. Another path for reflection might be to bring the status of the members closer to the status of magistrates, a solution that would follow the Flemish example of appointing magistrates to some of the positions at VRM. The length of the mandate could be longer and fixed independently of the legislature, and the financial conditions could be fixed in law rather than be left dependent upon government-adopted regulation.

As concerns possible relationships of members with the industry, it may be noted that there are rules of incompatibility as well as a duty of abstention when a conflict of interest arises. The members of the CAC, for instance, have to annually disclose their possible connections with audiovisual media interests in a closed letter to the chairman. Transparency could be extended to such information, so that the public could actually verify for itself the independence of its regulators.

Securing financial independence

The funding of the regulatory authorities may be secured by law or a management contract, but it nevertheless remains true that the budget is decided on a yearly basis by the government. The regulators may find themselves with little or no lever of action if governments decide not to fully respect their contractual engagements. To prevent the executive from sanctioning the regulators through the lessening of their financial independence, the budget of the regulatory authorities could be directly attached to the budget of the parliament instead of being an object of political appreciation in the hands of the Minister.

Small, open media markets
Belgian media landscapes are relatively small and – to varying degrees (Van Besien 2010) – open to the influence of audiovisual media services from neighbouring European countries. The most striking illustration of this phenomenon may be the decision of the most important commercial broadcaster on the French-Community market to re-localize its activity with its parent company in Luxembourg. The regulatory authority has vainly attempted to re-assert its jurisdiction over RTL Belgium (Derieux 2009). Even if the three Belgian regulatory authorities are willingly intensely involved in European cooperation with their peers, there is no consistent, coordinated regulatory action in the field of audiovisual media services at the European level. To be sure, the minimal harmonization effectuated by the AVMS Directive (European Parliament and the Council of the European Union 2010) left room for national discrepancies in legislation and allows operators to opt for the lesser-regulated territories. The result of the current state of law is that the most powerful commercial broadcaster can escape French-Community regulation (which is stricter than regulation in Luxembourg, notably in the field of advertising).[19] Other commercial broadcasters claim that it amounts to unfair competition that they should still be heavily regulated while their powerful competitor has evaded to a land of lighter regulation. The public service media argue similarly. As a consequence, it is the effectiveness of the whole regulatory system in the television sector that is somewhat put into question. The VRM does not face similar problems with such intensity, as the foreign-based media have smaller audience shares.

Interestingly, however, representatives of RTL Belgium routinely partake in seminars and meetings organized by the CSA. While the regulatory authorities need to be independent, the efficiency of their pragmatic action requires that they remain close to the actors, making them a crossroads of all possible influences. This openness – as illustrated for instance by the consultative processes – may sometimes be their better chance at exerting some influence over the forces of politics and the market.

How effectively can regulatory authorities' independence be organized? A comparative inquiry

Even though, as outlined, the German and Belgian media landscapes differ from each other, some aspects can be compared as media authorities, legislators and media operators faced similar questions arising from the federal structure. This holds true for the cooperation between regulators, the regulation in the field of public service broadcasting as well as the question of how to organize funding in a federal state *independently* from the state?

Cooperation in federal states

Cooperation through law

In Belgium and in Germany, the legislatures, the media operators, as well as the media authorities were and are compelled to cooperate because of the federal structure of the states. However, as this paragraph will explore, to a very different degree. In Belgium like in Germany, historical reasons in the course of the creation of the two countries shaped the political landscape and thus also the media landscape. After the federalization process initiated in the 1970s, Belgium became a federal state with three distinct Communities vested with legislative powers: the Flemish, the French and the German-speaking Community, operating alongside the federal government. In the case of Germany, federalization took place after World War II, as the Allied Forces organized the political spheres anew in line with their jurisdictions, which resulted in the creation of the different states (*Länder*) and, finally, the adoption of the Basic Law in 1949. Since the re-unification process in 1990, Germany comprises sixteen states.

A first fault line of potential conflicts that cause ineffective regulatory structures may occur in the relationship between state and federal legislatures in the field of media policy. Cooperation through law requires as a prerequisite a clear legal competence to act in this regard. Whereas the Belgian constitution clearly ascribes the Communities the power to enact legislation regarding matters related to media content and structures, in the case of Germany it was the Federal Constitutional Court which had to rule on the respective area of competences in 1961. The Court stipulated that it was for the states to decide on the structure and basic content regulation, while the federal level was responsible for the technical infrastructure. The tensions surrounding the competences in Germany had their origins in the decision of the Allied Forces to establish state broadcasting stations based on the principles of public service broadcasting and thus, de facto, to give the states the authority to decide on the legal framework. The idea was to establish a public communicative sphere which was independent from the state and governed by the main societal groups. It was thus the states which enacted legislation and in some cases interstate treaties to provide for a legal frame for the regional broadcasting stations. Once established, it was not possible for the Federal Government to change this situation any more and therefore the Federal Government attempted instead to establish a separate countrywide broadcaster. The envisaged *Deutschland-Fernsehen-GmbH* was not provided with a truly independent internal regulatory authority, because its raison d'être was to counterbalance the alleged impartial existing public service broadcasters. Since this endeavour was terminated by the Federal Constitutional Court, the Federal Government could not proceed to establish – in terms of independence – an inefficient governing body within the *Deutschland-Fernsehen-GmbH*.

A second fault line may occur in the cooperation among the public service broadcast organizations themselves. The six regional public service broadcasting organizations which existed in 1950 paved the way for the first forms of cooperation. It was their task to produce a common television channel, since it was simply too expensive to cover the necessary costs of establishing one on their own, especially for the smaller stations. Based on an agreement among the stations, the ARD was established as working consortium. The agreement, rather unusual as it was not enacted in the form of statutory law (Humphreys 1994: 151), was the first countrywide cooperation between regional situated broadcasting operators. Interestingly, each station remained, and still remains, responsible for the programmes produced and aired, even when this is done within the framework of the working consortium ARD. The popular news programme in the evening, *Tagesschau*, is produced by the North-German-Broadcasting (NDR), which is fully responsible for the content and the editorial decisions. The decision for a cooperative structure has influenced the governing system as well. Each Broadcasting Council of the currently existing nine regional public service broadcasters is responsible for the programmes aired or presented online. Although comprehensive cooperation is necessary, this federal structure of independent governing bodies has proven until now to work efficiently.

In the case of the Belgian public service broadcasters, cooperation in the form of interstate treaties or agreements among the operators was not necessary, since they originated as one national institution that later split along linguistic lines. Moreover, they broadcast to separate audiences, in the French, Flemish and German-language Communities respectively. The differentiated media landscape covering three language communities and thus three different audiences did not compel the broadcasters to work as close together as it was the case with the ARD.

With the advent of commercial broadcasting from 1984 onwards, the different states in Germany were compelled to act and have incrementally developed cooperative supervision structures. However, in the beginning very little, if any, cooperation existed. The states established distinct state media authorities under public law, with jurisdiction only regarding the state. Commercial broadcasters sought to find advantages by applying for a licence at more than one state media authority to gain a good bargaining position. When it came to deciding on the transmission of satellite signals covering the whole country, state governments had to decide collectively, but were not able to do so. Three different interstate treaties were applicable, resulting in disputes about supervisory competences. It became clear that issues of transmission, licensing and supervision had to be organized cooperatively, because short-sighted political influences on the governing structures posed the risk of losing any regulatory possibilities. An efficient and independent supervision of commercial broadcasting was at stake and in question because of the federal political structure. In 1987, all eleven West German states enacted the first Interstate Broadcasting Treaty, paving the way for further gradual developments. In 2008, all sixteen state legislatures introduced a joint body, the ZAK, to licence and supervise the countrywide outlets of commercial broadcasters. Comparable to the structure of the public service broadcaster ARD and because of constitutional requirements (Hain 2009: 28), the media authorities of the individual states retain responsibility, while the ZAK issues binding decisions on the cases. Interestingly, the Belgian regulatory authorities have not faced the same difficulties. Because of the structure of the media landscape of French, Flemish and German-language broadcasting, there was no need to cooperate regarding countrywide commercial broadcasters, for instance. Thus the Belgian lawmakers were not compelled to enact cooperative measures.

Cooperation in federal states prompted by media convergence: The influence of the Internet

Technical developments in the wake of digitalization and the advent of the Internet introduced a new situation that affects the federal cooperation among actors in the states as well as the legislature's competences. Problems have arisen regarding how to discuss and prepare the necessary legal solutions, which legislature is competent to enact relevant legislation and how regulatory media authorities should cooperate. As media outlets converge, it has become increasingly difficult to distinguish between solely individual telecommunication and mass communication in terms of broadcasting, because the Internet as technical backbone can provide both services. Furthermore, the Internet allows for a single person to reach a potential mass audience, which constitutes a new form of media. These developments compelled the responsible authorities to coordinate their activities and the legislatures to establish common content requirements.

First, Belgian and German constitutional law assigns telecommunication competences to the federal level, while broadcasting falls into the remit of the states (Van Besien 2010: 17). This creates the need to establish common solutions in legal questions. In the Belgian case, the governments and legislatures involved are obliged by the Constitutional Court's case law to coordinate their actions (Van Besien 2010: 17). In Germany, however, the federal and state governments and legislatures repeated the debates that had already taken place regarding the legislative competences over broadcasting, but now in the field of online competences. While the Federal Government referred to the telecommunication aspect of online communication, the states feared to lose competences. The distinction between telecommunication and broadcasting thus predominates current legislation and cooperation among regulators, inasmuch as the Interstate Broadcasting Treaty *of the sixteen states* provides for content regulation of all online outlets and the *federal* Act on Telemedia stipulates data protection requirements, copyright protection as well as general regulations on accountability of online services.

Second, the cooperation among regulators in Belgium merits attention when it comes to implementation and supervision. The three media regulators of the Communities and the federal electronic telecommunications regulator BIPT are working together in a joint body, the Conference of Regulators for the Sector of Electronic Communications (CRC) on the basis of a *cooperation agreement* of the regulators involved. In contrast with the Belgian cooperative approach of the three regulators, the German telecommunication regulator and the media state authorities may informally share information or submit comments to federal or state legislative procedures, but do not maintain a joint body comparable to the Belgian Conference of Regulators for the Sector of Electronic Communications. A joint body of media experts, state and federal representatives in the form of an expert commission was proposed in an expert opinion in the year 2000 (Hoffmann-Riem, Schulz and Held 2000: 199), but has not yet been introduced. The German Federal Parliament's cultural committee initiated a discussion among politicians and media experts in the Commission on Internet and Digital Society, which took on issues such as net neutrality, access to Internet, green IT and copyright questions, among others. Although not focusing on specific contested areas of legislation among the federal and state legislatures, this Commission evidences the undertaking of the Federal Parliament to seek common solutions for problems resulting from the digital developments.

Third, the concrete supervision of media content in a converged environment also merits attention. This aspect is important as it addresses the work of regulatory authorities regarding online content and thus the position of free and independent media in the Internet. The combination of federally divided competences and converged media outlets poses a challenge to all actors involved and raises the question of how effective regulatory authorities in federal states can work, whether in the field of cooperation, independence from the state or transparency for the user. In Belgium, the online media fall under the jurisdiction of the regulatory authorities in accordance with the definition of the concept of audiovisual media services in the AVMS-Directive (including linear and non-linear services) (European Parliament and the Council of the European Union 2010). The online printed press remains un-regulated whereas the emergence of new forms of media is to be analysed on a case-by-case basis. The Belgian VRM considers a website to be under its jurisdiction when it consists mainly of audiovisual content, and it does not supervise the printed press' online presence. In 2011, the Belgian CSA led a public consultation on the 'perimeter of regulation' during which its proposed guidelines were open to commentaries from the sector and the public. A recommendation on the topic has been adopted in March 2012. Additionally, existing general law is applied to the Internet by ordinary courts. The situation in Germany is more complicated. The German Commission for the Protection of Minors in the Media (KJM) supervises all online content concerning potential adverse influences for minors. As the Commission is composed of representatives of state media authorities, members of the state governments' departments for the protection of minors and federal representatives, cooperation and harmonization are a key objective – but at the cost of an independent regulatory body. Supervision of online outlets of German public service broadcasters lies with the respective Broadcasting Councils. The public service broadcasters' federal organization with its clearly assigned remits poses no threat to the efficiency and the independence. State media authorities, however, operate in a broader field. Some of the state media laws provide for regulatory mechanisms regarding online services that are comparable to broadcasting, but no cooperative organ exists, as it is the case with the German ZAK for the supervision of broadcasting. Furthermore, the Interstate Broadcasting Treaty stipulates that state legislatures are entitled to decide which state authority (e.g. the state's media authority or a governmental department) assumes the task of supervising whether online content adhere to the treaty's legal provisions, the general state law as well as libel provisions (Art. 59 para. 2 Interstate Broadcasting Treaty). As a result, in some states (*Länder*) the independent state media authority supervises online content while in others it is an administrative department of the government. This regulation exemplifies the difficulties of finding a common approach within a federal state in this regard, considering no harmonization could be agreed on. It points also to a field in which further research by mass communication and legal scientists could be promising in order to set out basic structures.

Regulation and independence in the field of public service broadcasting

The regulation of public service media differs significantly between the German model of internal regulation and the Belgian situation where one regulatory authority has jurisdiction over both commercial and public broadcasters. In both cases, however, the issue of political influence over public service media remains as a source of continuous tension.

The German public service broadcasters are managed by the General-Directors, whose work is controlled by an administrative council regarding fiscal matters and a Broadcasting Council, which is responsible for approving programmes and generally supervising the operation of the broadcaster. These bodies are attached to each public service broadcaster in Germany: it is thus an internal organ of the public service broadcaster that is entrusted with the role of regulator. That body is composed only in minority by representatives of political parties or the public authorities: it is mainly the 'people' that is represented in the composition of the councils. More precisely, organized societal forces such as trade unions, churches and cultural associations are invited to appoint their delegates to the regulatory assemblies. In other words, regulation is effectuated by members of the general public in the interest of the general public, according to the consensus that may emerge from the discussions among the various social groups. In contrast, the public service broadcasters in Belgium are managed by a general director and a board of directors who are appointed by the Community Governments. The board of directors reflect the political composition of parliament. The power to represent the general interest in the management of the public service broadcasting thus largely remains in the hands of the political parties: it is mediated through the views and processes of the political parties. The directors, however, may not hold a political mandate, which introduces a formal distance between public authorities and the board.

In Belgium, the regulatory authorities have a general jurisdiction over both private and public sectors: regulation of the public service broadcasting is, in contrast with the German situation, external to the broadcaster. The regulator is therefore less prone to identifying with the interests of the public service broadcaster, a situation that may occur within the Broadcasting Councils in Germany. It is worth observing that the German State media authorities, in return, tend to identify with, and stand for, the interests of the commercial broadcasters. A unified supervision body might not alter this situation, because, as it is argued, it would not act neutral in issues where public service media and commercial broadcaster interests are confronted (Holznagel and Vollmeier 2003: 288) – the debate would simply become internalized. The German dual broadcasting system with its settled positions of regulatory authorities and the Belgian dual broadcasting system with unified regulatory bodies simply have different ways to resolve the tensions inherent to the coexistence of public and commercial media.

The autonomy of the regulatory bodies is guaranteed through a number of provisions that have been described above; however, it is worth remembering that the members of the deciding organs do have a link with the political parties, too. The independent operation of the external regulation may therefore be nuanced by the intermediation of politics. Interestingly, the studies on the culture of 'circles of friends' described in the German context of internal regulation suggest that the Broadcasting Councils, although composed of civil society organizations, may reflect the political opposition between the two main political parties: the discussion culture that actually governs the decision in the regulatory organs appears to be open to political influence to some degree. However, further research would be necessary to make comprehensive and thorough statements in this regard.

Nomination and appointment procedures of the regulatory authorities: Who chooses the regulators?

The media regulatory authorities in both countries under study govern media operators and adopt – in different degrees, according to their remit – regulatory decisions. As we saw, external regulators like the Belgian VRM or CSA monitor compliance with audiovisual regulations, including impartiality of information, protection of minors and rules on advertising. As they can impose fines and even withdraw licences, their position is important. The same holds true for the German state media authorities as well as their joint bodies with authority over countrywide commercial broadcasting. As described in the case of the German Commission on Concentration in the Media (KEK), merger control mechanisms can be influential and thus prone to economic or political pressure. The Broadcasting Councils overseeing the public service broadcasters in Germany enjoy an even broader mandate than the external authorities, since they elect the General-Director and adopt basic programme principles.

As the independence of regulatory authorities constitutes a core value in both Belgium and Germany and is protected through various means, the nomination and appointment procedures are of crucial importance. Essentially, once appointed to the body, a member is only bound by the applicable laws and regulatory mechanisms. Thus the question arises how this 'hinge' might be prone to political or economic influence.

Fundamentally, nomination and appointment procedures are organized in line with the federal structure of the media regulatory system. The responsible authorities are not a single institution, but state parliaments and governments as well as societal groups. However, the possible degree of political influence varies, as the Belgian legislatures concede political forces a predominant position in the nomination and appointment procedure, while in Germany the laws give precedence to societal forces and civil society organizations.

The governments of the Flemish, French and German-speaking Communities in Belgium appoint the members of the respective organs of the three regulatory authorities, for a five-year renewable term or, in the case of the German-speaking Community, for the duration of the legislative period. In the case of the French Community's CSA, the Community Parliament is mandated as well. Suggestions may be advanced by the stakeholders, but the final decision remains with the government (or parliament) and thus the political parties. Legislation provides for requirements in terms of incompatibility rules (excluding for instance regulatory authority members from parliamentary or governmental positions) and in terms of expertise, which may temper party political influence. However, the respective members may espouse party positions within the organs, instead of following their individual expertise or personal judgment.

The German model gives – generally – societal groups precedence in the appointment procedure. The state broadcasting laws concerning the nine regional public service broadcasting stations always provide for a majority of representatives of societal groups, nominated and appointed by the groups themselves. Besides rules regarding incompatibility (members of state media authorities or of other public service Broadcasting Councils are excluded) and basic expertise in the field of broadcasting, the respective societal group or civil society association is free to choose whom to delegate. Thus societal groups decide on the composition of the body, but the political parties and in some cases individual governmental representatives can remain represented in the body as well, because legislation does not exclude party or governmental representatives in regulatory authorities. The appointment procedure of the ZDF's Television Council constitutes the sole exception for German national public service broadcasters and resembles the Belgian model, as members can be nominated by the respective group but have to be appointed by the heads of the states, if possible consensually.

As with the Broadcasting Councils, in the case of twelve of the fourteen state media authorities the societal groups enjoy the right to appoint the members of the respective organ, as provided in the state media law. However, similar to the Belgian case, parliaments appoint the experts for the state media authorities' council of Hamburg and Schleswig-Holstein as well as Berlin-Brandenburg. Furthermore, the heads of the state governments appoint six experts of the German Commission on Concentration in the Media (KEK). Unlike the Belgian case, the legislatures have conceded the societal groups and civil societies a strong position – complemented, however, with a governmental and parliamentary role or representation in the regulatory authority themselves or in the election respectively appointment procedures for some of the regulatory bodies.

It would be an interesting task to examine whether the Belgian or the German model gives *actual* precedence to independent decisions by the respective regulatory authorities or whether one allows for more (undue) state influence than the other. Such a study would, however, have to carve out comparable parameters and would also have to define undue state influence with regard to regulatory performance.

Funding: The role of the political actors in the funding scheme

The financial autonomy of the German regulatory authorities, for both public and commercial media, rests upon a complex procedure that aims at preventing state influence (see above). This process determines, for a period of four years, the licence fee that serves as the basis for the income of the public service broadcasters, their Broadcasting Councils and by extension the state media authorities responsible for the supervision of the commercial broadcasters. A group of sixteen experts contributes to determining the appropriate level of financing on an objective basis. The state legislatures hold only a limited power of intervention regarding the confirmation of the amount of the licence fee and the percentage of the licence fee to be paid to state media authorities. Despite the federal structure of public service broadcasters' regulatory authorities as well as the state media authorities, it is a single body that prepares and thus significantly shapes the budget. An efficient and also independent mechanism was found to provide the financial basis for a federally structured supervisory system. In the case of Belgium, the funding of the regulatory authorities seems to be more prone to political influence. To be sure, the financial arrangements are covered by a contract that should secure income: however, the budget is subjected to government approval on a yearly basis, and the regulators may not have much protection in case the government does not fully respect the financial agreements.

Conclusion

This chapter illustrates and outlines the different legal safeguards that ensure the regulatory authorities' efficiency and independence in Belgium and Germany. Furthermore, we sought to investigate their actual independence, mainly based on the research carried out for the MEDIADEM project. In following this approach, it became clear that our work can carve out research questions, as a first and necessary step, as well as systematically present some critical observations pertaining to the actual independence of regulatory authorities. In order to arrive at scientifically sound results, it would be necessary to carry out comprehensive research that could combine a mass communication science and legal approach to verify (or falsify) our observations. For instance, it would be interesting to know more about the actual independence of German Broadcasting Council members and the alleged party influence. The question arises whether the 'circles of friends' with their political affiliations are still as influential as was the case twenty years ago. Concurrently, the Belgian model of political party appointments and the actual influence of party positions could be subject of a research project.

It also became clear that the federal political structure of each country reverberates in its media authority structure. This is evidenced in the existence of three different regulatory authorities in Belgium as well as their high number in Germany. Based on the available research results, we were able to ascertain that regulatory authorities in federal states face a complex structure in their regulatory work and that they need time and resources for cooperation, but no compelling evidence could be found that the federal structure impedes regulatory independence. The reasons for this are different in each country: in Belgium, the media landscape is distinct between the Communities and therefore the jurisdiction of the authorities is too. In this case, the federal structure itself outlines the remit. In Germany, the state media authorities had to learn to cooperate, which has resulted in 2008 in a joint body: the Commission on Licensing and Supervision (ZAK). But it seems that this cooperative approach satisfies the needs of media supervision in a federal state. That was not always the case, as the federal supervision of commercial broadcasters and the distinct vested interests of state governments put the system at risk in its early times in the 1980s. Other factors can influence the efficiency and also the independence of the regulatory authorities, but they stem from political or economic attempts to exert undue influence and not from the federal structure. But again, this is uncharted terrain and it would be illuminating to carry out further comparative research.

Notes

1 At the time of writing, P.-F. Docquir holds a 2007–2012 mandate as vice-president of the High Council for Audiovisual (Conseil supérieur de l'audiovisuel, CSA). Views expressed here are personal and do not reflect any official position of the CSA. Please see http://about. me/pfdocquir.
2 At the time of writing, Sebastian Müller was researcher at the Bielefeld University. The opinions made in the text reflect his personal views.
3 See generally http://mediadem.eliamep.gr for detailed information and results.
4 According to Black's Law Dictionary: 'Federalisms connotes the relationship and distribution of power between the national and regional governments within a federal system of government'.
5 For a more detailed overview of the German media landscape and its legal framework see Müller and Gusy (2010).
6 For a more detailed overview of Belgium's media landscape and its legal and regulatory framework, see Van Besien (2010) and Docquir and Van Besien (2012).
7 The Constitutional Court's jurisdiction is twofold. For one part, it arbitrates on conflicts about the respective competences of the different components of the state (indeed, it was named the 'Arbitrage' Court from its creation in 1980 until 2007); for the other part, it acts as guardian of the fundamental rights protected by the Constitution.
8 See http://www.csa.be/documents/1573.
9 http://www.epra.org.
10 When it deals with issues related to the protection of minors, the second chamber expands to include four additional experts, two of whom must come from the field of psychology, psychiatry or pedagogy, while the two others need to be (somehow) involved with the promotion of the interests of children or families.

11 Members of the Board also take part in the work of the Advisory College.

12 Members of the CAC or the advisory college may not be members of any organization that does not respect the principles of democracy and human rights.

13 The fact that the SI is not independent from the CAC (since the Board, whose members sit in the CAC, has authority over the SI) has led the ECJ to conclude that the CSA had no power to request a preliminary ruling, as it lacked the independence required of 'tribunals' in the sense of Art. 267 Treaty EU (ECJ, C-517/09, Dec. 22, 2010). The matter was subsequently discussed in the Parliament of the French Community and the Minister mentioned the possible revision of the status of SI (CRIc No48-Cult.8 (2010–2011), p. 20 ff.), but the situation remained unchanged at the time of writing.

14 http://www.csa.be, http://www.medienrat.be, http://www.vlaamseregulatormedia.be.

15 A good approach illustrates the INDIREG Final Report (Hans Bredow Institute for Media Research et al 2011) for Estonia, Hungary, Italy, Netherlands, Slovenia, United Kingdom, Macedonia and Bosnia and Herzegovina.

16 Exceptions exist in the case of MDR and Radio Bremen.

17 The decision concerned the regulatory body for the markets of gas and electricity but its relevance extends to all regulatory authorities.

18 In the case of the CSA, the government's formal decision to appoint members mentions the political affiliation of the appointees.

19 On the other hand, the divergence between the positions presented before the ECJ by the CSA (request for preliminary ruling) and the French-Community government (whose lawyer argued that there was no need to answer the request) illustrates the actual independence of the regulatory body.

References

Arbeitsgemeinschaft der Landesmedienanstalten (2011), *Jahrbuch 2010/2011. Landesmedienanstalten und privater Rundfunk in Deutschland*/Yearbook 2010/2011. State Media Authorities and Private Broadcasting in Germany, Berlin: Vistas Verlag.

Basic Law for the Federal Republic of Germany (2012).

Bavarian Broadcasting Act (2009).

Belgian Constitutional Court (2010), Dec. 2010–130, Nov. 18, 2010, see http://www.const-court.be.

Brosius, H.-B., Rössler, P. and Schulte zur Hausen, C. (2000), 'Zur Qualität der Medienkontrolle: Ergebnisse einer Befragung deutscher Rundfunk- und Medienräte/About Quality in Media Supervision: Results of a Survey of German Broadcasting and Media Councils', *Publizistik*, 4, pp. 417–441.

Bumke, U. (1995), *Die öffentliche Aufgabe der Landesmedienanstalten*/The Public Duty of State Media Authorities, Munich: C. H. Beck.

Cooperation Agreement of 17 November 2006, *Moniteur belge*, 28 December 2006, 75371.

Dehousse, F., Verbiest, T., and Zgajewski, T. (2007), *Introduction au droit de la société de l'information*/Introduction to the Law of the Information Society, Larcier, Brussels.

Delvax, D. (2008), 'Les contrôles administratifs pesant sur les autorités administratives indépendantes/Administrative Judicial Control of Independent Administrative Authorities', *Revue de droit de l'ULB/Review of Law of the Université Libre de Bruxelles*, 37, pp. 107–136.

Derieux, E. (2009), 'Exclusion d'un double contrôle/Exclusion of Double Control', *Auteurs & Médias*, 3, p. 306.

Docquir, P.-F. and Van Besien, B. (2012), 'Media Policy in Belgium: How a Complex Institutional System Deals with Technological Developments', in E. Psychogiopoulou (ed.), *Understanding Media Policy: a European Perspective*, Palgrave Macmillan.

Dörr, D. (2004), 'Die Vorschriften im Rundfunksstaatsvertrag zur Sicherung der Meinungsvielfalt/ The Regulation to Safeguard Pluralism of Opinion in the Interstate Broadcasting Treaty', *Zeitschrift für Wettbewerbsrecht*, pp. 159–190.

Dörr, D. (2009), 'Die Mitwirkung des Verwaltungsrats bei der Bestellung des ZDF-Chefredakteurs und das Problem der Gremienzusammensetzung/Participation of the Administrative Council in the Appointment of the ZDF-Chief Editor and the Problem of the Organ Composition', *Kommunikation & Recht*, 9, pp. 555–559.

Dumont, C. (2010), 'Le Conseil supérieur de l'audiovisuel, une autorité de régulation indépendante/ The High Council for the Audiovisual Sector: An Independent Regulatory Authority', *Courrier hebdomadaire du CRISP/CRIPS's Weekly Courier*, 9/2010 (n° 2054–2055), pp. 5–88.

Eifert, M. and Hoffmann-Riem, W. (1999), 'Die Entstehung und Ausgestaltung des dualen Rundfunksystems/The Development and the Arrangement of the Dual Broadcasting System', in D. Schwarzkopf (ed.), *Rundfunkpolitik in Deutschland. Band 1*, Munich: dtv, pp. 50–116.

European Commission (2007), Decision C (2007) 1761, State aid E 3/2005, of 24 April 2007 on the financing of public service broadcasters in Germany.

European Parliament and the Council of the European Union (2010), Directive 2010/13/EU of the European Parliament and of the Council of 10 March 2010 on the coordination of certain provisions laid down by law, regulation or administrative action in Member States concerning the provision of audiovisual media services (Audiovisual Media Services Directive), Official Journal of the European Union of 15.4.2010 L 95/1.

Federal Constitutional Court (2007), judgement of 11 September 2007, no. 1 BvR 2270/05 et al., in *Multimedia und Recht* (MMR), p. 770.

Federal Constitutional Court (1994), judgement of 22 February 1994, no. 1 BvL 30/88, in *Neue Juristische Wochenschrift* (NJW), p. 1942.

Federal Constitutional Court (1961), judgement of 28 February 1961, no. 2 BvG 1, 2/60, in *BVerfGE*, 12, p. 205.

Flemish Community Act on Radio and Television Broadcasting, 27 March, 2009, *Moniteur belge*, 30 April 2009, 34470.

Flemish Community Framework Act on Administrative Policy, 18 July, 2003, *Moniteur belge*, 22 August 2003, 41667.

French Community Act on Audiovisual Media Services, 26 March 2009, *Moniteur belge*, 24 July 2007, 50609.

German Community Act of 27 June 2005, on audiovisual media services and film showings, *Moniteur belge*, 6 September 2005, 38892.

Gersdorf, H. (2003), *Grundzüge des Rundfunkrechts/Basic structures of broadcasting law*, Munich: C. H. Beck.

Gounalakis, G. and Zagouras, G. (2008), *Medienkonzentrationsrecht. Vielfaltsicherung in den Medien/ Law of Media Concentration, Ensuring Pluralism in the Media*, Munich: C. H. Beck.

Hahn, C. (2010), *Die Aufsicht des öffentlich-rechtlichen Rundfunks/Supervision of Public Service Broadcasting*, Frankfurt/Main: Peter Lang.

Hain, K.-E. (2009), *Grenzen der Zentralisierung von Zulassungs- und Aufsichtsentscheidungen im föderalen Rundfunksystem/Limitations in the Centralized Organisation of Supervision and Licence Decisions in a Federal Broadcasting System*, Berlin: Vistas Verlag.

Hans Bredow Institute for Media Research, Interdisciplinary Centre for Law & ICT (ICRI), Katholieke Universiteit Leuven; Center for Media and Communication Studies (CMCS), Central European University; Cullen International; Perspective Associates (eds., 2011), *INDIREG. Indicators for independence and efficient functioning of audio-visual media services regulatory bodies for the purpose of enforcing the rules in the AVMS Directive*, Study conducted on behalf of the European Commission, Final Report. February 2011.

Hoebeke, S. and Mouffe, B. (2005), *Le droit de la presse/Law of the Press*, Academia-Bruylant, Brussels.

Hoffmann-Riem, W., Schulz, W., and Held, T. (2000), *Konvergenz und Regulierung/Convergence and Regulation*, Baden-Baden: Nomos.

Holznagel, B. and Vollmeier, I. (2003), 'Gemeinsame oder getrennte Aufsicht? Ein Überblick über die verschiedenen Ansätze der Beaufsichtigung von öffentlichem und kommerziellem Rundfunk/Unified or separated supervision? Overview of the Different Models of Supervision of Public Service and Commercial Broadcasting', in P. Donges and M. Puppis (eds.), *Die Zukunft des öffentlichen Rundfunks*, Copenhagen: Halem, pp. 277–291.

Humphreys, P. J. (1994), *Media and Media Policy in Germany*, 2nd ed., Oxford and Providence: Berg Publishers.

Interstate Treaty on Broadcasting and Telemedia (Interstate Broadcasting Treaty) (2010).

Interstate Treaty on the Protection of Minors (2010).

Interstate Treaty on Second German Television (2009).

Interstate Treaty on Broadcasting Financing (2009).

Jarren, O. et al. (2001), *Der öffentliche Rundfunk im Netzwerk von Politik, Wirtschaft und Gesellschaft/Public Service Broadcasting in the Network of Politic, Economy and Society*, Baden-Baden: Nomos.

Jongen, F. (2003), 'Cinq ans plus un: un premier bilan du nouveau C.S.A./Five Years Plus One: a First Assessment of the New CSA', *Auteurs & Médias*, 2003: 6, pp. 422–432.

Jongen, F. (ed.) (2010), *La Directive Service de Médias Audiovisuels/The AVMS Directive*, Anthemis-Bruylant, Brussels.

KEK (2006), decision of 10 January 2006, no. KEK 293-1 bis 5.

Klass, N. (2011), *Unterhaltung ohne Grenzen? Der Schutzbereich der Menschenwürde in den Programmgrundsätzen der Medienstaatsverträge/Limitless Entertainment? The Scope of Protection of Human Dignity in the Programme Principles of Interstate Treaties on Media*, Berlin: Vistas Verlag.

Kommission für Jugendmedienschutz (2011), *Vierter Bericht/Fourth Report*, Erfurt und Munich: KJM.

Kommission zur Ermittlung des Finanzbedarfs der Rundfunkanstalten (KEF) (2009), *17. Bericht/17th Report*, Mainz: KEF.

Kommission zur Ermittlung der Konzentration im Medienbereich (KEK) (2011), *Vierzehnter Jahresbericht/Fourteenth Annual Report*, Potsdam: die medienanstalten.

Landesanstalt für Medien Nordrhein-Westfalen (2010), *'Menschenwürde im privaten Rundfunk': Mahrenholz ermutigt Medienaufsicht zu beherztem Vorgehen/'Human Dignity in Commercial Broadcasting': Mahrenholz Encourages Media Authority to Act Dauntlessly*, press release, 3 February 2010.

Mitteldeutscher Rundfunk (MDR) (2011), *Noch kein Nachfolger für MDR-Intendanten/Still no Successor for the MDR-General Director*, press release, 26 September 2011.

Müller, S. and Gusy C. (2010), 'The case of Germany', in: *Media Policies and Regulatory Practices in a Selected Set of European Countries, the EU and the Council of Europe*, Report for the MEDIADEM project (FP7-SSH-2009-A no. 244365), http://www.mediadem.eliamep.gr/wp-content/uploads/2010/05/BIR.pdf.

Potelle, P.-Y. (2003), 'Un nouveau statut pour le régulateur des télécommunications dans un secteur en pleine mutation/A New Status for the Regulator of Telecommunications in a Mutating Sector', *Revue du droit des technologies de l'information/Information Technologies Law Review*, 16, pp. 83–97.

Renson, A.-C. (2011), 'L'indépendance des autorités de régulation: la fin d'une controverse/Independence of Regulation Authorities: the End of Controversy', *Journal des Tribunaux/Journal of Courts*, pp. 349–350.

Schneider, N. (2011), 'Medienregulierung 2015/Regulation of Media 2015', *Funkkorrespondenz*, 2011: 33.

Schuler-Harms, M. (1995), *Rundfunkaufsicht im Bundesstaat/Broadcasting Supervision in a Federal State*, Baden-Baden: Nomos.

Schwotzer, B. (2011), 'Fernsehen in Deutschland 2009/2010/ Television in Germany 2009/2010', in ALM (ed.), *Programmbericht 2010. Fernsehen in Deutschland*, Berlin: Vistas Verlag, pp. 26–41.

State Media Law Rhineland-Palatinate (2010).

Stock, M. (1997), 'Konzentrationskontrolle in Deutschland nach der Neufassung des Rundfunkstaatsvertrags 1996/Supervision of media concentration in Germany according to the Interstate Broadcasting Treaty 1996', in M. Stock, H. Röper and B. Holznagel (eds.), *Medienmarkt und Meinungsmacht*, Berlin: Springer, pp. 1–78.

Van Besien, B. (2010), 'The Case of Belgium', in *Media Policies and Regulatory Practices in a Selected Set of European Countries, the EU and the Council of Europe*, Report for the MEDIADEM project (FP7-SSH-2009-A no. 244365), http://www.mediadem.eliamep.gr/wp-content/uploads/2010/05/BIR.pdf. Accessed 21 August 2013.

Van Besien, B. (2011), 'The Case of Belgium', in *Does Media Policy Promote Media Freedom And Independence?*, Case Study Reports for the MEDIADEM project (FP7-SSH-2009-A no. 244365), http://www.mediadem.eliamep.gr/wp-content/uploads/2012/01/Belgium.pdf.

West-German-Broadcasting Act (WDR-Broadcasting Act) (2009).

Westphal, D. (2007), *Föderale Privatrundfunkaufsicht im demokratischen Verfassungsstaat/ Federal Supervision of Commercial Broadcasting in a Democratic Constitutional State*, Berlin: Duncker & Humblot.

Westphal, D. (2008), 'Abschied vom Original. Zur Deformation der KEK durch den 10. Rundfunkänderungsstaatsvertrag/Parting of an original. About the deformation of KEK', *ZUM*, pp. 854–861.

Chapter 10

The independence of media regulatory authorities in Finland
and the UK: An assessment

Rachael Craufurd Smith
University of Edinburgh

Epp Lauk
University of Jyväskylä

Yolande Stolte
University of Edinburgh

Heikki Kuutti
University of Jyväskylä

Abstract

This article compares the measures taken to ensure the independence of media regulatory bodies from political and industry influence in Finland and the UK. It argues that Hallin and Mancini's models of media regulation continue to provide a useful framework for understanding at least some of the nuances in the way the two countries seek to regulate their media industries and to address the vulnerabilities to political or industrial influence that stem from those regulatory choices. Though regulatory transplants from one country to another may, for legal, cultural or economic reasons, be neither appropriate nor successful, we suggest that useful comparative lessons can be learned, particularly in relation to the potential benefits of co-regulation, the role of evidence-based rule making and the need to shape regulatory structures with the convergent nature of the media in mind.

Keywords: press freedom, Democratic Corporatist model, Liberal model, co-regulation, self-regulation, codes of ethics

Introduction

As members of the European Union and Council of Europe and signatories to the European Convention on Human Rights, both Finland and the United Kingdom (UK) accord a high level of respect to press freedom, political rights and civil liberties. Finland is a small Nordic country with a potential media market limited to its population of 5.36 million, which is 90 per cent Finnish-speaking and 5.4 per cent Swedish-speaking. Finnish media policy is oriented towards the relaxation of statutory regulation, with a preference for flexible and directive regulation rather than bureaucratic, restrictive regulatory regimes. Within a framework that is maximally supportive of freedom of expression, legal regulation focuses on guaranteeing responsible use of this freedom and holding the media accountable to society. Finnish media regulatory authorities have no coercive power, nor the power to sanction journalists, editors or publishers, but are mainly responsible for monitoring the media organizations' compliance with the laws and regulations.

The UK, with a population of over 62 million, has a greater capacity to develop its media markets and has a diverse media sector. The present coalition government has expressed a strong commitment to reducing regulatory constraints on industry (HM Government

2010), and future proposals for the communications sector are likely to have a marked deregulatory dimension (Hunt 2011). The main communications regulator in the UK, the Office of Communications (Ofcom), also has a preference for 'light-touch' regulation and co-regulatory structures wherever possible, in line with the general direction of European Union (EU) communications policies (Ofcom 2008).

Given the emphasis that the EU and Council of Europe place on freedom of the press and the independence of media regulatory bodies, one would expect the two countries to adopt a broadly similar approach to regulation in the media field. Philosophical, cultural and economic factors, however, lead states to interpret and balance press freedom, political rights and civil liberties in markedly different ways. Hallin and Mancini, in their comparison of media systems, considered Finland and the UK to exemplify different models, with Finland representative of the Northern European or Democratic Corporatist model and the UK of the North Atlantic or Liberal model (Hallin and Mancini 2004). Though these models share certain commonalities, notably a high level of professionalization and reliance on rational legal authority as opposed to clientelism, the differences have important implications for the scale and nature of state intervention in the media field. The Northern European model, shaped by a history of consensus politics and organized pluralism, involves institutionalized forms of self-regulation, significant state intervention and strong support for public service broadcasting. The Liberal model, grounded in majoritarian government and individualized representation, is reflected by non-institutionalized forms of self-regulation and reliance on the market, though UK support for public service media brings it closer to the Northern European model in this respect.

In this chapter, we explore whether these models enable us to understand the regulatory structures and practices that shape the provision of media goods and services in Finland and the UK today. In particular, we examine how the two countries have sought to insulate the various regulatory bodies from inappropriate commercial or political pressures. Regulatory independence can be supported, more or less directly, by a cluster of organizational strategies that relate to the mode of appointment and term of office of key personnel; structure and remit; operating procedures, notably with regard to transparency and consultation; method and sufficiency of funding; and accountability (Hans Bredow Institute for Media Research, et al. 2011; Gilardi and Maggetti 2010). As the Council of Europe has stated, 'independent broadcasting regulatory authorities can only function in an environment of transparency, accountability, clear separation of powers and due respect for the legal framework in force' (Council of Europe 2008: recitals).

We focus on these factors below in our consideration of specific media regulators in the two countries, comparing similarities and differences in the levels of independence from both formal and de facto perspectives (see Chapter 5 in this book by Stephan Dreyer). We consider first the public and commercial audiovisual media sectors, before turning our attention to press self-regulation. We explain the laws and practices that shape regulation in each field, drawing on policy documents, academic literature and interviews carried out with regulators and journalists as part of our participation in the EU-funded MEDIADEM research project, which explores policies to promote free and independent media (MEDIADEM 2012). Our chapter thus seeks to feed into wider debates about both the continuing relevance of Hallin and Mancini's models and the effectiveness of certain regulatory strategies in promoting regulatory independence in the media field. We start, by way of background, with a brief explanation of the constitutional and public law principles that apply in each country.

Constitutional and public law principles relating to the independence of regulatory authorities in Finland and the UK

As noted above, both Finland and the UK are signatories to the European Convention on Human Rights (ECHR) and member states of the European Union (EU). In Finland, the ECHR is given effect through constitutional guarantees and the Act on the Exercise of Freedom of Expression in Mass Media (especially s. 1) (Finnish Parliament 2003), whereas in the UK, consequent on the doctrine of the supremacy of parliament, 'Convention rights' are protected by virtue of the Human Rights Act 1998, an ordinary act of parliament (UK Parliament 1998b).

Two provisions of the ECHR are directly relevant in this context. First, Art. 10, which protects freedom of expression, requires state parties to justify any restriction on this freedom on the basis of limited exceptions set out in Art. 10(2) or as a result of the need to balance conflicting Convention rights. In the case of *Manole and Others v Moldova* (European Court of Human Rights 2009), the European Court of Human Rights also recognized that states may be under a positive duty to regulate the media to ensure that they reflect the diversity of political views in their country. Any attempt by a state or government to regulate the media for partisan political advantage would thus be considered a disproportionate restriction on freedom of expression and the right to access information. Drawing on the requirements imposed by Art. 10, the Council of Europe passed a recommendation and declaration in 2000 and 2008 respectively on the independence and functions of regulatory authorities for the broadcasting sector, which identify how regulatory independence can be strengthened in relation to each of the various components of the regulatory process (Council of Europe 2000; 2008). Second, Art. 6 ECHR requires that the determination of a person's civil or criminal rights, which encompasses the right to freedom of expression, must be carried out by an independent and impartial tribunal.

The EU Charter of Fundamental Rights has parallel provisions to Arts. 10 and 6 ECHR in its Arts. 11 and 47, the former explicitly noting the importance of media pluralism. In secondary EU law, increasing emphasis has been placed on the need for national regulatory authorities, particularly those regulating core utilities, to be independent from both political and industry interests. Key guiding principles have also been developed by the Court of Justice in relation to data protection supervision in the case of *European Commission v Federal Republic of Germany* (Court of Justice of the European Union 2010) (see Chapter 4 in this book by David Stevens). In the communications sector, the 2009 Framework Directive for electronic communications networks and services explicitly requires national telecommunications regulatory bodies to be protected from external pressures or political influence that might jeopardize their independent judgment (European Parliament and the Council of the European Union 2009: recital 13 and new Art. 3a). Specific attention is paid to the protection of officials from removal from office on political grounds and the provision of sufficient funds to enable the body to fulfil its tasks efficiently. These provisions apply to 'converged' regulators, present in both the UK and Finland, with responsibility for telecommunication services as well as for television and radio broadcasts. Although the Audiovisual Media Services (AVMS) Directive (European Parliament and the Council of the European Union 2010), which regulates television broadcasts and 'television-like' on-demand services, does not formally require regulatory independence, it does specifically refer to independent regulatory bodies in recital 94, stimulating further research by the EU into regulatory standards in the field (European Parliament and the Council of the European Union 2010; Hans Bredow Institute for Media Research, et al. 2011).

Finland has advanced domestic democratic traditions and a developed civil society and civic culture. According to World Audit.org, using data from Transparency International's Corruption Perceptions Index (CPI), Finland ranked second lowest in corruption levels among 150 countries in December 2011 (World Audit 2011). Finland is characterized by the openness of its economy, technology and government proceedings (Lewis 2005). It has a strong tradition of transparent decision making and access to information: the world's first Freedom of Information Act, adopted by the Swedish Parliament in 1766 (Anders Chydenius Foundation 2006), also covered Finland, then part of the Swedish Kingdom. The Act abolished censorship and declared public access to government documents. During 1772–1809 the Act was suspended, but the principle of transparency of public affairs has remained central in Finland, as in all Nordic countries (Björkstrand and Mustonen 2006: 6).

The basic guidelines relating to regulatory bodies and their practices in Finland derive from the country's constitution, adopted in 1919 and last amended in 1999. By virtue of Art. 12 everyone has the right of expression and the right to disseminate and receive information without prior restraint. The same Article is the basis for requiring that state authorities act in a transparent and open fashion, providing that everyone has the right to freely access documents and records in the possession of the authorities. The Act on Openness of Government Activities (Finnish Parliament 1999) establishes the principle that official documents (those in the possession of, prepared by, or delivered to, an authority) shall be in the public domain unless there is a specific reason for withholding them. The application of the Act is very broad: in addition to public authorities it also applies to *ad hoc* bodies that exercise public authority.

The Freedom of Expression Act (Finnish Parliament 2003) provides further detail on how these constitutional provisions apply to all types of mass media, including online media. The main principle underpinning the Act is set out in s. 1, which provides that 'interference with the activities of the media shall be legitimate only in so far as it is unavoidable, taking due note of the importance of the freedom of expression in a democracy subject to the rule of law'. Legally binding restrictions on the freedom of expression in Finland must be in accordance with Art. 10 para. 2 of the European Convention of Human Rights.

The Finnish Constitution (Finnish Parliament 1999) does not specifically determine the structure of, or guarantees relating to, media regulatory authorities. Instead, their functions, structures and operating conditions are established by separate acts and government decrees. The Act on Communication Administration (Finnish Parliament 2001) establishes the duties of the Finnish Communications Regulatory Authority (FICORA); the Act on the Finnish Competition Authority (Finnish Parliament 1988) regulates the activities of the Finnish Competition Authority (FCA). According to these Acts, FICORA operates under the Ministry of Transport and Communications and the FCA under the Ministry of Employment and the Economy, both as independent units of these ministries. The Act of Yleisradio Oy (Finnish Parliament 1993) is the basis of the Finnish public service broadcasting operations. Finland does not have a dedicated ministry for the communications sector and responsibility for preparing and implementing new legislation relating to the mass media is dispersed among different ministries, such as the Ministries for Justice, Education and Culture, Transport and Communications, and Employment and the Economy.

In Finland, transparency and openness are key conventions supported by legislation, which, in combination, contribute to the actual independence of, and public trust in, the regulatory authorities, and the fairness of their activities. The posts of public officials are defined with reference to required expertise and secured by the Act on Civil Servants (Finnish Parliament 1994). There is very little room for nepotism. The Finnish Criminal Code (Finnish Parliament 1889) contains provisions intended to protect the independence and impartiality of public officials: Chapter 16 deals with offences against public authorities and offences in office (e.g. giving and accepting bribes). The Act on Civil Servants establishes three exclusive conditions for removing public officials from their posts: (1) if the job is terminated, (2) if the job requirements diminish to an extent that there is insufficient work for a full time job and (3) if the public official outrageously violates the terms of, or fails in performing, their duties (The Act on Civil Servants, §§ 27, 33).

The UK does not have a formal written constitution and key Articles of the ECHR, including Arts. 6 and 10, are given effect to by the Human Rights Act 1998 (UK Parliament 1998b). The Act requires 'public authorities', a term broad enough to cover state regulatory bodies such as the Competition Commission and the main communications regulator Ofcom; private regulatory bodies carrying out public functions such as the Press Complaints Commission (see High Court (QBD) 2001); courts and tribunals; and persons whose functions are of a 'public nature', to act in conformity with 'Convention rights' unless unambiguously prevented from doing so by primary legislation (s. 6). In interpreting Convention rights, public bodies are required to 'take into account' judgements of the European Court of Human Rights (s. 2). Moreover, so far as it is possible to do so, primary legislation and subordinate legislation must be read and given effect to in a way that is compatible with Convention rights (s. 3).

Unlike Finland, there is no formal constitutional requirement relating to the transparency of public bodies, though the UK and Scotland have passed specific Freedom of Information laws, which establish a general right of access to information held by public authorities (Freedom of Information Act 2000 and Freedom of Information (Scotland) Act 2002) (UK Parliament 2000; Scottish Parliament 2002). The communications regulator Ofcom is covered by this legislation, as is the public broadcaster, the BBC, in respect of information held for purposes other than those of journalism, art or literature (Freedom of Information Act 2000, Schedule 1). Recognition of the importance of a free press has underscored the UK's commitment to self-regulation in the print sector and limited regulatory intervention regarding online services.

The UK is a unitary state, but specific legislative powers have been devolved to the Welsh, Scottish and Northern Irish nations. Competence in relation to the broadcast media, spectrum management and competition policy has, however, been retained by the central Westminster Parliament, which has tended to be controlled by powerful single party government majorities, elected on a 'first past the post' basis. The present coalition government, formed by the Conservative and Liberal Democrat parties, thus constitutes a relatively novel arrangement and the implications for the media sector have yet to be clearly established. The ability of the government to dominate proceedings in Parliament, implement devolved powers, and direct the exercise of certain royal prerogatives, has led to the executive exercising considerable power in relation to the setting-up and financing of the various media regulatory bodies and the appointment of their key officials. Alternating terms of office have, however, discouraged governments from using this power solely for their own advantage and a number of conventions and more or less formalized practices have developed to moderate government influence and guarantee a significant degree of regulatory independence.

Key among the conventions that govern these appointments are the seven 'Nolan Principles of Public Life', established in 1995 (Nolan 1995: 14). These call for holders of public office to be selfless and have integrity; to be objective, accountable, open and honest; and to show leadership. The Nolan principles led to improvements in the way in which key public appointments are made in order to reduce the risk of patronage and cronyism. In particular, a Commissioner for Public Appointments was established, whose remit is to ensure that appointments are made on merit and conform to a code of practice (Commissioner for Public Appointments 2012); posts are advertised publicly; and independent assessors are involved in the selection of suitable short lists. Final selection of the individual to fill key posts will in most instances, however, remain with the government, it being argued that the government is ultimately accountable to parliament for the operation of executive bodies under its control (Commissioner for Public Appointments 2011). The key UK regulatory bodies concerned with the media operate under the auspices of the Department for Culture, Media and Sport ('DCMS') and the Department for Business, Innovation and Skills ('DBIS').

A brief overview of the regulatory landscape

The main Finnish regulatory bodies in charge of implementing, and supervising compliance with, media-related laws and regulations are the communications regulator FICORA and the competition authority FCA. Fulfilment of the same functions in relation to public service broadcasting is entrusted to the Administrative Council of the Finnish Broadcasting Company (YLE) and is based on a combination of statutory and self-regulatory measures. The most authoritative self-regulatory body operating in the media field is the Council for the Mass Media (CMM), supported by the Union of Journalists in Finland (UJF) and the Federation of the Finnish Media Industry (Finnmedia). Advertising is regulated by the Consumer Protection Act (Finnish Parliament 1978) and the Council of Ethics in Advertising. The Finnish Centre for Media Education and Audiovisual Media is responsible for preventing audiovisual content harmful for minors and for age classification of audiovisual products. There is no specific regulation relating to media markets or media ownership and these issues are regulated by the Competition Act (Finnish Parliament 2011) under the supervision of the FCA.

In the UK, a wide variety of bodies are active in regulating the mass media. Media-specific state, co-regulatory and self-regulatory regimes are all employed alongside the operation of generally applicable statutory and common law provisions, overseen by the courts. The number of media-specific regulators grew in the latter part of the twentieth century, reflecting technological and economic developments (Levy 2001: 33; Milwood-Hargrave and Livingston 2009). This changed in 2003, when five distinct regulatory bodies operating at the time were merged to form one 'converged' communications regulator, 'Ofcom'. This has not, however, prevented new regulators, such as the Authority for Television on Demand (ATVOD), from emerging.

In constitutional terms, it is considered important that the printed press operates free from specific government control and the sector has to date been regulated by a self-regulatory body, the Press Complaints Commission (PCC), though as discussed further in the section on self-regulation in the media sector below, this is now under review. The audiovisual media, on the other hand, have, from their inception, been subject to state regulation, with Ofcom enjoying extensive powers in relation to both commercial and public service broadcasters. The oldest public service broadcaster in the UK, the BBC, is still largely free from statutory regulation and is subject to its own system of internal regulation, with limited oversight by Ofcom. Advertising is subject to both co- and self-regulatory regimes overseen by the Advertising Standards Authority (ASA).

In addition, there are a number of 'niche' regulatory bodies, such as the British Board of Film Classification (BBFC) and the Internet Watch Foundation, which oversee specific aspects of the media industry (Mac Síthigh 2011). Competition issues can be addressed by a range of bodies, including Ofcom, the Office of Fair Trading and the Competition Commission, although the government plays a decisive role in deciding whether certain media mergers should be evaluated and blocked on media plurality grounds. At the local level, elected local authorities are authorized to licence cinemas within their areas and licences are usually awarded to show films certified by the BBFC (UK Parliament 1985).

The plethora of regulators responsible for different types of media content has led to a complex system of regulation in need of rationalization (Fielden 2011; Mac Síthigh 2011). In the converging media environment the boundaries between different types of media content and different media regulatory bodies are fading, putting pressure on the current regulatory structure. This is exacerbated by the perceived failure of self-regulation in the print sector to protect the public from phone-hacking and other illegal activities. The recent Leveson Inquiry into press standards is expected to have long-term implications for the future regulation of the mass media (Leveson Report 2012).

We start our detailed examination by considering the specific regulatory regimes adopted for the main public service broadcasters, before moving on to consider how the remaining public service companies (in the UK) and commercial television and radio operators are regulated.

Legacy regulation of core public service broadcasters

In both Finland and the UK the main public service broadcasting institutions are subject to 'organization-specific' regulatory regimes. The Finnish Broadcasting Corporation (YLE) and the British Broadcasting Corporation (BBC) both commenced operations as private companies but converted to public service broadcasters in 1934 and 1927 respectively. Their distinct regulatory regimes stem from the perceived importance of these organizations as key public service institutions, playing a central role in informing, educating and entertaining the public and reflecting all aspects of the nation back to itself. They also serve as benchmarks of high quality journalism.

Both YLE and the BBC currently provide a wide range of national television channels as well as national, regional and local radio services and online services (detailed in: YLE 2012b; BBC 2011). Both seek to reach majority and minority audiences, with YLE operating in 30 localities and offering services in Finnish, Swedish and Sami. YLE programmes and content reach almost 95 per cent of the Finnish people (YLE 2011). The BBC offers dedicated news and parliamentary coverage and provides services in Gaelic and Welsh. The BBC World Service provides services in 27 different languages internationally, while the commercial subsidiary BBC Worldwide exploits the BBC's archives and intellectual property on international markets.

Organizational structure, powers and functions

Both institutions combine elements of state and self-regulation and may be considered to exemplify forms of 'co-regulation'. In the Finnish context, the organization of YLE is regulated by the law regarding the Finnish Broadcasting Company, the Act on Yleisradio Oy (Finnish Parliament 1993), and its funding by the Act on the State Television and Radio Fund (Finnish Parliament 1998). Parliament, therefore, shapes the basic objectives and operating structure of the organization. YLE takes the form of a state-owned (99.98 per cent) limited company that is engaged in public service provision; it is not allowed to sell advertising or produce sponsored programmes (Act on Yleisradio Oy, ss 1 and 12). YLE does not need a licence and has an unlimited operating term. The Act also determines the duties and the organization of YLE. In addition, YLE has itself established internal guidelines for its journalists and programme production (YLE 2005). In this way the state legally ensures the formal independence of YLE from the government and stability of its operations.

By contrast, the BBC is a public corporation set up by Royal Charter (Department of Culture Media and Sport 2006. Although it is constituted under the royal prerogative, the Crown acts on the advice of the government of the day. The Charter is supplemented by an agreement between the BBC and the government, which provides further detail as to the BBC's operating conditions and funding (Department of Culture Media and Sport 2006. The Charter is awarded for a period of ten years, which affords some stability for the Corporation but is less protective than YLE's unlimited term, in that the BBC will be particularly aware of government concerns at times when the Charter and licence fee are being negotiated.

The government rather than parliament, as in the Finnish context, consequently determines the BBC's main institutional and operational provisions, and although parliament is given an opportunity to debate both the Charter and Agreement prior to adoption it cannot require changes. The power of government in this context renders the BBC vulnerable to partisan political pressure, leading to calls for the Corporation to be put on a statutory basis (House of Lords 2005: paras 31–32). But when it was initially suggested in 1926 that the BBC should be created by act of parliament, the minister responsible argued that this 'might give the public the idea that the […] Corporation was […] "a creature of Parliament and connected with political activity"' (Scannell and Cardiff 1991: 37). The Charter has rather paradoxically therefore been defended on the basis that it distances the BBC from political pressure (House of Lords 2005: para. 36). Debate on this issue is ongoing and it is possible that the situation may be reviewed prior to the next charter in 2016 (House of Lords 2011: 12).

Both YLE and the BBC have governing bodies that perform a number of governance and regulatory functions, setting key objectives, appointing key officials, and ensuring that the broadcasters comply with their public service remits. The autonomy of these governing bodies is an important indicator of their independence. YLE is administered by an Administrative Council (AC) with 21 members, elected by parliament in the first session of the parliamentary term. According to the law, the members of the AC should include representatives from the fields of science, art, education, business and economics, as well as from different social and language groups. In practice, the AC is elected from among the members of parliament according to the number of seats each party has in parliament. The parliamentary groups nominate their representatives to the AC who are then appointed by parliament. The members of the AC elect a chairman and a vice-chairman from among themselves. In addition, YLE employees have two representatives on the AC, who have the right to be heard at meetings but no right to vote. The term of office of the members of the AC continues until the election of new members of the AC by parliament.

Appointment by parliament makes the AC directly accountable to it, but does not restrict its independence in deciding about matters that have a significant impact on the company's activities and organization. The AC elects and dismisses the Board of Directors and its Chairman, oversees how YLE fulfils its public service tasks, and reviews and approves the annual report of the Board of Directors. The political influence of the AC is, however, limited by its remit: the AC's functions do not extend to any intervention in the day-to-day activities of YLE, and the AC does not appoint or dismiss managers, responsible editors or journalists either.

The Act on Yleisradio Oy (Finnish Parliament 1993) stipulates that the Board of Directors (BD) should consist of five to eight members, who cannot be members of the AC or the company's senior management. Currently, there are eight members of the BD. The BD independently elects and dismisses the company's Director-General and senior management and decides upon their salaries and other terms of office. It also appoints the responsible editors required by the Freedom of Expression Act (Finnish Parliament 2003), summons the Ordinary General Meeting and prepares its agenda. The BD decides the budget for the following year and delivers annual reports of the company's operations to FICORA. The BD does not, however, intervene in day-to-day programme production, which is the responsibility of the editors they have appointed to lead the production departments.

The BBC Trust is the BBC's sovereign body, combining both governance and regulatory functions. Not only does it set the BBC's main strategic objectives and approve key budget lines, it also ensures compliance with the BBC's obligations under its Charter and Agreement in the interests of the licence fee payer and hears appeals on editorial matters from the Editorials Complaints Unit (Department for Culture, Media and Sport 2006: Charter, Art. 24). The Trust appoints the Chairman of the Executive Board and approves the Director-General, if a separate appointment, as well as the non-executive members of the Executive Board. Unlike the YLE's BD, the Executive Board has a majority of members from within the organization. Day-to-day operational activities are overseen by the Executive Board, which includes the Director-General.

The Trust replaced the Board of Governors in 2006 in light of the Hutton Inquiry, established to consider the circumstances surrounding a BBC report based on an interview with government scientist Dr. David Kelly. The report suggested the government had deliberately exaggerated the military threat posed by Iraq prior to the invasion in 2003 (Lord Hutton 2004). The Board of Governor's initial robust defence of the report, prior to a full investigation, led to the conclusion that it had become too close to the Corporation it was intended to oversee (House of Lords 2011: 10). The BBC Trust was thus established with the explicit goal of clearly demarcating the regulatory and operational arms of the BBC. Art. 9 of the Charter states that the Trust must maintain its independence from the Executive Board and must not seek to exercise its functions. In contrast to the AC in Finland, BBC employees have no representation, even non-voting, on the BBC Trust. The Trust is assisted by a dedicated Trust Unit, with staff solely accountable to the Trust, not the BBC executive (Department for Culture, Media and Sport 2006: Charter, Art. 43). The Trust is guaranteed sufficient financial support from BBC funds to cover its own expenses and those of the Trust Unit.

Although measures are in place to ensure that the BBC Trust does not become involved in the day-to-day operations of the Corporation, it nevertheless sets the BBC's main strategic objectives and has a close interest in the broadcaster's success and good standing. The Trust's wide remit may lead to suspicions that it will favour the BBC when deciding appeals relating to BBC compliance with editorial standards or when determining the scale of BBC services. New services are subject to a formal Public Value Test (PVT), under which Ofcom reports on the potential impact of the service on market operators, while the Trust assesses the public value of the service and whether this outweighs any negative effects highlighted by Ofcom (BBC Trust 2007). Industry representatives have, for example, expressed concern that the Trust avoided a formal PVT in relation to the 'You View' television delivery system, which could have a significant impact on commercial competitors (House of Lords 2011: 43).

In relation to political influence on the Trust, the government maintains a degree of leverage through its control over key appointments, BBC finances, and the Agreement with the BBC, which is 'regularly changed' (House of Lords 2011: 51). Although the Queen technically appoints the twelve members of the Trust, this is done on the advice of the government and, in particular, the Prime Minister. Appointments follow the Public Appointments Code, noted above in this chapter's section on constitutional and public law principles relating to the independence of regulatory authorities, with vacancies publicly advertised and at least one independent assessor on the initial selection panel. Prior to the appointment of the most recent Trust Chairman, the House of Commons Culture, Media and Sport Committee was given the opportunity to question the preferred candidate, though the House of Lords, the second parliamentary chamber, was not afforded the same facility (House of Commons, Culture, Media and Sport Committee 2011). Trustees are appointed for terms of up to five years, which may be renewed, and their remuneration is fixed by the Secretary of State. They can be removed not only for failure to perform their duties but by Order in Council and by decision of the Trust. These rather open-ended provisions mean that they are not fully protected from removal on political grounds and the power of renewal could exert an indirect influence over particular Trustees.

Chairmen tend to be closely affiliated with the political party in government at the time of their appointment, though there have been exceptions. In practice, a limited range of fairly establishment interests and political affiliations tend to be represented, with a clear emphasis on business, legal or media expertise (Freedman 2008: 161). A number of current trustees have previously been involved in the enforcement of competition policy and privatization initiatives, or with the regional press, which sees the BBC as a potential threat, particularly in relation to its online activities. Freedland has suggested that the emphasis on commercial and business experience could result in the Trust being populated 'not with fearless fighters for licence fee payers and the public interest, but with executives from the media and other industries who see their role in representing the BBC *as part of and in relation to the wider commercial UK media environment*' (Freedman 2008: 161). Such experience could, however, enable the BBC to better identify and respond to external challenges, and three of the current Trustees have worked for the BBC in the past and strongly espouse the BBC's commitment to independent reporting and its cultural and creative role. Four trustees are specifically designated to represent English, Scottish, Welsh and Northern Irish interests respectively. The Trust is also responsive to the four audience councils that represent viewers in the devolved nations.

Despite potential pressure points, a number of internal controls and protocols have been introduced, designed to constrain extraneous political influence. Art. 6 of the BBC Charter clearly states that 'the BBC shall be independent in all matters concerning the content of its output, the times and manner in which this is supplied, and in the management of its affairs'. The Trust is required to ensure that the independence of the BBC is maintained (Department for Culture, Media and Sport 2006: Art. 23). As noted above, there are procedures to ensure that the Trust is suitably funded and the Trust's Code of Practice requires Trustees to follow the Nolan principles and to avoid conflicts of interest (BBC Trust 2010). Trustees are allowed to be members of political organizations or parties but not to hold office in a political party or be actively involved in partisan political activities (BBC Trust 2010: s. 7.1).

Transparency and accountability

In relation to YLE, the AC is ultimately accountable to parliament, submitting a report every second year on the implementation of the public service and on the fulfilment of its own supervisory obligations (YLE 2012b). According to recent amendments to the Act on Yleisradio Oy (Finnish Parliament 1993), which come into force in 2013, the public service function of YLE will be better secured. The AC will be required to evaluate in advance the public service nature and possible market impact of significant new YLE services and products. An official in the parliament's Transport and Communications Committee will prepare and present the pre-evaluation to AC. Reports to parliament will from this date be submitted annually (YLE 2012c).

In order to further strengthen the independence of supervision, the communication authority FICORA is also involved in overseeing and evaluating YLE. The BD reports annually to FICORA on financial, technological, organizational, personnel and management matters, as well as on the compliance of the previous year's activities with the legal acts of YLE's regulation. On the basis of FICORA's evaluation, the government may propose legal amendments if considered necessary. FICORA has no right to impose sanctions if any shortcomings have been found, as its sanctioning powers apply only to commercial broadcasters.

In relation to the BBC Trust, a register of Trustees' interests is published, which covers political and financial interests, including those of family members (BBC Trust 2012). In addition, Art. 27 of the Charter states that the principal points of Trust proceedings, and the reasons behind important decisions, must be made public. Details of the Trust's main activities and rulings are thus available on the Trust website. Minutes of Trust meetings are also posted online within three weeks of meetings. These identify the matters raised, reports submitted and conclusions reached, though they provide relatively little detail on the substance of discussions and do not indicate the views of specific Trustees.

In terms of accountability, the BBC is required to report on an annual basis to parliament (Department for Culture, Media and Sport 2006: Art. 45). The annual report, available online, is a means by which the BBC accounts to licence fee payers, exposing the BBC to wider scrutiny than that of the government alone, and is an important element in ensuring overall independence. Maintaining a high level of public approval for its activities is an important concern for the BBC, as it strengthens its position when subject to political pressure. The BBC's financial management is reviewed by the National Audit Office (NAO), through arrangements with the DCMS. The NAO is not authorized to make recommendations relating to the BBC's journalism or content policy (House of Lords 2011: 41). Ofcom has independent powers to consider complaints about BBC programmes, save those relating to accuracy, impartiality and the coverage of elections or referenda (House of Lords 2011: 28), while regulatory decisions of the BBC are subject to judicial review as, for example, in the *R (ProLife Alliance) v BBC* case (House of Lords, Appellate Committee 2004).

Funding

Funding is a key mechanism through which influence can be exerted; therefore it is important to apply a model of funding that is not dependent on any political interest group, business or person etc. In Finland, up to the end of 2012, YLE's operations will be financed mainly by television fees of €252 annually; YLE programmes carry no advertising. The fee is collected by FICORA and directed into a special radio and television fund, operating under the Act on State Television and Radio Fund (Finnish Parliament 1998).

As the fee system did not work efficiently (according to estimates, one in four viewers did not pay, significantly reducing YLE's budget), a new financing model was introduced at the beginning of 2013, which will make the funding more stable and independent. YLE will now be funded by a special YLE-tax, collected by the Finnish tax authorities and directed into the radio and television fund. The sum will be progressive and specific to each taxpayer (€50–140 a year depending on the taxpayer's annual income; persons with income below a determined level will not have to pay the tax). In addition, enterprises and companies will pay YLE-tax according to their turnover. The tax applies to all taxpayers regardless of whether they have a television set or not. The basic idea behind the tax is that YLE offers its service to, and should be accountable to, the whole Finnish people: according to studies, every Finn uses the services of YLE in one form or another (e.g. online). According to the new arrangements, YLE will receive a fixed amount of €500 million annually, index-linked. This cannot be changed without amending the law. The tax revenue will technically be included in the state budget, and directed to the State Television and Radio Fund, from which YLE receives its finances. FICORA administers the Fund together with the State Treasury.

The new Finnish model, designed to guarantee long-term financial stability for the public sector, contrasts with the currently difficult position of the BBC. The BBC is primarily funded by the licence fee, which is set by the government after consultations with the

Corporation, and collected by an agent on behalf of the BBC (House of Lords 2011: 49). In 2007, the licence fee was agreed for a period of six years. The amount is approved each year by parliament, which votes to transfer funds to DCMS to cover the cost of the fee, which is then transferred to the BBC. In the UK those who watch or record TV *as it is broadcast* need to have a TV licence. Therefore those who only use catch-up or on-demand services do not require a licence (TV Licensing 2012). The annual fee is currently £145.50, though individuals over 75 are exempt.

The distinct nature and form of collection of the licence fee, though considered a hypothecated tax, renders it less likely to be played off in discussions over the allocation of resources among government departments. Nevertheless, the government's ability to set the level of the licence fee is one mechanism by which it can strategically influence the scale of BBC services. The process in which the BBC and the coalition government came to an agreement in 2010 to freeze the licence fee until renewal of the Charter in 2016 was heavily criticized for its secrecy and speed, providing no opportunity for licence fee payers or parliament to comment on the proposal (House of Lords 2011; Levy 2012: 107). In real terms, the BBC will experience cuts of around 16 per cent, with a potentially significant impact on its output (BBC Trust 2011). In addition, the licence fee is increasingly being used to fund activities outside BBC services, notably to support digital switchover and broadband rollout, thereby diluting the link between the licence fee payer and the Corporation on which the BBC's independence partly depends.

Concluding observations

The Hallin and Mancini models remain relevant to our understanding of how Finland and the UK have chosen to regulate their core public service providers. Both countries continue to emphasize the importance of public service and professional autonomy in the audiovisual sector, but Finland seeks to ensure a socially and politically representative regulatory system, adopting a parliamentary model that is characteristic of at least some Democratic Corporatist countries (Hallin and Mancini 2004: 169–179); while in the UK the role of parliament is sidelined and that of government enhanced, with preference for a smaller, less overtly political, Trust (Hallin and Mancini 2004: 235).

The complex, culturally dependent 'ecology' of independence is also well illustrated by the two regimes. In relation to the BBC Trust, government retains the power to appoint key personnel, to shape the Trust's terms of operation, and to determine the level of available funding. But a long tradition of public service, reflected in the Nolan principles, has led to a range of formal requirements and conventions that in practice constrain government influence. These include independent oversight of appointments; explicit requirements of independence in governing documents and supplementary codes; prohibitions on political or financial activities that could give rise to conflicts of interest; and publication of members' interests. These constraints are reinforced by the

BBC's accountability to parliament and, ultimately, the courts together with widespread public support for a service that is generally considered politically independent and thus a trustworthy provider of news and information. A variety of civil society organizations play an important role in highlighting potential political or industrial pressures on the media (Jempson and Powell 2011).

This equilibrium rests, however, on a considerable measure of self-restraint and could relatively easily be undermined. At times of political or financial crisis the BBC can be under considerable government pressure to adopt the 'official line', as the Hutton Inquiry illustrated (Hallin and Mancini 2004: 235; Freedman 2008: 142–143). More recently, concerns have been voiced over discussions between senior BBC executives and members of the Prime Minister's office regarding BBC coverage of the coalition government's spending cuts (Goodwin 2012: 74) and over pressure on the BBC relating to coverage of the 2012 London mayoral election (Mulholland 2012). Though the existence of political pressure by itself is not indicative of a lack of independence, BBC editors and staff need to know that they will find robust support for responsible independent journalism from the Trust, even in the face of government criticism. Government influence on the make-up of the Trust and selection of its Chair could undermine faith in this commitment.

In Finland, YLE is a creature of statute not government, and parliament plays a role in appointing key regulatory personnel. But parliamentary control can lead to greater rather than less politicization and it is notable that the Finnish Parliament has chosen to appoint its own members to the AC in line with political groupings. Unlike the case of the BBC Trust, therefore, elected politicians are directly involved in regulation. But in Finland, as in the UK, checks have been put in place to address concerns stemming from the particular system: the AC cannot influence programme content and YLE's internal guidelines (YLE 2005) strictly emphasize the importance of political independence and a commitment to the ideal of public service. It is the BD which independently manages the practical operation of YLE by appointing responsible editors and deciding on the budget. The Finnish approach indicates that a politically representative mechanism for regulating the public sector is possible without undermining the broadcaster's independence or public trust. The new tax-based mechanism for financing YLE may also provide a more secure basis for long-term funding than the BBC licence fee, subject to periodic and opaque negotiations with the government of the day.

The distinct regulatory regimes that apply to YLE and the BBC serve to emphasize the special constitutional status of these two organizations. But both of them also create the risk of the regulatory body becoming, or being seen to be, unduly close to the industry it oversees. This is particularly relevant where there are potential conflicts of interest between the public broadcaster and other industry actors, for instance where new online public services are proposed (Goodwin 2012). Clearly, there is a judgement call to be made as to which type of body is best equipped to make evaluations of this type. The policy issues inherent in determining the scale and scope of public service media suggest that a body such as the Finnish AC, reflecting a range of political and social interests, could here be more appropriate than a more technocratic regulatory body such as Ofcom, or even the government-appointed BBC Trust. In Finland, the AC will be made responsible for this duty from 2013 onwards, so the impact of this strategy on YLE's activities cannot yet be evaluated.

Media-specific state and co-regulatory bodies

In both Finland and the UK audiovisual services have been the main targets of state regulation, leaving the printed press free from specific state control. Intervention in the audiovisual sector has been justified on the perceived greater immediacy and public impact of radio and television services and the need to allocate spectrum to prevent interference.

In Finland, the main regulatory body for commercial audiovisual services is FICORA, while the Finnish Centre for Media Education and Audiovisual Media is primarily concerned with preventing the exposure of minors to harmful content in audiovisual programmes and films, and advancing media literacy. In the UK, oversight of the commercial broadcasting sector and public service broadcasters other than the BBC rests with the state regulator, Ofcom, while co-regulator ATVOD is concerned with on-demand audiovisual media services.

Organizational structure, powers and functions

In Finland, FICORA's core objectives are to promote 'an information-secure society and interference-free communications networks, effectively functioning communications markets and securing the interests of consumers' (FICORA 2012). Its obligations include monitoring the functionality of electronic communications networks and reporting potential information security threats. FICORA monitors the commercial broadcasters' compliance with the terms and conditions of their licences and the regulations of the Act on Radio and Television Operations (Finnish Parliament 1998). FICORA plans and administers the use of radio frequencies, communication network numbers and network addresses to ensure effective electronic communication connections. The decision-making powers of FICORA, however, are mostly limited to the economic and technical aspects of broadcasting regulation. The authority also grants short-term radio licences; long-term licences are granted by the government (FICORA 2012). FICORA also plays a role in supervising YLE (see 'Transparency and accountability' above).

FICORA's formal independence is secured by law (Finnish Government 2001), which determines the framework of its functions, supervisory power and operational structure. In addition, it defines the duties of the Director-General, and the mode of appointment and employment criteria for personnel. The Director-General is appointed by the government following a public application procedure, where government ministers select the best candidate. When making appointments, the relevant expertise of the candidate is more decisive than political leanings. Dismissal of the Director-General is possible only in accordance with the Act on Civil Servants or on the basis of a court decision. In practice, these procedures are strictly followed, which definitely increases the credibility of the regulator in society.

Other personnel are appointed or employed by the Director-General unless otherwise provided in FICORA's rules of procedure. The Director-General and directors of units must have a Master's degree, management skills and good knowledge of the duties covered by the post. Additionally, the Director-General must have managerial experience. The Decree does not specify the qualifications for employees, stating only that they must possess 'the skill and ability necessary for the successful discharge of the duties in question' (Finnish Government 2001, s. 7).

The actual independence of FICORA is confirmed by the fact that the Director-General has broad authority to define the structure of the organization and its rules of procedure, including the duties of the various units and personnel. The Director-General can appoint advisory boards to assist decision making but in practice most matters are resolved by the Director-General or a civil servant employed within FICORA to whom responsibility for the issue has been delegated. The selection process of a Director-General, the nature of the Director-General's duties, the law, accountability to the government and public scrutiny are all designed to balance the considerable power concentrated in this position. Although misuse of this power is possible, such cases are not known in Finland.

FICORA's sanctioning powers apply only to commercial broadcasters. The sanctions available are issuance of a reminder, conditional fine or penalty fine. FICORA cannot terminate a licence. In fact, neither FICORA nor the Finnish government, which is the main licensing authority, have ever terminated a broadcast licence. For breach of the provisions of the Act on Television and Radio Operations (Finnish Parliament 1998) by a broadcaster, FICORA can propose that the Market Court impose a fine (from €1000 to €1 million). The maximum fine has never been imposed. Any penalty fine, proposed by FICORA, cannot be more than 5 per cent of the broadcaster's turnover during the previous year. The highest fine levied so far (in 2011) was €50,000, imposed on Pro Radio Oy for severe violation of its licence conditions. In practice, FICORA rarely imposes penalties and more often imposes conditional fines. The decisions of FICORA can be appealed to the general administrative courts and suspended only by the court. The next level of appeal is to the Supreme Administrative Court (Karppinen and Nieminen 2012: 135–136).

In the UK, Ofcom carries out a broadly similar range of duties to FICORA. It was established by the New Labour administration, which came to power in 1997, and takes the form of a statutory corporation, created by the Office of Communications Act 2002 (UK Parliament 2002b). In taking over from five previously distinct regulatory authorities, Ofcom was intended to offer a more coherent regulatory approach better able to respond to media convergence, though it was afforded very little competence in the Internet field. Ofcom's emphasis on stakeholder participation, consultation and empirical research reflects a commitment to evidence-based, accountable and transparent policy making at one remove from government (Lunt and Livingstone 2012: 38–40). Ofcom's duties are specified in the 2003 Communications Act (UK Parliament 2003) and comprise an overarching obligation to further 'the interests of citizens in communications matters [...] and consumers in relevant markets, where appropriate by promoting competition' (s. 3(1)). These interests at times coincide but at others conflict, thereby projecting Ofcom into a contested policy arena. Depending on the context, Ofcom has either responded to the policy challenge by mapping out alternatives; sought to achieve a consensual resolution based on dialogue and consultation or a strong evidential base; or has itself put forward its own preferred policy solutions (Lunt and Livingstone 2012: 157–159, 183).

Key responsibilities include overseeing the award of television and radio licenses and the operation of electronic communications networks more generally; agreement of public service remits with commercial public service broadcasters and monitoring their enforcement; setting and enforcing a programme code for television and radio services; acting as a co-regulator with ATVOD and the Advertising Standards Authority (ASA); and ensuring that radio and television markets are competitive. Ofcom shares the competence to review the conformity of BBC content with editorial standards with the BBC Trust, save, as noted above, where a complaint relates to the accuracy or impartiality of BBC programmes, which are matters reserved for the BBC alone (House of Lords 2011: paras 26–29).

Strategic guidance and oversight is provided by the Ofcom Board, comprising a non-executive Chair and executive and non-executive members: there are currently nine members in all. As with the BBC Trust, the government is able to shape the general outlook of the Board, with the Secretaries of State for DBIS and DCMS jointly appointing the Chair and the non-executive members. Executive members, which must be fewer in number than non-executive members, include the Chief Executive. The Chief Executive is appointed by the Chair and the other non-executive members of the Board with the approval of the Secretary of State. When appointing members to the Board, the Secretaries of State are required to ensure that candidates do not have financial or other interests that could prejudice their ability to act impartially (Schedule to the 2002 Act). Appointments are for renewable terms and members can be removed by the Secretary of State on grounds that include prejudicial financial arrangements, incapacity, misbehaviour or lack of fitness to perform the duties of the post. Ofcom employees are appointed after an open applications process on the basis of relevant expertise and merit.

Although the executive is able to make strategic appointments to Ofcom's governing board, a number of measures help to insulate Ofcom from political and other commercial influence. Internal guidelines state that it:

> is essential that Ofcom should establish and maintain a reputation for impartiality, integrity and high professional standards [...] this means that there must never be any legitimate reasons for people outside Ofcom to suspect that our decisions may be influenced by

the private interests of Non-Executive Board members; or that Non-Executive Board members may be able to profit from information available to them through their work.

(Ofcom 2012)

In particular, such members are not allowed to hold shares in companies, a significant part of whose activities consist of broadcasting or providing electronic communications networks or services, or to engage in certain media or political activities, notably by acting as a candidate for national or local political office. Any potential conflict of interest, which also extends to family members, must be notified to the Corporation's Secretary (Ofcom 2012). Ofcom also maintains a register of members' interests and Board Members are not allowed to immediately take up employment with regulated firms when they leave Ofcom.

Statutory and non-statutory measures relating to consultation also help to ensure that Ofcom acts impartially in carrying out its day-to-day regulatory functions. Ofcom is required by statute to receive advice from a number of committees and advisory panels (Communications Act 2003: ss. 14–21). These include the Consumer Panel, a separate statutory body established by s. 16 of the Communications Act 2003 (UK Parliament 2003) to represent the interests of consumers and provide a counterweight to large corporate interests (Lunt and Livingstone 2012: 75). Ofcom also has a number of internal advisory committees, including the England, Northern Ireland, Scotland and Wales Advisory Committees, the Ofcom Spectrum Advisory Board and the Older Persons and Disabled Persons Advisory Committee. In particular, a specific Content Board with representatives of the four nations, members with considerable broadcasting experience and lay members meets to give advice to the Board or to make content-related decisions where the Board has delegated power to it. Ofcom is required to carry out an impact assessment whenever it puts forward 'important' proposals (UK Parliament 2003: s. 7). Specific guidance on impact assessment procedures underlines the importance of both formal and informal consultations and a commitment to ensuring that all those who may be affected are identified and that consultations are suitably representative (Ofcom 2005: paras 5.18–5.21).

The Authority for Television on Demand (ATVOD) regulates UK on-demand audiovisual programme services, a task carried out by FICORA in Finland. ATVOD started as a self-regulatory body set up by the industry, reflecting the UK's reluctance to submit audiovisual media services relayed over the Internet to sector-specific state regulation. It became an independent co-regulatory body in order to bring the UK into line with its EU obligations under the AVMS Directive (European Parliament and the Council of the European Union 2010). A similar move from a self-regulatory to a co-regulatory body took place when the ASA took over broadcast advertising regulation from Ofcom. The move from a self- to a co-regulatory structure led to a restructuring of ATVOD in order to ensure it would operate sufficiently independently from the industry it regulates, as well as to ensure its priority would lie with customer protection.

ATVOD is set up as a private company, limited by guarantee. It is currently led by an independent chair and a board consisting of five independent and four non-independent members. 'Independent' is defined in ATVOD's articles of association as having 'no relevant consultancy contracts, directorships or other employment, or significant financial interests, in a company regulated by ATVOD' (ATVOD 2006). Positions on the ATVOD board are publicly advertised, and considered by a recruitment panel which includes 'a person of independence and distinction with no connection to either the industry or to ATVOD'. The appointment of the Chairman is done in consultation with Ofcom. Independent members are appointed by a recruitment panel with a majority of independent persons, and non-independent members by a panel consisting of an equal number of independent and non-independent persons. There is no government influence on the board, other than indirectly through Ofcom, which is likely a result of ATVOD starting life as a self-regulatory body.

Transparency and accountability

FICORA is a transparent body, open to public scrutiny in all aspects of its activities. All documents concerning its operation are freely accessible on the Authority's website, although the law does not require this level of transparency. The documentation includes all decisions, regulations and guidelines issued by FICORA, various reports on specific issues and FICORA's annual reports. In order to assess broadcasters' compliance with the licensing terms, FICORA orders analyses on the programme supply and content of broadcasting stations from external research institutions, such as universities. FICORA reports to the Ministry of Transport and Communications. The general practice in Finland is that subordinate institutions report to their respective ministries, not to the government or parliament (Kuutti 2012c).

In the UK, s. 3(3) of the Communications Act 2003 (UK Parliament 2003) requires Ofcom to have regard to 'the principles under which regulatory activities should be transparent' and 'accountable'. As noted, Ofcom maintains a register of Board members' interests and is legally required to carry out impact assessments which entail publication and a high level of visibility for its proposals. It is also under a statutory duty to publish the results of any research it carries out (Communications Act 2003: s. 15). Extensive information on Ofcom's structure, remit and policies is published on the corporation's website.

Ofcom submits its financial accounts annually to the Secretary of State and the National Audit Office (NAO), which has in the past called for Ofcom's objectives to be more clearly set out to enable an assessment of its effectiveness (National Audit Office 2010). Ofcom also submits an annual report detailing how it has performed its functions over the course of the preceding year to the Secretary of State. Its main line of accountability is thus to the government, though the NAO's report on the accounts and Ofcom's annual report are both laid before parliament for information (see Schedule to the Office of Communications Act 2002). Ofcom's decisions are open to judicial review, as illustrated by the 2005 case of *R (Grieson) v Ofcom* (High Court (QBD), UK 2005), while its competition-related rulings can be appealed to the Competition Appeal Tribunal.

ATVOD publishes a register of members' interests on their website, as well as the policy and processes for recruiting board members and a code of conduct for board members. The code of conduct contains provisions stating that independent members must take care to remain independent for the duration of their term of office. Minutes of Board Meetings are similarly published online as well as scope determinations and complaint determinations.

ATVOD consults quarterly with the ATVOD industry forum, consisting of representatives of notified services, to discuss regulatory services, obtain input on draft consultations at an early stage, and obtain the industry perspective and expertise. Trade associations are invited to attend. A strong industry input on consultations and regulation through the industry forum could affect ATVOD's independence from the industry. There is no similar process for regular consultation with consumers, though ATVOD has consulted publicly on key regulatory issues, with documents published on its website. Decisions regarding the scope of ATVOD's jurisdiction can be appealed to Ofcom, and final decisions from both Ofcom and ATVOD are open to judicial review.

Funding

Financially, FICORA is independent from the government or state budget. The largest proportion of its income comes from fees charged for radio transmitter licences, short-term radio and television licences, .fi domain names and telephone network numbers. The fee for collecting television fees is also included in FICORA's income. The charges payable to the state are determined by special acts and decrees. According to the current Director-General of FICORA, Merja Saari, the budget has been sufficient for FICORA's needs. There has not been any public discussion about its financing in the media. Some voices in the government have suggested an increase in the price of licences, but no actual changes have been made in this respect (Kuutti 2012c). It can be concluded that the legal arrangements concerning the operation of FICORA support its independence from political institutions and economic interests.

Ofcom also receives funding from fees for the award of operating licences and various administrative charges, but this is coupled with a government grant from DCMS. Sections 38 and 347 of the Communications Act 2003 (UK Parliament 2003) require Ofcom to raise income from each of the sectors it regulates, such that it covers the costs of regulating that sector. As part of a more general programme of public spending cuts, the decision was made to reduce Ofcom's funding by just over 28 per cent over the four years beginning April 2011, while at the same time imposing on Ofcom a number of new responsibilities, including the regulation of postal services (Ofcom 2011; Sweney 2011). Some of these cuts have been reflected in lower fees for the commercial sector. These financial cutbacks are likely to constrain Ofcom's capacity to maintain the high level of independent research and investigation that have characterized its 'evidence-led' approach to regulation in the past, and certain activities, such as its regular reviews of media ownership and public service broadcasting, will be scaled back (Ofcom 2011; Sweney 2011).

By contrast, ATVOD is funded solely by annual fees levied on the organizations that it regulates. The scale of the fees is decided jointly by ATVOD and Ofcom. Initially, a flat fee of £2,900 was levied, which was considered problematic by small-scale providers of video on-demand services. In 2011, therefore, a progressive three-band fee structure, based on the turnover of the service provider, was introduced, with three concessionary rates for non-commercial, micro-scale and small-scale providers.

Concluding observations

Despite Finland and the UK falling under different Hallin and Mancini media system models, the regulation of commercial broadcasting in the two countries displays some surprising similarities. Key officials of FICORA and Ofcom are appointed by the respective governments but their extensive powers are balanced by specific obligations, public and media scrutiny and judicial review. Media regulators in Finland appear to be better insulated from financial pressures than those in the UK, with Ofcom subject to a reduction in spending as the government seeks to reduce further regulatory costs on industry.

Ofcom's powerful position in the UK communications market has enabled it to act both as referee and influential policy entrepreneur, notably in its reviews of public service broadcasting (Lunt, Livingstone and Brevini 2012). Its evidence-based approach to policy-making, coupled with a commitment to wide-ranging consultation with all stakeholders, strengthens its claim to be a neutral body acting at one remove from government. Underlying value judgements and priorities cannot, however, be completely excluded and it is here that the open and at times conflicting policy objectives specified in the governing statutory provisions become problematic. A number of commentators have, for instance, suggested that Ofcom has tended to emphasize the interests of competition and industry over those of citizens and failed to adequately disentangle citizen from consumer interests (Freedman 2008: 96–101, 119; Lunt and Livingstone 2012: 189, 192).

Ofcom's commitment to transparent and representative consultation backed by empirical research may, paradoxically, also pose challenges for civil society organizations that rarely have the resources or man-power to match the engagement of large industry players. Coalition proposals to disband the independent Consumer Panel, which Ofcom consults at an early stage in policy development, could further weaken the ability of civil society organizations to engage in the development of policy both at the national and European levels (Lunt and Livingstone 2012: 76).

Lunt and Livingstone suggest that it would be naive to conclude that Ofcom is not subject to political pressures in relation to specific controversial issues (Lunt and Livingstone 2012: 115, 180) but it is nevertheless apparent that Ofcom has created a new, more open, accountable and egalitarian environment in which policy issues can be debated within society. Though there is evidence of industry lobbying being effective in certain contexts (Freedman 2008: 96), Ofcom has also stood up to powerful industry actors in a number of high-profile competition rulings and advisory opinions, notably regarding the proposed merger of News Corporation and BSkyB (Ofcom 2010b).

In this respect Ofcom may be a victim of its own success as an independent regulator, in that the coalition government has acted not only to reduce Ofcom's income but also to repatriate some of its policy-making powers to 'ministers responsible to Parliament' (Lunt and Livingstone 2012: 150). Given the at times highly opaque nature of government policy formation and increasing evidence of the influence that powerful media organizations have had on the direction of that policy in the past, this is likely to weaken rather than enhance the stake that citizens have in the development of media policy. One final observation is that although the creation of 'super-regulator' Ofcom was intended to rationalize a complex regulatory environment there remains considerable complexity in the UK context, with the relationship between ATVOD, Ofcom, the BBC Trust and the Press Complaints Commission, discussed in more detail below, remaining difficult for even those well versed in the communications field to understand.

Competition authorities and media pluralism

Because general competition authorities are not sector-specific, they tend to receive limited attention in works on media regulation. We discuss them briefly here, however, because of the important role that they can play in furthering media pluralism and because of the novel situation in the UK where the Competition Commission can be involved not merely in the assessment of competition concerns, but also in determining whether a merger could undermine media plurality.

As noted above, media markets and media ownership are regulated in Finland by the Competition Act (Finnish Parliament 2011) under the supervision of the FCA. The Decree on the Finnish Competition Authority (Finnish Government 1993) sets out the tasks of the FCA, which are: investigating conditions of competition; examining restrictions on competition; taking measures to eliminate the harmful effects of competitive restraints; and taking initiatives to promote competition and to dismantle any restrictive regulations and orders. The FCA deals with cases involving media competition and mergers in the same way it deals with competition in other fields of the economy and trade.

New competition rules entered into force in early 2011 under the Competition Act (Finnish Parliament 2011), which enhance the FCA's independence and autonomy, notably in determining its operating priorities. There is no political interference; the Ministry does not have a power of veto over FCA decisions. Only the general framework for action in the following year, key aims and focus, is agreed in annual meetings with the Ministry of Employment and the Economy.

In the UK, a number of authorities have concurrent powers to ensure that markets operate competitively. The Office of Fair Trading (OFT) investigates potential anti-competitive or abusive practices under the Competition Act 1998 (UK Parliament 1998a) and can refer certain mergers or market arrangements to the Competition Commission for further investigation under the terms of the Enterprise Act 2002 (UK Parliament 2002a). Members of the Competition Commission are appointed by DBIS for eight years, following an open competition. Similarly, the OFT recruits staff based on an open competition. Alongside these general competition regulators, Ofcom has specific powers under ss. 316–318 of the Communications Act 2003 (UK Parliament 2003) to ensure 'fair and effective competition' among licensed or connected services, with oversight by the Competition Appeal Tribunal. Ofcom has thus made a number of important competition-related decisions in the media field, for instance fixing a minimum wholesale price for the sale of premium sports rights (Ofcom 2010a).

In the competition context, the question of regulatory independence in the UK arises most directly in relation to the operation of the 'media plurality' test for proposed media mergers, under s. 58 of the Enterprise Act 2002 (UK Parliament 2002a). Such investigations are triggered by the government minister responsible, who is also empowered to decide, after seeking advice from Ofcom and, potentially, the Competition Commission, whether the merger should be allowed to proceed. The minister's decision is subject to review by the Competition Appeal Tribunal. Controversy over two recent cases relating to actual or proposed media acquisitions by BSkyB and News Corporation respectively has brought the legitimacy of these procedures into question (BBC News 2011; Arnott 2010). In particular, evidence presented to the Leveson Inquiry, set up to investigate press ethics, suggests that News Corporation may have had access to advance or confidential information from the minister's office relating to the progress of the investigation (Plunkett and O'Carroll 2012).

One way to address the concern that government ministers may be too close or antagonistic to specific media interests to maintain the required degree of impartiality when making 'quasi-judicial rulings' of this type is to remove them from the regulatory framework altogether. It is possible that decision-making power could be transferred to an independent authority, such as Ofcom, in future legislation, though the coalition ministers most closely involved in the recent cases disagree as to the desirability of devolving what is in part a policy decision to an independent body.

Self-regulation in the media sector

In both Finland and the UK there has been a long tradition of media self-regulation. This is most evident in the field of the print media, though a number of other media sectors, for instance advertising and cinema, have also relied to a significant extent on self-regulatory regimes. Self-regulation can only work when the respective bodies (Press Councils or Press Complaint Commissions or Ombudsmen) are autonomous from the industry they are supposed to regulate and independent from political and economic interests. The independence of a press council directly relates to the principles of their composition and financing, and the rules and procedures governing their work (Lauk and Jufereva 2010).

The Finnish system of media self-regulation, unlike in most other European countries, seems to work efficiently, supported by a high level of journalistic professionalism, reflexive journalism culture and developed civic ethos.

Apart from the Freedom of Expression Act (Finnish Parliament 2003), there is no specific legislation for the print media in Finland. Otherwise, certain provisions of the Criminal Code (Finnish Parliament 1889), the Competition Act (Finnish Parliament 2011) etc. apply. More directly, the activities of the Council for the Mass Media (CMM), Finnmedia and the Union of Journalists in Finland (UJF) affect the performance of the print media and their online versions. The CMM provides a self-regulatory system for all Finnish media, not merely the printed press; the Federation of the Finnish Media Industry (Finnmedia) is the employers' trade association (Finnmedia 2012); and the UJF is the journalists' trade union (UJF 2012).

In the UK, the Press Complaints Commission (PCC) has for over twenty years operated the self-regulatory regime for the press. Although the PCC sought to balance the rights of individuals with press freedom, concerns that the PCC had grown too close to the industry it was supposed to regulate and had failed adequately to investigate allegations of phone-hacking led to a loss of trust on the part of the public and politicians in the institution. As a result, in February 2012, the PCC announced it was moving to a 'transitional' phase, pending reform (PCC 2012c). The PCC has itself proposed a new structure (Lord Hunt 2012), but any new model will need to take into account the findings of Lord Justice Leveson's wide-ranging inquiry into 'the culture, practices and ethics of the press' (Leveson Report 2012; see also Information Commissioner's Office 2006: paras 5.6–5.11).

At time of writing the future structure of press regulation in the UK was, therefore, far from clear. The Leveson Report favours a co-regulatory regime, with a reformed self-regulatory body continuing to monitor standards and address complaints relating to those newspapers that choose to participate. This would, however, be supplemented by a system of arbitration, backed-up by enhanced incentives for participation, and a statutory body designed to ensure the maintenance of standards (Leveson Report 2012). Statutory intervention is, however, seen by many in the industry as the 'thin end of the wedge', opening the door to government intervention and a loss of independence. Alternative proposals currently under consideration include the adoption of a Royal Charter (O'Carroll 2012), which in practice could afford the government even more influence; oversight by a charitable trust (Sabbagh 2013) or a strengthened system of self-regulation.

Alongside the PCC, the National Union of Journalists is a campaigning organization that responds to consultations in the media field and operates a code of conduct, which sets out core ethical standards for British journalism (NUJ 2008 and 2011). All journalists joining the union must sign that they will strive to adhere to the code. In this chapter we focus on the CMM and the PCC both because of their key roles and because interesting comparisons can be drawn in relation to their effectiveness and standing. We also note key proposals in the Leveson Report designed to address some of the shortcomings of the current UK regime.

Organization, powers and functions

The CMM is a self-regulatory body established in 1968 by publishers and journalists in Finland. Its principal tasks are to provide guidance on good professional practice and defend freedom of speech and publication. An important function of the Council is to deal with complaints by individuals or organizations, where they seek a non-judicial resolution in contested cases. The CMM seeks to maintain and increase the credibility of the Finnish mass media, and to a degree, has succeeded in doing so.

Nearly all Finnish media organizations and news agencies have committed themselves to the CMM's objectives and its Guidelines for Journalists, by joining a Basic Agreement. These objectives and guidelines become automatically binding on any journalist working for a CMM member organization. The collective membership is also reflected in the way in which complaints to the CMM are dealt with: these are always directed against the media organization and not a particular journalist. The editor-in-chief responds to the CMM's requests concerning complaints in the name of the news organization.

The PCC primarily regulated the printed press in the UK, but it also covered online versions of newspapers or magazines as well as online-only publications where the editor and publisher subscribed to the Editor's Code of Practice (the Code) (PCC 2009). The Leveson Report has not proposed substantial changes to this remit. Unlike the CMM, news agencies, with the exception of the Press Association, were not formally covered, nor did the PCC regulate the audiovisual media, save for video content posted on newspaper or magazine websites that were subject to the paper's editorial control. As in Finland, the self-regulatory nature of the PCC meant that only those publications that subscribed to the Code were covered by it and there were therefore publications that fell outside the PCC's remit, most notably the newspaper group Northern & Shell, which withdrew after a funding dispute. The Code set out ethical standards in relation to matters such as accuracy, privacy, and the protection of minors. Although the co-regulatory regime proposed by Lord Justice Leveson is a voluntary one, the Report proposes certain incentives to encourage the press to subscribe, notably potential protection from exemplary damages or the payment of costs in legal proceedings (Leveson Report 2012: recommendation 26).

The PCC focused on resolving disputes between individuals and the press that were referred to it, through processes of mediation or adjudication. It did not monitor press standards generally across the UK and its powers of investigation were limited. The PCC was thus primarily a reactive institution, though it did publish guidance notes and occasionally initiated investigations, for instance where it was unlikely that the person harmed or those involved would make a complaint (e.g. where the press had made payments to criminals). Editors and publishers were responsible for ensuring editorial material complied with the Code and were, therefore, responsible for the journalists on their staff. Neither the CMM nor the PCC could impose fines to enforce compliance with their respective Guidelines and Code, but they could oblige an editor to publish an adjudication against their organization. The Leveson Report has proposed that any future regulatory body should not only have wider investigatory powers, but also competence to impose financial sanctions, and it is likely that this will be taken up in any future regulatory scheme (Leveson Report 2012: recommendation 19, see also Hunt 2012 for a self-regulatory approach to this issue).

The CMM in Finland operates on the basis of the Basic Agreement signed by the news media, which form a supporting association for the Council (the last Agreement came into force on 1 October 2011). The supporting association approves the Guidelines for Journalists (the ethical code), which are the basis for the CMM's adjudications. Any person who considers that there has been a breach of good professional practice by the media may bring this to the attention of the CMM. The CMM handles complaint investigations free of charge, within an average timeframe of two months. The Chairman may also resolve matters independently that clearly do not involve a breach of good professional practice and are of no significant importance (JSN 2008). If the complainant is not satisfied with the decision of the Chairman, the CMM will deal with the complaint. Where a complaint is upheld, news media have to publish the decision unchanged in their online version and should run a news item about the decision in the print version or in the relevant broadcast. It is a generally accepted practice that all the news media follow this requirement. Where important principles are at stake, the CMM can itself initiate an investigation. It can also issue policy statements regarding questions of professional ethics.

Since the beginning of 2013, the CMM has comprised thirteen members appointed for three years (JSN 2012). In addition, the supporting association elects the Chairperson of the CMM for a period of three years and two vice-chairs on an annual basis. A chair may be re-elected only once. The supporting association also elects eight members of the CMM from among journalists and publishers as well as personal auxiliary members (who attend the meetings when the regular member is unable to attend). The members of the CMM must be professionally experienced, competent in ethical questions, and represent both the print and digital media. Appointments must be agreed unanimously within the supporting association. Five members of the Council and their auxiliaries, representing the public, are chosen by the CMM itself. The representatives of the public are not permitted to be in the service of the mass media nor in related positions of trust (e.g., member of a Board of a news organization). Two of the representatives of the public, plus their personal auxiliary members, must, where possible, have a special grounding in matters concerning freedom of speech or ethical questions (JSN 2011a: Art. 5). Inclusion of the representatives of the public makes the work of the CMM more transparent, and also more credible for the wider public.

After their term of office has ended, members of the Council, aside from the chair, cannot be immediately re-elected (but they can be re-elected to the Council after a time out of office). The election of the members is transparent and based on an open call. When making decisions, all members of the CMM act and vote as independent individuals, not as representatives of their related organizations. However, when a complaint against a news organization which one of the members belongs to is adjudicated, this member withdraws from the decision making.

The PCC in the UK was composed of seventeen members, of which ten were 'lay' or public members, with no connection to the newspaper or magazine industry, and seven were press members, selected from among senior editors of publications signed-up to the Code. Journalists did not, therefore, sit on the board of the PCC. The lay presence was thus more pronounced than on the CMM, though industry representation was less diverse. The Chair of the PCC was a lay member appointed by the Press Standards Board of Finance (PressBof), a finance body made up of industry members that operated independently from the PCC (PCC 2012b). The Chair of the PCC formed, together with two other lay members, the Nominations Committee, responsible for recommending appointments and reappointments of the lay members of the PCC as well as liaising with PressBof over the appointment and reappointment of press members (PCC 2012a). An independent assessor from outside the PCC was appointed to oversee the process (PCC 2012a).

The Code was reviewed and updated by the Editors Code of Practice Committee (Code Committee), which operated independently from the PCC (Editors Code of Practice Committee 2012). This Committee consisted of thirteen members, all from the national and regional newspaper and magazine industry, and its chairman was a senior industry figure. The level of lay influence thus varied depending on whether a decision was being taken by the PCC or the important Code Committee, the latter having no lay involvement at all. The Leveson Report proposes significant improvements to the independence of any future regulatory body, such as an independent appointments panel and a Board with a majority of individuals independent of the press and without serving editors, members of the House of Commons or members of government (Leveson Report 2012: recommendations 1–5). Journalists could in future, therefore, be members of any regulatory Board. Leveson does, however, propose that serving editors should be able to sit on any future Code Committee because of their expertise (Leveson Report 2012: recommendation 7).

Transparency and accountability

To be effective, self-regulatory bodies must be open to public scrutiny and their activities and decision-making mechanisms should be transparent. The meetings of the CMM are not public, but everyone has the right to access the documentation of the CMM (e.g. the minutes of the meetings etc.). All adjudications of the CMM beginning from 1994 are available on its website. The website also contains the Basic Agreement, statistics, annual reports and information on the member organizations. Adjudications are also regularly published in the monthly journal of the Newspaper Association.

For decades self-regulation in Finland has functioned as a 'middleman' between judicial regulation and absolute freedom of expression. Self-regulation covers a certain 'grey area' where the statutory regulators are reluctant to enter. The CMM does not exercise legal jurisdiction, and the ethical evaluation of journalistic activities is kept separate from legal judgements. The CMM does not simultaneously deal with cases that are the subject of legal proceedings. However, decisions of the CMM upholding specific complaints are sometimes relied on in legal proceedings, a tendency which the CMM strongly condemns. According to the CMM, this practice generates problems: by using the Guidelines for Journalists in legal practice, the courts extend their authority to a sphere (journalism ethics) that, under the rule of law, is not a judicial field (JSN 2002). The purpose of the Guidelines is completely different from statutory regulation of the media – they define ethical principles for journalists. Constitutionally, lawsuits, sentences, fines or compensation can only be based on the law. An important purpose of the CMM is to resolve conflicts through out-of-court settlements and its decisions are not open to judicial review.

In the Finnish context, although the CMM meets the Minister of Justice once a year to discuss issues arising in the field of self-regulation, the CMM is accountable only to the supporting association and is not subject to any state or institutional control. Pressure on the CMM may, however, sometimes come from inside the media. For example, in a case in 2011, a number of newspaper editors-in-chief criticized the CMM for dismissing a complaint concerning an YLE broadcast. Their concern appeared to be that the decision, favourable to the media, could have damaged the trustworthiness of the CMM among the public (JSN 2009). As a result of this case and accompanying criticisms, amendments were made to the Guidelines for Journalists: if an anonymous source has been used in a story of high public interest and societal importance, and causing negative publicity, the news organization must demonstrate how the reliability of the source had been verified (JSN 2011b: s. 14).

Although the state authorities never directly interfere in the activities of the CMM, they have introduced a few general measures, such as the introduction of product placement, that relate directly to media ethical issues (Kuutti 2012a). As the CMM has always strongly opposed product placement, it will not adjudicate on cases raising concerns in this field.

The PCC during its operation published a wide range of documents, including a register of members' interests, rules on conflict of interests, as well as minutes of Commission meetings. It also produced an extensive database of complaints investigated by the PCC since 1996 and published monthly complaint summaries. Details of internal deliberations regarding code amendments were not, however, published (Media Standards Trust 2009: 25). Complaints on the handling of a case by the PCC could be taken up with the 'Independent Reviewer', who would investigate and report its findings to the PCC.

Unlike the CMM, PCC decisions were subject to judicial review (Court of Appeal, UK 1997). In areas such as privacy, the courts afforded the PCC 'a margin of discretion', where they were reluctant to interfere, as confirmed in *R (Ford) v The Press Complaints Commission* (High Court (QBD), UK 2001). It is important to note that a member of the public had the choice of taking a complaint to the PCC or to court, if there was a recognized civil cause of action such as defamation or invasion of privacy. The main advantages of the PCC were that it resolved complaints relatively quickly and there were no costs involved, save those that the individual incurred on their own account, for instance if they decided to employ a legal advisor. As noted above, however, the PCC was widely considered 'media friendly', unwilling to take allegations of press failings seriously or to do anything that would 'discomfort [the press] or make its life difficult' (House of Lords

2008: para. 222, citing Lord Puttnam; Seymour-Ure 2009). Where the editor of the publication against which a complaint was made was a member of the PCC, the perceived bias could push complainants to start court proceedings, as in the case of the McCanns, whose daughter went missing while on holiday in Spain (House of Commons 2010: 358).

Funding

The financing of the CMM is the responsibility of the supporting association in accordance with the Basic Agreement. The members of the supporting association cover expenses of the CMM with their annual membership fees, but the association also accepts state support through the Ministry of Justice. State support made up about 32–33 per cent of the budget since 2008, but nearly half of it in earlier years. This financial support is not automatic and has to be separately applied for (Kuutti 2012a).

The PCC did not receive any state support and was funded by a levy on its members, raised by the Press Standards Board of Finance (PressBof). The PCC argued that by leaving the setting and collection of fees to PressBof the PCC was better able to maintain its independence from the industry that funded it. The dependence of the PCC on PressBof as the sole form of financing nevertheless exposed the PCC to influence from this body, an organization made up solely of industry members, and thus indirectly to industry pressure. These concerns were exacerbated by the fact that PressBof, like the Code Committee, was not a transparent organization: it did not publish the names of companies that subscribed, nor how much individual companies paid (Media Standards Trust 2009: 25, 29; Media Standards Trust 2011). Here, too, the Leveson Report has proposed a more structured and clearly calibrated system of funding for the future (Leveson Report 2012: recommendation 6).

Concluding observations on the CMM and PCC

It is in the field of media self-regulation that Finland and the UK have diverged most radically, not so much in terms of formal structures but in relation to the two regimes' relative success. Although the CMM has been publicly criticized for being 'toothless', as it has no power to sanction except for obliging media outlets to print the adjudications related to them, the authority and independence of the CMM and its adjudications have never been publicly questioned. Through its statements, guidelines and adjudications, the CMM has a say in the ethical issues of journalism and definitely influences the way the journalists work. In a survey in 2011, 79 per cent of Finnish journalists agreed that the CMM has an impact on their work and 90 per cent regarded the ethical code to be important (MediaAct 2011). Within the larger Northern European context, it seems that the Finnish CMM, along with the Norwegian Pressens Faglige Utvalg, is among the few self-regulatory bodies that are influential and appreciated by journalists. By contrast, the PCC's close links to industry and its inability to address serious ethical failings undermined its credibility, with various options for reform currently under active consideration (Leveson Report 2012).

What explains the very different outcomes in the two countries? It is unlikely to relate to the availability of sanctions, since the PCC and CMM had broadly equivalent powers, though instances in which newspapers afforded insufficient prominence to PCC adjudications suggest even these limited sanctions were not taken seriously in the UK (House of Commons 2010: paras 570–572). The smaller scale of the industry in Finland, with potentially tighter peer control, and the cultural conventions of Finnish society (such as high respect for privacy, trust in the authorities, compliance with the law etc.) could be significant factors. The CMM's broader remit to proactively enhance industry standards, not merely react to complaints, may also have led to allegations of unethical behaviour being addressed at an earlier stage and more tenaciously pursued.

In the UK, the extremely challenging nature of the print market imposes competitive pressures, both economic and professional, on journalists and their newspapers. These factors discourage journalists from speaking out about abuses and suggest that effective measures to protect whistleblowers and their anonymity at the individual company level are needed to supplement independent external regulatory oversight (see Leveson Report 2012: recommendations 46–47). Although the PCC Code was widely incorporated into journalists' contracts of employment, this constraint proved ineffective in a culture where a cynical attitude to Code compliance had taken hold. The Chairman of the PCC, Lord Hunt, has proposed that in the future a specific individual within each media organization should be entrusted with the task of monitoring compliance with ethical standards, serving to devolve regulatory oversight still further to the institutions involved (Lord Hunt 2012).

Of note also is the fact that the Finnish system incorporates not merely editors but also journalists drawn from all media sectors, television and radio as well as the press, with their different reporting cultures. This may also be characteristic of the Democratic Corporatist model with it commitment to enhancing cooperation among different social groups, workers and employees, and journalistic professionalism (Hallin and Mancini 2004: 191). By contrast, the PCC in the UK has come to be associated with a specific section of the print industry, namely editors and, through them, press owners. Even after the inclusion of a majority of lay members on the PCC, the strategically important Code Committee and PressBof continued to be made up solely of editors. To command trust, it is clearly not enough for only part of the regulatory body to be structurally independent from vested interests.

Other self-regulatory bodies

In Finland, many media organizations have internal codes of ethics and in-house guidelines that regulate their performance. The Council of Ethics in Advertising issues statements on whether or not an advertisement or advertising practice is ethically acceptable using its own Code.

In the UK, apart from the PCC, there are a number of other self-regulatory bodies active in media content regulation, such as the British Board for Film Classification and the Advertising Standards Authority, which also participates with Ofcom in a co-regulatory scheme for advertising on broadcast television and on-demand video content (Mac Síthigh 2011). The Internet Watch Foundation (IWF) is a self-regulatory, independent organization established by UK Internet service providers working to minimize the online availability of potentially criminal child sexual abuse content. It is funded by the EU and by industry and operates a notice-and-takedown system. The IWF is governed by a ten-member board with an independent chair, six independent trustees, and three industry trustees. All independent Board members are chosen by an open selection procedure following national advertising (IWF 2003). The IWF has been heavily criticized for a lack of transparency in removal actions and a lack of clarity in blocking criteria (Kelly and Cook 2011: 340). It has recently introduced new policies and guidelines to improve its transparency (IWF 2011).

As a regulatory body, the IWF is of particular interest in the sense that, unlike most other regulators, it is set up as a charity. The IWF converted in 2004 from a not-for-profit company to charitable status. Charitable status brings a number of tax advantages and may enhance accountability: the IWF has brought all constitutional documents into line with the Companies Act 2006 (UK Parliament 2006b) and the Charities Act 2006 (UK Parliament 2006a) and is now monitored by the Charity Commission, to which it is required to submit an annual report and accounts. As noted above, a charitable trust has been suggested as one way of ensuring independent oversight of a new press regulator (Sabbagh 2013).

Conclusion

Our examination of media regulation in Finland and the UK indicates that there is no one single factor that guarantees regulatory independence; rather, independence is underpinned by a combination of legal rules, conventions and socio-cultural factors. Ensuring complete structural separation from both the state and industry is inherently difficult and may not even be desirable, though a clear understanding of, and responsiveness to, potential pressure points is essential. In practice, only a minority of regulatory authorities enjoy the full characteristics of an independent authority entrusted with regulatory powers (Jacobzone 2005: 34). Mostly, we can find a variety of advisory bodies, ethical councils and agencies with varying degrees of subordination to ministries or industry. This is the case in the UK and Finland, where a number of regulatory bodies have more or less close links either with the state or industry.

But both Finland and the UK display considerable commitment to regulatory independence in the media field and there are clear parallels in the structures they employ to achieve this objective, notably in their preference for a high level of regulatory autonomy in relation to the main public service broadcasters YLE and the BBC; for self-regulation in the print sector; and for professional state regulation in relation to commercial broadcasting. But there are also marked differences in the relative size, composition and operating terms of key regulatory bodies; the degree of protection from removal for office holders; the specificity with which required official qualifications are set out; and the degree of financial security of the institutions themselves.

Constitutional structures and traditions clearly have an impact on the level at which protections are built into each system. In Finland, over-arching principles of freedom of expression and access to information are enshrined in the constitution. General laws, including laws relating to the appointment, dismissal and probity of public officials, establish important principles for media governance. The transparency and openness of the media regulatory authorities give them reliability and public trust. As a result, the need for specific media regulation is limited. Those laws that do regulate the media and their supervisory bodies do not contradict the professional principles and conventions of journalists and media organizations.

In the UK, regulatory independence has been supported by a mix of less well entrenched conventions that govern the behaviour of public bodies generally and specific requirements built into the governing frameworks of the various media regulators. Decisions taken by public authorities must also be in conformity with the Human Rights Act (unless unambiguously precluded by UK primary legislation) and the main media regulatory bodies in the UK, including (to date) the PCC, are subject to judicial review, which extends to control over bias.

We find that the various models identified by Hallin and Mancini continue to provide a useful framework for understanding at least some of the nuances in the ways the two countries seek to regulate their media industries and to address the vulnerabilities to political or industrial influence that stem from those regulatory choices. In particular, Finland, in line with the Democratic Corporatist model, has designated a politically and socially representative regulator for public service broadcaster YLE, in practice populated by members of parliament. In addition, a strong commitment to professionalization in the media sector has led to a self-regulatory system that is both inclusive of all aspects of the industry and financially supported by the state. In the UK, recent Labour administrations have, in line with the Liberal model, pursued a deregulatory agenda, notably in removing restrictions on media ownership, yet they also established a powerful media regulator, Ofcom, specifically tasked with taking into account the interests of consumers and citizens as well as industry. Under the current coalition administration, Ofcom's policy-making powers have been scaled back, indicating a shift in the balance of power back to government, though government may well seek to divest itself of its controversial regulatory powers in the field of media pluralism. Indeed, it is government, not parliament, which retains many of the levers of power within the UK, particularly in relation to key appointments to media regulatory bodies. The UK has displayed an ongoing (though now badly shaken) commitment to self-regulation in the press sector, and a willingness to experiment with light-touch forms of co-regulation in advertising and on-demand services, even at the cost of creating a complex and increasingly incoherent regulatory system.

The variable success of self-regulation in the two countries underlines the fact that superficially similar structures can have quite different regulatory outcomes in politically, economically, and culturally diverse environments. Although the self-regulatory mechanisms in Finland have similar weaknesses as elsewhere (adherence to the ethical code is voluntary, the CMM has no punitive power etc.), they still seem to have a relatively high authority among journalists and news media organizations. In the UK by contrast, the PCC, with its more limited remit in terms of media sectors covered and role, has failed to command the trust of politicians or the public. The Finnish case also illustrates that state support need not be inherently problematic for regulatory independence, even in the sensitive print field. Without this support the CMM would face financial difficulties that would seriously endanger its ability to safeguard journalistic standards.

Self-regulatory bodies, by their very nature, run the risk of being perceived as servants of the industry they regulate. From this perspective, the example of ATVOD in the UK suggests that a move from a self- to a co-regulatory regime may preserve some of the responsiveness to industry that self-regulation offers, while at the same time guaranteeing greater independence from industry when making decisions. In particular, more open appointments processes; policies relating to conflicts of interests; formal commitments to impartial processes with lay representation; and consultation, transparency and accountability mechanisms can all be put in place. Though there has traditionally been limited appetite for even attenuated state regulation of the printed press in the UK (Ponsford 2012), co-regulation backed by a range of incentives could encourage wider participation in the regime, even if voluntary, enhance independence from industry, and facilitate more effective sanctions. As noted, co-regulation was the favoured solution proposed by Lord Justice Leveson (Leveson 2012). The relatively relaxed attitude to state regulation in the audiovisual context, with its accompanying checks and controls, contrasts markedly with past rejection of state regulation in the context of the press.

Political, economic and cultural factors therefore play an important role in the operation of the various regulatory regimes. For this reason, although the comparison between Finland and the UK highlights certain distinct strengths and weaknesses, piecemeal transplantation of specific aspects would not be without risk and could be positively damaging for regulatory independence. Application of the parliamentary model of regulation in the UK could, for example, result in a system completely dominated by government interests, given the tendency for elections to result in strong single-party majorities in the House of Commons. Keeping this caveat in mind, we nevertheless suggest that the UK could draw from Finland's high-level recognition of press freedom and regulatory transparency as well as its more representative system for regulating the public broadcasting sector. In addition, aspects of Finland's more inclusive system of self-regulation, applicable across all media sectors and engaging journalists as well as representatives of the public, could prove relevant when considering press reform in the UK and the demands of a converging media environment. In Finland, further consideration might be given to the role that co-regulation can play in ensuring the consistent application of ethical standards and effective enforcement, as well as to Ofcom's experience as a regulator committed to evidence-based rule making. For both countries, the greatest challenge will be to adapt their previously fragmented regulatory systems in order to provide citizens with a coherent, comprehensible and effective regulatory framework suited to our increasingly integrated online world.

References

Anders Chydenius Foundation (2006), *The World's First Freedom of Information Act*, Kokkola: Anders Chydenius Foundation, http://www.chydenius.net/pdf/worlds_first_foia.pdf. Accessed 22 May 2012.

Arnott, C. (2010), 'Media Mergers and the Meaning of Sufficient Plurality: A Tale of Two Acts', *The Journal of Media Law*, 2: 2, pp. 245–275.

ATVOD (2006), *Articles of Association*, adopted 22 June 2011, http://www.atvod.co.uk/uploads/files/ATVOD_Articles_of_Association.pdf. Accessed 22 May 2012.

BBC (2006), *Agreement with the Secretary of State for Culture, Media and Sport*, July 2006, Cmn 6872.

BBC (2012), *Quality First: Annual Report and Accounts 2010/2011*, http://www.bbc.co.uk/annualreport/. Accessed 22 May 2012.

BBC News (2011), 'Rupert Murdoch BSkyB take-over gets government go-ahead', *BBC News*, 3 March.

BBC Trust (2007), *Public Value Test (PVT): Guidance on the conduct of the PVT*, http://www.bbc.co.uk/bbctrust/assets/files/pdf/regulatory_framework/pvt/pvt_guidance.pdf. Accessed 22 May 2012.

BBC Trust (2009), *Local Video, Public Value Test, Final Conclusions*, 23 February, http://www.bbc.co.uk/bbctrust/assets/files/pdf/consult/local_video/decision.pdf. Accessed 22 May 2012.

BBC Trust (2010), *Code of Practice*, September, http://www.bbc.co.uk/bbctrust/assets/files/pdf/about/how_we_operate/code_of_practice.pdf. Accessed 22 May 2012.

BBC Trust (2011), *Delivering Quality First*, October, http://www.bbc.co.uk/bbctrust/assets/files/pdf/review_report_research/dqf/dqf.pdf. Accessed 22 May 2012.

BBC Trust (2012), *Register of Interests*, January, http://www.bbc.co.uk/bbctrust/assets/files/pdf/about/trustees/register_of_interests.pdf. Accessed 22 May 2012.

Björkstrand, G. and Mustonen, J. (2006), 'Introduction: Anders Chydenius' Legacy Today', in J. Mustonen (ed.), *The world's first Freedom of Information Act: Anders Chydenius' legacy today*, Kokkola: Art-Print Ltd, pp. 4–8.

Cambini, C. and Rondi, L. (2010), *Regulatory Independence, Investment and Political Interference: Evidence from the EU*, http://zope2.wiwi.hu-berlin.de/Professuren/vwl/mt/forschung/cambini. Accessed 22 May 2012.

Commissioner for Public Appointments (2011), *Review of Public Appointments Regulation: A Consultation*, June, http://publicappointmentscommissioner.independent.gov.uk/wp-content/uploads/2012/02/consultation-paper.pdf. Accessed 22 May 2012.

Committee on Standards in Public Life (1998), *The Seven Principles of Public Life*, available at: www.public-standards.gov.uk/Library/Seven_principles.doc. Accessed 22 May 2012.

Competition Commission (2011), *Annual Report and Accounts*, http://www.competition-commission.org.uk/governance/annual-report-and-accounts. Accessed 26 January 2012.

Council of Europe (2000), *Recommendation Rec(2000)23 of the Committee of Ministers to member states on the independence and functions of regulatory authorities for the broadcasting sector*, 20 December 2000.

Council of Europe (2006), *Declaration of the Committee of Ministers on the guarantee of the independence of public service broadcasting in the member states*, 27 September 2006.

Council of Europe (2008), *Declaration of the Committee of Ministers on the independence and functions of regulatory authorities for the broadcasting sector*, 26 March 2008.

Court of Appeal, UK (1997), *R v Press Complaints Commission, ex p Stewart Brady*, EMLR 185.

Court of Justice of the European Union (2010), *European Commission v Federal Republic of Germany*, case C-518/07.

Curran, J. and Seaton, J. (2010), *Power without Responsibility: Press, Broadcasting and the Internet in Britain*, 7th revised ed., London, New York: Routledge.

Department for Culture, Media and Sport (2006), *Royal Charter for the Continuance of the BBC*, Cm 6925, October.

Editors Code of Practice Committee (2012), *Editors' Code of Practice*, http://www.editorscode.org.uk. Accessed 26 January 2012.

European Commission (2008), *Commission opens three new cases on independence and effectiveness of telecoms regulators in Latvia, Lithuania and Sweden*, press release IP/08/1343, 18 September 2008, http://europa.eu/rapid/. Accessed 22 May 2012.

European Commission (2009), *Communication from the Commission on the application of State aid rules to public service broadcasting*, Official Journal of the European Union of 27.10.2009 C 257/1.

European Commission (2010), *Telecoms: Commission welcomes new Slovak rules on independence of telecoms regulator; ends legal action*, press release IP/10/806, 24 June 2010, http://europa.eu/rapid/. Accessed 22 May 2012.

European Court of Human Rights (2009), *Manole and Others v Moldova*, App no.13936/02, 17 December (final).

European Parliament and the Council of the European Union (2007), Directive 2007/65/EC of the European Parliament and of the Council of 11 December 2007, amending Council Directive 89/552/EEC on the coordination of certain provisions laid down by law, regulation or administrative action in Member States concerning the pursuit of television broadcasting activities, Official Journal of the European Union of 18.12.2007 L 332/27, consolidated in Directive 2010/13/EU (Audiovisual Media Services Directive), see below.

European Parliament and the Council of the European Union (2009), Directive 2009/140/EC of the European Parliament and of the Council of 25 November 2009, amending Directives 2002/21/EC on a common regulatory framework for electronic communications networks and services, 2002/19/EC on access to, and interconnection of, electronic communications networks and associated facilities, and 2002/20/EC on the authorisation of electronic communications networks and services, Official Journal of the European Union of 18/12/2009 L337/37.

European Parliament and the Council of the European Union (2010), Directive 2010/13/EU of the European Parliament and of the Council of 10 March 2010 on the coordination of certain provisions laid down by law, regulation or administrative action in Member States concerning the provision of audiovisual media services (Audiovisual Media Services Directive), Official Journal of the European Union of 15/4/2010 L 95/1.

FCA (Finnish Competition Authority) (2011), 'About Us', http://www.kilpailuvirasto.fi/cgi-bin/english.cgi?luku=about-us&sivu=about-us. Accessed 26 January 2012.

Fielden, L. (2011), *Regulating for Trust in Journalism: Standards Regulation in the Age of Blended Media*, Oxford: Reuters Institute for the Study of Journalism.

Ferrell Lowe, G. and Steemers, J. (eds.) (2012), *Regaining the Initiative for Public Service Media*, Gothenburg: Nordicom.

FICORA (2012), 'Providing versatile, effective and secure communications connections for everyone in Finland', http://www.ficora.fi/en/index/viestintavirasto/esittely.html. Accessed 26 January 2012.

Finnish Government (1993), *Decree on Finnish Competition Authority (66/1993)*, Helsinki.

Finnish Government (2001), *Decree on Communication Administration (697/2001)*, Helsinki, http://www.finlex.fi/en/laki/kaannokset/2001/en20010697.pdf. Accessed 26 January 2012.

Finnish Parliament (1889), *The Criminal Code of Finland (39/1889)*, Helsinki, http://www.finlex.fi/en/laki/kaannokset/1889/en18890039.pdf. Accessed 26 January 2012.

Finnish Parliament (1978), *Consumer Protection Act (38/1978)*, Helsinki, http://www.finlex.fi/en/laki/kaannokset/1978/en19780038.pdf. Accessed 26 January 2012.

Finnish Parliament (1988), *Act on the Finnish Competition Authority (711/1988)*, Helsinki.

Finnish Parliament (1993), *Act on Yleisradio Oy (1380/1993)*, Helsinki, http://www.finlex.fi/en/laki/kaannokset/1993/en19931380.pdf. Accessed 26 January 2012.

Finnish Parliament (1994), *Act on Civil Servants (750/1994)*, Helsinki.

Finnish Parliament (1997), *Criminal Procedure Act (689/1997)*, Helsinki, http://www.finlex.fi/en/laki/kaannokset/1997/en19970689.pdf. Accessed 26 January 2012.

Finnish Parliament (1998), *Act on the State Television and Radio Fund (745/1998)*, Helsinki, http://www.finlex.fi/en/laki/kaannokset/1998/en19980745.pdf. Accessed 26 January 2012.

Finnish Parliament (1999), *The Constitution of Finland (731/1999)*, Helsinki, http://www.finlex.fi/en/laki/kaannokset/1999/en19990731.pdf. Accessed 26 January 2012.

Finnish Parliament (2001), *Act on Communication Administration (625/2001)*, Helsinki, http://www.finlex.fi/en/laki/kaannokset/2001/en20010625.pdf. Accessed 26 January 2012.

Finnish Parliament (2003), *Freedom of Expression Act: Act on the Exercise of Freedom of Expression in Mass Media (460/2003)*, Helsinki, http://www.finlex.fi/en/laki/kaannokset/2003/en20030460.pdf. Accessed 26 January 2012.

Finnish Parliament (2011), *Competition Act (948/2011)*, Helsinki, http://www.finlex.fi/en/laki/kaannokset/2011/en20110948.pdf. Accessed 26 January 2012.

Finnmedia (2012), 'The tasks of Finnmedia', http://www.vkl.fi/en/finnmedia. Accessed 26 January 2012.

Freedman, D. (2008), *The Politics of Media Policy*, Cambridge: Polity Press.

Gilardi, F. (2005), 'Evaluating independent regulators', in OECD, *Designing Independent and Accountable Regulatory Authorities for High Quality Regulation. Proceedings of an Expert Meeting in London, United Kingdom, 10–11 January 2005*, pp. 101–125.

Gilardi, F. and Maggetti, M. (2010), *The Independence of Regulatory Authorities*, http://www.maggetti.org/Sito/Publications_files/gilardi_maggetti_handbook.pdf. Accessed 22 May 2012.

Goodwin, P. (2012), 'High noon. The BBC meets "The West's Most Daring Government"', in G. F. Lowe and J. Steemers (eds.), *Regaining the Initiative for Public Service Media*, Gothenburg: Nordicom, pp. 63–76.

Hallin, D. C. and Mancini, P. (2004), *Comparing Media Systems: Three Models of Media and Politics*, Cambridge: Cambridge University Press.

Hans Bredow Institute for Media Research; Interdisciplinary Centre for Law & ICT (ICRI), Katholieke Universiteit Leuven; Center for Media and Communication Studies (CMCS), Central European University; Cullen International; Perspective Associates (eds., 2011), *INDIREG. Indicators for independence and efficient functioning of audio-visual media services regulatory bodies for the purpose of enforcing the rules in the AVMS Directive*, Study conducted on behalf of the European Commission, Final Report. February 2011.

High Court (QBD), UK (2001), *R (Ford) v The Press Complaints Commission* EWHC Admin 683.

High Court (QBD), UK (2005), *R (Grieson) v Ofcom* EWHC 1899.

HM Government (2010), *Reducing regulation made simple: less regulation, better regulation and regulation as a last resort*, http://www.bis.gov.uk/assets/biscore/better-regulation/docs/r/10-1155-reducing-regulation-made-simple.pdf. Accessed 22 May 2012.

House of Commons, Culture, Media and Sport Committee (2010), *Press standards, privacy and libel: Second Report*, HC paper HC362-I, 9 February.

House of Commons, Culture, Media and Sport Committee (2011), *Pre–appointment hearing with the Government's preferred candidate for Chairman of the BBC Trust*, HC Paper HC 864-I, 10 March.

House of Lords, Appellate Committee (2004), *R (ProLife Alliance) v BBC* 1 AC 185.

House of Lords, Communications Committee (2005), *The Review of the BBC's Royal Charter*, First Report of Session 2005/2006, HL paper 50-I, November.

House of Lords, Communications Committee (2008), *The Ownership of the News, First Report of Session 2007–2008*, HL 122-I, June.

House of Lords, Communications Committee (2011), *The Governance and Regulation of the BBC, Second Report*, HL Paper 166, 29 June.

Hunt, J. (2011), 'A communications review for the Digital Age. Open letter to all those who work in fixed or mobile communications, television, radio, online publishing, video games, and other digital and creative content industries', 16 May 2011, http://www.culture.gov.uk/images/publications/commsreview-open-letter_160511.pdf. Accessed 22 May 2012.

Hunt (David James Fletcher, Lord) (2012), *Towards a New System of Self-regulation*, 9 March, http://www.pcc.org.uk/assets/0/Draft_proposal.pdf. Accessed 2 June 2012.

Information Commissioner's Office (2006), *What Price Privacy?*, HC Paper 1056, 2006, London: HMSO, http://www.ico.gov.uk/upload/documents/library/corporate/research_and_reports/what_price_privacy.pdf. Accessed 22 May 2012.

IWF (Internet Watch Foundation) (2003), *Board Members Handbook*, available at: http://www.iwf.org.uk/accountability/governance/board-handbook. Accessed 26 January 2012.

IWF (Internet Watch Foundation) (2011), *Annual report 2010*, http://www.iwf.org.uk/accountability/annual-reports/2010-annual-report. Accessed 22 May 2012.

Jacobzone, S. (2005), 'Designing Independent and Accountable Regulatory Authorities. A Comparative Overview across OECD Countries', in OECD, *Designing independent and accountable regulatory authorities for high quality regulation. Proceedings of an Expert Meeting in London, United Kingdom, 10–11 January 2005*, pp. 33–36.

Jempson, M. and Powell, W. (2011), 'United Kingdom: From the Gentleman's Club to the Blogosphere', in T. Eberwein, S. Fengler, E. Lauk and T. Leppick-Bork (2011), *Mapping Media Accountability – in Europe and Beyond*, Copenhagen: Herbert von Halem Verlag, pp. 194–216.

JSN (Julkisen Sanan Neuvosto/ Council for Mass Media in Finland) (2002), *Council Resolution 3206/L/02*.

JSN (Julkisen Sanan Neuvosto/ Council for Mass Media in Finland) (2008), 'The Council for Mass Media in Finland', http://www.jsn.fi/en/Council_for_Mass_Media/the-council-for-mass-media-in-finland. Accessed 26 January 2012.

JSN (Julkisen Sanan Neuvosto/ Council for Mass Media in Finland) (2009), *Yle, TV2 Silminnäkijä, 4193/4199/YLE/09*, http://www.jsn.fi/sisalto/4193--4199-yle-09/?year=2011&search=4199%2fYLE%2f09. Accessed 2 February 2012.

JSN (Julkisen Sanan Neuvosto/ Council for Mass Media in Finland) (2010), *JSN Vuosikertomus/ CMM Annual Report 2010*, http://www.jsn.fi/jsn/tilastot-ja-vuosikertomukset. Accessed 22 May 2012.

JSN (Julkisen Sanan Neuvosto/ Council for Mass Media in Finland) (2011a), *The Basic Agreement of the Council for Mass Media*, http://www.jsn.fi/en/Council_for_Mass_Media/basic-agreement/. Accessed 26 January 2012.

JSN (Julkisen Sanan Neuvosto/ Council for Mass Media in Finland) (2011b), 'Guidelines for Journalists and an Annex', http://www.jsn.fi/en/guidelines_for_journalists/. Accessed 26 January 2012.

JSN (Julkisen Sanan Neuvosto/ Council for Mass Media in Finland) (2012), Neuvoston jäsenmäärä kasvaa kahdella/ The number of the members of the CMM will increase by two, http://www.jsn.fi/uutiset/neuvoston-jasenmaara-kasvaa-kahdella/. Accessed 29 December 2012.

Jyrkiäinen, Jyrki (2010), 'Media landscape: Finland', *European Journalism Centre*, http://www.ejc.net/media_landscape/article/finland/. Accessed 22 May 2012.

Karppinen, K. and Nieminen, H. (2012), 'Example Cited by Hungarian Government: Finland. Expert Assessment', in Center for Media and Communication Studies (CMCS), *Hungarian Media Laws in Europe: An assessment of the consistency of Hungary's media laws with European practices and norms*, Budapest: Central European University, http://cmcs.ceu.hu/. Accessed 22 May 2012.

Kelly, S. and Cook, S. (eds.) (2011), *Freedom on the Net 2011: A Global Assessment of Internet and Digital Media*, Washington DC; New York: Freedom House, 18 April.

Kuutti, H. (2012a), *Interview with Ilkka Vänttinen, CMM secretary*, 5 January 2012.

Kuutti, H. (2012b), *Interview with Seppo Reimavuo, FCA Assistant Director*, 12 January 2012.

Kuutti, H. (2012c), *Interview with Merja Saari, FICORA Director-General*, 12 January 2012.

Larsen, A., Pedersen, L. H., Sørensen, E. M. and Olsen, O. J. (2005), 'Independent Regulatory Authorities in Europe', in SNF-SESSA, *Conference: Harmonising Effective Regulation*, Bergen, Norway, 3–4 March, http://www.sessa.eu.com/documents/wp/D73.1-Larsen.pdf. Accessed 22 May 2012.

Lauk, E. and Jufereva, M. (2010), '"Reversed Censorship"? Assessing Media Self-regulation in the Baltic Countries', *Medialni Studia/Media Studies*, 1, pp. 31–46.

Leveson Report (2012), *An Inquiry into the Culture Practices and Ethics of the Press: Report*, Stationery Office, 29 November, http://www.official-documents.gov.uk/document/hc1213/hc07/0780/0780.asp. Accessed 10 January 2013.

Levy, D. (2001), *Europe's Digital Revolution: Broadcasting Regulation, the EU and the Nation State*, London: Routledge.

Levy, D. (2012), 'PSB Policymaking in Comparative Perspective. The BBC and France Télévision' in G. Ferrell Lowe. and J. Steemers (eds.) (2012), *Regaining the Initiative for Public Service Media*, Gothenburg: Nordicom, pp. 97–112.

Lewis, R. (2005), *Finland, Cultural Lone Wolf*, London: Intercultural press.

Lord Chancellor and Secretary of State for Justice (2011), *Draft Defamation Bill*, Cm 8020, March.

Lord Hutton (2004), *Report of the Inquiry into the Circumstances Surrounding the Death of Dr David Kelly C.M.G.*, HC 247, 28 January.

Lunt, P. and Livingstone, S. (2012), *Media Regulation. Governance and the Interests of Citizens and Consumers*, London, Los Angeles and New Delhi: Sage Publications.

Lunt, P., Livingstone, S. and Brevini, B. (2012), 'Changing Regimes of Regulation. Implications for Public Service Broadcasting', in G. F. Lowe and J. Steemers (eds.), *Regaining the Initiative for Public Service Media*, Gothenburg: Nordicom, pp. 113–128.

Mac Síthigh, D. (2011), 'Co-regulation, Video-on-demand and the Legal Status of Audio-visual Media', *International Journal of Digital television* 2: 1, p. 51.

MediaAct (2011), *Preliminary Results of the Media Accountability and Transparency-project survey among Journalists of 12 Countries*, http://www.mediaact.eu/. Accessed 22 May 2012.

Media Standards Trust (2009), *A More Accountable Press: Is Self-Regulation Failing the Press and the Public?*, http://mediastandardstrust.org/wp-content/uploads/downloads/2010/07/A-More-Accountable-Press-Part-1.pdf. Accessed 22 May 2012.

Media Standards Trust (2011), 'MST response to Northern & Shell exit from the system of press self-regulation', 11 January, http://mediastandardstrust.org/mst-news/mst-response-to-northern-shell-exit-from-the-system-of-press-self-regulation/. Accessed 22 May 2012.

MEDIADEM (2012), 'Project', http://www.mediadem.eliamep.gr/. Accessed 2 June 2012.

Millwood-Hargrave, A. and Livingstone, S. (2009), *Harm and Offence in Media Content: A Review of the Evidence*, Bristol: Intellect.

Mulholland, H. (2012), 'Guto Harri threatened to turn UK press against BBC', *The Guardian*, 27 May.

National Audit Office (NAO) (2010), *The Effectiveness of Converged Regulation*, HC 490, November. November 2010C: 490, 2010–2011

Nolan (1995), *Standards in Public Life*, http://www.archive.official-documents.co.uk/document/cm28/2850/285002.pdf. Accessed 22 May 2012.

NUJ (National Union of Journalists) (2008), 'About us', http://www.nuj.org.uk/innerPagenuj.html?docid=27. Accessed 26 January 2012.

NUJ (National Union of Journalists) (2011), *NUJ Code of Conduct*, http://media.gn.apc.org/nujcode.html. Accessed 26 January 2012.

O'Carroll, Lisa (2012), 'Royal charters: what are they and how do they work?', *guardian.co.uk*, 7 December.

Ofcom (2005), *Better Policy Making: Ofcom's Approach to Policy Making*, July, http://www.ofcom. org.uk/about/policies-and-guidelines/better-policy-making-ofcoms-approach-to-impact-assessment/. Accessed 22 May 2012.

Ofcom (2008), *Identifying appropriate regulatory solutions: principles for analysing self- and co-regulation – Statement*, 10 December, http://stakeholders.ofcom.org.uk/consultations/coregulation/statement/. Accessed 11 June 2012.

Ofcom (2010a), *Pay TV statement*, 31 March, http://stakeholders.ofcom.org.uk/binaries/consultations/third_paytv/statement/paytv_statement.pdf. Accessed 2 June 2012.

Ofcom (2010b), *Report on public interest test on the proposed acquisition of British Sky Broadcasting Group plc by News Corporation*, 31 December, http://www.culture.gov.uk/images/publications/OfcomPITReport_NewsCorp-BSkyB_31DEC2010.pdf. Accessed 11 June 2012.

Ofcom (2011), *Ofcom announces budget reduction and savings*, 31 March, http://media.ofcom.org.uk/2011/03/31/ofcom-announces-budget-reduction-and-savings/. Accessed 2 June 2012.

Ofcom (2012), *Non-executive Ofcom board members' interests in companies in the communications sector*, http://www.ofcom.org.uk/about/policies-and-guidelines/policy-on-conflicts-of-interest/. Accessed 26 January 2012.

OFT (Office of Fair Trading) (2010), *Transparency: A statement on the OFT's approach*, May, http://www.oft.gov.uk/shared_oft/consultations/668117/OFT1234.pdf. Accessed 22 May 2012.

PCC (Press Complaints Commission) (2006), *Memorandum of Association of the Press Complaints Commission*, http://www.pcc.org.uk/assets/111/PCC_Articles_of_Association.pdf. Accessed 22 May 2012.

PCC (Press Complaints Commission) (2009), *PCC's remit extended to cover online-only publications*, press release, 14 December, http://www.pcc.org.uk/news/index.html?article=NjEwOQ. Accessed 22 May 2012.

PCC (Press Complaints Commission) (2012a), 'Who's who: Nominations committee', http://www.pcc.org.uk/about/whoswho/nominations.html. Accessed 26 January 2012.

PCC (Press Complaints Commission) (2012b), 'Who's who: Press Standards Board of Finance (Pressbof)', http://www.pcc.org.uk/about/whoswho/pressbof.html. Accessed 26 January 2012.

PCC (Press Complaints Commission) (2012c), *Minutes of PCC meeting held Wednesday 21 February 2012*, http://pcc.org.uk/assets/559/Minutes_Februry_2012.pdf. Accessed 2 June 2012.

PCC Governance Review Panel (2010), *The governance of the Press Complaints Commission: An independent review*, July, http://www.pcc.org.uk/assets/441/Independent_Governance_Review_Report.pdf. Accessed 22 May 2012.

Plunkett, J. and O'Carroll, L. (2012), '"Congrats on Brussels!" Texts Reveal Hunt's Close Alliance with Murdoch. Culture Secretary's Evidence to Leveson Inquiry Reveals Extent of Relationships with Key Players in News Corp's Bid for BSkyB', *The Guardian*, 31 May.

Ponsford, D. (2012), 'Lord Leveson: The State Cannot Licence Journalists', *Press Gazette*, 12 January.

Press Gazette (2011), 'David Cameron Sounds Death Knell for PCC', *Press Gazette*, 8 July.

Prosecutor General (2004), 'VKS Menettely Sananvapausrikoksissa', http://www.vksv.oikeus.fi/Etusivu/VKSnmaarayksetjaohjeet/Sananvapausrikosasiat/VKS20041Menettelysananvapausrikoksissa. Accessed 22 May 2012.

Puppis, M. (2010), 'Media Governance: A New Concept for the Analysis of Media Policy and Regulation', *Communication, Culture & Critique*, 3: 2, pp. 134–149.

Reporters Without Borders (2012), *Press Freedom Index 2011/2012*, http://en.rsf.org/press-freedom-index-2011-2012,1043.html. Accessed 26 January 2012.

Sabbagh, D. (2013), 'Leveson reforms could be made by charitable trust, says industry group', *guardian.co.uk*, 10 January.

Saurwein, F. (2011), 'Regulatory Choice for Alternative Modes of Regulation: How Context Matters', *Law & Policy*, 33: 3, pp. 334–36.

Scannell, P. and Cardiff, D. (1991), *A Social History of British Broadcasting: 1929–1939: Serving the Nation*, Oxford: Basil-Blackwell.

Scottish Parliament (2002) *Freedom of Information (Scotland) Act 2002*, London: HMSO.

Seymour-Ure, C. (2009), 'A more accountable press', *The Political Quarterly*, 80: 3, pp. 416–419.

Sweney, M. (2011), 'Ofcom to cut budget by 20% this year. Regulator to make "majority of cuts" in 2011 as part of four-year savings plan to meet government spending targets', *The Guardian*, 31 March.

TV Licensing (2012), 'Technology: devices and online', http://www.tvlicensing.co.uk/check-if-you-need-one/topics/technology-devices-and-online-top8/. Accessed 22 May 2012.

UJF (2012), 'The Union of Journalists in Finland', http://www.journalistiliitto.fi/en/union/. Accessed 26 January 2012.

UK Parliament (1985), *Cinemas Act 1985*, London: HMSO.

UK Parliament (1998a), *Competition Act 1998*, London: HMSO.

UK Parliament (1998b), *Human Rights Act 1998*, London: HMSO.

UK Parliament (2000), *Freedom of Information Act 2000*, London: HMSO.

UK Parliament (2002a), *Enterprise Act 2002*, London: HMSO.

UK Parliament (2002b), *Office of Communications Act 2002* London: HMSO.

UK Parliament (2003), *Communications Act 2003*, London: HMSO.

UK Parliament (2006a), *Charities Act 2006*, London: HMSO.

UK Parliament (2006b), *Companies Act 2006*, London: HMSO.

World Audit (2011), *Democracy table December 2011*, http://www.worldaudit.org/democracy.htm. Accessed 26 January 2012.

YLE (2005), *Ohjelmatoiminnan säännöstö/Guidelines of Broadcasting*, http://avoinyle.fi/www/fi/liitetiedostot/ots.pdf. Accessed 22 May 2012.

YLE (2011), *YLE happy with the conclusions of the Parliamentary groups*, http://avoinyle.fi/www/en/index.php?we_objectID=497. Accessed 26 January 2012.

YLE (2012a), 'Administrative Council', http://avoinyle.fi/www/en/organisation/administrative_council.php. Accessed 26 January 2012.

YLE (2012b), 'This is Yle', http://avoinyle.fi/www/en/index.php. Accessed 26 January 2012.

YLE (2012c), Parliament reaches consensus on YLE reform. Ministry of Transport and Communications press release 15.06.2012, http://www.lvm.fi/web/en/pressreleases/-/view/4114935. Accessed 29 December 2012.

Chapter 11

Independence through intervention? International intervention
and the independence of the Communications Regulatory Agency
in Bosnia and Herzegovina

Tarik Jusić
Analitika - Centre for Social Research

Abstract

The establishment and operation of the Communications Regulatory Agency in Bosnia and Herzegovina is widely recognized as one of the most successful media reform projects in the country since the end of the war in late 1995. The good performance and the high level of independence of the Agency have been attributed to an advanced legal framework and a strong internal culture of independence. Nevertheless, with international presence decreasing, concerns have been voiced about the sustainability of the current level of the agency's independence. This chapter attempts to investigate these assumptions, linking them to the relevant theoretical concepts about the impact of broader socio-political contexts on the independence prospects of broadcasting regulatory agencies, as well as with theoretical concepts regarding the sustainability of institutions created through external international intervention.

Keywords: Bosnia and Herzegovina, Communications Regulatory Agency (CRA), culture of independence, politicization

Introduction

Bosnia and Herzegovina is a new democracy, without significant experience in democratic self-governance (Malcolm 1994; Dizdarević, et al. 2006: 21–22). It was only in 1990 that democratization of the country began: the country adopted amendments to its constitution, introducing a multi-party democratic political system and a market economy, while the first free parliamentary elections took place on 18 November 1990. Nevertheless, the first attempt at democratization failed after only a year, and by the time its independence was internationally recognized on 6 April 1992,[1] the country was already in a full-scale war that lasted until late 1995, with devastating consequences (Ministry for Human Rights and Refugees of Bosnia and Herzegovina 2003: 7; The World Bank 2004). The war ended with the signing of the 1995 General Framework Agreement for Peace in Bosnia and Herzegovina, known as the Dayton Peace Accords after the city of Dayton where it was signed (hereafter, the 'DPA'); the DPA was brokered by international actors led by the United States (Dizdarević, et al. 2006: 22–23.).

Within such a context, the establishment of an independent regulatory agency (IRA) for communications in Bosnia and Herzegovina – the Communications Regulatory Agency (CRA) – is often heralded as a successful example of the introduction of a regulatory agency in a post-conflict society. It has been argued that the good performance of the CRA in terms of its independence can in significant degree be attributed to the quality of its governing law and a strong internal 'culture of independence' (Hans Bredow Institute for Media Research, et al. 2011: 299–300; Council of Europe 2008a). Nevertheless, concerns have been expressed that with the reduced presence of the international community in Bosnia and Herzegovina, the sustainability of the current level of the CRA's independence might be endangered (Hans Bredow Institute for Media Research, et al. 2011: 299). It is the intention of this chapter to test these assumptions and investigate the prospects for ensuring long-term sustainability of the independency of the CRA.

It is understood that the case of Bosnia and Herzegovina merits special attention because of several peculiarities. First, the creation of the CRA, its governing Law on Communications of Bosnia and Herzegovina (Parliamentary Assembly of Bosnia and Herzegovina 2003b) and its institutional design are direct products of intense international intervention. Second, there is still a strong international presence in the country led by a UN-appointed High Representative, who is entrusted with broad powers in order to ensure the implementation of the peace agreement that stopped the war in 1995. Third, it is a post-conflict society still characterized by strong tensions between its three major ethnic groups (Bosniaks, Croats and Serbs). In order to balance out political tensions, complex power-sharing arrangements have been introduced. Those arrangements guarantee the influence of the representatives of the three ethnic groups on decision making and on the distribution of seats at all levels of government through grand coalitions, consensual decision making, and veto powers. This results in a rather cumbersome and often inefficient policy process. Since the end of the war in 1995, the country has been gridlocked in a deep political crisis, where key parties are often unable to compromise and reach agreements on any major issue, and international actors have had to intervene to move political processes forward.

It is well established that formal independence alone cannot explain the actual level of independence of IRAs, since other context-specific factors might influence the outcome as well. Findings from relevant literature point to numerous factors influencing the actual level of media freedoms and of the independence of regulatory agencies in different countries (Hans Bredow Institute for Media Research, et al. 2011: 301). When considering the influence of structural factors on the development of independent media, Hallin and Mancini (2004) differentiate between three main types of media systems with characteristic media system constellations. Their model features two sets of dimensions, with the first set characterizing the media system (i.e. political parallelism, professionalization, the role of the state in the media system) and the second set referring to the main features of a country's political system and culture (i.e. a political history featuring patterns of conflict or consensus, majoritarian or consensus government, individualized v organized pluralism, the role of the state and the rational legal authority). (For a detailed explanation of Hallin and Mancini's approach, see Chapter 2 in this book by Irion and Radu.) Additionally, Zielonka and Mancini (2011: 2) emphasize the importance of the *politicization of the state* for understanding the relationship between politics, state institutions, and the broader political culture in a society. The politicization of the state results in the capture of state structures by political actors, a high level of informality, and weak formal institutions and rule of law, as means of extracting resources from these structures (Zielonka and Mancini 2011: 2–3).

This chapter considers in particular the type of government, the politicization of the state, the culture of independence and the role of external intervention as decisive variables that determine the actual independence of the CRA in Bosnia and Herzegovina. The first part of the chapter provides an overview of the formal independence of the CRA, followed by an analysis of its de facto independence in the current context, with a special focus on the impact of state politicization and the culture of informality on the de facto independence of the agency. The third part offers an in-depth analysis of the role power-sharing arrangements and consensus politics might play in respect to ensuring the independence of the CRA. In the fourth section, the role of international assistance and scrutiny is analysed, while the fifth part reflects upon the concept of the culture of independence and its relevance for understanding the overall prospects for CRA's independence. A conclusion includes a summary of key findings and suggestions of potential subjects for further research.

Formal independence of the CRA

Following the common distinction in literature, independence of a regulatory agency is considered at formal and de facto levels (see Chapter 5 in this book by Dreyer; Hans Bredow Institute for Media Research, et al. 2011: 28). The Council of Europe Recommendation Rec(2000)23 of the Committee of Ministers to member states on the independence and functions of regulatory authorities for the broadcasting sector (Council of Europe 2000) provides detailed instructions on what the preconditions are for an IRA in the broadcasting sector (see Chapter 3 in this book by Valcke, Voorhoof and Lievens). In relation to this Recommendation, the INDIREG study for the European Commission on indicators for the independence and efficient functioning of audiovisual media services regulatory bodies operationalizes five key dimensions (Hans Bredow Institute for Media Research, et al. 2011: 32):

- status and powers (the nature and extent of statutory documents, institutional arrangements, decision-making powers, rule-making powers etc.),
- financial resources (the level of control over the resources needed for normal functioning of the IRA, e.g. a stable source of funding, salary policies),
- autonomy of decision-makers (nomination, appointment, tenure and dismissal procedures),
- knowledge/expertise requirements for board and staff members,

- accountability and transparency (formal accountability, auditing requirements, transparency requirements, procedural legitimacy).

It is generally assumed that a high level of formal independence significantly contributes to the de facto independence of regulatory agencies. Furthermore, the source of recognition of IRAs is an indicator of the significance attributed to a regulatory agency's independence. Recommendation Rec(2000)23 of the Council of Europe explicitly states that the independence of regulatory authorities should be granted by clear rules and procedures. First, if its independence is formally recognized, it is assumed that the regulator will be prone to act in a more independent manner. Second, the higher in the legal order the source of recognition of IRA, the higher the likelihood for independent functioning of the regulatory authority, since the obligation will be an overriding principle to be followed in all cases (Hans Bredow Institute for Media Research, et al. 2011: 371). Third, the higher the source of recognition, the more difficult it would be to amend it and change the level of independence granted to the regulatory authority (Hans Bredow Institute for Media Research, et al. 2011: 371). Hence, the independence of a regulatory authority should be granted in legal texts.

The formal independence of the CRA is granted by the Law on Communications of Bosnia and Herzegovina, which complies with high international standards as defined by the Council of Europe's Recommendation Rec(2000)23. The law provides mechanisms for the protection of the CRA from political pressures and powers for the efficient regulation of the broadcasting and telecommunications sector in an accountable and transparent manner. Hence, on a formal level, the law provides the CRA with significant safeguards for independence:

- It is established as an independent and a non-profit institution equipped with both policy-setting and policy-implementing duties and powers. It is responsible for the regulation of the broadcasting and telecommunications sectors, the allocation of frequencies to broadcasters, including public service broadcasters, and frequency spectrum management.
- The CRA has at its disposal a set of enforcement measures ranging from oral and written warnings to inspections, financial penalties, and ultimately the revocation of a license (Art. 46). It also has monitoring and information collection powers, in order to be able to assess compliance with licensing conditions and regulations.
- The CRA's decision-making bodies are the CRA Council and the Director General. The Council is responsible for strategic issues and implementation of the law, and adopts codes of practice and rules for broadcasting and telecommunications. The Council consists of seven members, nominated by the Council of Ministers of Bosnia and Herzegovina on the basis of a list submitted by the CRA Council with twice as many candidates as there are positions, and appointed by the Parliament of Bosnia and Herzegovina within 30 days after the submission of the nominations. If the Parliament

rejects a nomination, the Council of Ministers has to nominate another candidate from the list. The members of the CRA Council have a four-year term that is renewable once. Decisions in the CRA Council are made by majority vote. A legal review of the Council's decisions can be initiated before the State Court of Bosnia and Herzegovina (Art. 47).

- The CRA is managed by a Director General (Art. 40) who is nominated by the CRA Council and approved by the Council of Ministers of Bosnia and Herzegovina. The Council receives reports from the Director General. Appeals against decisions of the Director General are directed to the Council, whose decisions are final and binding in an administrative procedure.
- Candidates for the positions of Director General or the members of the CRA Council must have experience in the telecommunications or broadcasting sector, and cannot hold a position at the legislative or executive level of government or be members of political party organs. In addition, the Director General cannot have any financial relation with a telecommunications operator or broadcaster, whereas Council members, in case of a conflict of interest, must abstain from the decision-making process (Art. 39).
- The law provides incompatibility rules for key CRA staff in respect to other state and party functions, while financial relationships with stakeholders from communications sectors are only required to be declared in the case of a conflict of interest. The Director General and senior staff cannot have financial relationships with stakeholders. However, there are no rules that prevent Council members from being employed by regulatees after their term in office.
- The authority to dismiss members of the CRA Council before their term expires rests with the Parliament of Bosnia and Herzegovina, whereas the Director General can be dismissed by the Council of Ministers of Bosnia and Herzegovina. The dismissal of the members of the Council and the Director General can take place in the case of illness; conviction of a crime punishable by imprisonment; a conflict of interest; failure of the Director General to perform his/her duties; and violation of the agency's Code of Ethics (Art. 42).
- The modalities of CRA's funding are stipulated in Art. 44 of the Law on Communications. The budget for each fiscal year is first adopted by the CRA Council and then submitted by the Director General to the Council of Ministers for approval. Until the final budget is approved by the Council of Ministers, the CRA operates according to the budget adopted by the CRA Council. The CRA's budget consists of revenues from license fees and grants or donations received by the agency. When grants are received for specific tasks or projects, they are accounted for separately, and are not part of the approved budget. Fines collected from enforcement measures by the agency are remitted to the Council of Ministers, and are included in the budget of the institutions of Bosnia and Herzegovina.
- The CRA staff fall into the category of civil servants, in accordance with the Law on Civil Service in the Institutions of Bosnia and Herzegovina (Parliamentary Assembly

of Bosnia and Herzegovina 2002). But the Law on Communications stipulated that the agency had the right to employ 'officers and staff as may be necessary for the efficient performance of its functions' and to 'determine which positions fall under the scope of the Law on Civil Service' (Art. 43). This means that the CRA could operate its own salary scheme, especially in respect to expert positions.

- With respect to the CRA's accountability, Art. 44 of the Law on Communications stipulates that the agency is subject to an annual audit review by the Supreme Audit Institution (SAI). Additionally, the agency prepares an annual report of its activities and finances that is submitted to the Council of Ministers of Bosnia and Herzegovina. Through these reporting procedures, the agency is accountable to the parliament and the government of Bosnia and Herzegovina.

- The Freedom of Access to Information Act (Parliamentary Assembly of Bosnia and Herzegovina 2000) requires all public institutions and companies to provide access to the information in their possession. The laws do not require that the CRA's decisions must be published. With respect to procedural legitimacy, the CRA is required by Art. 38 of the Law on Communications, before adopting any rules, to publish a draft rule and allocate at least fourteen days for public consultations. The CRA regularly practices public consultation (CRA 2012a; CRA 2011a).

Hence, the Law on Communications provides a good formal basis for good performance and the independence of the CRA. However, in recent years, several of the government's legal initiatives have eroded the formal independence of the CRA, especially in respect to the status of its staff members, its financial independence and its formal status in relation to the Council of Ministers, whereas the significance of the Law on Communication in those areas has been reduced. In many cases, provisions of new laws are in conflict with provisions of the Law on Communications, but that has not prevented the Council of Ministers or the Parliament of Bosnia and Herzegovina from enforcing new legal obligations and practices on the CRA:

- Contrary to the Law on Communications, the exemption from the civil service rule was revoked in 2008 by the Law on Salaries and Compensations in Institutions of Bosnia and Herzegovina (Parliamentary Assembly of Bosnia and Herzegovina 2008). As a result, the salaries of certain CRA employees decreased significantly (Hans Bredow Institute for Media Research, et al. 2011: 300), thus decreasing the ability of the CRA to retain or recruit experienced staff.

- Art. 17 of the amended Law on Ministries and Other Bodies of Administration in Bosnia and Herzegovina (Parliamentary Assembly of Bosnia and Herzegovina 2003a) includes the CRA in the list of autonomous administrative bodies. This renders the CRA a managing organization to the government (Hans Bredow Institute for Media Research, et al. 2011: 301). In its 2010 Progress Report on Bosnia and Herzegovina, the European Commission declared that this is not in line with the relevant EU provisions and with specific national legislation, since the independence of the CRA is enshrined in the Law on Communications (European Commission 2010: 51). The Commission's 2011 Progress Report insists that 'amendments to the Law on Ministries and Other Bodies of Administration in Bosnia and Herzegovina remain to be adopted in order to ensure the CRA's independence' (European Commission 2011: 16).

- Despite the fact that the CRA is a self-financed body, according to Art. 9(4) of the Law on Financing of State Institutions of Bosnia and Herzegovina (Parliamentary Assembly of Bosnia and Herzegovina 2004), its budget is included in the state budget, so the Agency has no direct control of its funds. In effect, if the state budget is not adopted in time, CRA funding depends on decisions regarding the temporary financing of state institutions. This means that such a situation de facto renders irrelevant the provision of Art. 44 of the Law on Communications, which stipulates that the CRA can operate according to the budget adopted by the CRA Council until the final budget is approved by Bosnia and Herzegovina's Council of Ministers.

Overall, the Law on Communications provides a solid formal basis for ensuring a good performance and relatively high level of independence of the CRA. Nevertheless, subsequent legal interventions have significantly reduced both its independence from the government and its capacity to perform its statutory functions. In the case of the legal framework relevant to the CRA, one can identify what Zielonka and Mancini (2011: 6) call 'floating laws and procedures': legal documents are adopted and amended frequently and in haste, with little or no public debate, which results in contradictory and conflicting laws. The consequence is 'legal uncertainty and regulatory chaos' that ultimately demotes formal rules and promotes informality (Zielonka and Mancini 2011: 6).

State politicization, informality and the CRA

For an adequate implementation of legal norms, a country should have a specific type of political culture that favours formal rules over informality – what Max Weber calls *rational legal authority*, understood 'as a form of rule based on adherence to formal and universalistic rules of procedure' (Hallin and Mancini 2004: 55). Where rational legal authority is strongly developed, broadcasting regulatory agencies are 'likely to be relatively autonomous from control by government, parties, and particular politicians, and to be governed by clear rules and procedures' (Hallin and Mancini 2004: 56).

In contrast to rational legal authority stands what Zielonka and Mancini (2011: 2) call the *politicization of the state*, which is recognized as a 'distinctive, common feature across the whole of Central and Eastern Europe' (Zielonka and Mancini 2011: 2). It is a context in which political parties and various vested interests attempt to 'conquer' state institutions in order to extract resources from them. In such cases, the:

> administration and law are shaped by the *ad hoc* needs of political agents rather than by *a priori* policy objectives which aim at providing public goods. [...] Actors are not treated as equal, norms do not have universal application and there is only a selective accountability in such a politicised state. [...] Informal networks and rules are extremely important in such a politicised state and they undermine formal institutions and the rule of law. State structures appear weak, volatile and prone to capture by political competitors.
>
> (Zielonka and Mancini 2011: 3)

The case of Bosnia and Herzegovina demonstrates a high level of politicization of the state and an absence of strong rational legal authority. This can be seen in the subsequent analysis of the actual implementation of laws and rules related to the functioning and independence of the CRA.

Notwithstanding its formal limitations, the CRA is regarded as highly successful in performing its statutory roles and functions. It introduced significant changes to the broadcasting sector in the country. A major achievement was in the area of policy making and regulation, where the agency introduced a set of rules and regulations relevant for the broadcasting and telecommunications sectors. The most substantial recent accomplishment in this area was a comprehensive update of the regulatory framework for audiovisual media in Bosnia and Herzegovina in late 2011. By adopting the set of new rules and codes, the Council of the CRA largely harmonized the country's regulatory framework with the European Union Audiovisual Media Service Directive.

A crucial achievement of the CRA was the introduction of licensing procedures for broadcasters, and the actual process of issuing long-term licenses. The first round of issuing long-term licences in 2002 reduced the number of licensed broadcasters by half without any major incidents. The broadcasting industry was quick to comply with the new standards set by the CRA (CRA 2003), and order was introduced in this previously rather chaotic sector.

Overall, the CRA sees a high level of compliance with the rules, decisions and sanctions it issues to broadcasters. According to CRA's own analysis of violations of rules and regulations, it issued a total of 640 sanctions in the 1998–2011 period, with a more or less continuous increase of sanctions since 2003 (CRA 2012b: 18). Ten sanctions involved revocations of broadcasting licences.

Nevertheless, although the agency is capable of introducing and enforcing rules and regulations, it is also facing significant problems and obstacles that threaten its independence and functionality. These pressures and problems primarily come from the state and entity governments, legislative bodies and occasionally broadcasters and other media that are closely affiliated with political parties and the government, such as public service broadcasters.

First, the appointment of the Director General and the members of the CRA Council are seen as politicized, while the legally prescribed procedures for nomination and appointments are largely ignored by the government and the parliament of Bosnia and Herzegovina. For example, when the term of the Director General ended in 2007, the CRA Council followed the procedure prescribed by the Law on Communications and submitted its nomination to the government. However, the Council of Ministers failed to approve the nomination, as the vote on the matter resulted in a tie, with four votes against and four in support of the nomination (Halilović 2008). Instead, the Council of Ministers ordered the CRA to publish a new public invitation for the position. The CRA refused to abide by this order, since the law does not allow for such an option; it only allows the Council of Ministers to reject the suggested candidate if legal procedures were not respected. The CRA also has no legal obligation to provide the Council of Ministers with a list of candidates, and can suggest only one candidate. Finally, Art. 36 of the Law on Communications stipulates that the Council of Ministers is not allowed to 'interfere in the decision-making of the Agency in individual cases'.

In response to these developments, the president of the CRA Council sent a protest letter to the Council of Ministers in October 2007 stating that such actions undermine the CRA Council and the legal procedures. The president also wrote that 'it is apparent from the comments accompanying the conclusion that the Council of Ministers was not in possession of the relevant facts and did not discuss them, and that it is rather obvious that a political action was in question, absolutely going against the Law on Communications and the role of the Agency' (Halilović 2008). As a consequence, the CRA has been without a formally appointed Director General since 2007, and the incumbent Director General has been performing his function in a technical mandate for over four years (Halilović 2008; Hans Bredow Institute for Media Research, et al. 2011; European Commission 2009).

These developments have had a negative impact on the administrative and policy-making capacity of the agency:

> Since the start of the debate on the procedure for appointing the CRA's director general, and in the absence of a sector policy, the adoption of several decisions on broadcasting and telecommunications prepared by the CRA has been delayed by the executive. [...] The overall situation at the CRA also hampers its administrative capacity.
>
> (European Commission 2009: 52)

The controversy surrounding the election of the new Director General of the CRA was very much present in the media discourse as well. Accusations and criticism of the work of the CRA were often ethnically charged, with newspapers from Republika Srpska accusing the regulatory agency of working in favour of the largest Bosniak political party, SDA (*Stranka Demokratske Akcije* – Party of Democratic Action). The leaders of key political parties started publicly speculating that the next Director General of the CRA should be ethnically Croat (Halilović 2008).

In addition, when the term in office of the CRA Council members expired in 2009, the Council followed the procedure as set out by the Law on Communications and submitted a list of candidates to the Council of Ministers. The Council of Ministers submitted a slate of seven candidates it had selected from the list to the Parliament of Bosnia and Herzegovina, but the parliament refused to appoint the candidates, without giving any specific explanation. The Council of Ministers did not submit a new, revised list to the parliament, so no appointments were made, and the CRA Council continued to operate in a technical mandate (Hans Bredow Institute for Media Research, et al. 2011: 177–178; European Commission 2011: 16).

After the Parliament of Bosnia and Herzegovina failed to appoint new members to the CRA Council, the Council's compensation payments were suspended in 2009, although it continued to operate in a technical mandate. They were later on resumed, but the compensation amount was cut by half (European Commission 2010: 51).

Finally, after the 2010 general elections, during the negotiations about the distribution of seats in the new Council of Ministers and other public institutions, the six political parties which had received the most votes publicly discussed how the positions of directors of formally independent agencies, including the CRA, should be distributed on party- and ethnically-based principles, in spite of the fact that the appointment procedure for the position of the CRA's Director General is defined by the Law on Communications and precludes political influence and ethnic criteria (for more details, see Karabegović 2012).

The appointment of the members of the Management Board of the state-level public broadcaster (BHRT) provides another example of how the CRA's authority has been undermined. With the aim of reducing political influence on the appointment of the members of the Management Board, Art. 26 of the Law on Public Broadcasting Service of Bosnia and Herzegovina (Parliamentary Assembly of Bosnia and Herzegovina 2005) stipulates that the CRA should submit nominations for the board's potential members to the Parliament of Bosnia and Herzegovina, which is then required to appoint the members from among the proposed list of candidates. However, the House of Peoples, the second chamber of the Parliament of Bosnia and Herzegovina, whose task it is to protect the vital national interest of the three dominant ethnic groups, blocked the appointment of candidates from the list submitted by the CRA. The Management Board includes one member for each of the three major ethnic groups, and the CRA submits a separate list of candidates for each post. The list of candidates for the member from the Serb ethnic group was submitted to the Parliament of Bosnia and Herzegovina in 2009, and the list of candidates for the member from the Croat ethnic group was submitted in 2010. However, no candidate from either of the lists was accepted, and the parliament asked the CRA to repeat the procedure. The CRA rejected this request, arguing that there is no legal basis for the repetition of the procedure. This stand-off between the CRA and parliament has continued since then (CRA 2011a: 17). Hence, although the CRA followed the legal procedure, this issue remained unresolved even in 2012. This is a strong example of how the agency's authority has been undermined by key state institutions; in this particular case it appears that the proposed candidates were not appointed because they were not seen as politically acceptable by the ethnic parties that have veto powers in the House of Peoples of the Parliament of Bosnia and Herzegovina (Gorinjac 2011).

Another notable example of the direct political pressure being exerted on the CRA took place in 2006, when the State Investigation and Protection Agency (SIPA), which is primarily concerned with organized crime issues, spent several weeks at the premises of the CRA investigating alleged criminal activities. Although the investigation yielded no results, the CRA never received an official notice that the proceedings were closed (Halilović 2008).

Since its establishment, the CRA has faced continuous financial pressures from the Council of Ministers of Bosnia and Herzegovina. For example, in December 2002, the High Representative intervened, imposing the 'Decision Amending the Structure of Expenditures of the Communications Regulatory Agency for 2002' after the agency's budget for 2002 was decreased by 25 per cent compared to 2001. As a result, the agency was left without the funds needed to function effectively (Open Society Institute 2005: 280–281). The problem with the decrease of the CRA's budget was later resolved through Art. 9(4) of the Law on Financing of State Institutions of Bosnia and Herzegovina, which stipulates that the Council of Ministers cannot reduce the proposed budget by more than 20 per cent. Another incident occurred in 2005 when the Council of Ministers of Bosnia and Herzegovina decided to redirect 1.1 million BAM (€550,000) from the CRA bank account for the purpose of funding satellite channels of the public broadcasters. In a statement given to a daily paper, the Director General of the CRA accused the Council of Ministers of Bosnia and Herzegovina of illegal actions directed against the agency (Lazović 2005). Finally, although the CRA seems to be adequately funded, it is arguably understaffed. There are currently eighteen employees for the broadcasting sector, with a total of 32 planned for (Hans Bredow Institute for Media Research, et al. 2011: 178).

In keeping with the policy of obstruction and political pressures described above, annual reports of the CRA have not been acknowledged or even included in the agenda of the Council of Ministers of Bosnia and Herzegovina since 2007 (Hans Bredow Institute for Media Research, et al. 2011: 178; 299).

In addition, the agency is undergoing pressure from the broadcasting and telecommunications industry. For example, in 2010, the CRA issued a penalty to the public broadcaster Radio-Television of Republika Srpska (RTRS) because it started using a frequency to test its digital TV programme without previously obtaining a licence, and failed to comply with the CRA's request to stop this illegal broadcasting (CRA 2010c). The RTRS responded by publicly attacking the agency, questioning its transparency and fairness, and undermining the credibility of the CRA's Director General (CRA 2010d). Eventually, the CRA had to resort to enforcement proceedings before the Court of Bosnia and Herzegovina to collect the penalty from the RTRS (CRA 2012b: 23).

Evidently, there are strong and continuous pressures on the CRA in general and on its decision-making bodies in particular, aimed at limiting the agency's autonomy. The above examples point to the rather low level of rational legal authority and high level of state politicization, coupled with a proportionally high level of informality. As a consequence, the rules and laws often are not applied and even the legislative bodies are comfortable in ignoring the laws they themselves enacted, the case in point being the systematic refusal of the parliament and the Council of Ministers of Bosnia and Herzegovina to interact with the CRA in accordance with rules and procedures prescribed by the relevant laws.

It seems that when the decisions of the CRA clash with political preferences and government mechanisms of control over broadcasting, they are regularly blocked or simply ignored. Nevertheless, when the CRA focuses on more technical issues, such as the introduction and enforcement of rules and regulations, the obstacles and pressures are much less obvious.

In short, although a solid legal basis is crucial for the proper functioning of an independent regulatory body, it cannot explain de facto independence by itself. This is obvious in the case of the CRA, which has experienced a reduction in the formal protection of its independence, combined with continuous political pressures and obstacles to its functioning, and yet still tries to resist such pressures and maintain a high level of independence. The politicization of the state, coupled with a high level of informality, disrespect and selective application of rules and procedures, make the legal framework less relevant.

Power-sharing and consensus politics

Bosnia and Herzegovina is an ethnically and territorially divided country, with complex power-sharing arrangements that have been introduced to mitigate conflicts and keep the country together. It is established as a highly decentralized democratic state consisting of two entities, the Serb-dominated Republika Srpska and the Bosniak-Croat Federation of Bosnia and Herzegovina (hereafter: the Federation), as well as the District of Brčko, a separate self-government unit independent of the two entities' territories, placed under the sovereignty of the state. Moreover, the Federation consists of ten cantons, four of which have a Bosniak majority, four a Croat majority and two which are ethnically mixed. Each of the ten cantons has a constitution and a legislature of directly elected representatives, in charge of enacting cantonal legislation.

As a result, state-level institutions have weak competences,[2] whereas the entities are given a high degree of autonomy and powers. Major ethnic groups (Croats, Serbs and Bosniaks) and territorial units (Federation of Bosnia and Herzegovina and Republika Srpska) have been granted extensive veto powers for the protection of their vital national interests at various levels of government, to prevent the domination of a majority ethnic group in a particular administrative unit and to enforce consensual decision making. An ethnic rotation principle is introduced throughout the government (Constitution of Bosnia and Herzegovina, Art. IX.3). For example, Bosnia and Herzegovina has a three-member rotating Presidency that consists of a Bosniak and a Croat directly elected from the Federation territory, and a Serb elected from the Republika Srpska territory. As a consequence, the country has a rather limited capacity for efficient decision making, as the complex power-sharing principles with ethnic and territorial veto rights and ethnically based allocations of major positions in public office dominate governance.

Inevitably, the type of government in the political system of a country influences how regulatory authority is delegated to an IRA. Hallin and Mancini (2004: 50–53) build on the distinction Lijphart made regarding whether the political system is based on majoritarian or consensus politics. This is of special importance if one focuses on highly polarized political systems with a strong presence of power-sharing mechanisms. Such cases are often characterized by multi-party systems, coalition governments, a lack of clear distinction between government and opposition, and high levels of political parallelism in the media system. In such a system, direct control over broadcasting by the government in power is rather difficult since it creates political turmoil and damages the credibility of media institutions (Hallin and Mancini 2004: 52).

In addition, the theory of veto points (Tsebelis 2002; Hammond 2003; Hans Bredow Institute for Media Research, et al. 2011: 18) suggests that the number of veto players, which is by definition larger in power-sharing than in majoritarian systems, will affect the stability of policy arrangements. According to Gilardi, 'the number of veto points can be considered an additional safeguard for making credible policy commitments, which renders the benefits of delegation to independent regulators greater' (Hans Bredow Institute for Media Research, et al. 2011: 19). However, Voltmer emphasizes that a specific pattern 'arises when the political contest is fragmented into multiple small groups, none of which is able to control the scene over a substantial period of time. Where these groups are unable to reach compromise and form coalitions, this type of fragmented pluralism can result in a permanent stalemate and the inability of governments to make binding decisions' (Voltmer 2012: 229–230).

Hence a complex consociational power-sharing model, with deep ethnic cleavages and a highly decentralized administrative structure which reflects the power-sharing arrangements with a large number of veto points, can have two rather contradictory effects when it comes to the issue of the sustainability of the CRA's independence.

On the one hand, the political elite is frequently pushing for the introduction of ethnic and territorial criteria when it comes to the appointment of the Director General and the Council of the CRA. This has proven a major obstacle for the formal appointment of the Director General and the members of the CRA Council. In a similar fashion, the candidates that were nominated by the CRA for the board of the state-level public service broadcaster BHRT were rejected by the Parliament of Bosnia and Herzegovina primarily because of ethnic criteria used by parliament to assess the nominees. The principle of ethnic proportional representation that is embedded in the power-sharing arrangements governing Bosnia and Herzegovina, and often goes hand-in-hand with the country's strong culture of political parallelism, is used as a tool to justify the political pressure on the CRA and to undermine the decision-making autonomy of the agency.

Furthermore, due to the complex power-sharing arrangements as well as the cumbersome process of negotiation involved in the formation of the state government (which took more than a year after the last general elections in 2010), the country is late year after year in adopting the state budget (European Commission 2011). This has a negative effect on all state institutions and independent agencies, including the CRA, as their funding under such circumstances often depends on a temporary state budget, with ever stricter rules and conditions in place for accessing such funds. Additionally, large coalitions and power-sharing arrangements with extensive veto rights have proven, in the case of Bosnia and Herzegovina, to have a very negative effect on the efficiency of policy-making at the state level. As a consequence, the government often fails to make decisions (or makes them only with significant delays) that are necessary for the implementation of activities in various fields, including the sector of broadcasting and telecommunications (European Commission 2011: 50–51).

It cannot be ruled out that the different forms of pressure that are exerted on the CRA and similar agencies are in fact often used as leverage in broader negotiations among ruling political parties, and therefore aren't necessarily directly linked to the issue of independence of the regulatory agency. The effect of all this on the CRA, however, is increasing financial uncertainty and a limited capacity to perform its functions.

On the other hand, the large number of veto players and the broad coalition governments could potentially also provide some safeguards for the CRA's independence. The need for technical expertise and credible policy commitments is even more pronounced in such a volatile, polarized and inefficient political system. The acceptance of this need is illustrated by how none of the parties involved is actually questioning the need for the CRA to exist.

Furthermore, the existence of a relatively independent regulatory agency that is not directly controlled by any of the dominant ethnic groups or numerous parties is actually in the interest of most of those parties and groups, since each of them knows that it alone could not gain full control over the agency, and they do not want any other party or group to be able to do so either. This recognition increases the benefit of delegation to an independent regulatory agency for all involved parties and stakeholders (Hans Bredow Institute for Media Research, et al. 2011: 19).

The very fact that power-sharing in Bosnia and Herzegovina includes numerous veto points provides an important safeguard too, since it prevents any individual player from being able to adopt and implement any radical policy that could significantly endanger the independence of the CRA. For example, no major changes to the Law on Communications have been made so far, whereas other laws that have been introduced and that have, to a certain degree, limited the CRA's formal level of independence such as The Law on Civil Service in the Institutions of Bosnia and Herzegovina, the Law on Ministries and Other Bodies of Administration in Bosnia and Herzegovina and the Law on Financing of Institutions of Bosnia and Herzegovina (Parliamentary Assembly of Bosnia and Herzegovina 2004) have not gravely undermined the agency's overall functionality or diminished its autonomy so far.

In addition, although the CRA has been in direct conflict with the Council of Ministers and the Parliament of Bosnia and Herzegovina for over four years, these state bodies did not have the power or will to significantly alter the status of the agency to eliminate its autonomy. The political landscape is not homogenous, and there is a wide plurality of political interests, some of which do support the CRA. For example, the rejection of the CRA Council's candidate for the position of Director General by the Council of Ministers of Bosnia and Herzegovina was not due to an anonymously hostile vote, but an evenly split one (Halilovic 2008).

International intervention and the CRA

Media restructuring efforts that are undertaken after the end of wars and conflicts, such as the Allied Occupation Forces' efforts to influence the shape of the new media systems in Germany and Japan after the Second World War and, more recently, international efforts in Bosnia and Herzegovina after 1995 and in Kosovo after 1999, generally aim to prevent national monopolies over the sources of information and to limit the effects of political and ethnic propaganda in conflict-torn states. The results of those interventions have been mixed at best (Price and Thompson 2002; Rhodes 2007). For example, in the case of the Western Balkans, research to date suggests that media systems developed unevenly across their subsystems, with more success in some areas and less in others (Kumar 2006: 662). International-led reform efforts had little impact on national broadcast media that remain under strong political influence. Often, independent media and their supporting institutions remain financially donor-dependent, while legal and regulatory reforms are stalled (Kumar 2006: 662; CIMA 2008: 33; Rhodes 2007: 29).

The literature focused on institutional development through foreign aid and intervention suggests that, so far, foreign aid has had limited measurable success in improving institutions in recipient countries. Studies demonstrate that inherent beliefs and institutions of a society create strong incentives for powerful individuals and organizations to prefer the status quo and preserve the existing institutional arrangements. Lessons from development assistance efforts show that international aid providers, through their funds and consultants, cannot easily overcome such a heritage, if at all (Shirley 2005: 12–14). Funding agencies and intermediary implementation agencies face legacies of undemocratic structures, politicians and traditions, which render the creation of enabling laws and policies difficult or impossible (Price 2002: 57).

According to development aid literature, in the instances where enduring institutional changes occurred, local elites in power normally welcomed such foreign ideas. However, in cases where powerful local support is absent, chances for achieving enduring improvements in the institutions by means of external intervention are rather small (Shirley 2003: 32–33). Studies also suggest that reforming institutions through conditionality – i.e. by means of a list of specific changes the country is required to enact before funds or other benefits are released – does not correspond with the experience of institutional change (Shirley 2003: 33). When the required institutional changes are not an integral part of the existing belief systems and norms, and there is a lack of political support, the intervention will generally fail to produce sustainable change (Shirley 2003: 34). As a consequence, the recipient country is likely to suffer from the 'transplant effect' – the mismatch between pre-existing conditions and transplanted solutions, which weakens the effectiveness of the imported institutional arrangements (Berkowitz, et al. 2003: 171).

All these lessons are highly relevant for understanding the post-war development of Bosnia and Herzegovina, which has heavily depended on international presence and support. According to a World Bank report, 48 donor countries and 14 international organizations pledged almost $5 billion and disbursed $3.7 billion during the 1996–1999 period for post-war reconstruction and development programmes in the country (The World Bank 2004: 2). In 1995, the Dayton Peace Accords (Annex 10, Art. V.) established the Office of the High Representative (OHR), which was to monitor, facilitate and coordinate activities of the civilian aspects of the implementation of the peace agreement (DPA, Annex 10, Art. I.2; II.1), while a 60,000 strong international military Implementation Force (IFOR) was initially tasked with enforcing the implementation of the military aspects of the peace accords. The High Representative was and still is nominated by the Steering Board of the Peace Implementation Council (PIC),[3] and endorsed by the United Nations Security Council. Following the continuous obstruction of the implementation of the DPA by local political elites, the mandate of the High Representative was strengthened at the PIC conference in December 1997 in Bonn, Germany, when he was given the powers to remove from office public officials who obstruct the DPA, as well as to impose laws in cases where Bosnia and Herzegovina's legislatures fail to do so, and as the High Representative sees fit.

As the political gridlock in the country continued to block decision-making processes, it became inevitable for the OHR and other international actors to intervene in order to move the country towards democratization and a stable peace. The OHR used its new powers extensively in the subsequent years. For example, a decision by the High Representative established the Court of Bosnia and Herzegovina at the state level on 9 May 2002, and the Office of the Prosecutor of Bosnia and Herzegovina on 7 May 2002 (Dizdarević, et al. 2006: 24). The OHR used its powers to amend the constitutions of the two entities and to remove elected politicians from entity and state legislatures, and even from the state Presidency.[4] International development agencies and donors funded numerous projects, aimed at post-war reconstruction, reconciliation and institution-building. Moreover, during the run-up to the first post-war election in late 1996, it became clear that the media in Bosnia and Herzegovina remained under strong political influence, exhibiting an almost total disregard for basic standards of professional journalism and impartiality. This had a rather negative impact on the implementation of the civilian aspects of the peace agreement, undermining the chance for free and fair elections, as opposition parties were prevented from accessing mainstream media. Moreover, some media outlets continued to incite distrust in and hatred against international peace-implementation organizations, political opponents and 'other' ethnic groups (Media Experts Commission 1998; Kurspahić 2003; Thompson and De Luce 2002).

It is against this backdrop that the international community first attempted to introduce some basic regulatory principles and mechanisms in the media landscape of the country. In early 1996, the OSCE, which had the mandate to organize elections, established the Media Experts Commission (MEC), tasked with ensuring the compliance of the media with electoral rules and regulations issued by the Provisional Electoral Commission (Media Experts Commission 1998: 10). Nevertheless, the media and political parties largely ignored the work of the Media Experts Commission in the 1996 election campaign (Open Society Institute 2005: 285). It was only after the OHR was given extensive powers at the Bonn and Sintra conferences[5] of the PIC in 1997 that some order started to be introduced in the media system, so elections in 1998 could be held in a more democratic atmosphere. The mandate of the MEC expired after the elections, on 31 October 1998 (Media Experts Commission 1998: 19). Subsequently, and especially in the period of 1998–2002, a great extent of international intervention focused on the media, involving, in addition to the OHR, a wide range of institutions, donors and development agencies that included the European Commission, Open Society Foundation, OSCE, USAID, the World Bank, and many others. According to Rhodes, over €87 million was invested in media development projects in Bosnia and Herzegovina between 1996 and 2006 (Rhodes 2007: 15).

As a next step, the OHR established the Independent Media Commission (IMC) in June 1998 (OHR 1998), which was tasked with the management of frequency spectrum allocation, issuing broadcasting licenses, drafting and enforcing codes for broadcasters, and dealing with complaints (Open Society Institute 2005: 286; Hans Bredow Institute for Media Research, et al. 2011: 92). Another OHR decision three years later (OHR 2001) ordered the merger of the IMC and the Telecommunications Regulatory Agency into the Communications Regulatory Agency of Bosnia and Herzegovina (CRA), a new converged regulatory body in charge of both the broadcasting and telecommunications sector (Open Society Institute 2005: 276; Hans Bredow Institute for Media Research, et al. 2011: 176, Thompson and De Luce 2002). The CRA's legal status was established on 21 October 2002 by the High Representative's decision to impose the Law on Communications, since the Council of Ministers of Bosnia and Herzegovina failed to do so after eighteen months of futile attempts (Open Society Institute 2005: 276). With the introduction of the Law on Communications, the formal preconditions were set for the transition of the CRA from an internationally imposed and run institution to a local independent state agency.

Considering the crucial role of international actors, especially the OHR, in establishing the CRA, the Agency has significantly benefited from international scrutiny whenever the government attempted to interfere with its independence. The efforts of international actors ranged from the OHR's outright interference in policy processes to ensure the agency's financing (OHR 2002) to international monitoring and regular warnings and protest letters by international organizations such as the OSCE, Council of Europe, and the European Commission directed at the Council of Ministers of Bosnia and Herzegovina. Additionally, the issue of CRA's independence has taken a prominent place in the regular annual European Commission progress reports on Bosnia and Herzegovina (European Commission 2009; 2010; 2011).

The conflict between the CRA and the Council of Ministers of Bosnia and Herzegovina regarding the appointment of the Director General of the agency has provoked harsh reactions from the OSCE, European Union (EU) and Council of Europe, and the

US Embassy in Sarajevo. The European Union leveraged a conditionality mechanism to ensure that the Council of Ministers of Bosnia and Herzegovina would comply with requirements concerning the CRA, making it a precondition for the country's progress in the process of signing the Stabilisation and Association Agreement (Halilović 2008). The reactions from the OHR were much milder, however, which was perhaps linked to the transition from OHR-driven policy-making to a more significant role of the European Union in the country's transition and reforms.

As Bosnia and Herzegovina negotiates its way towards EU accession, the use of Bonn powers by the OHR has significantly decreased, from its peak of 158 decisions in 2004 to only 10 decisions in 2011 (OHR 2012). After the signing of the Stabilization and Association Agreement (SAA) with the European Union in 2008, Bosnia and Herzegovina embarked on additional structural and institutional reforms under the watchful eye of the EU. Although there have been announcements about the OHR's closing and full transition to an Office of the EU Special Representative (EUSR) for six years (and the High Representative held both positions simultaneously between 2002–2011), the PIC extended OHR's mandate indefinitely. This decision made it clear that the PIC still considers it necessary for the OHR to monitor the civilian aspects of the DPA (and to use the Bonn powers). Whereas analysts remain divided on the question of whether Bosnia and Herzegovina still needs the OHR's strong presence and the use of Bonn powers in light of continuous political crises and slow reform, or whether the country should instead be guided by the EU's soft power approach, it is evident that a continuation of the extensive intervention that took place in the late 1990s and early 2000s is not a likely scenario. A separate EU Special Representative (EUSR), simultaneously the Head of the Delegation of the European Union to Bosnia and Herzegovina, was appointed in 2011. The EUSR is in charge of monitoring the accession progress of Bosnia and Herzegovina towards the European Union.

Hence, although the OHR's role in scrutinizing the government has decreased, the European Union is taking on a much more prominent role, and the presence of other international actors continues. The experience from other post-communist countries shows that during the EU accession process, compliance with EC requirements and standards is very high, but after EU accession is complete, political actors tend to interfere with the independence of IRAs again (Hans Bredow Institute for Media Research, et al. 2011: 90). However, Bosnia and Herzegovina still has a long way to go before it potentially becomes a member of the European Union, given that it still hasn't even fulfilled the criteria for submitting a formal application for membership.

One can say that the intensity and nature of international scrutiny has changed, but that the presence of relevant international actors is still significant and will remain relevant for some time. This is clearly an important factor to be taken into consideration when trying to understand the resilience of the CRA in the face of mounting pressures on its independence from the government. Moreover, by the very nature of the process of Europeanization, Bosnia and Herzegovina will inevitably remain under the influence of international standards.

Nevertheless, according to lessons from literature on development discussed at the beginning of this section, the chance that an independent agency that has emerged as a result of international intervention is able to maintain its independent status depends on the extent to which the introduced changes correspond with the context as a whole. Newly created or transformed institutions that do not build upon, and relate to, other relevant institutions and subsystems could have a difficult time sustaining themselves after external support ends. Such institutions might remain anomalous with respect to the institutional context of the society, which could limit the chances for their long-term sustainability and effectiveness (Berkowitz, et al. 2003).

Clearly, the CRA falls into the category of institutions that run the risk of suffering from the consequences of the 'transplant effect', considering the intensity, extent and duration of international assistance. The agency owes its existence, independence and statutory powers to the decisive role played by the OHR and international assistance efforts. The exemplary performance of the CRA, its respect for laws and procedures, and the high level of independence from political parties and government are in sharp contrast to the high level of politicization of the state, a culture of informality, and overall disregard for the rule of law. Hence, the still strong presence of the international community and the prospects of joining the European Union are certainly a plausible explanation for why the CRA is still not fully subordinated to local political interests in such a hostile context. Consequently, there is a significant danger that the CRA's independence will be eroded proportional to the decrease of international involvement and scrutiny.

Nevertheless, one has to take into account the time factor: The CRA now exists for over ten years, and has become an integral part of the broadcasting and telecommunication sector in the country. The role it performs is vital for the normal functioning of these financially and politically important sectors, which certainly gives it some leverage when international support eventually ends. In other words, the process of approximation of the agency to the context is taking place. Today, the CRA is integrated into the formal legal and institutional framework of the country, which is significant when considering the prospects of sustaining its formal and de facto independence.

Culture of independence and the CRA

Setting aside the question of formal legal frameworks, de facto autonomous regulatory agencies are likely to be found 'in longstanding democracies with relatively low levels of corruption, where the transparency of public bodies in general is ensured and where independent media and a vibrant civil society keep the regulatory authority's work under close scrutiny' (Council of Europe 2008b). In other words, institutional development in general may significantly be conditioned by cultural factors, such as political culture, civil society development, the history of democratization, and other values, beliefs, and norms. In their seminal work tracing the cultural roots of different outcomes of institutional development in the South and the North of Italy, Putnam, et al. (1993) have demonstrated how significant the effect of different cultural norms can be on the institutional development and functioning of institutions, even under the same formal legal framework.

According to Machet (2007: 4), 'a culture of independence and transparency is a key to the well-functioning system' and a strong culture of independence can compensate for a general lack of rules (see also Chapter 1 in this book by Schulz). The importance of context and culture for the development of IRAs is strongly emphasized in the 2008 Declaration on the independence and functions of regulatory authorities for the broadcasting sector (Council of Europe 2008a), adopted by the Committee of Ministers of the Council of Europe on 26 March 2008. The Declaration signposts that:

> a 'culture of independence', where members of regulatory authorities in the broadcasting sector affirm and exercise their independence and all members of society, public authorities and other relevant players including the media, respect the independence of the regulatory authorities, is essential to independent broadcasting regulation.
>
> (Council of Europe 2008a)

Such a culture of independence should therefore be fostered by all member states, by creating an environment of transparency, accountability, clear separation of powers and due respect for the legal framework, which is necessary for the independent regulatory authorities to function properly. Civil society and the media are expected to support the development of the 'culture of independence' by performing their watchdog functions and warning about any infringements on regulators' independence, while broadcasting regulatory authorities should 'contribute to the entrenchment of a "culture of independence" and, in this context, develop and respect guidelines that guarantee their own independence and that of their members' (Council of Europe 2008a).

Hence the concept of a culture of independence has an external and internal dimension – the external dimension relating to the role of the government, civil society and media, while the internal dimension concerns the role of the regulatory agency itself in promoting a culture of independence.

The external dimension largely corresponds with the key characteristics of the three models outlined by Hallin and Mancini (2004). The capacity of governments, civil society and the media to contribute to the development of a culture of independence will depend on the level of political parallelism, the professionalization of the media, the role of the state in the media system, as well as the democratic tradition and political history of a country.

Accordingly, all evidence points to the fact that Bosnia and Herzegovina has a generally low level of external culture of independence, which can be traced back to a lack of democratic tradition and a weak civil society. The failure of the country's first experience with democracy from late 1990 until early 1992, the subsequent devastating war, and the post-war failure of local political elites to steer the country towards a more stable democracy without pressure from the OHR and other international actors, all point to a persistent lack of democratic capacity and democratic culture among the power elites in Bosnia and Herzegovina. Additionally, a high level of politicization of the state, as demonstrated in previous sections, strongly supports this finding.

Overall, the country is characterized by a weak civil society and an undeveloped civic culture. Although the freedom of assembly and association is granted by the Constitution of Bosnia and Herzegovina, 'cases of violence and threats against human rights advocates and civil society organizations have been reported, mostly involving activists investigating suspected corruption' (European Commission 2010: 17). According to a 2009 UNDP report, less than 20 per cent of adults in Bosnia and Herzegovina are members of a civil society association, a club or a similar type of organization (in comparison with, for example, 80 percent in Norway and 90 percent in Sweden). Such a low association membership is indicative of limited civic participation and general suspicion towards civic and political engagement (UNDP 2009: 59–65). Moreover, there seems to be a general dependence of civil society organizations on international funding, and a rather limited capacity of civil society to participate in policy formulation and to cooperate with the government (Maglajlić and Hodžić 2006; Kotlo and Hodžić 2006).

In addition, the level of professionalism in the media sector is rather low. Self-regulatory mechanisms, such as Press Councils and Press Codes, fail to take a foothold in the local journalism community. There is a general lack of high-quality journalism and investigative reporting; pressures on journalists have been mounting in recent years while journalistic solidarity has been rather low (IREX 2010; 2011; Rhodes 2007: 36). Media and journalists faced increased pressures during the electoral campaign in 2010, and the coverage of elections to a significant level reflected the needs of the more powerful political parties (IREX 2011: 15).

The internal dimension of a culture of independence relies on key individuals within an IRA, especially on their attitudes towards the concept of independence and legal and other safeguards for an IRA's independence. This means that IRAs and their key officials need to adhere to the rule of law, live up to the standards they themselves have set for the broadcasting sector, and function according to the principles of effectiveness, transparency and accountability. Furthermore, it implies an active role on the part of key personnel within the IRA when it comes to resisting external pressures. In other words, the internal dimension emphasizes the important role regulatory agencies themselves have when it comes to affirming their independence. The IRAs have an important role to play in helping the culture of independence take a foothold in a society, which means that IRAs can also be important agents of change towards more open, professional and independent systems in contexts with a weak external culture of independence.

A number of facts point to the possibility that the CRA has managed to develop a relatively strong internal culture of independence, as it stands its ground amid growing political pressures over the past few years:

- The way the CRA operates in practice – as regards its decision making, enforcement of decisions, accountability and transparency – is indicative of a high level of internal culture of independence. The agency's transparency and the procedural legitimacy it enforces are indicators of a strong commitment to the values and principles of accountability in its activities. The agency publishes all its decisions and its annual reports on its website, in both the local and English language. The website of the agency provides easy access to all relevant documents and information, and access to additional information and documents may be requested in line with the Freedom of Access to Information Act.

- The fact that the CRA Council and Director General are consistent and persistent in fighting external pressures and strictly abiding by the laws demonstrates that the key decision-making bodies and individuals within the agency have internalized the principles of a culture of independence.
- Apart from publishing draft rules, the CRA regularly organizes regional consultation meetings with licensees, and when needed, consultations with other relevant institutions and industry representatives.

The CRA's ability to develop a relatively strong internal culture of independence can probably be linked to other important factors that are crucial for its operations: the adequacy of the legal framework, the expertise and profile of its staff, and the general respect it enjoys in the media and communications industry, to name only a few. Nevertheless, special attention should be dedicated to the role of international support in the development of the CRA's internal culture of independence. Since the CRA originated as an international assistance project and was then slowly transformed into a fully locally run agency under the watchful eye of the OHR and the international community, one can assume that this specific institutional history and the strong influence of international organizational procedures and rules have had a decisive effect on the creation of the strong internal culture of independence.

However, the agency's internal culture of independence contradicts a rather weak external culture of independence in the society at large. The CRA cannot count on significant support for its independence among a large number of civil society organizations or the media, let alone politicians and political parties. Consequently, the external support for its independence is reduced to a handful of civil society organizations, a few media outlets, and again, the international community.

Conclusion

One of the main characteristics of the context in which the CRA in Bosnia and Herzegovina operates is a high level of politicization of the state, coupled with an underdeveloped rational legal authority, undermined formal institutions, and weak state structures that are prone to capture by political interests. The result is a widespread culture of informality, clientelism and selective application of rules and norms. As a consequence, both formal and the de facto independence of the agency are significantly undermined. The CRA faces increasing financial uncertainty, while its capacity to perform its primary function is notably reduced. This is the single most serious threat to the sustainability of the current level of CRA's independence and to the proper exercise of its statutory functions.

Current power-sharing arrangements, with their numerous veto points and the politics of consensus, clearly play an important role in shaping the prospects for a sustainable independence and functioning of the CRA. The power-sharing system in Bosnia and Herzegovina is notorious for its inefficiency in decision making, which may have a detrimental effect on the CRA's capacity to function normally amid political gridlock. However, power-sharing can provide safeguards for the CRA's independence by preventing any single political party or coalition of parties to easily take control of the agency.

Although the CRA managed to develop a relatively strong internal culture of independence, it appears that the agency cannot count on substantial support for its independence from civil society organizations, the media, or politicians. In light of the negative consequences of state politicization, the dominant culture of informality, the absence of an enabling environment, and the prolonged political crisis and stalemate in the decision-making process in the country, the importance of the assistance by international actors becomes apparent. The international scrutiny is an important factor in ensuring that the independence and exemplary performance of the CRA is to be safeguarded and sustained. A still strong presence of the international community and the promise of European Union membership are probably the most important reasons why the CRA has managed to preserve its independence for so long.

Further research is needed to better understand the prospects of sustainability of IRAs that have been created through international assistance programmes. Future research should investigate, in a comparative perspective, how specific factors in different post-conflict countries influence the independence of the IRAs from politics. Another possible line of inquiry could offer deeper insights into the complex interaction between power-sharing mechanisms and IRAs, and its consequences for the independence of the agencies. Additional studies could be dedicated to the potential educational and transformative role of IRAs in a transitional, post-conflict context, offering an insight into the potential capacities of these institutions to positively influence their environments.

Notes

1   On 29 February and 1 March 1992, a referendum took place on the independence of Bosnia and Herzegovina from Yugoslavia (Malcolm 1994: 230–231); at that time, Slovenia, Croatia and Macedonia had already become independent states, whereas Serbia, Montenegro and Bosnia and Herzegovina were still part of Yugoslavia. International recognition of the independence of Bosnia and Herzegovina came on 6 April 1992 at the meeting of the Committee of Ministers of the European Community in Brussels (Dizdarević, et al. 2006: 22; Malcolm 1994: 234).

2   The state-level institutions of Bosnia and Herzegovina are responsible for foreign policy; foreign trade policy; customs policy; monetary policy; finances of institutions and international obligations of the country; immigration, refugee and asylum policy and regulation; international and inter-entity criminal law enforcement, including relations

with Interpol; establishment and operation of common and international communications facilities; inter-entity transportation regulation; and air traffic control (see the General Framework Agreement of 1995, Annex 4, Article 3.1).

3   The PIC was established as a result of a Peace Implementation Conference held in London on 8–9 December 1995 for the purpose of mobilizing international support for the DPA. The PIC comprises 55 countries and international agencies that give support to the peace process in different ways, such as financially, or by providing troops or directly running country operations; a fluctuating number of observers is also involved. See OHR, *The Peace Implementation Council and its Steering Board*, http://www.ohr.int/ohr-info/gen-info/#6 (accessed 31 May 2012).

4   All OHR decisions are available at: http://www.ohr.int/decisions/archive.asp. Accessed 13 February 2012.

5   At a ministerial meeting of the PIC Steering Board in Sintra, Portugal, in May 1997, the High Representative was given 'the right to curtail or suspend any media network or program whose output is in persistent and blatant contravention of either the spirit or letter of the Peace Agreement' (OHR 1997).

References

Berkowitz, D., Pistor, K. and Richard, J.-F. (2003), 'The Transplant Effect', *The American Journal of Comparative Law*, 51, pp. 163–87.

CIMA – Center for International Media Assistance (2008), *Empowering Independent Media, U.S. Efforts to Foster Free and Independent News around the World. Inaugural Report*, Washington, D.C.: National Endowment for Democracy.

Council of Europe (2000), *Recommendation No. R (2000) 23 of the Committee of Ministers to Member States on the Independence and Functions of Regulatory Authorities for the Broadcasting Sector*, http://www.coe.int/t/dghl/standardsetting/media/doc/cm/rec%282000%29023&expmem_EN.asp. Accessed 19 February 2013.

Council of Europe (2008a), *Declaration of the Committee of Ministers of 26 March 2008 on the Independence and Functions of Regulatory Authorities for the Broadcasting Sector*.

Council of Europe (2008b), *Appendix to the Declaration of the Committee of Ministers of 26 March 2008 on the independence and functions of regulatory authorities for the broadcasting sector*.

CRA (2003), *Annual Report of the Communications Regulatory Agency for the Year 2002*, Communications Regulatory Agency of Bosnia and Herzegovina (CRA), http://rak.ba/eng/index.php?uid=1273696422. Accessed 15 February 2012.

CRA (2004a), *Annual Report of the Communications Regulatory Agency for the Year 2003*, Communications Regulatory Agency of Bosnia and Herzegovina (CRA), http://rak.ba/eng/index.php?uid=1273696422. Accessed 15 February 2012.

CRA (2004b), *Report on Cases of Violation of Rules and Regulations in 2003*, Communications Regulatory Agency of Bosnia and Herzegovina (CRA), http://rak.ba/eng/index.php?uid=1273696230. Accessed 30 May 2012.

CRA (2005a), *Annual Report of the Communications Regulatory Agency for the Year 2004*, Communications Regulatory Agency of Bosnia and Herzegovina (CRA), http://rak.ba/eng/index.php?uid=1273696422. Accessed 15 February 2012.

CRA (2005b), *Report on Cases of Violation of Rules and Regulations in 2004*, Communications Regulatory Agency of Bosnia and Herzegovina (CRA), http://rak.ba/eng/index.php?uid=1273696230. Accessed 30 May 2012.

CRA (2006a), *Annual Report of the Communications Regulatory Agency for the Year 2005*, Communications Regulatory Agency of Bosnia and Herzegovina (CRA), http://rak.ba/eng/index.php?uid=1273696422. Accessed 15 February 2012.

CRA (2006b), *Report on Cases of Violation of Rules and Regulations in 2005*, Communications Regulatory Agency of Bosnia and Herzegovina (CRA), http://rak.ba/eng/index.php?uid=1273696230. Accessed 30 May 2012.

CRA (2007a), *Annual Report of the Communications Regulatory Agency for the Year 2006*, Communications Regulatory Agency of Bosnia and Herzegovina (CRA), http://rak.ba/eng/index.php?uid=1273696422. Accessed 15 February 2012.

CRA (2007b), *Report on Cases of Violation of Rules and Regulations in 2006*, Communications Regulatory Agency of Bosnia and Herzegovina (CRA), http://rak.ba/eng/index.php?uid=1273696230. Accessed 30 May 2012.

CRA (2008a), *Annual Report of the Communications Regulatory Agency for the Year 2007*, Communications Regulatory Agency of Bosnia and Herzegovina (CRA), http://rak.ba/eng/index.php?uid=1273696422. Accessed 15 February 2012.

CRA (2008b), *Report on Cases of Violation of Rules and Regulations in 2007*, Communications Regulatory Agency of Bosnia and Herzegovina (CRA), http://rak.ba/eng/index.php?uid=1273696230. Accessed 30 May 2012.

CRA (2009a), *Annual Report of the Communications Regulatory Agency for the Year 2008*, Communications Regulatory Agency of Bosnia and Herzegovina (CRA), http://rak.ba/eng/index.php?uid=1273696422. Accessed 15 February 2012.

CRA (2009b), *Report on Cases of Violation of Rules and Regulations in 2008*, Communications Regulatory Agency of Bosnia and Herzegovina (CRA), http://rak.ba/eng/index.php?uid=1273696230. Accessed 30 May 2012.

CRA (2010a), *Annual Report of the Communications Regulatory Agency for the Year 2009*, Communications Regulatory Agency of Bosnia and Herzegovina (CRA), http://rak.ba/eng/index.php?uid=1273696422. Accessed 15 February 2012.

CRA (2010b), *Report on Cases of Violation of Rules and Regulations in 2009*, Communications Regulatory Agency of Bosnia and Herzegovina (CRA), http://rak.ba/eng/index.php?uid=1273696230. Accessed 30 May 2012.

CRA (2010c), *Radio- Televizija Republike Srpske kažnjena novčanom kaznom u iznosu od 100.000 KM*, press release, Communications Regulatory Agency of Bosnia and Herzegovina (CRA), 21 January 2010, http://rak.ba/bih/aktuelnost.php?uid=1269562154&root=1270195155. Accessed 28 January 2012.

CRA (2010d), *RAK odbacuje tvrdnje kolegija JP RTRS*, press release, Communications Regulatory Agency of Bosnia and Herzegovina (CRA), 19 March 2010, http://rak.ba/bih/aktuelnost.php?uid=1270626925&root=1270195155. Accessed 28 January 2012.

CRA (2011a), *Annual Report of the Communications Regulatory Agency for the Year 2010*, Communications Regulatory Agency of Bosnia and Herzegovina (CRA), http://rak.ba/eng/index.php?uid=1273696422. Accessed 15 February 2012.

CRA (2011b), *Report on Cases of Violation of Rules and Regulations in 2010*, Communications Regulatory Agency of Bosnia and Herzegovina (CRA), http://rak.ba/eng/index.php?uid=1273696230. Accessed 30 May 2012.

CRA (2012a), *Godišnji izvještaj Regulatorne agencije za komunikacije za 2011. Godinu/Annual Report of the Communications Regulatory Agency for the Year 2010*, Communications Regulatory Agency of Bosnia and Herzegovina (CRA), http://rak.ba/bih/index.php?uid=1272548129. Accessed 30 May 2012.

CRA (2012b), *Izvještaj o slučajevima kršenja pravila u 2011.godini/Report on Cases of Violation of Rules and Regulations in 2011*, Communications Regulatory Agency of Bosnia and Herzegovina (CRA), http://rak.ba/bih/index.php?uid=1272548169. Accessed 30 May 2012.

Dizdarević, S. et al. (eds.) (2006), *Democracy Assessment in Bosnia and Herzegovina*, Open Society Fund Bosnia and Herzegovina.

European Commission (2009), *Bosnia and Herzegovina Progress Report*, http://ec.europa.eu/enlargement/pdf/key_documents/2009/ba_rapport_2009_en.pdf. Accessed 31 May 2012.

European Commission (2010), *Bosnia and Herzegovina Progress Report*, http://ec.europa.eu/enlargement/pdf/key_documents/2010/package/ba_rapport_2010_en.pdf. Accessed 31 May 2012.

European Commission (2011), *Bosnia and Herzegovina Progress Report*, http://ec.europa.eu/enlargement/pdf/key_documents/2011/package/ba_rapport_2011_en.pdf. Accessed 31 May 2012.

Evans, P. (2004), 'Development as Institutional Change: The Pitfalls of Monocropping and the Potentials for Deliberation', *Studies in Comparative International Development*, Winter 2004, 38: 4, pp. 30–52.

Ford, J. T. (2005), *Independent Media Development Abroad*, GAO – United States Government Accountability Office, July 2005.

Gagliardone, I. (2011), 'From Mapping Information Ecologies to Evaluating Media Interventions', in Annenberg School for Communication at the University of Pennsylvania et al., *Workshop: Evaluating Media's Impact in Conflict Countries*, Caux, Switzerland, 13–17 December 2011.

Gorinjac, E. (2011), 'RAK mora dva puta raditi isti posao: Novi Parlament BiH također želi podobne u UO BHRT-a', *Sarajevo-x.com*, 29 August, http://www.sarajevo-x.com/bih/novi-parlament-bih-takodjer-zeli-podobne-u-uo-bhrt-a/110829097. Accessed 28 January 2012.

Halilović, M. (2008), 'Disciplining Independent Regulators: Political Pressures on the Communications Regulatory Agency of Bosnia and Herzegovina', *Puls demokratije/Puls of Democracy*, 10 July, http://arhiva.pulsdemokratije.net/index.php?id=1060&l=en. Accessed 29 May 2012.

Hallin, D. C. and Mancini, P. (2004), *Comparing Media Systems: Three Models of Media and Politics*, Cambridge University Press.

Hallin, D. C. and Mancini, P. (2012), 'Conclusion', in D. C. Hallin and P. Mancini (eds.), *Comparing Media Systems Beyond the Western World*, Cambridge: Cambridge University Press.

Hammond, T. H. (2003), 'Veto Points, Policy Preferences, and Bureaucratic Autonomy in Democratic Systems', in G. A. Krause and K. J. Meier (eds.), *Politics, Policy, and Organizations: Frontiers in the Scientific Study of Bureaucracy*, Ann Arbor: University of Michigan Press.

Hans Bredow Institute for Media Research, Interdisciplinary Centre for Law & ICT (ICRI), Katholieke Universiteit Leuven; Center for Media and Communication Studies (CMCS), Central European University; Cullen International; Perspective Associates (eds., 2011), *INDIREG. Indicators for independence and efficient functioning of audio-visual media services regulatory bodies for the purpose of enforcing the rules in the AVMS Directive*, Study conducted on behalf of the European Commission, Final Report. February 2011.

Hozić, A. A. (2008), 'Democratizing Media, Welcoming Big Brother: Media in Bosnia and Herzegovina', in K. Jakubowicz and M. Sükösd (eds.), *Finding the Right Place on the Map: Central and Eastern European Media Change in a Global Perspective*, Bristol: Intellect.

IREX (2010), *Media Sustainability Index 2010: Bosnia and Herzegovina*, IREX, http://www.irex.org/system/files/EE_MSI_2010_Bosnia%20%20Herzegovina.pdf. Accessed 31 May 2012.

IREX (2011), *Media Sustainability Index 2011: Bosnia and Herzegovina*, IREX, http://www.irex.org/sites/default/files/EE_MSI_2011_Bosnia.pdf. Accessed 31 May 2012.

Jusić, T. (2006), 'The Media in a Democratic Society', in S. Dizdarević et al. (eds.), *Democracy Assessment in Bosnia and Herzegovina*, Open Society Fund Bosnia and Herzegovina.

Jusić, T. (2010), *Media landscape: Bosnia and Herzegovina*, European Journalism Center, http://www.ejc.net/media_landscape/article/bosnia_and_herzegovina/. Accessed 31 May 2012.

Jusić, T. and Džihana, A. (2008), 'Bosnia and Herzegovina', in S. B.-Hrvatin, M. Thompson and T. Jusić (eds.), *Divided They Fall: Public Service Broadcasting in Multiethnic States*, Sarajevo: Mediacentar Sarajevo.

Jusić, T. and Palmer, K. L. (2008), 'The Media and Power-Sharing: Towards an Analytical Framework for Understanding Media Policies in Post-Conflict Societies. Public Broadcasting in Bosnia and Herzegovina', *Global Media Journal – Polish Edition*, 1: 4, http://www.globalmediajournal.collegium.edu.pl/. Accessed 31 May 2012.

Karabegović, D. (2012), 'Novi presedan: Vlast će nadzirati partijski kadrovi', *Radio Free Europe/Radio Liberty*, 13 January, http://www.slobodnaevropa.org/content/vlast_ce_nadzirati_partijski_kadrovi/24451124.html. Accessed 29 January 2012.

Kotlo, R. and Hodžić, E. (2006), 'Government Responsiveness – Is Government Responsive to the Concerns of its Citizens?' in Srđan Dizdarević et al. (eds.), *Democracy Assessment in Bosnia and Herzegovina*, Open Society Fund Bosnia and Herzegovina.

Kumar, K. (2006), 'International Assistance to Promote Independent Media in Transition and Post-conflict Societies', *Democratization* 13: 4, pp. 652–667.

Kurspahić, K. (2003), *Zločin u 19:30 – Balkanski mediji u ratu i miru/Prime-Time Crime: Balkan Media in War and Peace*, Mediacentar Sarajevo and South East Europe Media Organization (SEEMO).

Lazović, T. (2005), 'Huseinović priprema tužbu protiv Dokića', *Dnevni avaz/Daily Voice*, 25 October, p. 10.

Machet, E. (2007), 'The Independence of Regulatory Authorities', in EPRA (European Platform of Regulatory Authorities), *25th EPRA meeting*, Prague, 16–18 May, EPRA.

Maglajlić, R. A. and Hodžić, E. (2006), 'Political participation – Is there full citizen participation in public life?' in S. Dizdarević et al. (eds.), *Democracy Assessment in Bosnia and Herzegovina*, Open Society Fund Bosnia and Herzegovina.

Malcolm, N. (1994), *Bosnia: A Short History*, London: Macmillan London Limited.

Media Experts Commission (Komisija eksperata za medije) (1998), *Završni izvještaj: Mediji u izborima/Final Report: Media in Elections*, OSCE Mission in Bosnia and Herzegovina.

Ministry for Human Rights and Refugees of Bosnia and Herzegovina (2003), *Comparative Indicators on Refugees, Displaced Persons and Returnees: Property Laws Implementation and Reconstruction in Bosnia and Herzegovina from 1991 to 30 June 2003*, http://www.internal-displacement.org/8025708F004CE90B/%28httpDocuments%29/0121944D04546D33802570B700587A58/$file/comparative+indicators+-+part+one.PDF. Accessed 12 January 2012.

OHR (1997), *Political Declaration from Ministerial Meeting of the Steering Board of the Peace Implementation Council*, adopted at Sintra PIC Steering Board Ministerial Meeting, 30 May, http://www.ohr.int/pic/default.asp?content_id=5180. Accessed 31 May 2012.

OHR (1998), *Decision of the High Representative on the Establishment of the Independent Media Commission in Bosnia and Herzegovina*, Office of the High Representative (OHR),

11 June 1998, http://www.ohr.int/decisions/mediadec/default.asp?content_id=95. Accessed 27 January 2012.

OHR (2001), *Decision of the High Representative Combining the Competencies of the Independent Media Commission and the Telecommunications Regulatory Agency*, Office of the High Representative (OHR), 2 March 2001, http://www.ohr.int/decisions/mediadec/default. asp?content_id=75. Accessed 27 January 2012.

OHR (2002), *Decision of the High Representative on Amending the Structure of Expenditures of the Communications Regulatory Agency for 2002*, Office of the High Representative (OHR), 2 December 2002, http://www.ohr.int/decisions/archive.asp. Accessed 13 February 2012.

Open Society Institute (2005), *Television Across Europe: Regulation, Policy, and Independence (Volume 1)*, Budapest: Open Society Institute/EU Monitoring and Advocacy Program.

Palmer, K. L. (2001), 'The Power-Sharing Process: Media Reforms in Bosnia and Herzegovina', in Harvard University, *3rd annual Kokkalis Graduate Student Workshop*, Cambridge, Massachusetts, 9–10 February.

Parliamentary Assembly of Bosnia and Herzegovina (2000), *Freedom of Access to Information Act*, Official Gazette of Bosnia and Herzegovina, 28/00, 45/06.

Parliamentary Assembly of Bosnia and Herzegovina (2002), *Law on Civil Service in the Institutions of Bosnia and Herzegovina*, Official Gazette of Bosnia and Herzegovina 19/02, 35/03, 4/04, 17/04, 26/04, 37/04, 48/05, 2/06, 32/07, 43/09, 8/10.

Parliamentary Assembly of Bosnia and Herzegovina (2003a), *Law on Ministries and Other Bodies of Administration in Bosnia and Herzegovina*, Official Gazette of Bosnia and Herzegovina 5/03, 42/03, 26/04, 42/04, 45/06, 88/07, 35/09, 59/09, 103/09.

Parliamentary Assembly of Bosnia and Herzegovina (2003b), *Law on Communications of Bosnia and Herzegovina*, Official Gazette of Bosnia and Herzegovina 31/03.

Parliamentary Assembly of Bosnia and Herzegovina (2004), *Law on Financing of State Institutions of Bosnia and Herzegovina*, Official Gazette of Bosnia and Herzegovina 61/04.

Parliamentary Assembly of Bosnia and Herzegovina (2005), *Law on Public Broadcasting Service of Bosnia and Herzegovina*, Official Gazette of Bosnia and Herzegovina 92/05.

Parliamentary Assembly of Bosnia and Herzegovina (2008), *Law on Salaries and Compensations in Institutions of Bosnia and Herzegovina*, Official Gazette of Bosnia and Herzegovina 50/08.

Price, M. (2002), *Mapping Media Assistance*, The Programme in Comparative Media Law and Policy, Centre for Socio-Legal Studies, University of Oxford.

Price M. and Thompson M. (eds.) (2002), *Forging Peace: Intervention, Human Rights, and the Management of Media Space*, Edinburgh: Edinburgh University Press.

Putnam, R., Leonardi, R. and Nanetti, R. Y. (1993), *Making Democracy Work: Civic Traditions in Modern Italy*, Princeton University Press.

Rhodes, A. (2007), *Ten Years of Media Support to the Balkans – An Assessment*, Stability Pact for South Eastern Europe.

Robinson, G. J. (1977), *Tito's Maverick Media: The Politics of Mass Communications in Yugoslavia*, Chicago: University of Illinois Press.

Shirley, M. M. (2003), *Institutions and Development*, Working Paper, http://www.iim.uni-flensburg.de/vwl/upload/lehre/sose08/MaEuS/w-shirley2003institutionsanddevelopment. pdf. Accessed 4 February 2012.

Shirley, M. M. (2005), *Can Aid Reform Institutions?*, Working Paper, http://www.isnie.org/ISNIE05/Papers05/shirley.pdf. Accessed 4 February 2012.

Shirley, M. M. (2008), *Institutions and Development: Advance in New Institutional Analysis*, Edward Elgar Publishing Ltd.

Snyder, J. and Ballentine, K. (1996), 'Nationalism and the Marketplace of Ideas', *International Security* 21: 2, pp. 5–40.

The World Bank (1997), *Bosnia and Herzegovina: From Recovery to Sustainable Growth*, The World Bank.

The World Bank (2004), *Bosnia and Herzegovina: Post-Conflict Reconstruction and the Transition to a Market Economy: An OED Evaluation of World Bank Support*, The International Bank for Reconstruction and Development/The World Bank, http://www.oecd.org/dataoecd/22/62/35282080.pdf. Accessed 15 February 2012.

Thompson, M. (1994), *Forging War: the Media in Serbia, Croatia and Bosnia Herzegovina*, London: Art. 19.

Thompson, M. and De Luce, D. (2002), 'Escalating to Success? The Media Intervention in Bosnia and Herzegovina', in M. E. Price and M. Thompson (eds.), *Forging Peace: Intervention, Human Rights and the Management of Media Space*, Edinburgh: Edinburgh University Press.

Tsebelis, G. (2002), *Veto players: How Political Institutions Work*, Princeton: Princeton University Press.

Voltmer, K. (2012), 'How Far Can Media Systems Travel? Applying Hallin and Mancini's Comparative Framework outside the Western World', in D. C. Hallin and P. Mancini (eds.), *Comparing Media Systems Beyond the Western World*, Cambridge: Cambridge University Press.

Zielonka, J. and Mancini, P. (2011), *Executive Summary: A Media Map of Central and Eastern Europe*, Media and Democracy in Central and Eastern Europe: An ERC Project based at the Department of Politics and International Relations of the University of Oxford in collaboration with the Department of Media and Communications, The London School of Economics and Political Science, http://mde.politics.ox.ac.uk/images/stories/summary_mdcee_2011.pdf. Accessed 20 February 2013.

Chapter 12

Concluding chapter: Independence in context

Wolfgang Schulz

This book outlines the role of independence of the media and its regulatory agencies, building on the outcome of the INDIREG project and the preliminary findings of the MEDIADEM project. Starting point for the discussions in this book is the relationship between media freedom and regulation. Freedom of expression and freedom of the media are shared values within Europe and protected under Article 10 ECHR as well as by most of the national constitutions. Proceeding from that starting point, Part I of the book assesses the independence of regulators within the audiovisual sector, whereas the second part explores the relevance of the culture of independence on the basis of case studies and comparative analysis. Interestingly, although the analyses depart from different theoretical backgrounds and paradigms, the findings they arrive at are to a great extent consonant or at least overlapping.

The aim of this concluding chapter is to identify those compatible findings. It will first look into the results regarding the notion of independence, which will lead to a reflection on the relativity of independence and, finally, show the importance of the cultural context.

Formal and informal independence

One of the consistent conclusions of the analyses in this book concerns the assumption made in previous research that one has to differentiate between formal and informal independence.[1] The findings presented in this book underpin the necessity of this distinction. They present sets of indicators for both aspects of independence, and, furthermore, show the links between them.

The findings regarding these indicators of both formal and informal independence broaden and deepen the understanding of the influencing factors identified in previous studies. Applying the concept of governance has added a new theoretical layer that allows for identifying the resources which – to make use of the INDIREG terminology – drive the dependencers as well as the autonomizers of a given institution (cf. Chapter 5 in this book by Dreyer). It also creates a link between the concept of independence and regulation theory, which can be further explored in future research. To influence an entity like a regulator means to (partly) control it; thus research on dependence looks at the other side of such control: autonomizing factors. The concept of dependencing and autonomizing factors might contribute to the understanding of independence of organizations in general, not just in the media sector.

Having said that, one has to accept that deriving concrete indicators to measure formal and informal independence is associated with a certain degree of arbitrariness: there is no theory that would provide for creating a method to exactly deduce a matrix of indicators. Therefore the catalogues of indicators in studies already done are not identical with those which MEDIADEM and INDIREG provide. However, the overlapping is significant and they create a proxy with which empirical research can work.

What makes it even harder to construct and interpret those indicators is that many criteria can mean contradictory things. The revolving door mechanism can serve as an example. Its manifestation can indicate that a regulator is an attractive employer and people from the industry gladly decide to work with and within it, which would suggest an empowered regulator. There are experts on board with a deep, first-hand understanding of the developments and strategies of the industry players, they speak their language and may even foresee their moves. However, the revolving door mechanism also entails the risk of having staff members who might still hold loyalties towards the industry, or who operate with a business-orientated mindset rather than acting in a public spirit. Only an in-depth case study can demonstrate what effect prevails for a specific regulator.

Another of those ambivalent indicators is the length of tenure: the longer the term of the boards members, the more chance they have to develop the necessary expertise; but on the other hand the risk of capture is also likely to grow the longer a committee is in office. Thus a nine-year term in combination with a high degree of influence exercised by the party in power on the nomination process can weaken the autonomy of the regulator considerably. Such ambiguous factors might be the ones that should be looked into in more depth in future research, including the interplay of those factors.

Several case studies and country comparisons can be found in this book. They are an excellent source of examples of how skilled governments, especially, are in inventing shrewd ways to circumvent mechanisms formally guaranteeing independence. In case you cannot directly influence a media regulator by cutting its budget, for example, you can make use of your power to broaden the remit and thus the workload of the institution, or obstruct the appointment of new staff – and in this way achieve a similar result (cf. Chapter 11 in this book by Jusić). Mechanisms to create transparency can also be used to make the regulator more accountable to the government, stakeholders or the general public and steer it in a specific direction. The mere fact that political parties have a greater organizational capacity and linkage force than civil society actors can give them a disproportionate power in governing councils, as they can create informal circles that influence the decision-making process (cf. Chapter 9 in this book by Docquir, Gusy and Müller). Such examples, too, underscore the need to look at informal or real independence.

In terms of how further research on independence should be developed, the findings of this book emphasize how assessing only formal independence may yield findings of relatively little significance. Studies should include an assessment of de facto indicators as well if they are to produce meaningful results. This is true, at least, if you want to measure whether a regulatory agency is in fact independent. Certainly, there are formal aspects that can be regarded as essential for a regulator to function independently, and a lack of those is a strong indication that the regulator cannot be independent in practice. However, the presence of such essentials is, in itself, by no means a guarantee that it actually functions that way.

Relativity of independence

Another common finding of the chapters in this book reflects how both research projects came up with a working definition of independence that is based on the relativity of independence. It is not feasible to frame independence as something absolute, as an abstract level that can be defined in a consistent way for all regulatory purposes and regardless of the political, economic and cultural context, the analyses in this book suggest. It has been demonstrated that the current status of the media system is the result of (at least) two developments: the development of the media – which all states face in a similar way (e.g. convergence) – and the development of the political system, which varies considerably (cf. Chapter 2 in this book by Irion and Radu). Thus it does not come as a surprise that relatively similar formal settings – as in Finland and UK – have resulted in rather different outcomes (cf. Chapter 10 in this book by Craufurd-Smith, Stolte and Kuutti).

The definition of independence has to take into account the dynamic relationships between the regulator and the different stakeholders, in which the regulator is positioned within a parallelogram of power. The book makes use of governance theory to make this concept more concrete. All the articles demonstrate that absolute independence is neither desirable nor an adequate theoretical concept.

The aim for which an independent regulator was set up in the first place also has to be taken into account when one tries to understand what independence actually entails in a specific case. For the analysis reflected in this book, this meant trying to understand the specific role of media regulation in a free society (cf. Chapter 1 in this book by Schulz).

This relative concept does, however, create problems for those who want to contra factually guarantee independence of regulators, like the European institutions do. Creating a structure of independent national regulators has become a common policy tool in European regulation. The telecommunication sector as well as data protection can serve as examples here: regarding data protection, the European Court of Justice held that 'Data Protection Authorities need to be completely independent'[2] – whatever that means and whatever the reason for that might be. The analysis in this book has demonstrated that the level of regulation vis-à-vis independence of authorities differs from sector to sector (cf. Chapter 4 by Stevens). The AVMS Directive does not stipulate such a strict harmonization as there is concerning data protection; nevertheless, there are requirements for the member states here as well, as Chapter 4 by Stevens explains.

Within the European Union, the independence of regulatory agencies in the member states also serves a specific goal that is not relevant when there is no such supranational level: independence makes it easier for regulators to form networks across borders. The most prominent example of this process is the telecommunications sector, where the cooperation between regulators has now led to the formation of a Body of European Regulators for Electronic Communications (BEREC). Such supranational linkages can help achieve (European) regulatory goals. However, within the power game of European politics, they also serve the interest of the European institutions, especially the European Commission, in having direct access to regulatory bodies, rather than having to communicate via the national governments with their own political interests.

Normatively the independence of media regulators is to be seen in the broader context of media independence. Independence is in this case not only a means to secure the effectiveness and efficiency of regulation: influenced regulators can endanger the freedom of the media as a whole. The studies in this book show that, at least in theory, all examined countries accept the need for media freedom. Societies depend on free media to create a medium of reflection. State influence on the media creates the risk of turning the process of public opinion making upside down. In view of this, securing the independence of media regulators can be framed as a part of guaranteeing free media. In this book the authors argue that the independence of media regulators from state influence is to be considered a guarantee which states are bound to under Article 10 (1) ECHR.[3]

This normative context, in particular, constitutes a factor which distinguishes media regulation from regulation in other sectors. It demonstrates why it is meaningful to explore the independence of media regulators separately, instead of developing a general concept of regulatory independence and just applying it to the regulatory agencies in this and every other sector.

This point also, however, raises the normative questions about regulatory independence that have not been extensively covered in this book, but are of growing interest in both the academic and the political discourse. The debate about independent regulators – like the debate on other modern forms of regulation – has been focused for some time on the effectiveness and efficiency of regulators and, by doing so, has neglected to some extent the aspect of democratic legitimation and accountability. Independence from the parliament, i.e. elected politicians, is by definition associated with a reduced level of legitimation. That does not mean to say that this cannot be adjusted by other means, but the establishment of independent regulators is therefore not by definition desirable.

Finally, the concept of governance allows analysis to also include the dependence of regulators on other stakeholders, apart from politicians and the state, such as the industry or pressure groups. How these types of dependence can also hamper the independence of regulators in the media sector is demonstrated in this book (cf. Chapter 7 by Klimkiewicz, regarding the Polish 'Rywingate' scandal).

Culture of independence

The theoretical chapters in this book as well as the case studies and country comparisons all point to the importance of soft context-factors; above all, what we in this book call 'culture of independence'. The culture of independence in a society or a sub-section of a society can be framed as the *assumptions people make about the independence of institutions*. Therefore, it is fundamentally shaped by *informal norms, practices, perceptions and expectations* vis-à-vis independence.

It is plausible to assume that the past record of the decision making of institutions can influence this set of factors. In a society where even courts, formally the pinnacles of independence of the legal system, do not act impartially, expectations concerning the actions of newly established actors like regulatory authorities will not be particularly high. This does not need to be a problem in itself, because it enables other actors to design adequate strategies to protect their interests. It does, however, shape expectations.

In a culture of informality, clienteles and a selective application of rules, the prospects for a media regulator performing its task autonomously, following only its regulatory aim, are not favourable, to say the least (cf. Chapter 11 in this book by Jusić).

The different chapters of this book offer an ample choice of examples to illustrate the importance of cultural contexts. For example, the comparison of Finland and the UK in Chapter 10 of this book by Craufurd-Smith, Stolte and Kuutti demonstrates that even in two countries with similar legal frameworks which both changed their system to enable more self-regulation, those frameworks can, once in effect, lead to different working systems in practice. Thus superficially similar structures can have quite different regulatory outcomes in different (socio-)cultural environments. However, as this case demonstrates, political and economic factors interfere as well.

Another relevant case might be the German neo-corporate structures which emerged after World War II, which brought the phenomenon of 'circles of friends' that aggregate around political parties and can be used to indirectly influence decision-making procedures in boards, including, for example, regulatory authorities (cf. Chapter 9 in this book by Docquir, Gusy and Müller). The special case of Bosnia and Herzegovina demonstrates that the political culture can be changed by interventions from outside. The presence of the international community that played a significant role in the country has – at least – influenced the perception of institutions. Additionally, the case study demonstrates that outside intervention creates a dynamic process, the outcome of which cannot be easily foreseen. In cases where the legal and cultural influences from outside are not linked to existing legal and cultural contexts within the country, however, the resulting impact on the regulator might not be stable – especially when the external influence fades.

When research outside the inner circle of cultural studies takes refuge to the concept of 'culture', this can be a sign that the effects being observed cannot be explained sufficiently by the data at hand: culture, in such cases, serves as a kind of vague residual category. By at least partly taking the expectations of actors vis-à-vis each other into account when measuring de facto independence, we at least try to describe the cultural context. Building on that, future studies should further elaborate the identification of informal norms, practices, perceptions and expectations in the field to broaden our understanding of de facto or 'real' independence.

Independence means a regulator has more leeway, and that can mean that individuals and their preferences can get to play a more prominent role. It has been demonstrated for other aspects of modern regulation, such as self-regulatory arrangements, that in the perception of other actors the entire success of the endeavour can rely on individual chairpersons of a regulator.[4] If it is plausible to assume the relevance of such phenomena for de facto independence as well, this is an additional aspect for future research to explore.

Against this background it seems even more important to promote transparency and create the means to increase the accountability of media regulators. However, transparency – i.e. bringing procedures into the open – only has a regulatory effect if there are shared rules against which the procedures can be measured, and if malpractice can and will be scandalized. If nobody cares, transparency is powerless. Thus, one strategy to strengthen the media and their regulators can be to change the configuration of actors involved – e.g. by including observers from abroad.

Outlook

Media regulation is a rather complex process. Normatively the whole system, as well as each single decision taken by a regulator, possibly infringes the fundamental rights of a media actor or outlet. Regulation, understood as a process, requires the regulator to establish itself within the field and maintain an adequate working distance to all actors. This positioning is by no means static but part of a sometimes highly dynamic process, which can change as new actors enter the scene, additional tasks are introduced and new challenges emerge or resurface.

One key change which is touched upon in some chapters of this book is the increasing relevance of Internet-based services and the respective functional changes in the information ecology associated with them. While in the traditional media sector the set of actors had been limited and the structure of the field did not change rapidly, this is not true for online media.

The need to integrate new actors in the regulatory system can mean having to change the normative framework, and this gives parliament and government an opportunity, at least, to modify the formal factors that shape independence too. Additionally, the structure of the industry is changing. New actors might oppose the attempts to be regulated, or at least the expectations vis-à-vis the regulator might change significantly. This might mean that the regulator requires additional institutional support, which can come at a price in terms of its independence. The MEDIADEM project is conducting some valuable research in that respect; however, further efforts are needed to acquire a full understanding of the effects of those developments on the independence of regulators.

There is another effect of the rise of online media which can influence the factors that frame independence. All over the world attempts to tamper with the freedom of the Internet have provoked an intense public response, with protests which erupted online first then being reflected in the traditional media, since journalists are as a rule rather sensitive when it comes to censorship issues. That the Internet makes it easy to draw at least such partial public attention to actions that are deemed inappropriate can turn out to be an important autonomizer for regulators. Transparency is certainly not a magic wand to solve all regulatory problems, as we are occasionally made to believe. However, as long as the impartiality of decision making is a shared value, greater transparency means that attempts to infringe with that impartiality come with a risk for the infringer, and makes it less likely for those infringements to occur. 'Regulation watch' can therefore be a tool to foster the independence of regulators. However, its efficacy depends on relevant stakeholders being able to recognize the relevance of the information provided.

Within the knowledge society, knowledge becomes more and more important as a regulatory resource. Strengthening the regulator means – as is clearly demonstrated in this book and the underlying studies – providing it with internal expertise as well as the means to acquire external knowledge when needed. This is, of course, associated with another important source of regulation: money. Adequate financial resources are paramount.

Finally, policy-wise, the findings of this book at least suggest that the modelling of regulators follows trends and imitation strategies. There seems to be some shared understanding of what a 'modern regulator' should look like. The findings here can lead to a more rational choice of regulatory models, reflecting the pros and cons and – again –specific sectoral requirements as well as political, economic and cultural contexts.

Regarding future research, the deliberations reflected in this book suggest that further research could try to provide a more structural basis for the notion of 'cultural context' or, in this case, 'culture of independence'. In many studies a reference to 'culture' merely constitutes a confession that the differences found in a country comparison cannot be explained by the data available. However, it seems like an effort to describe the specific configuration of actors involved and identify the relevant patterns would be feasible. The study of informal norms within a society or a community can further help to broaden the picture.

Notes

1 Cf. Chapter 1 of this book; striking examples can be found in the comparison of the regulatory system in Greece and Italy in Chapter 8.

2 Court of Justice of the European Union, Judgment of 9 March 2010, *Commission of the European Communities v Federal Republic of Germany*, case C-518/07, paras 31–37.

3 Cf. European Court of Human Rights (Grand Chamber), Judgment of 7 June 2012, *Centro Europa 7 S.R.L. and Di Stefano v Italy*, Application no. 38433/09, http://cmiskp.echr.coe.int/ tkp197/view.asp?action=html&documentId=909275&portal=hbkm&source=externalbydo cnumber&table=F69A27FD8FB86142BF01C1166DEA398649. Accessed 4 September 2013.

4 Schulz, Wolfang and Held, Thorsten: *Regulated Self-Regulation as a Form of Modern Government: An Analysis of Case Studies from Media and Telecommunications Law*, p. 10 ff.

Contributors' biographies

Federica Casarosa is a research assistant at the European University Institute, Department of Law. She graduated in Private Comparative Law at the University of Pisa and obtained a Master of Research in Law from the European University Institute (2003). In 2008, she successfully defended her PhD thesis on the role of information in online contracting, analysing in particular the protection provided to consumers in the pre-contractual phase. She has worked as a consultant for FAO and as a Jean Monnet Fellow at the Robert Schuman Centre for Advanced Studies. Her research interests focus on new media law and regulation, and on child protection in the media sector. Her works appeared on several Italian and international journals, such as the *European Review of Private Law*, the *Journal of Internet Law* and *Diritto dell' Informazione e dell' Informatica*.

Rachael Craufurd Smith is a senior lecturer at the University of Edinburgh. Before becoming an academic, she gained considerable experience working both in private legal practice and as an adviser on media law and policy for the BBC. She teaches media law at both undergraduate and postgraduate levels and supervises a range of PhD research students working in the media field. Rachael Craufurd Smith has written widely on the impact of constitutional guarantees, fundamental rights and international and domestic laws on media pluralism and diversity. More recently, her research has focused on the impact of convergence on established domestic regulatory regimes and the evolving relationship between individuals and the mass media. She is a member of the Europa Institute and Co-director of the AHRC Script Centre, based in the School of Law of the University of Edinburgh. She is also an editor of The Journal of Media Law, launched by Hart Publishing in 2009 to provide scholarly and critical analysis of media law developments, and currently leads the UK team on the EU-funded research project 'European media policies revisited: valuing and reclaiming free and independent media in contemporary democratic systems (MEDIADEM)'.

Pierre-François Docquir is an independent researcher and expert in the fields of human rights law, media law and regulation. He received his Ph.D. in law from the Université Libre de Bruxelles (ULB) in January 2009 for a doctoral dissertation entitled 'Freedom of Expression in the worldwide communication networks: proposals for a theory of the right of access to privately- owned public spaces' (prix Alice Seghers 2010). Pierre-François held the 2007–2012 mandate as the vice-president of the Conseil supérieur de l'audiovisuel (CSA – the independent regulatory authority for audiovisual media in French-speaking Belgium). He is a member of the editorial board of the Revue du droit des technologies de l'information (Information Technology Law Review – http://www.rdti.be). He was the scientist in charge of the ULB – MEDIADEM team from April 2010 to September 2012. Web and social networks via http://about.me/pfdocquir.

Stephan Dreyer is Senior Researcher in the field of media regulation and media policy at the Hans Bredow Institute for Media Research. After studying Law at the University of Hamburg, he has been a member of the Department for Media and Telecommunications Law at the institute since 2002. His research concerns the law and legal concepts applicable to new media services as well as new online and distribution platforms. One of his thematic priorities at the institute is the protection of minors against harmful media content. A further emphasis of research and a main interest beside data protection issues are legal and regulatory questions related to online video games and virtual worlds. In the context of his PhD thesis, he is investigating the difficulties as well as the determinants of legal decisions under uncertainty within current systems of youth media protection. He has been a contributing senior researcher within the EU funded INDIREG project.

Christoph Gusy is professor of Law at the University of Bielefeld with expertise in public and constitutional law, general theory of state and constitutional history. He was vice rector of the University from 1998 to 2005 and has taught as a visiting professor at the University of Paris I (Panthéon/Sorbonne, 1998) and at the University of Strasbourg (Robert Schuman, 2000/2004). He has participated in many interdisciplinary research projects, focusing, amongst other issues, on political communication and the implementation of judgments from the European Court of Human Rights. Since April 2010, he is the scientist in charge of the German research team in the EU funded research project 'European media policies revisited: valuing and reclaiming free and independent media in contemporary democratic systems (MEDIADEM)'. He is the author of more than 20 books and around 200 essays.

Kristina Irion is Assistant Professor at the Department of Public Policy and Research Director, Public Policy, at the Center for Media and Communications Studies (CMCS) at Central European University in Budapest, Hungary. She obtained her Dr. iuris degree from Martin Luther University, Halle-Wittenberg, Germany, and holds a Masters degree in Information Technology and Telecommunications Law from the University of Strathclyde, Glasgow, UK. She has worked in the field of audiovisual media and electronic communications regulation and policy for ten years as an academic and professional. In 2010, as part of a European consortium under the lead of the Hans Bredow Institute in Hamburg she was the key public policy exert in a study for the European Commission on Indicators for independence and efficient functioning of audiovisual media services regulatory bodies (INDIREG).

Karol Jakubowicz is a distinguished scholar and expert in the field of media policy. He worked for Academia (at the University of Warsaw and as a visiting professor at the University of Dortmund and at the Amsterdam School of Communication) and as a journalist for many years. He has extensive experience working as an executive for Polish press, radio and television, as well as for the National Broadcasting Council of Poland. He has been active in the UNESCO, as chairperson of the Intergovernmental Council of the UNESCO Information for All Programme (2008–2010) and in other capacities, and the Council of Europe, in part as chairman of the Steering Committee on the Media and New Communication Services (2005–2006), He has been a member of the Digital Strategy Group of the European Broadcasting Union and is an expert working with the Council of Europe, UNESCO, the European Union and OSCE. His scholarly and other publications have been published widely in Poland and internationally.

Tarik Jusić is Executive Director at Analitika – Center for Social Research, Sarajevo, Bosnia and Herzegovina. He holds a PhD from the Institute for Media and Communication Studies, University of Vienna, Austria; an MA degree in Political Science from Central European University, Budapest, Hungary; and a BA degree in Journalism from the Faculty of Political Science, University of Sarajevo. From 2009 to 2013 he was an Assistant Professor at the Department of Political Science and International Relations, Sarajevo School of Science and Technology and from 2002 to 2011 he was a Programme Director and Lead Researcher at the Mediacentar Sarajevo.

Anna Kandyla is a research assistant at the Hellenic Foundation for European and Foreign Policy (ELIAMEP, Athens, Greece) working for the MEDIADEM project. She holds a bachelor's degree in Communication and Mass Media from the University of Athens and a Master's degree in Political Behaviour from the University of Essex, UK. She has worked as a research assistant at the Amsterdam School of Communications Research, University of Amsterdam, and at the Communication Unit of the Directorate General Interpretation of the European Commission. She has also held research positions in the field of market research. Her articles have appeared in *Comparative European Politics* and the *Journal of Common Market Studies*.

Beata Klimkiewicz is Assistant Professor at the Institute of Journalism and Social Communication, the Jagiellonian University, Cracow, Poland where she also received her Ph.D. from the Institute of Political Sciences. She was awarded with a number of fellowships at Oxford University, Columbia University, Robert Schuman Centre, European University Institute, Open Society Institute in Budapest and NIAS (Netherlands Institute for Advanced Study in the Humanities and Social Sciences). She has been involved in several research and policy projects in the area of media and communication studies including COST Action A30 East of West: Setting a New Central and Eastern European Media Research Agenda; Indicators for Media Pluralism in the Member States – Towards a Risk-Based Approach and

Indicators for the Independence and Effective Functioning of Audiovisual Media Services Regulatory Bodies (both studies for the European Commission) and Pilot Media Study on the Media Representations of Minorities, Migrants and Diversity Issues (for the EU Agency for Fundamental Rights). Most recent publications include Media Freedom and Pluralism: Media Policy Challenges in the Enlarged Europe published in 2010 by the CEU Press.

Heikki Kuutti is a research fellow in journalism in the Department of Communication, University of Jyväskylä, Finland. His doctoral theses focused on investigative reporting and the investigative nature of Finnish journalism. Previously, he has worked as a newspaper reporter and editor, journalism teacher and project researcher at the Academy of Finland and at the Jyväskylä University Media Institute. He has also been head of the Information Department of the Finnish Air Force. Besides his current activities he works as the president and managing director of Media Doc Ltd. Since April 2010 he led the Finnish team in the EU-funded MEDIADEM project.

Epp Lauk, Ph.D. is Professor of Journalism at the University of Jyväskylä, Finland. She has worked at the University of Tartu, and as Guest Professor at the University of Oslo and University of Stockholm. She has participated in numerous national and international journalism research and training projects and networks. Her publications include over 100 articles and book chapters and five edited or co-edited books on journalism cultures and history, media self-regulation, media and journalism in post-Communist countries, etc. She is chairperson of the Estonian Press Council, acting chair of the History Section of IAMCR and Board member of ECREA. She is also vice-chair of the Executive Committee of the world-wide project on journalism cultures 'Worlds of Journalism'. Epp Lauk was member of the Estonian team of the MEDIADEM project in 2010 and member of Finnish team in 2011–2013.

Michele Ledger has been working for Cullen International for 15 years. She has a law degree from the Université Libre de Bruxelles, Belgium and an LLM in international commercial law from Kent University. She is in charge of the media service of Cullen International which provides independent analysis and research for regulators and operators at the EU level and in a number of western European countries. She was a lead researcher on the INDIREG study, in charge of compiling and analysing the country data and in charge of developing the ranking tool to measure the level of formal independence and de facto independence of media regulatory authorities.

Sebastian Müller is a Researcher at the Law Faculty of the University of Bielefeld. He holds a PhD in Law on non-judicial mechanisms in the field of human rights protection. Parts of his thesis analysed the necessary structures for democratic participation in human rights protection and examined the role of the media in this respect. Since April 2010, he has been working in the EU-funded research project 'European media policies revisited: valuing and reclaiming free and independent media in contemporary democratic systems (MEDIADEM)'. Before joining the University in 2006, he had worked for domestic human rights non-governmental organizations, the Federal Commissioner for Migrants and Refugees of the Federal Government of Germany and the German Institute for Human Rights in Berlin. He has published on human rights, the role of the media in democracies and EU integration.

Eva Lievens holds a law degree from the University of Ghent (2002), a Masters degree in Transnational Communications and Global Media from Goldsmiths College, London (2003) and a PhD in Law from KU Leuven (2009). She has been a member of the Interdisciplinary Centre for Law & ICT (www.icri.be) since 2003 and is currently a Postdoctoral Research Fellow of the Research Fund Flanders, working on a project titled 'Risk-reducing regulatory strategies for illegal and harmful conduct and content in online social network sites'. Her research focuses on legal challenges posed by new media phenomena, such as the regulation of audiovisual media services, user-generated content and social networks. Eva is a member of the Advisory Committee of the BE SIC II-project (EU Safer Internet Programme) and the Belgian Film Evaluation Committee.

Evangelia Psychogiopoulou is a research fellow at the Hellenic Foundation for European and Foreign Policy (Athens, Greece). She holds a DEA in EU law from Paris I University, a Master of Research in Law degree from the European University Institute (Florence, Italy) and a PhD in Law from the same university. Her main areas of research are EU cultural and media policies and human rights protection. She has held research and management positions at the Academy of European Law (Florence, Italy), the Directorate-General Education and Culture of the European Commission and UNESCO. Her articles have appeared in *European Foreign Affairs Review*, *European Law Journal*, *European Law Review*, *Legal Issues of Economic Integration*, *European State Aid Law Quarterly* and *European Human Rights Cases*. She is also the author of *The Integration of Cultural Considerations in EU Law and Policies* (2008) and editor of *Understanding Media Policies: A European Perspective* (2012). She presently coordinates the MEDIADEM project.

Roxana Radu is a PhD candidate in political science at the Graduate Institute of International and Development Studies (Geneva, Switzerland) and a research fellow at the Center for Media and Communication Studies, Central European University (Budapest, Hungary). Her current research investigates the ways in which the governance of the Internet is negotiated in the framework of regional and global institutions. In 2010 she worked as a research assistant for the INDIREG study on Indicators for independence and efficient functioning of audiovisual media services regulatory bodies, and she has since contributed to several large-scale projects of the Open Society Foundations and the Global Development Network.

Wolfgang Schulz is Director of the Hans Bredow Institute for Media Research and Professor for Public Law and Media Law including its Theoretical Fundaments at the Faculty of Law at the University of Hamburg. At the Hans Bredow Institute, he leads the Media and Telecommunications Law Department. His work emphasizes problems of legal regulation with regard to media contents (particularly depictions of violence), questions of law in new media (above all in digital television) and the legal bases of journalism, but also the jurisprudential bases of freedom of communication and of the description of the systems of journalism and communications in systems theory. In addition, his works focus on new forms of regulation, for instance in the framework of concepts of 'regulated self-regulation'. He has been the project leader of the EU funded INDIREG project.

David Stevens is research manager (since 2005) and researcher (since 1998) at the Interdisciplinary Centre for Law & ICT (www.icri.be) of the Faculty of Law (www.law. kuleuven.be) of the Katholieke Universiteit Leuven (part of the Flemish ICT Research Institute iMinds, www.iminds.be). His expertise relates to the evolving role of governments and national regulatory authorities in the telecommunications and media sectors. The most important projects on this subject were funded by the Fonds voor Wetenschappelijk Onderzoek Vlaanderen (Fund for Scientific Research Flanders), the federal and regional governments and private and public market players. In 2009, David also defended a PhD on this matter. In the context of the INDIREG project, David was responsible for the legal requirements analysis on the independence of regulatory authorities in the European information and communications sectors.

Yolande Stolte graduated with an LLB degree in 2007 from the University of Leiden and obtained an LLM in Civil Law from the same university in 2008. She was awarded the VSB foundation scholarship to further specialize in her main field of interest: IP and media law. She used this to obtain an LLM in Innovation, Technology and the Law at the University of Edinburgh. After graduating in 2009 she has worked as a Research Fellow at the University of Edinburgh, while managing the online legal journal SCRIPTed and working towards a PhD on 'The legal protection of war correspondents in conflict zones'. She is currently working as a researcher on the EU-funded research project 'European media policies revisited: valuing and reclaiming free and independent media in contemporary democratic systems (MEDIADEM)' for the UK team in Edinburgh.

Peggy Valcke is research professor at KU Leuven, working at the Interdisciplinary Centre for Law & ICT (ICRI-iMinds) at the Faculty of Law, and assistant professor at HU Brussel. She is visiting professor at the University of Tilburg and has been visiting professor at Central European University in Budapest, Hungary in 2006–2007. She is a member of the scientific committee of the Centre for Media Pluralism and Media Freedom and of the Florence School of Regulation (both at the European University Institute in Florence). She is a member of the General Chamber in the Flemish Media Regulator and part-time member of the Belgian Competition Council. In 2010, she served as key legal expert in the INDIREG study for the European Commission on Indicators for independence and efficient functioning of audiovisual media services regulatory bodies, carried out by a European consortium under the lead of the Hans Bredow Institute in Hamburg.

Dirk Voorhoof (www.psw.ugent.be/dv) is a professor at Ghent University, and teaches courses in Media Law, Copyright Law and Journalism & Ethics. He is a member of the Flemish Regulator for the Media (since 2006). Dirk Voorhoof published a Handbook on Media Law (Larcier, Brussels, 2003/2007 and 2011, with P. Valcke) and a textbook on European Media Law (Knops Publishing, 2012–2013). He is a member of the editorial board of Auteurs & Media (Brussels) and Mediaforum (Amsterdam) and he regularly reports on recent developments in the case law of the European Court of Human Rights on issues related to media, journalism and freedom of expression, including in Iris, Legal Observations (newsletter), European Audiovisual Observatory, Strasbourg.